HARCOURT Math

Orlando   Austin   Chicago   New York   Toronto   London   San Diego

Visit *The Learning Site!*
www.harcourtschool.com

Copyright © 2004 by Harcourt, Inc.

All rights reserved. No part of this publication may be reproduced or transmitted in any form or by any means, electronic or mechanical, including photocopy, recording, or any information storage and retrieval system, without permission in writing from the publisher.

Requests for permission to make copies of any part of the work should be addressed to School Permissions and Copyrights, Harcourt, Inc., 6277 Sea Harbor Drive, Orlando, Florida 32887-6777. Fax: 407-345-2418.

HARCOURT and the Harcourt Logo are trademarks of Harcourt, Inc., registered in the United States of America and/or other jurisdictions.

For permission to reprint copyrighted material, grateful acknowledgment is made to the following sources:

Candlewick Press Inc., Cambridge, MA: Cover illustration by Nick Sharratt from *Isn't It Time?* by Judy Hindley. Illustration copyright © 1994 by Nick Sharratt. Cover illustration by Cynthia Jabar from *How Many, How Many, How Many* by Rick Walton. Illustration copyright © 1993 by Cynthia Jabar.

Harcourt, Inc.: Cover illustration from *The Great Kapok Tree: A Tale of the Amazon Rain Forest* by Lynne Cherry. Copyright © 1990 by Lynne Cherry. Cover illustration from *Pancakes for Breakfast* by Tomie dePaola. Copyright © 1978 by Tomie dePaola. Cover illustration from *Fish Eyes* by Lois Ehlert. Copyright © 1990 by Lois Ehlert. Cover illustration by Pamela Lofts from *Koala Lou* by Mem Fox. Illustration copyright © 1988 by Pamela Lofts.

Philomel Books, an imprint of Penguin Books for Young Readers, a division of Penguin Putnam Inc.: Cover illustration from *The Very Busy Spider* by Eric Carle. Copyright © 1984 by The Eric Carle Corporation.

Printed in the United States of America

ISBN 0-15-334740-6

4 5 6 7 8 9 10 030 10 09 08 07 06 05

Senior Author

Evan M. Maletsky
Professor of Mathematics
Montclair State University
Upper Montclair, New Jersey

Authors

Angela Giglio Andrews
Math Teacher, Scott School
Naperville District #203
Naperville, Illinois

Jennie M. Bennett
Houston Independent School District
Houston, Texas

Grace M. Burton
Professor, Watson School of Education
University of North Carolina at Wilmington
Wilmington, North Carolina

Lynda A. Luckie
K–12 Mathematics Coordinator
Gwinnett County Public Schools
Lawrenceville, Georgia

Joyce C. McLeod
Visiting Professor
Rollins College
Winter Park, Florida

Vicki Newman
Classroom Teacher
McGaugh Elementary School
Los Alamitos Unified School District
Seal Beach, California

Tom Roby
Associate Professor of Mathematics
California State University
Hayward, California

Janet K. Scheer
Executive Director
Create A Vision
Foster City, California

Program Consultants and Specialists

Janet S. Abbott
Mathematics Consultant
California

Elsie Babcock
Director, Mathematics and Science Center
Mathematics Consultant
Wayne Regional Educational Service Agency
Wayne, Michigan

William J. Driscoll
Professor of Mathematics
Department of Mathematical Sciences
Central Connecticut State University
New Britain, Connecticut

Lois Harrison-Jones
Education and Management Consultant
Dallas, Texas

Rebecca Valbuena
Language Development Specialist
Stanton Elementary School
Glendora, California

Unit 1

ADDITION AND SUBTRACTION CONCEPTS

Why Learn Math? .... A–D
Getting Ready: Patterns, Numbers, and Graphs .... E–I

School-Home Connection 1A–1B

CHAPTER 1
Addition Concepts 1
Check What You Know 2
1 Model Addition Stories 👆 HANDS ON 3
2 Use Symbols to Add 5
3 **Algebra:** Add 0 7
4 Problem Solving Strategy: Write a Number Sentence 9
Extra Practice 11
Review/Test • Standardized Test Prep 12–13
Math Game: Pet Numbers 14

Theme: My Favorite Animals

CHAPTER 2
Using Addition 15
Check What You Know 16
1 **Algebra:** Add in Any Order 👆 HANDS ON 17
2 Ways to Make 7 and 8 👆 HANDS ON 19
3 Ways to Make 9 and 10 👆 HANDS ON 21
4 Vertical Addition 23
5 Problem Solving Strategy: Make a Model 25
Extra Practice 27
Review/Test • Standardized Test Prep 28–29
Math Game: Tic-Tac-Sum 30

Theme: Getting to Know Us

CHAPTER 3
Subtraction Concepts 31

Theme: At the Beach

Check What You Know 32
1 Model Subtraction Stories 👋 HANDS ON 33
2 Use Symbols to Subtract 35
3 **Algebra:** Write Subtraction Sentences 37
4 Problem Solving Strategy: Make a Model 39
5 **Algebra:** Subtract All or Zero 41
Extra Practice 43
Review/Test • Standardized Test Prep 44–45
Math Game: Numbers in the Sand 46

CHAPTER 4
Using Subtraction 47

Theme: In the Classroom

Check What You Know 48
1 Take Apart 7 and 8 👋 HANDS ON 49
2 Take Apart 9 and 10 👋 HANDS ON 51
3 Vertical Subtraction 53
4 Subtract to Compare 55
5 Problem Solving Strategy: Draw a Picture 57
Extra Practice 59
Review/Test • Standardized Test Prep 60–61
It's in the Bag: Cat Pocket-Dots 62

Unit Wrap Up

Math Storybook: My Cat Biff .... A–D
Problem Solving On Location: Alabama 63
Challenge: Equals 64
Study Guide and Review 65
Performance Assessment 67
Technology: The Learning Site • Seashell Search 68

v

Unit 2

ADDITION AND SUBTRACTION FACTS TO 10

School-Home Connection 69A–69B

CHAPTER 5

Theme: Sea Life

Addition Strategies 69
Check What You Know 70
1 Count On 1 and 2 👋 HANDS ON 71
2 Use a Number Line to Count On 73
3 Use Doubles 👋 HANDS ON 75
4 Problem Solving Strategy: Draw a Picture 77
Extra Practice 79
Review/Test • Standardized Test Prep 80–81
Math Game: Doubles Bubbles 82

CHAPTER 6

Theme: On the Playground

Addition Facts Practice 83
Check What You Know 84
1 Use the Strategies 85
2 Sums to 8 87
3 Sums to 10 89
4 **Algebra:** Follow the Rule 91
5 Problem Solving Strategy: Write a Number Sentence 93
Extra Practice 95
Review/Test • Standardized Test Prep 96–97
Math Game: Building Numbers 98

vi

CHAPTER 7: Subtraction Strategies 99

Theme: Things in the Air

- Check What You Know 100
- 1 Use a Number Line to Count Back 1 and 2 101
- 2 Use a Number Line to Count Back 3 103
- 3 **Algebra:** Relate Addition and Subtraction HANDS ON 105
- 4 **Problem Solving Strategy:** Draw a Picture 107
- Extra Practice 109
- Review/Test • Standardized Test Prep 110–111
- Math Game: Up, Up, and Away 112

CHAPTER 8: Subtraction Facts Practice 113

Theme: Fun Food

- Check What You Know 114
- 1 Use the Strategies 115
- 2 Subtraction to 10 117
- 3 **Algebra:** Follow the Rule 119
- 4 Fact Families to 10 HANDS ON 121
- 5 **Problem Solving Skill:** Choose the Operation 123
- Extra Practice 125
- Review/Test • Standardized Test Prep 126–127
- It's in the Bag: Math Under the Sea 128

Unit Wrap Up

- **Math Storybook:** Under the Sea .... A–F
- **Problem Solving On Location:** Tennessee 129
- **Challenge:** Missing Parts 130
- **Study Guide and Review** 131
- **Performance Assessment** 133
- **Technology:** Calculator • Add and Subtract 134

Unit 3

GRAPHS, NUMBERS TO 100, AND FACTS TO 12

School-Home Connection 135A–135B

Chapter 9: Graphs and Tables 135

Theme: Favorites

Check What You Know 136
1 **Algebra:** Sort and Classify 👋 HANDS ON 137
2 Make Concrete Graphs 👋 HANDS ON 139
3 Make Picture Graphs 141
4 Read a Tally Table 143
5 Make Bar Graphs 145
6 **Problem Solving Skill:** Use Data from a Graph 147
7 Interpret Graphs 149
Extra Practice 151
Review/Test • Standardized Test Prep 152–153
Math Game: Graph Game 154

Chapter 10: Place Value to 100 155

Theme: Time for a Party

Check What You Know 156
1 Teen Numbers 👋 HANDS ON 157
2 Tens 👋 HANDS ON 159
3 Tens and Ones to 50 👋 HANDS ON 161
4 Tens and Ones to 100 👋 HANDS ON 163
5 **Algebra:** Different Ways to Make Numbers 165
6 **Problem Solving Skill:** Make Reasonable Estimates 167
Extra Practice 169
Review/Test • Standardized Test Prep 170–171
Math Game: Teen Spin 172

Chapter 11: Comparing and Ordering Numbers 173

Theme: Outdoor Fun

Check What You Know 174
1 **Algebra:** Greater Than 👋 HANDS ON 175
2 **Algebra:** Less Than 👋 HANDS ON 177
3 **Algebra:** Use Symbols to Compare 👋 HANDS ON 179
4 Order on a Number Line 181
5 Count Forward and Backward 183
6 **Problem Solving Skill:** Use a Model 185
Extra Practice 187
Review/Test • Standardized Test Prep 188–189
Math Game: Greater Steps 190

CHAPTER 12

Theme: Art Class

Number Patterns 191
Check What You Know 192
1 Skip Count by 2s, 5s, and 10s 193
2 **Algebra:** Use a Hundred Chart to Skip Count 195
3 **Algebra:** Patterns on a Hundred Chart 197
4 Even and Odd 199
5 Problem Solving Strategy: Find a Pattern 201
6 Ordinal Numbers 203
Extra Practice 205
Review/Test • Standardized Test Prep 206–207
Math Game: Even Skips 208

CHAPTER 13

Theme: Ways to Travel

Addition and Subtraction Facts to 12 209
Check What You Know 210
1 Count On to Add 211
2 Doubles and Doubles Plus 1 213
3 **Algebra:** Add 3 Numbers 👋 HANDS ON 215
4 Problem Solving Strategy: Write a Number Sentence 217
5 Count Back to Subtract 219
6 Subtract to Compare 221
Extra Practice 223
Review/Test • Standardized Test Prep 224–225
Math Game: Boats Full of Facts 226

CHAPTER 14

Theme: A Picnic

Practice Addition and Subtraction 227
Check What You Know 228
1 **Algebra:** Related Addition and Subtraction Facts 👋 HANDS ON 229
2 Fact Families to 12 👋 HANDS ON 231
3 Sums and Differences to 12 233
4 **Algebra:** Missing Numbers 235
5 Problem Solving: Choose a Strategy 237
Extra Practice 239
Review/Test • Standardized Test Prep 240–241
It's in the Bag: Animals' Picnic Basket 242

Unit Wrap Up

Math Storybook: The Animals' Picnic .... A–F
Problem Solving On Location: Indiana 243
Challenge: Represent Numbers in Different Ways 244
Study Guide and Review 245
Performance Assessment 247
Technology: Calculator • Skip Counting 248

Unit 4

GEOMETRY AND ADDITION AND SUBTRACTION TO 20

School-Home Connection 249A–249B

CHAPTER 15

Theme: Shapes in Our World

Solid Figures and Plane Shapes 249
Check What You Know 250
1 Solid Figures 🖐 HANDS ON 251
2 Faces and Vertices 🖐 HANDS ON 253
3 Plane Shapes on Solid Figures 🖐 HANDS ON 255
4 Sort and Identify Plane Shapes 🖐 HANDS ON 257
5 **Problem Solving Strategy:** Make a Model 259
Extra Practice 261
Review/Test • Standardized Test Prep 262–263
Math Game: Make That Shape 264

CHAPTER 16

Theme: On the Move

Spatial Sense 265
Check What You Know 266
1 Open and Closed 267
2 **Problem Solving Skill:** Use a Picture 269
3 Give and Follow Directions 271
4 Symmetry 🖐 HANDS ON 273
5 Slides and Turns 🖐 HANDS ON 275
Extra Practice 277
Review/Test • Standardized Test Prep 278–279
Math Game: On the Map 280

CHAPTER 17

Theme: Patterns All Around Us

Patterns 281
Check What You Know 282
1 **Algebra:** Describe and Extend Patterns 283
2 **Algebra:** Pattern Units 🖐 HANDS ON 285
3 **Algebra:** Make New Patterns 🖐 HANDS ON 287
4 **Problem Solving Skill:** Correct a Pattern 289
5 **Problem Solving Skill:** Transfer Patterns 291
Extra Practice 293
Review/Test • Standardized Test Prep 294–295
Math Game: Pattern Play 296

x

CHAPTER 18
Addition Facts and Strategies 297

Theme: Wildlife

Check What You Know 298
1 Doubles and Doubles Plus 1 HANDS ON 299
2 10 and More HANDS ON 301
3 Make 10 to Add HANDS ON 303
4 Use Make a 10 HANDS ON 305
5 **Algebra:** Add 3 Numbers 307
6 **Problem Solving Skill:** Use Data from a Table ... 309
Extra Practice 311
Review/Test • Standardized Test Prep 312–313
Math Game: Ten Plus 314

CHAPTER 19
Subtraction Facts and Strategies 315

Theme: In the Garden

Check What You Know 316
1 Use a Number Line to Count Back 317
2 Doubles Fact Families 319
3 **Algebra:** Related Addition and Subtraction Facts ... 321
4 **Problem Solving Skill:** Estimate Reasonable Answers ... 323
Extra Practice 325
Review/Test • Standardized Test Prep 326–327
Math Game: Fact Family Bingo 328

CHAPTER 20
Addition and Subtraction Practice 329

Theme: Arctic Life

Check What You Know 330
1 Practice the Facts 331
2 Fact Families to 20 333
3 **Algebra:** Ways to Make Numbers to 20 HANDS ON ... 335
4 **Problem Solving Strategy:** Make a Model ... 337
Extra Practice 339
Review/Test • Standardized Test Prep 340–341
It's in the Bag: The Hungry Prince's Crown ... 342

Unit Wrap Up

Math Storybook: The Hungry Prince .... A–H
Problem Solving On Location: New York 343
Challenge: Repeated Addition 344
Study Guide and Review 345
Performance Assessment 347
Technology: The Learning Site • Addition Surprise ... 348

Unit 5

MONEY, TIME, AND FRACTIONS

School-Home Connection 349A–349B

CHAPTER 21
Theme: At the Pizza Party

Fractions 349
Check What You Know 350
1 Halves 351
2 Fourths 353
3 Thirds 355
4 Problem Solving Strategy: Use Logical Reasoning 357
5 Parts of Groups 359
Extra Practice 361
Review/Test • Standardized Test Prep 362–363
Math Game: Pizza Party 364

CHAPTER 22
Theme: It's in the Bank

Counting Pennies, Nickels, and Dimes 365
Check What You Know 366
1 Pennies and Nickels HANDS ON 367
2 Pennies and Dimes HANDS ON 369
3 Count Groups of Coins 371
4 Count Collections 373
5 Problem Solving Strategy: Make a List 375
Extra Practice 377
Review/Test • Standardized Test Prep 378–379
Math Game: Finding Coins 380

CHAPTER 23
Theme: What's for Sale?

Using Money 381
Check What You Know 382
1 Trade Pennies, Nickels, and Dimes HANDS ON 383
2 Quarters HANDS ON 385
3 Half Dollar and Dollar HANDS ON 387
4 Compare Values 389
5 Same Amounts HANDS ON 391
6 Problem Solving Strategy: Act It Out 393
Extra Practice 395
Review/Test • Standardized Test Prep 396–397
Math Game: Shopping Basket 398

xii

CHAPTER 24

Telling Time 399

Theme: What Time Is It?

Check What You Know 400
1 Read a Clock 👋 HANDS ON 401
2 Problem Solving Skill: Use Estimation 403
3 Time to the Hour 👋 HANDS ON 405
4 Tell Time to the Half Hour 👋 HANDS ON 407
5 Practice Time to the Hour and Half Hour 409
Extra Practice 411
Review/Test • Standardized Test Prep 412–413
Math Game: Clock Switch 414

CHAPTER 25

Time and Calendar 415

Theme: All in My Day

Check What You Know 416
1 Use a Calendar 417
2 Daily Events 419
3 Problem Solving Strategy: Make a Graph 421
4 Read a Schedule 423
5 Problem Solving Skill: Make Reasonable Estimates 425
Extra Practice 427
Review/Test • Standardized Test Prep 428–429
It's in the Bag: Brown-Bag Grandfather Clock 430

Unit Wrap Up

Math Storybook: Is It Time? .... A–H
Problem Solving On Location: Louisiana 431
Challenge: Writing Fractions 432
Study Guide and Review 433
Performance Assessment 435
Technology: The Learning Site • Willy the Watchdog 436

xiii

Unit 6

MEASUREMENT, OPERATIONS, AND DATA

School-Home Connection 437A–437B

CHAPTER 26 — Length 437
Theme: Arts and Crafts

Check What You Know 438
1 Compare Lengths HANDS ON 439
2 Use Nonstandard Units HANDS ON 441
3 Inches HANDS ON 443
4 Inches and Feet HANDS ON 445
5 Centimeters HANDS ON 447
6 **Problem Solving Skill:** Make Reasonable Estimates 449
Extra Practice 451
Review/Test • Standardized Test Prep 452–453
Math Game: Ruler Race 454

CHAPTER 27 — Weight 455
Theme: At the Farm

Check What You Know 456
1 Use a Balance HANDS ON 457
2 Pounds HANDS ON 459
3 Kilograms HANDS ON 461
4 **Problem Solving Strategy:** Predict and Test 463
Extra Practice 465
Review/Test • Standardized Test Prep 466–467
Math Game: Gram Grab 468

CHAPTER 28 — Capacity 469
Theme: Fill It Up

Check What You Know 470
1 Nonstandard Units HANDS ON 471
2 Cups, Pints, and Quarts HANDS ON 473
3 Liters HANDS ON 475
4 Temperature 477
5 **Problem Solving Skill:** Choose the Measuring Tool 479
Extra Practice 481
Review/Test • Standardized Test Prep 482–483
Math Game: How Many Cups? 484

xiv

CHAPTER 29

Theme: In the Rain Forest

Adding and Subtracting 2-Digit Numbers 485
Check What You Know 486
1 Use Mental Math to Add Tens 487
2 Add Tens and Ones 👋 HANDS ON 489
3 Add Money 491
4 Use Mental Math to Subtract Tens 493
5 Subtract Tens and Ones 👋 HANDS ON 495
6 Subtract Money 497
7 Problem Solving Skill: Make Reasonable Estimates 499
Extra Practice 501
Review/Test • Standardized Test Prep 502–503
Math Game: Math Path 504

CHAPTER 30

Theme: Chances

Probability 505
Check What You Know 506
1 Certain or Impossible 507
2 More Likely, Less Likely 509
3 Equally Likely 511
4 Problem Solving Skill: Make a Prediction 513
Extra Practice 515
Review/Test • Standardized Test Prep 516–517
It's in the Bag: Cool Cat Hat 518

Unit Wrap Up

Math Storybook: Cat's Cool Hat ..... A-H
Problem Solving On Location: West Virginia 519
Challenge: Area 520
Study Guide and Review 521
Performance Assessment 523
Technology: Calculator • Find the Greatest Sum 524
Picture Glossary 525

Why Learn Math?

Look at each picture.
Decide what math skill is being used.

Explain It What are some things you do to use math?

Practice What You Learn

IT'S IN THE BAG

PROJECT You will make a math facts vest.

You Will Need

- Large brown bag
- Pattern tracer
- Scissors
- Construction paper
- Glue
- Tape
- Crayons

Directions

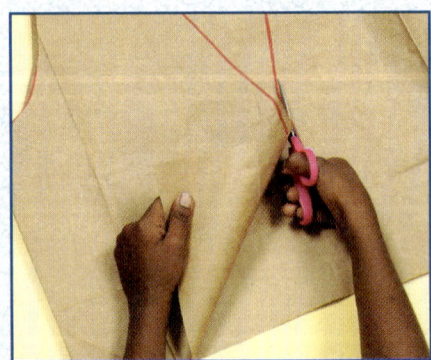
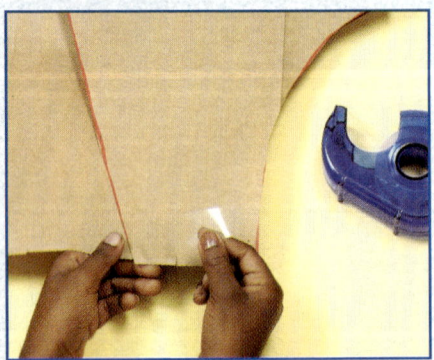

1. Pop out the sides of the bag. Lay the bag flat.
2. Trace the vest pattern 2 times, once on each side of the bag.
3. Trace two arm holes. Cut out two arm holes from two layers of the bag.
4. Cut the vest front from only the top layer of the bag.
5. Tape the front of the bag to the back of the bag. Make pockets. Use construction paper.

Show What You Learn

The checklist shows what you will do when you take a test.

I will:

- listen carefully.
- read carefully.
- follow directions.
- mark answers carefully.
- begin where told.
- begin when told.
- pay attention only to the teacher and the test.
- do the best I can.

_____
Name

Name _____

1. Color the triangles red.
   Color the squares and rectangles blue.
   Color the circles yellow.

2. Draw what comes next in this pattern.

E

REVIEW: Shapes and Patterns

Name _____

1. Get some 🟥 and 🟨. Sort.
   Make a graph.
   Write how many.

   How many 🟥 and 🟨?

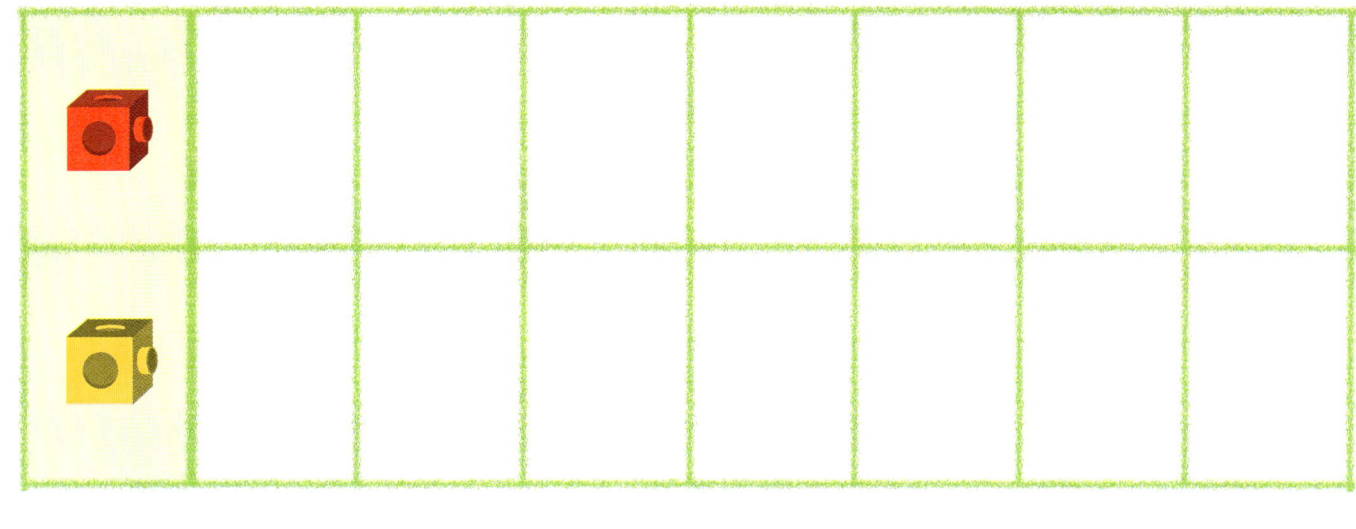

2. Write how many.

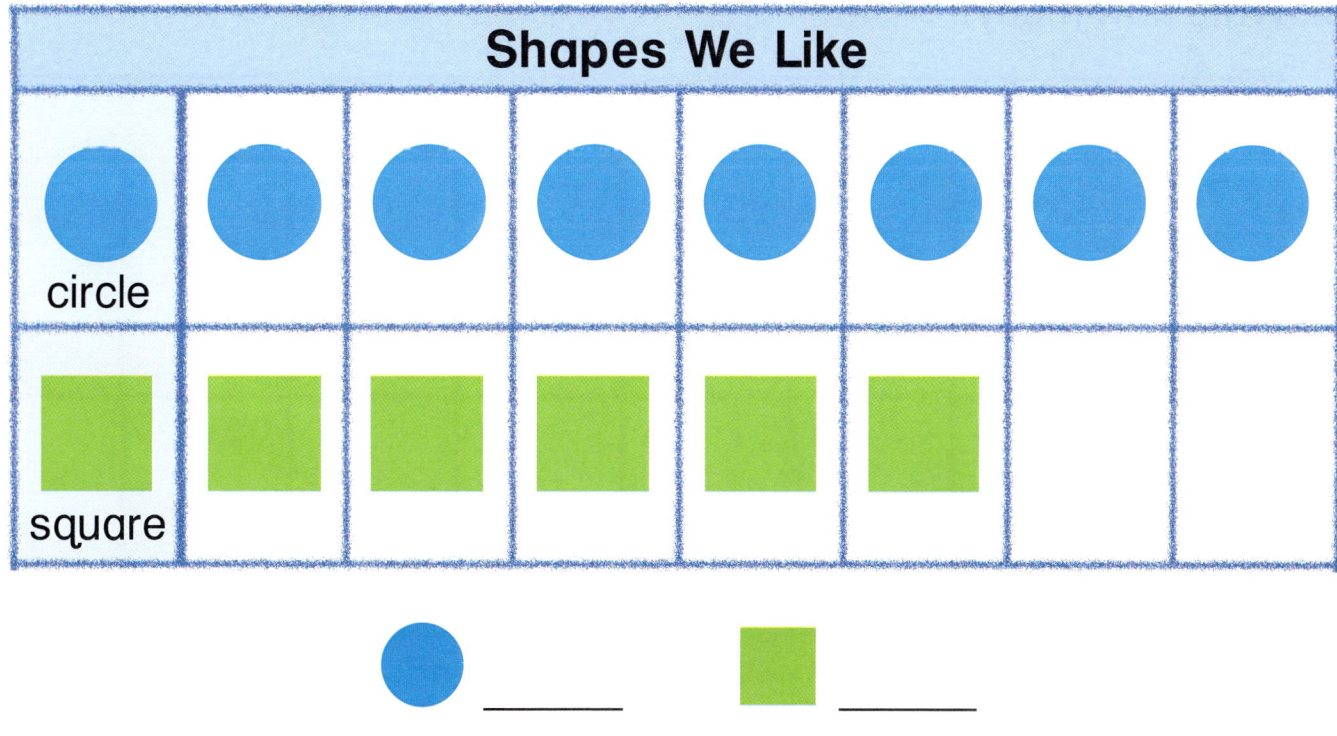

3. Which shape do more children like?
   Circle that shape.

REVIEW: Concrete Graphs/Picture Graphs

H

Name _____

1. Write how many.

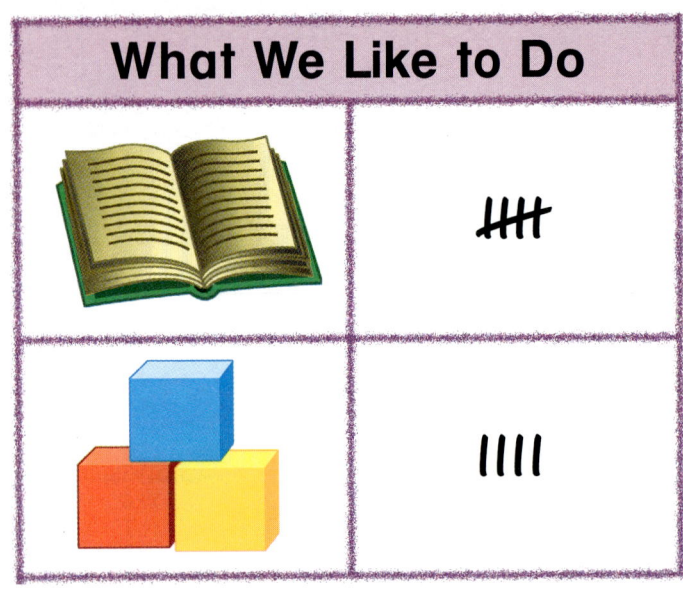

2. Which do more children like to do? Circle that picture.

3. Write how many.

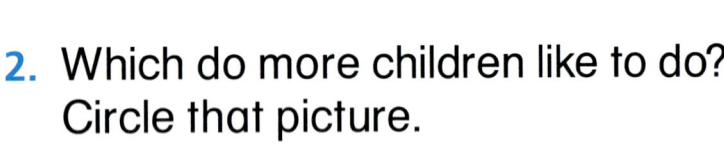

REVIEW: Tally Table/Bar Graph

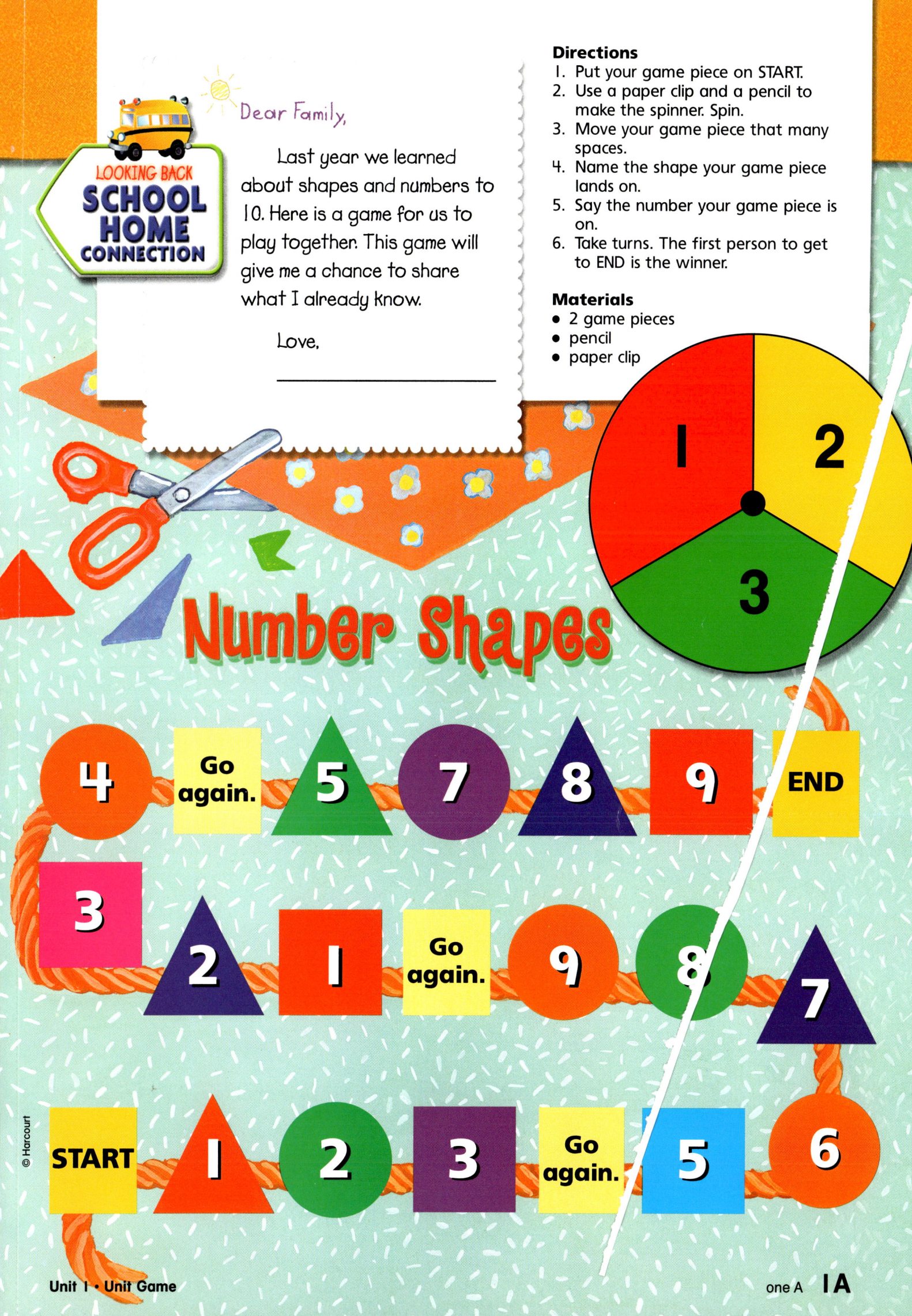

Dear Family,

During the next few weeks, we will learn to add and subtract through 10. Here is important math vocabulary and a list of books to share.

Love,

_____

Vocabulary

addition sentence
sum
subtraction sentence
difference

Vocabulary Power

4 + 1 = 5

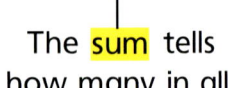

The sum tells how many in all.

4 + 1 = 5 is an addition sentence.

3 − 1 = 2

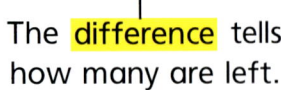

The difference tells how many are left.

3 − 1 = 2 is a subtraction sentence.

BOOKS TO SHARE

To read about addition and subtraction with your child, look for these books in your library.

Anno's Counting Book, by Mitsumasa Anno, HarperCollins, 1992.

Fish Eyes: A Book You Can Count On, by Lois Ehlert, Harcourt, 2001.

Roll Over! A Counting Song, illustrated by Merle Peek, Clarion, 1999.

Ten Little Mice, by Joyce Dunbar, Gulliver, 1992.

 Visit *The Learning Site* for additional ideas and activities. www.harcourtschool.com

CHAPTER 1
Addition Concepts

FUN FACTS

Cats have 4 sets of whiskers. Look on the chin, cheek, wrist, and eyebrow.

Theme: My Favorite Animals

Name _____

✓ Check What You Know

Zero

Count the . Write how many .

1.  _____

2.  _____

Count and Write the Numbers to 10

Count the ●. Write the number.

3. 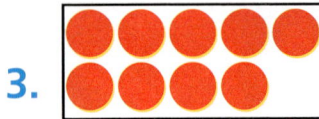 _____

4. 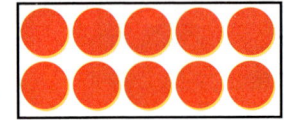 _____

Model Addition

Use 🟦 to show how many in all.

Draw the 🟦.
Write the number that tells how many in all.

5.

          4   1   _____

6.

          6   2   _____

Use this page to review important skills needed for this chapter.

Name _____

Model Addition Stories

Explore (Hands On)

Use 🟡 to show the story.
Draw the 🟡. Write how many in all.

1 big bird   1 little bird   __2__ in all

"There are 2 birds in all."

1.

1 ant   2 ants   _____ in all

2.

3 deer   3 deer come   _____ in all

Explain It • Daily Reasoning

What happens when more is added to a group?
Explain how you know.

Chapter 1 • Addition Concepts   three **3**

Practice

Use 🟡 to show the story.
Draw the 🟡. Write how many in all.

1.

3 big ducks   1 little duck   _____ in all

2.

2 big frogs   2 little frogs   _____ in all

3.

1 bee   4 bees come   _____ in all

HOME ACTIVITY • Have your child tell an addition story for each picture.

Name _____

Use Symbols to Add

Vocabulary
plus +
equals =
sum

Learn

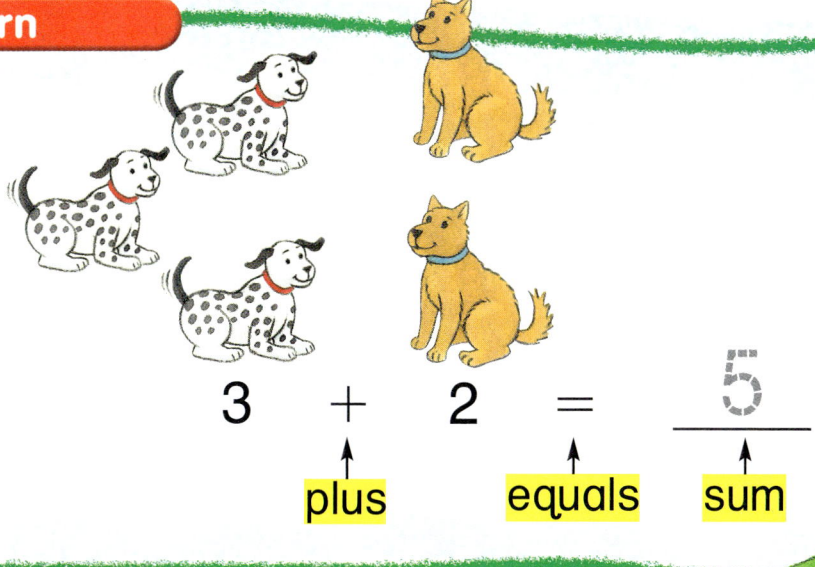

3 + 2 = 5

↑ plus ↑ equals ↑ sum

Check

Add. Write the sum.

1.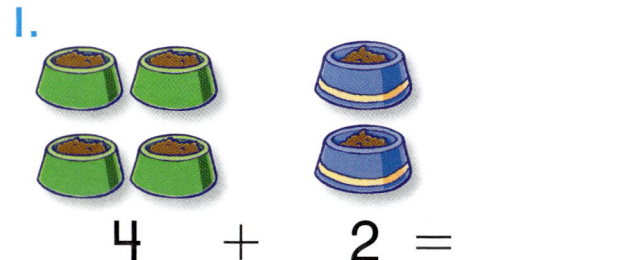

4 + 2 = ____

2. 3 + 3 = ____

3.

2 + 2 = ____

4.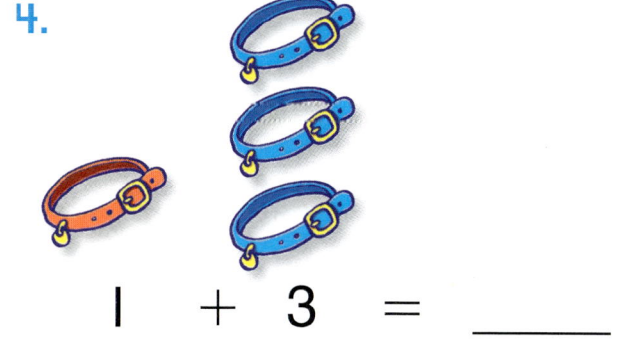

1 + 3 = ____

5.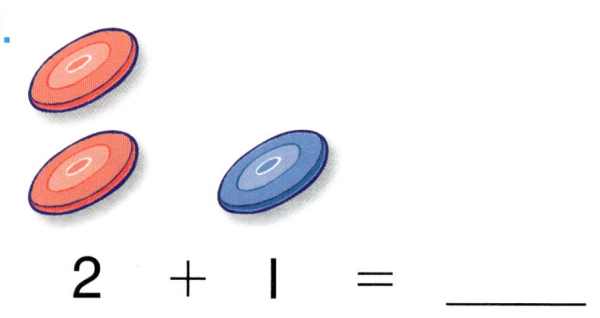

2 + 1 = ____

6.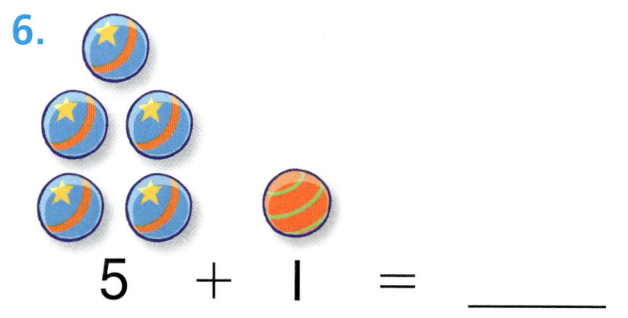

5 + 1 = ____

Explain It • Daily Reasoning

How could you find the sum for 1 + 4 without using pictures?

Chapter 1 • Addition Concepts

Practice and Problem Solving

Add. Write the sum.

1.

   3 + 1 = __4__

2.

   2 + 3 = ____

3.

   4 + 1 = ____

4.

   2 + 4 = ____

Problem Solving

Application

Use counters to show the story. Write the sum.

5. There are 5 black kittens.
   There is 1 gray kitten.
   How many kittens
   are there in all? _____ kittens

Write About It • Draw a picture. Show an addition story about a large dog and some small dogs. Write the sum.

HOME ACTIVITY • Ask your child to tell how he or she found each sum. Then have him or her draw pictures to show 1 + 5 and tell the sum. (6)

Name _____

Algebra: Add 0

Vocabulary
zero 0

Learn

Any number plus 0 equals the same number.

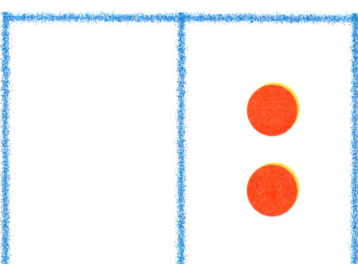

3 + 0 = __3__

0 + 2 = __2__

Check

Write the sum.

1.

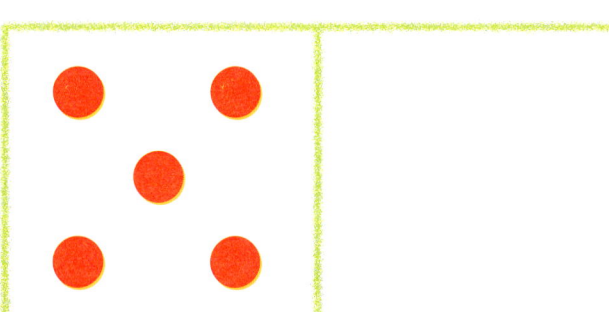

5 + 0 = ____

2.

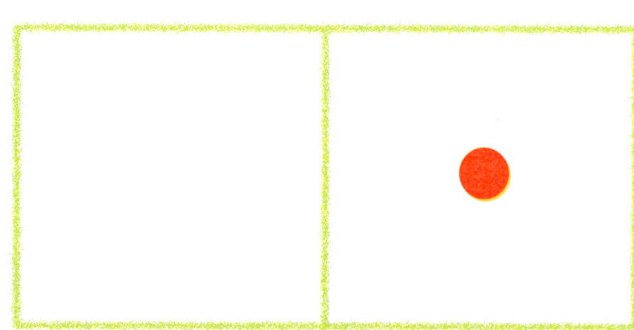

0 + 1 = ____

3.

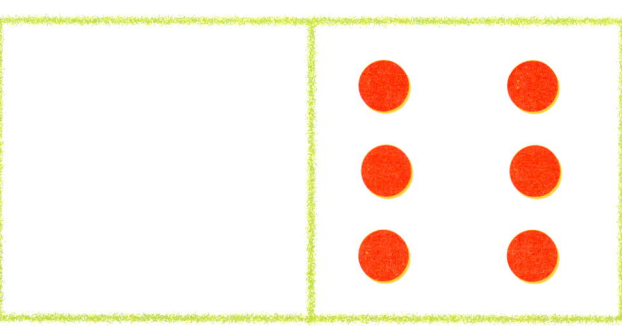

0 + 6 = ____

4.

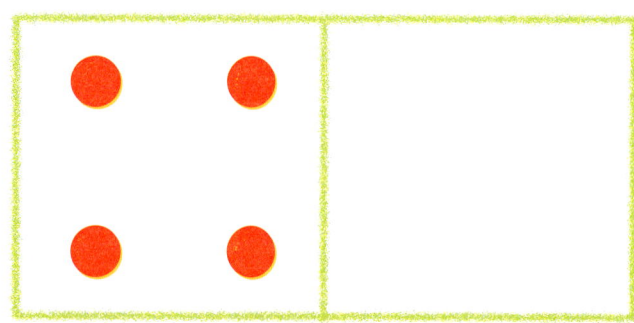

4 + 0 = ____

Explain It • Daily Reasoning

What happens when 0 is added to a number? Why?

Chapter 1 • Addition Concepts

Practice and Problem Solving

Draw circles to show each number.
Write the sum.

1. $1 + 0 = \underline{1}$

2. $1 + 1 = \underline{2}$

3. $1 + 2 = \underline{3}$

4. $0 + 3 = \underline{}$

5. $0 + 4 = \underline{}$

6. $0 + 5 = \underline{}$

7. $2 + 0 = \underline{}$

8. $2 + 1 = \underline{}$

9. $2 + 2 = \underline{}$

10. $0 + 0 = \underline{}$

11. $0 + 1 = \underline{}$

12. $0 + 2 = \underline{}$

Problem Solving
Application

13. Circle the problem that you think has the greatest sum. Write the sums to check.

$6 + 1 = \underline{}$ $6 + 2 = \underline{}$ $6 + 0 = \underline{}$

Write About It • Why does $6 + 0 = 6$?

HOME ACTIVITY • Ask your child to tell you the sums for $1 + 0$ through $6 + 0$.

Name _____

Problem Solving Strategy
Write a Number Sentence

Vocabulary
addition sentence

5 blue fish eat.

1 purple fish joins them.

(How many fish are there in all?)

UNDERSTAND

What do you need to find out?
Circle the question.

PLAN

How do you solve this problem?
Draw a picture.
Then write an addition sentence.

SOLVE

There are __5__ blue fish.

__1__ purple fish joins them.

5 ⊕ 1 ⊖ 6
fish

CHECK

Does your answer make sense?
Explain.

Draw a picture. Then write an addition sentence to solve.

THINK: What do I need to find out?

1. There are 4 fish.
   2 more fish come.
   How many fish are there in all?

___ ◯ ___ ◯ ___
fish

Chapter 1 • Addition Concepts

Problem Solving Practice

Draw a picture.
Then write an addition sentence to solve.

Keep in Mind!
Understand
Plan
Solve
Check

THINK: What do I need to find out?

1. 2 green fish swim.
   3 orange fish join them.
   How many fish are there in all?

   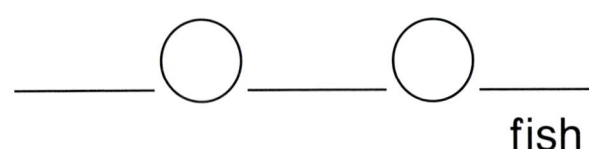
   ____ ◯ ____ ◯ ____ fish

2. Mike has 1 red fish.
   He gets 2 yellow fish.
   How many fish does he have in all?

   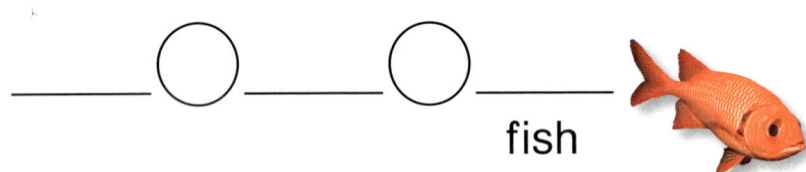
   ____ ◯ ____ ◯ ____ fish

3. 2 purple fish hide.
   4 blue fish join them.
   How many fish are there in all?

   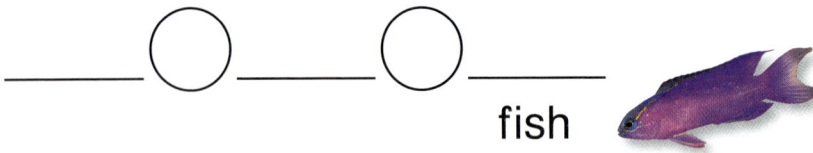
   ____ ◯ ____ ◯ ____ fish

4. Sue has 1 orange fish.
   She gets 1 blue fish.
   How many fish does she have in all?

   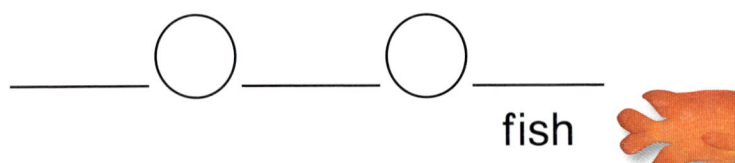
   ____ ◯ ____ ◯ ____ fish

HOME ACTIVITY • Have your child use small objects to show the addition stories on this page.

Name _____

Extra Practice

Add. Write the sum.

1.

   2 + 1 = ____

2.

   2 + 2 = ____

3.

   3 + 1 = ____

4.

   2 + 4 = ____

Draw circles to show each number. Write the sum.

5.

   4 + 0 = ____

6.

   4 + 1 = ____

7.

   4 + 2 = ____

Problem Solving

Draw a picture. Then write an addition sentence to solve.

8. 3 yellow fish swim.
   3 blue fish join them.
   How many fish are there in all?

   ____ ◯ ____ ◯ ____
           fish

Chapter 1 • Addition Concepts

eleven 11

Name _____

✓ Review/Test

Concepts and Skills

Add. Write the sum.

1.

   2 + 1 = ____

2.

   3 + 2 = ____

3.

   3 + 3 = ____

4.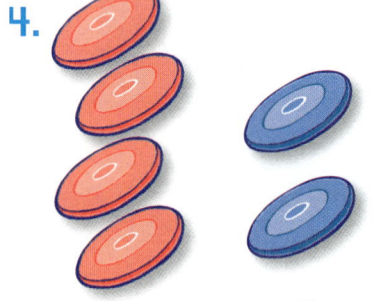

   4 + 2 = ____

Draw circles to show each number.
Write the sum.

5.

   5 + 0 = ____

6.

   5 + 1 = ____

7.

   5 + 2 = ____

Problem Solving

Draw a picture. Then write an addition sentence to solve.

8. There are 3 fish.
   2 more fish come.
   How many fish are there in all?

   ___ ◯ ___ ◯ ___
            fish

Name _____

⭐Standardized Test Prep
Chapter 1

Choose the answer for questions 1–4.

1. Which addition sentence tells about the picture?

   5 + 2 = 7   5 + 1 = 6   5 + 0 = 5   4 + 2 = 6
   ○   ○   ○   ○

2. Which addition sentence tells about the picture?

   4 + 0 = 4   4 + 1 = 5   3 + 1 = 4   4 + 2 = 6
   ○   ○   ○   ○

3. What is the sum for 4 + 0?

   0   4   5   40
   ○   ○   ○   ○

4. Which addition sentence tells how many there are in all?

   1 + 4 = 5   3 + 3 = 6   3 + 4 = 7   3 + 5 = 8
   ○   ○   ○   ○

Show What You Know

5. Write an addition sentence about this picture. Explain how you knew which numbers to use.

   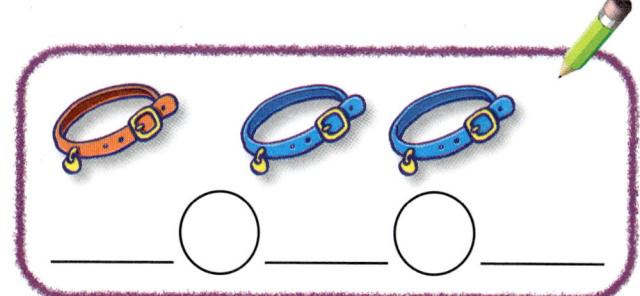

Chapter 1   thirteen 13

MATH GAME

Pet Numbers

Play with a partner.

1. Put your  at START.
2. Spin the .
3. Move your  that many spaces.
4. Find the sum.
5. If you are not correct, lose a turn.
6. The first player to get to END wins.

You will need

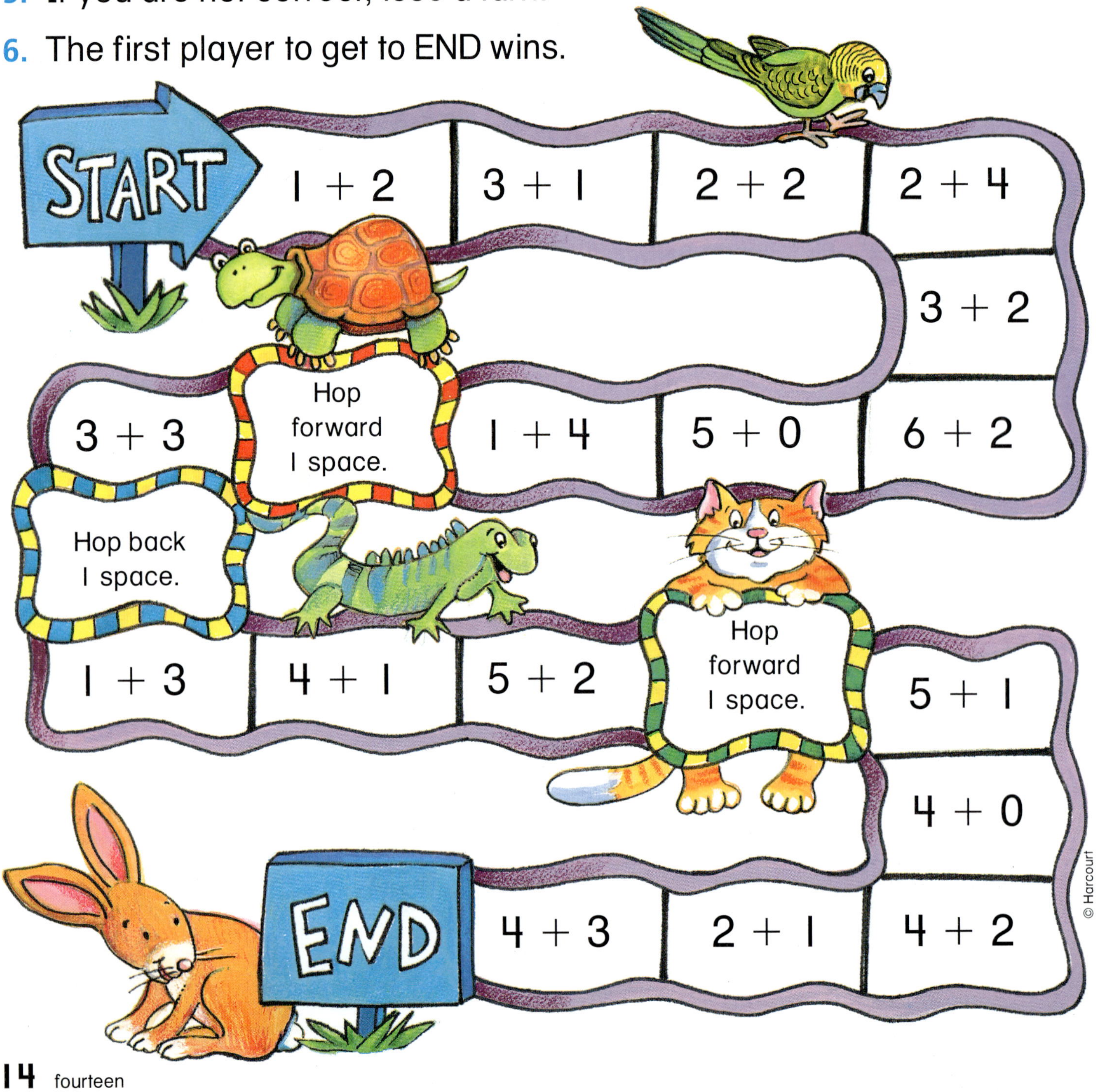

CHAPTER 2 Using Addition

FUN FACTS

Our 4 basic tastes are salty, sweet, bitter, and sour.

Theme: Getting to Know Us

Name _____

✓ Check What You Know

Make a Model: Names for Numbers

Use 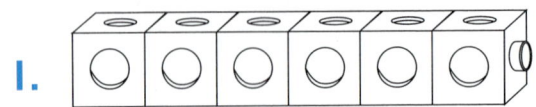 and  to make 6.

Color the ⬜. Write the numbers.

1.    ____  + ____  = 6

Use Pictures to Add

Add. Write the numbers.

2.

____ + ____ = ____

3.

____ + ____ = ____

4.

____ + ____ = ____

5.

____ + ____ = ____

Use Symbols to Add

Add. Write the sum.

6.

____ + ____ = ____

7.

____ + ____ = ____

16 sixteen   Use this page to review important skills needed for this chapter.

Name _____

Algebra: Add in Any Order

Vocabulary
sum

 **Explore**

"You can add in any order and get the same sum."

2 + 1 = __3__
sum

1 + 2 = __3__
sum

Connect

Use 🟥 and 🟦 to add. Write each sum.
Color to match.

1.

   4 + 1 = ____

2.

   1 + 4 = ____

3.

   3 + 2 = ____

4.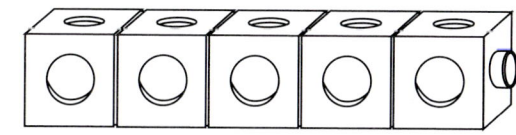

   2 + 3 = ____

5.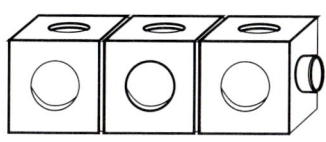

   3 + 0 = ____

6.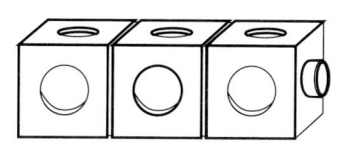

   0 + 3 = ____

Explain It • Daily Reasoning

What happens to the sum when you change the order of the numbers you are adding? Use 🟥 and 🟦 to prove your answer.

Chapter 2 • Using Addition

seventeen **17**

Practice and Problem Solving

Use  and 🟦 to add. Circle the addition sentences in each row that have the same sum.

1. (3 + 1 = __4__)   2. 2 + 1 = __3__   3. (1 + 3 = __4__)

4. 4 + 2 = ___   5. 2 + 4 = ___   6. 1 + 4 = ___

7. 3 + 3 = ___   8. 4 + 0 = ___   9. 0 + 4 = ___

10. 4 + 1 = ___   11. 5 + 1 = ___   12. 1 + 5 = ___

13. 2 + 3 = ___   14. 2 + 2 = ___   15. 3 + 2 = ___

Problem Solving

Application

Circle your answer.

16. Bob has 1 🟥 and 4 🟦.
Pat has 4 🟥 and 1 🟦.
Do they have the same number of cubes?
  Yes   No
Prove your answer.

Write About It • Show two ways to add 1 and 5. Tell why the sums are the same.

HOME ACTIVITY • Have your child use small objects to show 3 + 1 and 1 + 3 and then tell you why the two sums are the same.

18 eighteen

Name _____

Ways to Make 7 and 8

Vocabulary
plus
equals

Explore

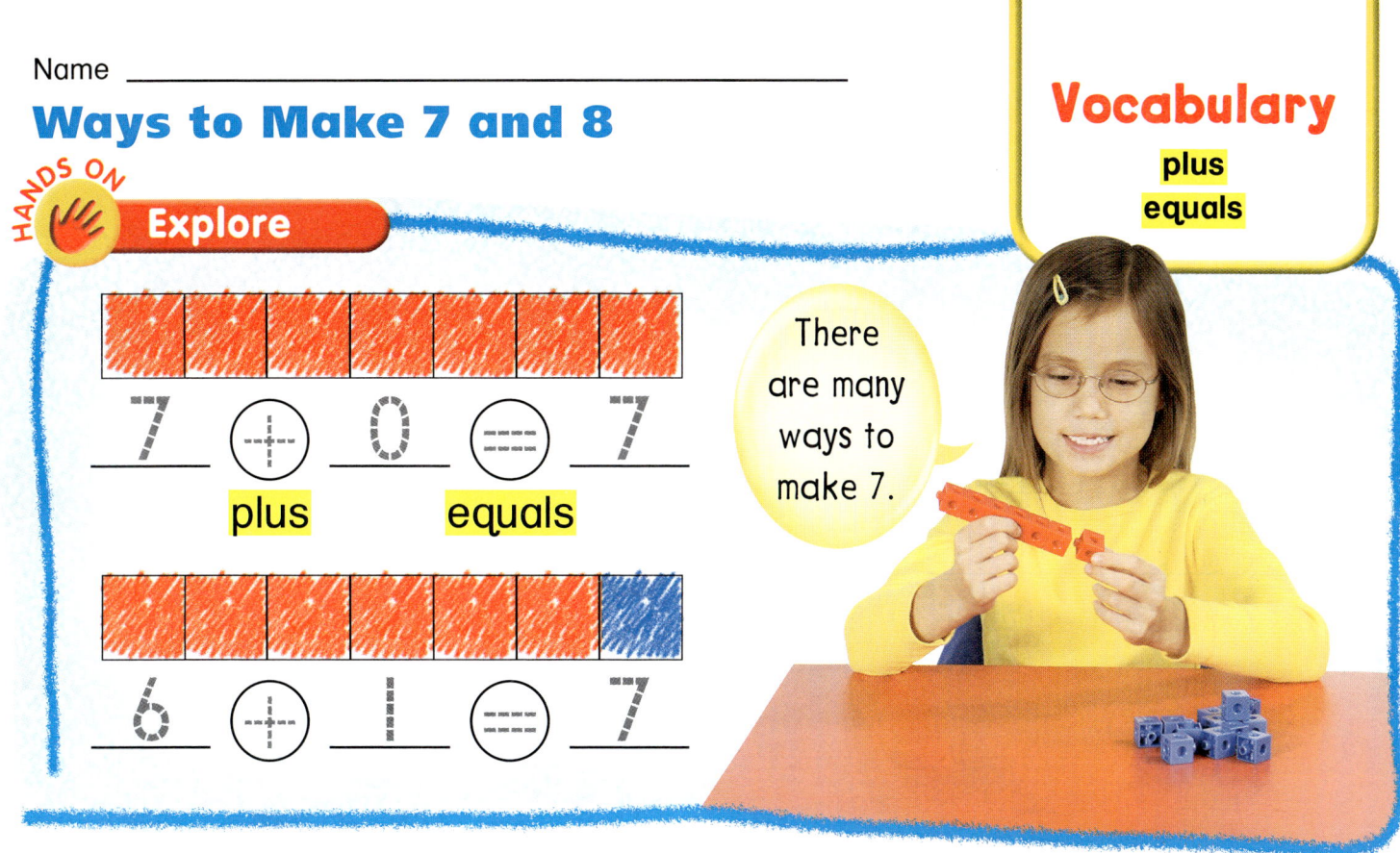

There are many ways to make 7.

7 + 0 = 7
plus   equals

6 + 1 = 7

Connect

Use 🟥 and 🟦 to make 7.
Color. Write the addition sentence.

1.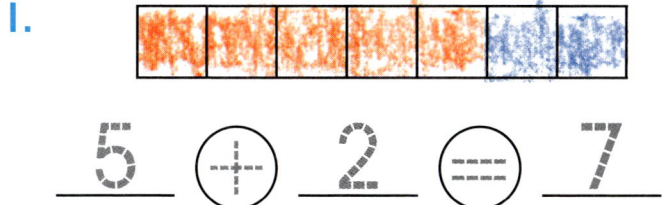

   5 + 2 = 7

2.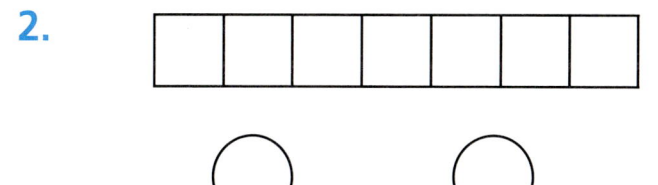

   ___ ○ ___ ○ ___

3.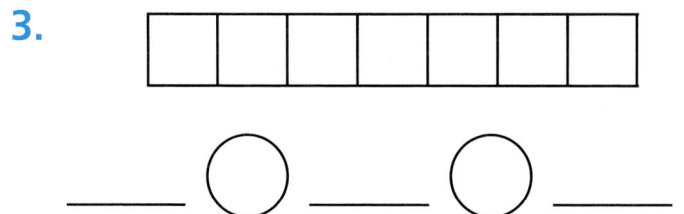

   ___ ○ ___ ○ ___

4.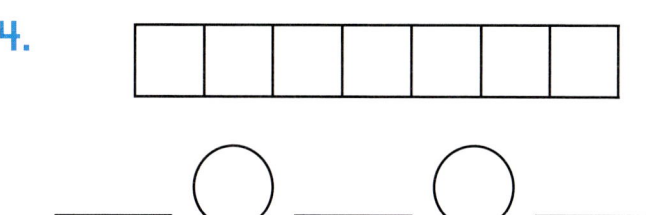

   ___ ○ ___ ○ ___

5.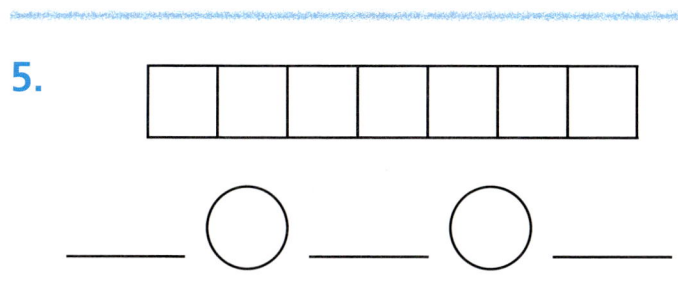

   ___ ○ ___ ○ ___

6.

   ___ ○ ___ ○ ___

Explain It • Daily Reasoning

If you have 3 🟥, how many 🟦 do you need to make 7? Use 🟥 and 🟦 to prove your answer.

Chapter 2 • Using Addition

Practice and Problem Solving

This is one way to make 8.

Use 🟥 and 🟦 to make 8.
Color. Write the addition sentence.

1. ___7___ ○+ ___1___ ○= ___8___

2. ___ ○ ___ ○ ___

3. ___ ○ ___ ○ ___

4. ___ ○ ___ ○ ___

5. ___ ○ ___ ○ ___

6. ___ ○ ___ ○ ___

7. ___ ○ ___ ○ ___

8. ___ ○ ___ ○ ___

Problem Solving
Visual Thinking

9. Write an addition sentence that tells about the picture.

   ___ ○ ___ ○ ___

 Write About It • How can you show 8 a different way? Draw cars to show how. Write the addition sentence.

🏠 **HOME ACTIVITY** • Have your child use small objects to show different ways to make 7 and 8.

20 twenty

Name _____

Ways to Make 9 and 10

Explore (Hands On)

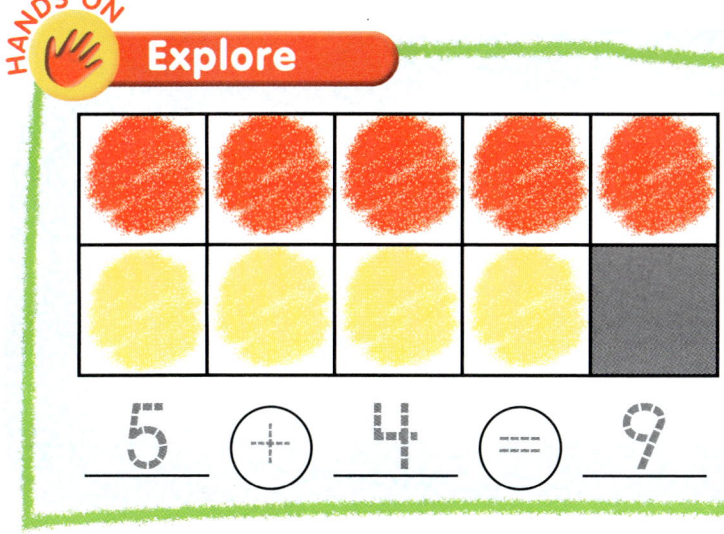

$\underline{5} \; \oplus \; \underline{4} \; \ominus \; \underline{9}$

"This is one way to make 9."

Connect

Use Workmat 7, 🔴, and 🟡 to make 9.
Draw and color. Write the addition sentence.

1.

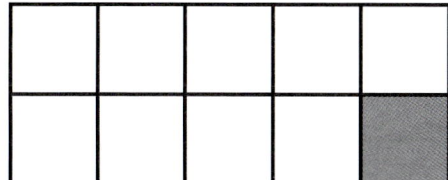

2.

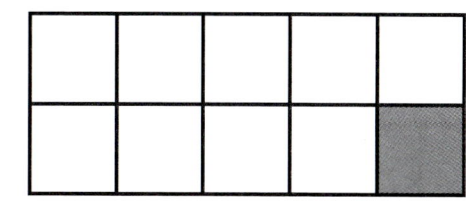

3.

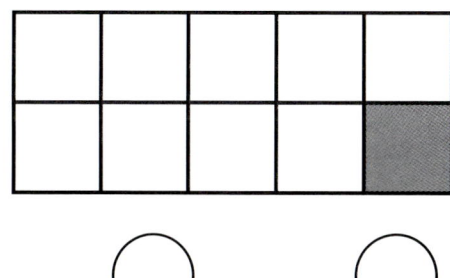

4.

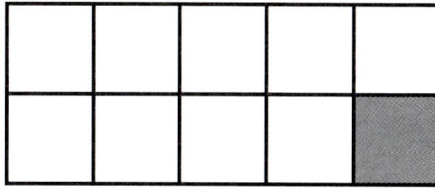

5.

6.

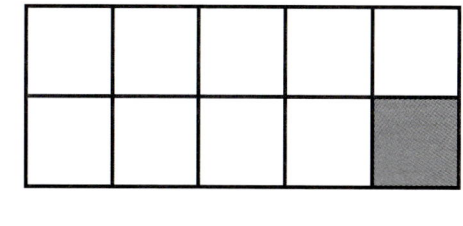

Explain It • Daily Reasoning

How could you use 🔴 and 🟡 to make 10?

Chapter 2 • Using Addition

Practice and Problem Solving

Use Workmat 7, 🔴, and 🟡 to make 10.
Draw and color. Write the addition sentence.

1.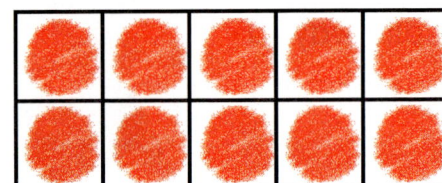

    + 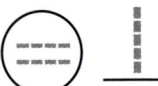 = 10

2.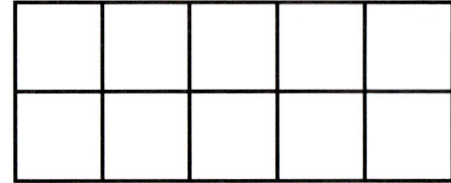

   ___ ○ ___ ○ ___

3.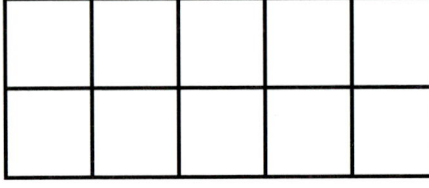

   ___ ○ ___ ○ ___

4.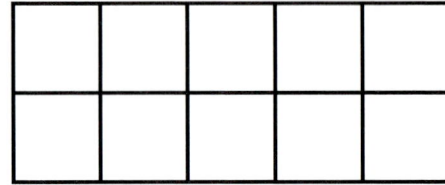

   ___ ○ ___ ○ ___

5.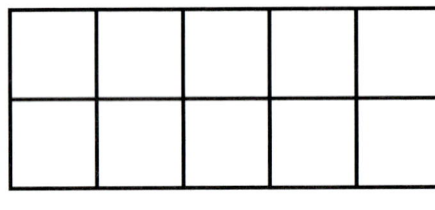

   ___ ○ ___ ○ ___

6.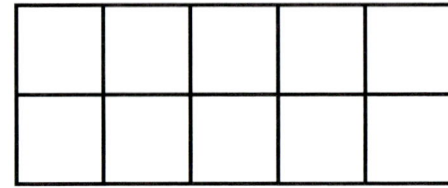

   ___ ○ ___ ○ ___

Problem Solving
Application

7. You have 5 pennies. How many more pennies do you need to make 10?

   _____ more pennies

 Write About It • You have 7 pennies. You need 10 pennies. Draw to show how many more pennies you need. Write the addition sentence.

🏠 **HOME ACTIVITY** • Have your child use small objects to show different combinations that make 9 and 10.

22 twenty-two

Name _____

Vertical Addition

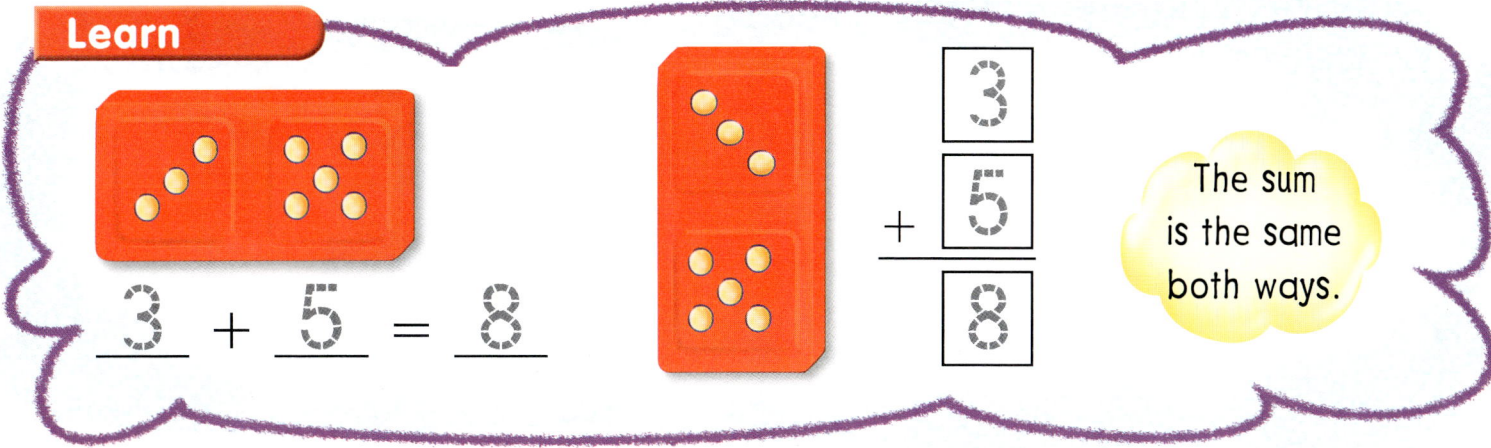

Learn

3 + 5 = 8

```
  3
+ 5
---
  8
```

The sum is the same both ways.

Check

Write the numbers to match the dots.
Write the sum.

1.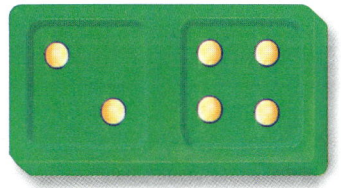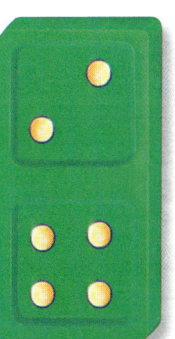

   ___ + ___ = ___

2.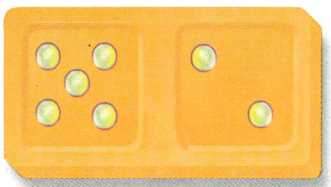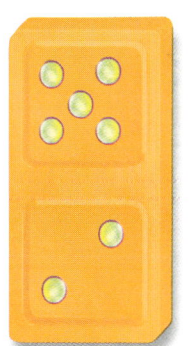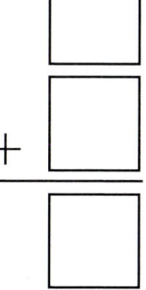

   ___ + ___ = ___

3.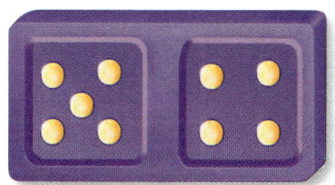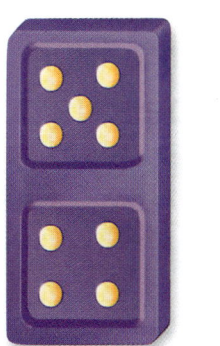

   ___ + ___ = ___

Explain It • Daily Reasoning

How are the problems in each row alike?
How are they different? Explain.

Practice and Problem Solving

Write the numbers to match the dots.
Write the sum.

1.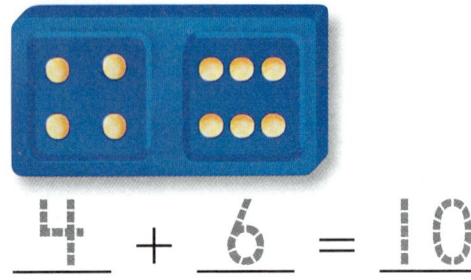

   $\underline{4} + \underline{6} = \underline{10}$

Write the sum.

2. 4
   +2
   ___

3. 6
   +2
   ___

4. 5
   +5
   ___

5. 7
   +2
   ___

6. 0
   +5
   ___

7. 2
   +2
   ___

---

8. 1
   +2
   ___

9. 5
   +4
   ___

10. 2
    +5
    ___

11. 4
    +6
    ___

12. 8
    +1
    ___

13. 0
    +6
    ___

---

14. 3
    +2
    ___

15. 2
    +3
    ___

16. 8
    +0
    ___

17. 3
    +6
    ___

18. 7
    +3
    ___

19. 4
    +0
    ___

Problem Solving
Application

20. Each person has 5 red pencils. They get some blue pencils. How many pencils does each person have now?

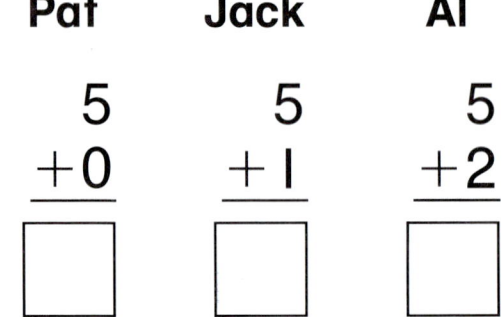

Pat	Jack	Al
5	5	5
+0	+1	+2
□	□	□

 Write About It • Look at Exercise 20. What pattern do you see?

 HOME ACTIVITY • Write addition problems both across and down for your child to solve.

Name _____

Problem Solving Strategy
Make a Model

How much do these cost altogether?

UNDERSTAND

What do you know?

Marbles cost __5__ ¢.   A giraffe costs __1__ ¢.

PLAN

How do you solve this problem?

Make a model.

SOLVE

Show 5 pennies.
Then show 1 penny.
Count the pennies.

__6__ ¢

CHECK

Explain why you think your answer is right.

Use 🪙 to show each price.

Draw the 🪙. Write how many there are in all.

THINK: What do I know?

1. How much do you spend for both?

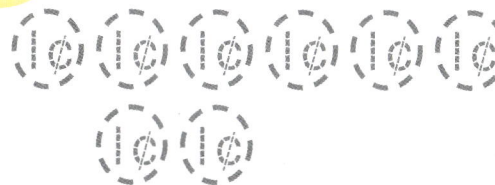

____ ¢

Chapter 2 • Using Addition

twenty-five **25**

Problem Solving Practice

Use 🪙 to show each price.
Draw the 🪙. Write how many there are in all.

Keep in Mind!
Understand
Plan
Solve
Check

1. How much will you spend if you buy both?

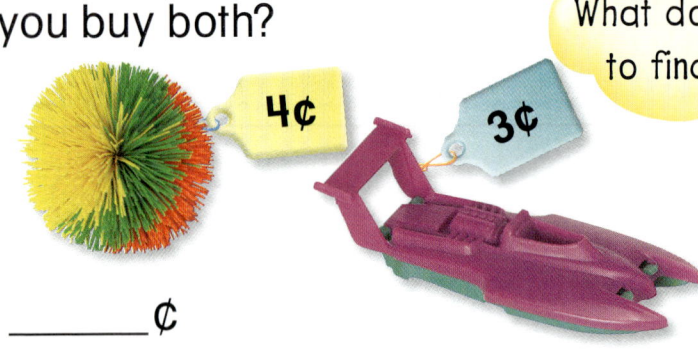

_____ ¢

THINK: What do I need to find out?

2. How much do these cost altogether?

_____ ¢

3. How much will you spend for both?

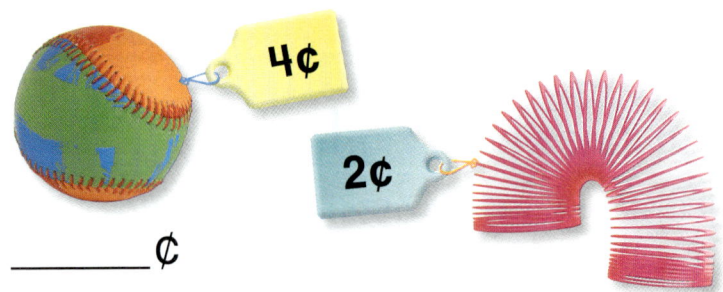

_____ ¢

4. How much will you spend if you buy both?

_____ ¢

HOME ACTIVITY • Choose two objects from pages 25 and 26. Have your child use pennies to show the total.

Name ______________________________

Extra Practice

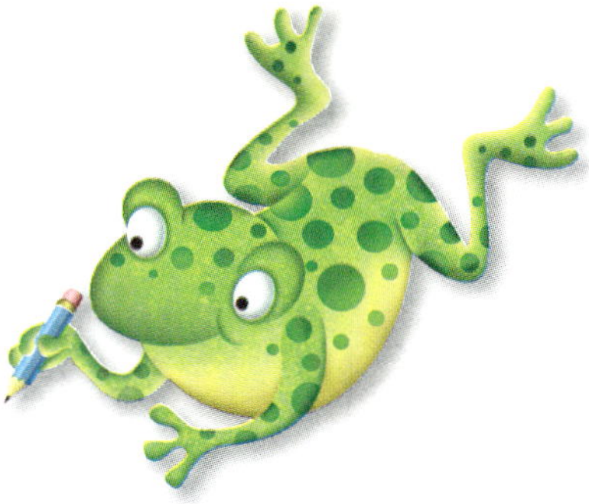

Add. Circle the addition sentences that have the same sum.

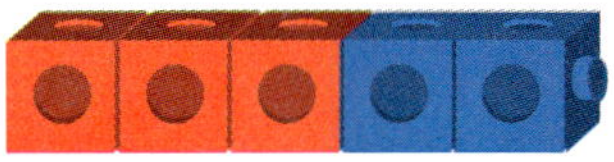 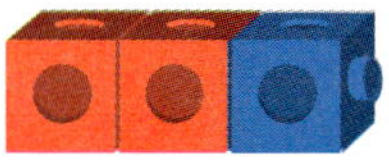 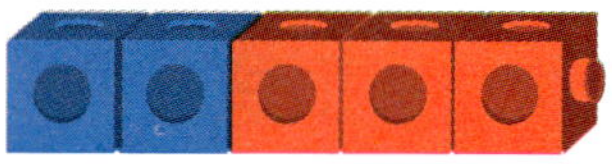

1. 3 + 2 = ____ 2. 2 + 1 = ____ 3. 2 + 3 = ____

Write two ways to make 7.

4. ____ ◯ ____ ◯ ____ 5. ____ ◯ ____ ◯ ____

Write two ways to make 9.

6. ____ ◯ ____ ◯ ____ 7. ____ ◯ ____ ◯ ____

Write the numbers to match the dots.
Write the sum.

8. 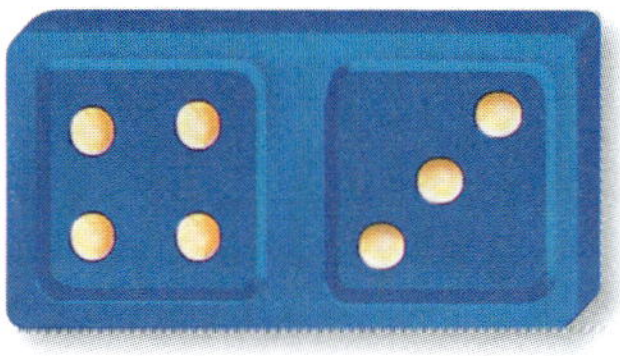

____ + ____ = ____

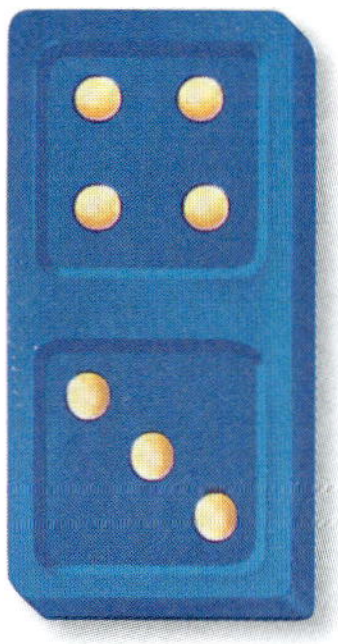

☐
+ ☐
☐

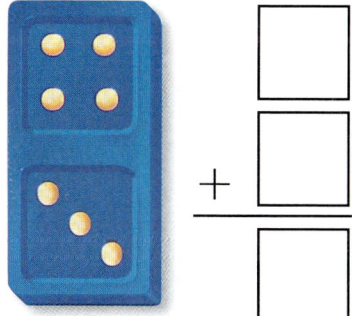

Problem Solving

Use (penny) to show each price. Draw the (penny).
Write how many there are in all.

9. How much will you spend for both?

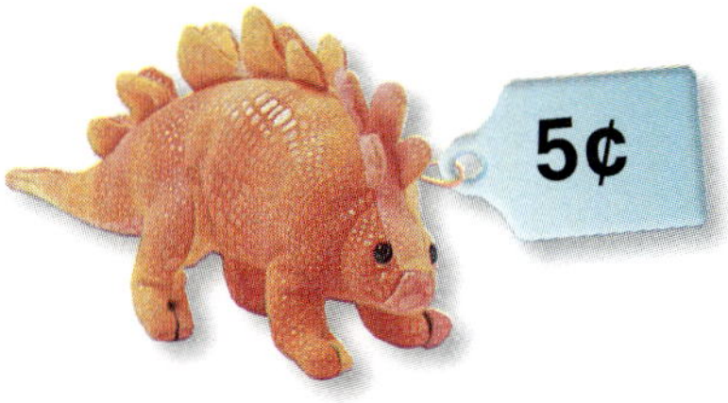

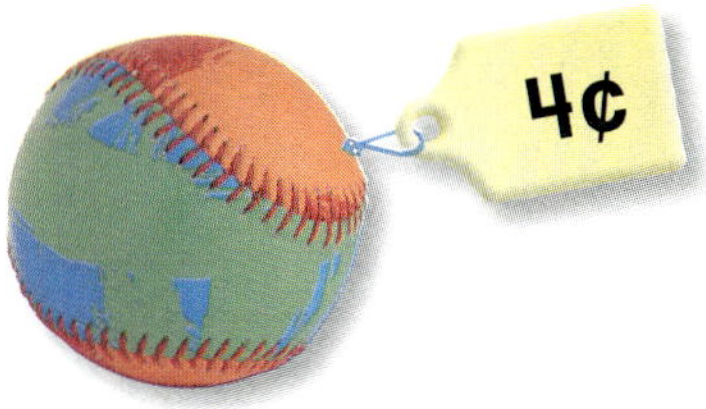

____¢

Name _____

✓ Review/Test

Concepts and Skills

Add. Circle the addition sentences that have the same sum.

1. 4 + 2 = ____   2. 2 + 4 = ____   3. 2 + 3 = ____

Write two ways to make 8.

4. ___ ◯ ___ ◯ ___   5. ___ ◯ ___ ◯ ___

Write two ways to make 10.

6. ___ ◯ ___ ◯ ___   7. ___ ◯ ___ ◯ ___

Write the numbers to match the dots. Write the sum.

8.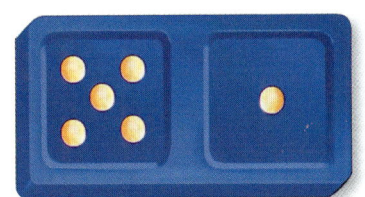

___ + ___ = ___

   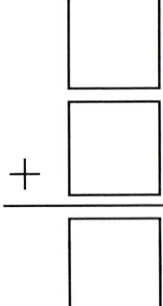

Problem Solving

Use  to show each price. Draw the 🪙. Write how many there are in all.

9. How much would you spend for both?

_____ ¢

28 twenty-eight

Name _____

⭐ Standardized Test Prep
Chapters 1–2

Choose the answer for questions 1–4.

1. Which is a way to make 8?

   5 + 1   4 + 4   6 + 4   3 + 2
   ○   ○   ○   ○

2. Which is another way to write 8 + 2 = 10?

     2   6   9   8
   +6   +2   +1   +2
   ──   ──   ──   ──
     8   8   10   10
   ○   ○   ○   ○

3. How much do these cost altogether?

   3¢   6¢   8¢   9¢
   ○   ○   ○   ○

4. What is the sum for 7 + 0?

   0   4   7   8
   ○   ○   ○   ○

Show What You Know

5. Write an addition sentence to show the sum of 6. Color some of the cubes red.

   Color the rest blue to explain your answer. Write another addition sentence that has the same sum.

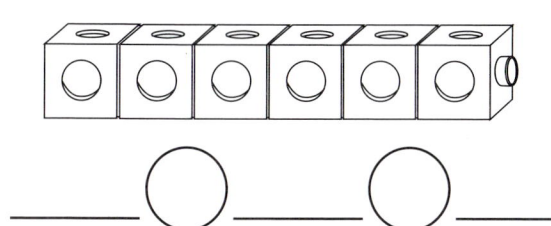

Chapter 2   twenty-nine **29**

Name _____

MATH GAME

Tic-Tac-Sum

Play with a partner.

1. One player uses 🔴.
   The other player uses 🟡.
2. Toss two 🎲.
3. Find the sum.
   Cover that number with a counter.
4. Your turn is over if that number is already covered.
5. The first player to get 4 counters in a row wins.

You will need

2 🎲

5 🔴   5 🟡

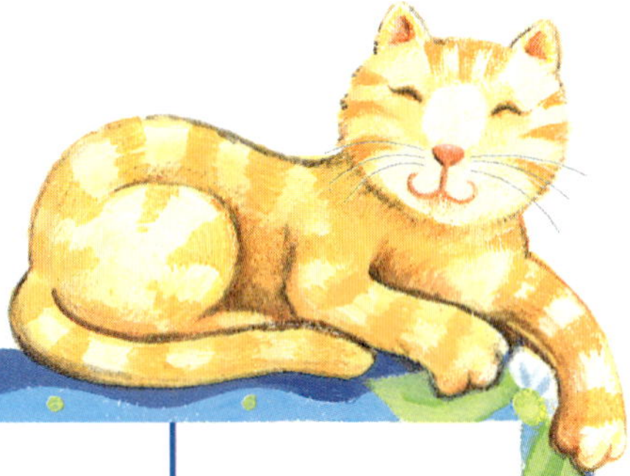

6	2	8	3
4	7	5	6
9	9	7	8
2	5	3	4

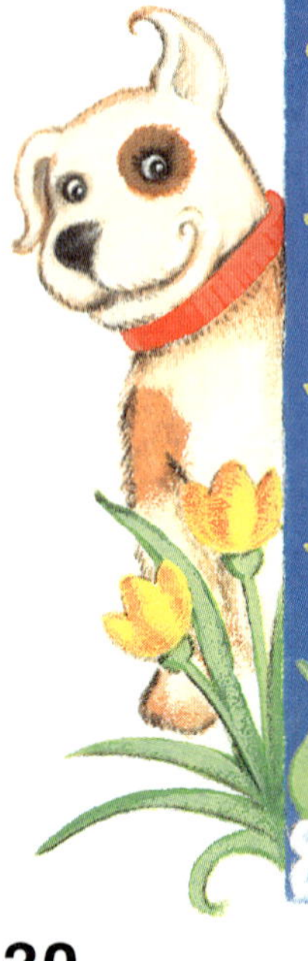

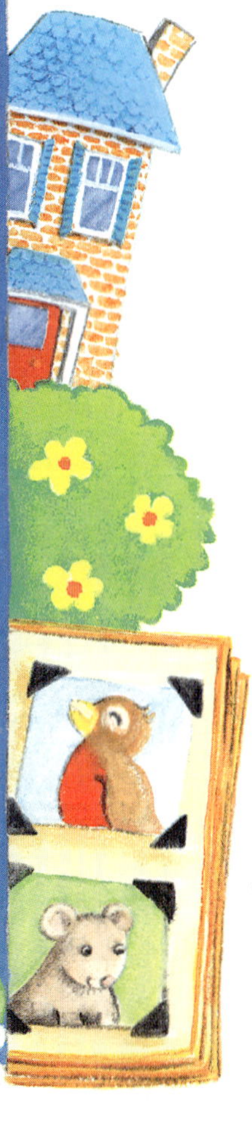

CHAPTER 3
Subtraction Concepts

FUN FACTS

Leatherback turtles are as long as 8 of your math books.

Theme: At the Beach

Name _____

✓ Check What You Know

Zero

Count the 🏈. Write how many are in each picture.

1.    _____

2.    _____

Model Subtraction

Use 🟦 to show the story.

Draw the 🟦. Mark an X on the 🟦 you subtract. Write how many are left.

3.

      3   1   _____

4.

      4   2   _____

5.

      3   2   _____

Name _____

Model Subtraction Stories

Explore

Use 🔴 to show the story. Draw the 🔴.
Cross out how many go away.
Write how many are left.

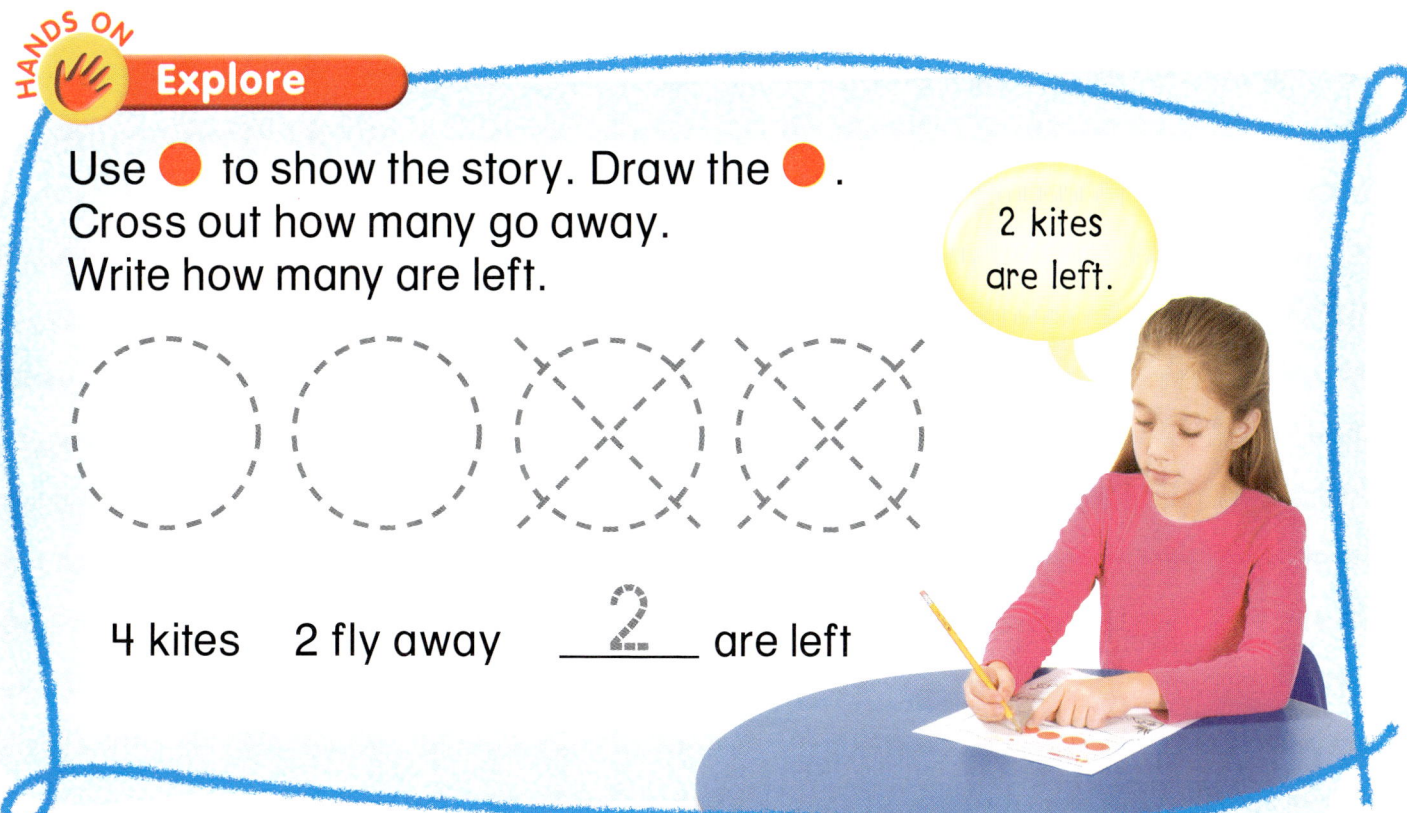

2 kites are left.

4 kites   2 fly away   __2__ are left

1.

3 boats   2 sail away   _____ is left

2.

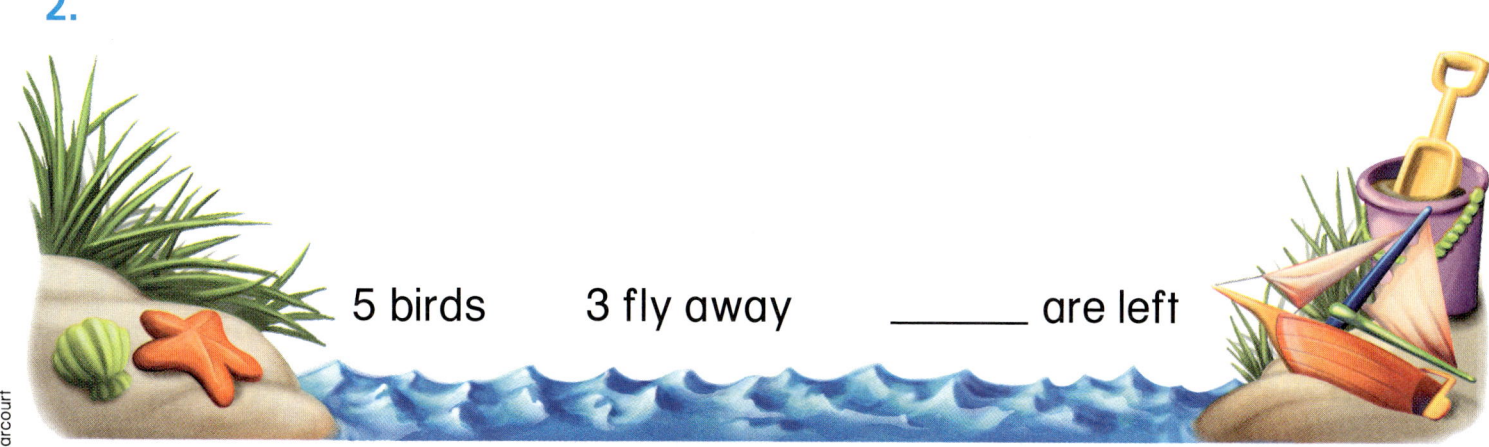

5 birds   3 fly away   _____ are left

Explain It • **Daily Reasoning**

When you take objects away from a group, are there **more** or **fewer** objects left? Why?

Chapter 3 • Subtraction Concepts

Practice

Use 🔴 to show the story. Draw the 🔴.
Cross out how many go away. Write how many are left.

1.
   4 bees   4 fly away   _____ are left

2.
   2 gulls   1 walks away   _____ is left

3.
   5 children   2 walk away   _____ are left

HOME ACTIVITY • Have your child use objects to show the subtraction stories on this page.

Name _____

Use Symbols to Subtract

Vocabulary
minus –
equals =
difference

Learn

5 – 3 = 2

minus — equals — difference

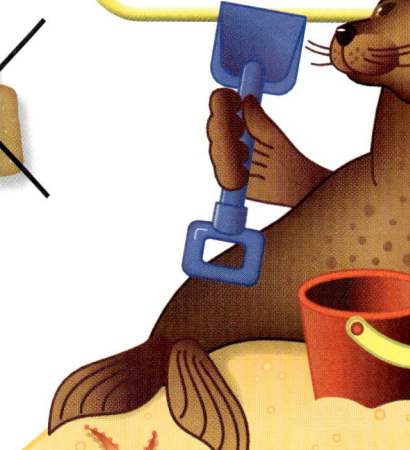

Check

Cross out pictures to subtract.
Write the difference.

1.    4 – 2 = ____

2.    6 – 3 = ____

3.    5 – 2 = ____

4.    3 – 1 = ____

Explain It • Daily Reasoning

What does the minus sign mean?
What does the equal sign mean? Explain.

Chapter 3 • Subtraction Concepts

Practice and Problem Solving

Cross out pictures to subtract.
Write the difference.

1.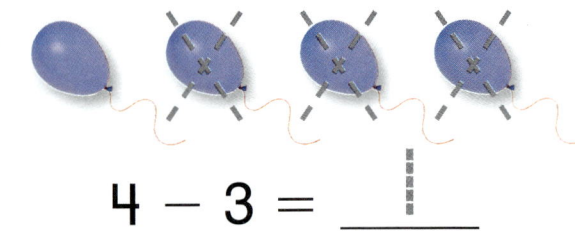

   4 − 3 = __1__

2.

   6 − 2 = _____

3.

   3 − 2 = _____

4.

   4 − 1 = _____

5.

   6 − 5 = _____

6.

   6 − 4 = _____

7.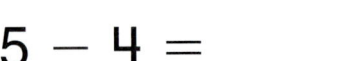

   5 − 4 = _____

8.

   2 − 1 = _____

Problem Solving
Logical Reasoning

Solve the riddle. Write the number.

9. I am greater than 4. I am less than 6. What number am I?

   _____

10. I am less than 3. I am greater than 1. What number am I?

    _____

 Write About It • Write a riddle about the number 4.

HOME ACTIVITY • Have your child draw pictures to show a subtraction problem. Then ask him or her to tell the difference.

Name _____

Algebra: Write Subtraction Sentences

Vocabulary
subtraction sentence

Learn

$6 - 2 = 4$ is a **subtraction sentence**.

Check

Write the subtraction sentence.

1.

2.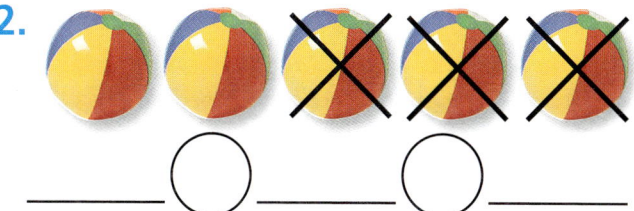

3.

4.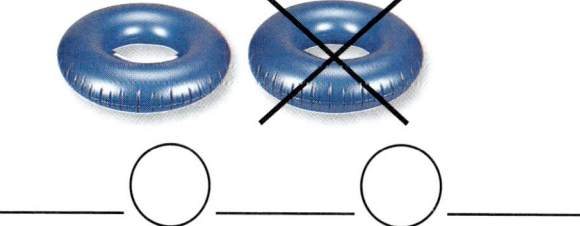

5.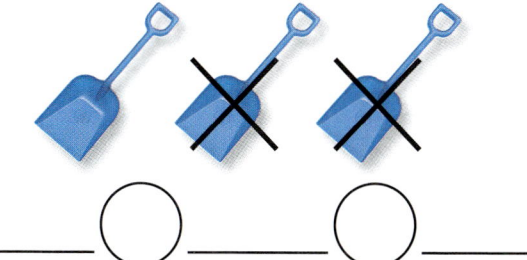

6.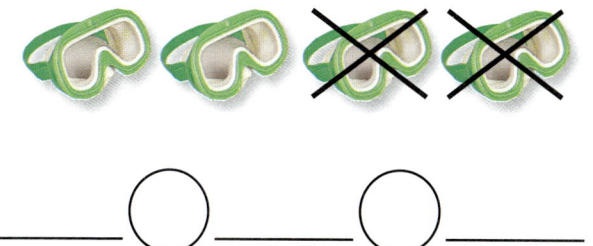

Explain It • Daily Reasoning

How can you use these numbers to write two different subtraction sentences? Explain.

Chapter 3 • Subtraction Concepts

thirty-seven **37**

Practice and Problem Solving

Write the subtraction sentence.

1.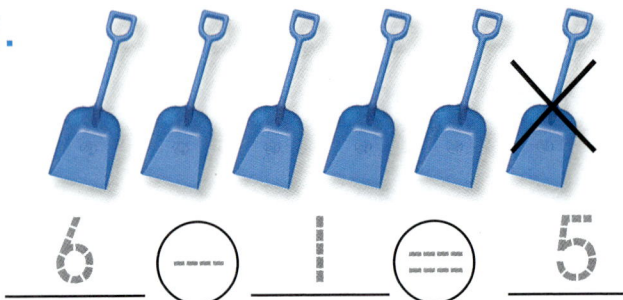
   6 ― 1 ◯ 5

2.
   ___ ◯ ___ ◯ ___

3.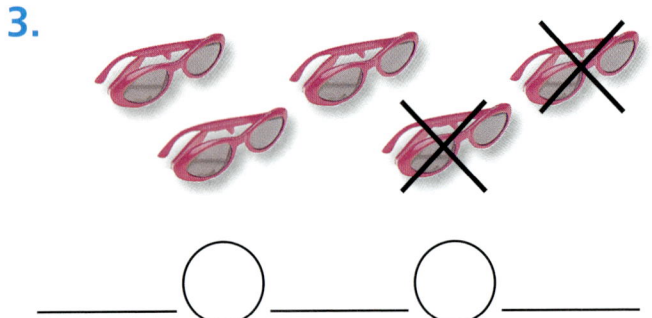
   ___ ◯ ___ ◯ ___

4.
   ___ ◯ ___ ◯ ___

5.
   ___ ◯ ___ ◯ ___

6.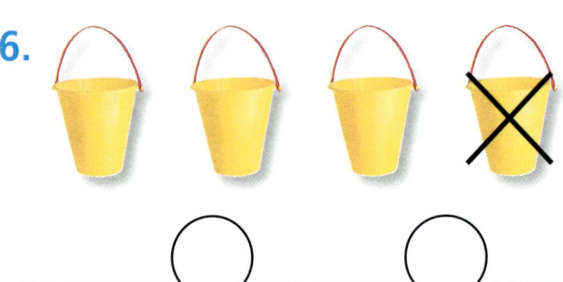
   ___ ◯ ___ ◯ ___

Problem Solving
Visual Thinking

Circle the picture that shows the subtraction sentence.

7. $4 - 3 = 1$

8. $3 - 1 = 2$

 Write About It • Look at Exercises 7 and 8. Explain why you circled the pictures you did.

🏠 **HOME ACTIVITY** • Have your child use objects to show subtraction stories. Then ask him or her to write the subtraction sentences.

Name _____

Problem Solving Strategy
Make a Model

3 butterflies are in the tree.

1 flies away.

How many are left?

UNDERSTAND

What do you need to find out?

Circle the question.
What do you know?

There are __3__ butterflies.

__1__ flies away.

PLAN

How do you solve this problem?

Use counters. Draw 3 counters. Cross out 1.

SOLVE

There are __2__ butterflies left.

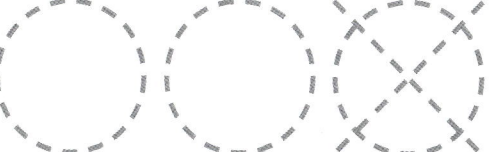

CHECK

Does your answer make sense?
Explain.

Use ● to subtract.
Draw the ●.
Write the difference.

1. Kathy finds 4 shells.
   She gives 2 away.
   How many shells
   does she have left?

   THINK:
   What do I need
   to find out?

   _____ shells

Chapter 3 • Subtraction Concepts

thirty-nine **39**

Problem Solving Practice

Use 🔴 to subtract.
Draw the 🔴.
Write the difference.

THINK: How can I solve the problem?

Keep in Mind!
Understand
Plan
Solve
Check

1. Steve sees 6 pelicans.
   2 fly away.
   How many pelicans are left?

   _____ pelicans

2. Lisa sees 5 fish.
   3 swim away.
   How many fish are left?

   _____ fish

3. Tim finds 3 shells.
   He gives 1 to Joe.
   How many shells does he have left?

   _____ shells

4. Ann sees 2 sand castles.
   1 gets washed away.
   How many sand castles are left?

   _____ sand castle

🏠 **HOME ACTIVITY** • Make up story problems like the ones in this lesson. Have your child use objects or draw pictures to solve the problems.

Name _____

Algebra: Subtract All or Zero

Vocabulary
zero 0

Learn

6 − 0 = __6__

When you subtract zero, you have the same number left.

6 − 6 = __0__

When you subtract all, you have zero left.

Check

Write the difference.

1.

3 − 0 = ____

2.

3 − 3 = ____

3.

4 − 4 = ____

4.

4 − 0 = ____

5.

2 − 0 = ____

6.

2 − 2 = ____

Explain It • Daily Reasoning

What happens when you subtract all of a group? Why?
What happens when you subtract 0 from a group? Why?

Chapter 3 • Subtraction Concepts

forty-one **41**

Practice and Problem Solving

Write the difference.

1.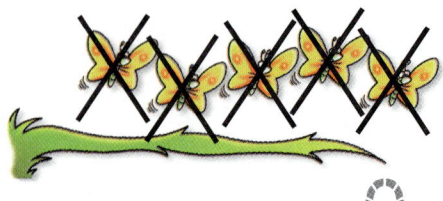
5 − 5 = __0__

2.
6 − 0 = __6__

3.
4 − 4 = ____

4.
2 − 0 = ____

5.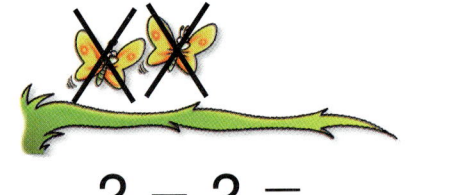
2 − 2 = ____

6.
1 − 1 = ____

7.
5 − 0 = ____

8.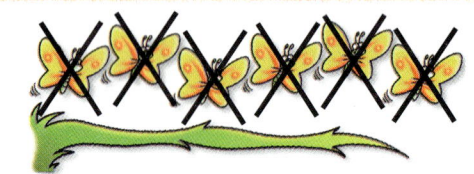
6 − 6 = ____

Problem Solving
Application

Write the subtraction sentence.

9. Maria sees 3 butterflies. All 3 fly away. How many are left?

____ ◯ ____ ◯ ____

 Write About It • Look at Exercise 9. Draw pictures to show your subtraction sentence. Explain if you subtracted all or zero.

HOME ACTIVITY • Have your child draw pictures to show 3 − 3 and 3 − 0. Ask your child to tell you how to find each difference.

Name _____

Extra Practice

Cross out pictures to subtract.
Write the difference.

1.

   4 − 3 = ____

2.

   5 − 2 = ____

Write the subtraction sentence.

3.

   ___ ◯ ___ ◯ ___

4.

   ___ ◯ ___ ◯ ___

Write the difference.

5.

   4 − 0 = ____

6.

   6 − 6 = ____

Problem Solving

Use to subtract.
Draw the ●.
Write the difference.

7. Joe sees 6 fish.
   2 swim away.
   How many fish are left?

   _____ fish

Chapter 3 • Subtraction Concepts

Name _____

✓ Review/Test

Concepts and Skills

Cross out pictures to subtract.
Write the difference.

1.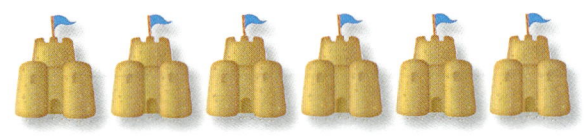

   6 − 3 = _____

2.

   5 − 4 = _____

Write the subtraction sentence.

3.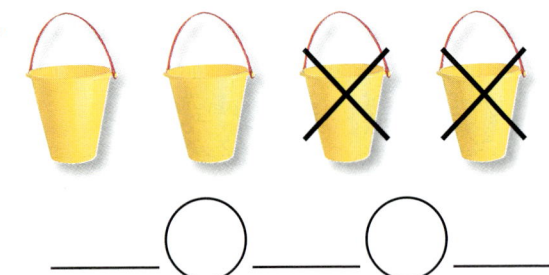

   ___ ◯ ___ ◯ ___

4.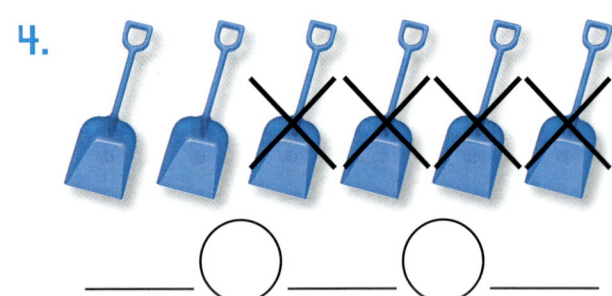

   ___ ◯ ___ ◯ ___

Write the difference.

5.

   5 − 0 = _____

6.

   6 − 6 = _____

Problem Solving

Use 🔴 to subtract.
Draw the 🔴.
Write the difference.

7. 5 ants are on a log.
   3 ants crawl away.
   How many ants are left?

   _____ ants

44 forty-four

Name _____

★Standardized Test Prep
Chapters 1–3

Choose the answer for questions 1–4.

1. Which subtraction sentence tells about the picture?

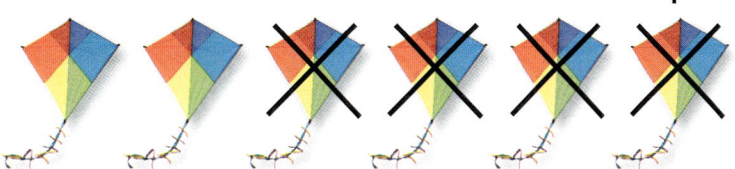

   6 − 6 = 0   6 − 3 = 3   6 − 4 = 2   6 − 1 = 5
      ○   ○   ○   ○

2. What is the difference?

   6 − 3 = ____

   3   6   8   11
   ○   ○   ○   ○

3. What is the difference for 4 − 0?

   4   3   2   1
   ○   ○   ○   ○

4. There are 3 bees. 2 fly away. How many are left?

   0   1   3   5
   ○   ○   ○   ○

Show What You Know

5. Write an addition sentence to show the sum of 8. Use and to explain your answer. Draw the and you use.

Chapter 3   forty-five **45**

MATH GAME

Numbers in the Sand

Play with a partner.

1. Put your 🎲 at START.
2. Toss the 🎲.
3. Move your 🎲 that many spaces.
4. Find the difference.
5. If you are not correct, lose a turn.
6. The first player to get to END wins.

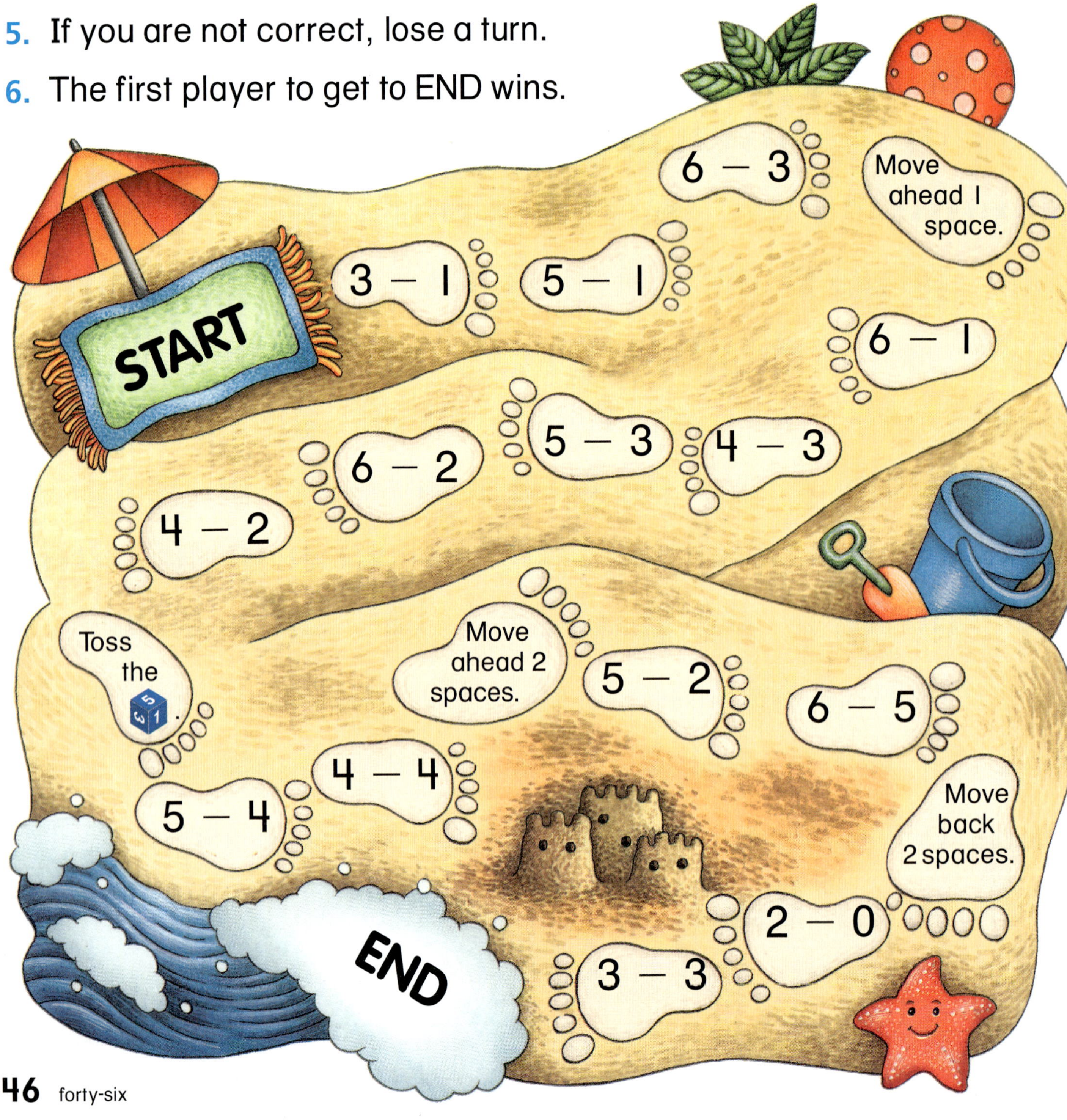

You will need

2 🎲   🎲

CHAPTER 4
Using Subtraction

FUN FACTS

There are three primary colors: red, yellow, and blue.

Theme: In the Classroom

Name _____

✓ Check What You Know

Use Pictures to Subtract

Subtract. Write the numbers.

1.

   ___ − ___ = ___

2.

   ___ − ___ = ___

3.

   ___ − ___ = ___

4.

   ___ − ___ = ___

Use Symbols to Subtract

Cross out pictures to subtract.
Write the difference.

5.

   $3 - 1 =$ ___

6.

   $6 - 1 =$ ___

7.

   $5 - 3 =$ ___

8.

   $4 - 3 =$ ___

Name _____

Take Apart 7 and 8

Vocabulary
subtraction sentence

Explore

I started with 7 cubes and then took one away.

7 − 1 = 6

subtraction sentence

Connect

Use 🎲 to show all the ways to subtract from 7.
Complete the subtraction sentences.

1. 7 − _0_ = _7_
2. 7 − ___ = ___
3. 7 − ___ = ___
4. 7 − ___ = ___
5. 7 − ___ = ___
6. 7 − ___ = ___
7. 7 − ___ = ___
8. 7 − ___ = ___

Explain It • Daily Reasoning

Continue the pattern.
What comes next?
Explain how you know.

7−0=7
7−1=6
7−2=5

Chapter 4 • Using Subtraction

Practice and Problem Solving

Use 🟥 to show all the ways to subtract from 8. Complete the subtraction sentences.

Remember to always start with 8 cubes.

1. 8 − 0 = 8

2. 8 − ___ = ___

3. 8 − ___ = ___

4. 8 − ___ = ___

5. 8 − ___ = ___

6. 8 − ___ = ___

7. 8 − ___ = ___

8. 8 − ___ = ___

9. 8 − ___ = ___

Problem Solving
Visual Thinking

Cross out some of the pictures. Write the subtraction sentence.

10.

___ ◯ ___ ◯ ___

11.

___ ◯ ___ ◯ ___

 Write About It • Explain what happens if you cross out all of the pictures in a group.

 HOME ACTIVITY • Have your child use small objects to show different ways to subtract from 8.

50 fifty

Name _____

Take Apart 9 and 10

 **Explore**

There are many ways to take apart 9.

$9 - 0 = 9$

$9 - 1 = 8$

$9 - 2 = 7$

Remember to look for a pattern.

Connect

Use  to show all the ways to subtract from 9. Complete the subtraction sentences.

1. $9 - \underline{0} = \underline{9}$
2. $9 - \underline{} = \underline{}$
3. $9 - \underline{} = \underline{}$
4. $9 - \underline{} = \underline{}$
5. $9 - \underline{} = \underline{}$
6. $9 - \underline{} = \underline{}$
7. $9 - \underline{} = \underline{}$
8. $9 - \underline{} = \underline{}$
9. $9 - \underline{} = \underline{}$
10. $9 - \underline{} = \underline{}$

Explain It • Daily Reasoning

How did using a pattern help you find the answers?

Chapter 4 • Using Subtraction

Practice and Problem Solving

Use to show all the ways to subtract from 10. Complete the subtraction sentences.

What are the different ways you can subtract from 10?

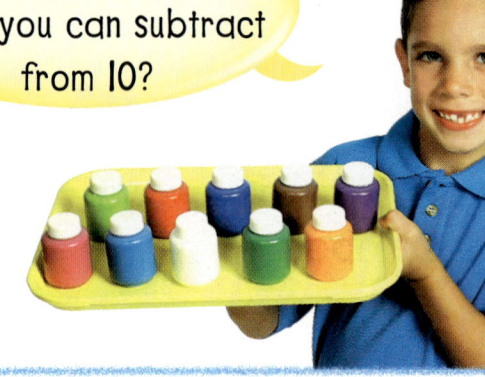

1. 10 − __0__ = __10__

2. 10 − ___ = ___

3. 10 − ___ = ___

4. 10 − ___ = ___

5. 10 − ___ = ___

6. 10 − ___ = ___

7. 10 − ___ = ___

8. 10 − ___ = ___

9. 10 − ___ = ___

10. 10 − ___ = ___

11. 10 − ___ = ___

Problem Solving
Algebra

Solve. Use to help you.

12. 7 − ■ = 3

■ = ___

13. 8 − ■ = 6

■ = ___

14. 7 − ■ = 5

■ = ___

 Write About It • Look at Exercise 14. Draw pictures to check your answer.

 HOME ACTIVITY • Have your child use small objects to show ways to subtract from 10.

Name _____

Vertical Subtraction

Learn

You can subtract across.

You can subtract down.

5 − 1 = __4__

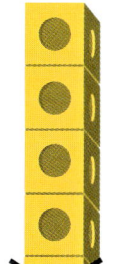

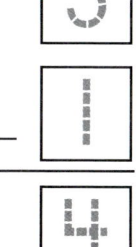

Check

Subtract across and down.

1.

   4 − 3 = ___

2.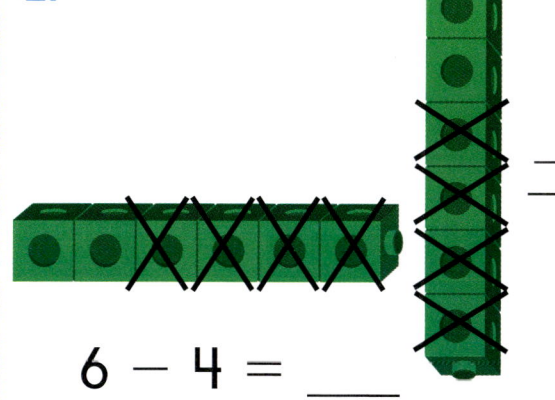

   6 − 4 = ___

3.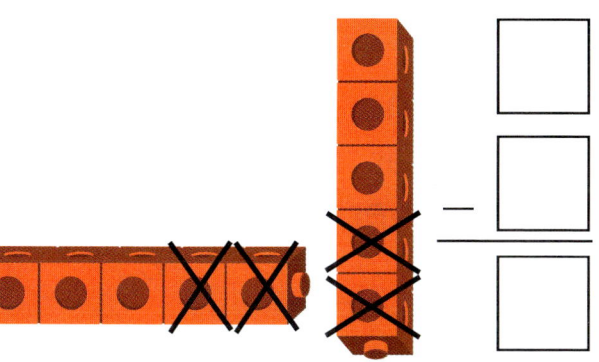

   5 − 2 = ___

4.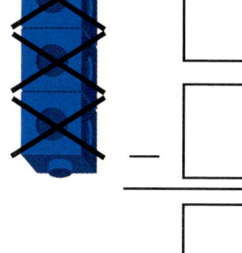

   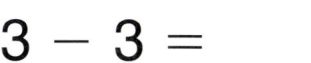

   3 − 3 = ___

Explain It • Daily Reasoning

Why is the answer the same for both ways of subtracting?

Chapter 4 • Using Subtraction

Practice and Problem Solving

Write the difference.

1.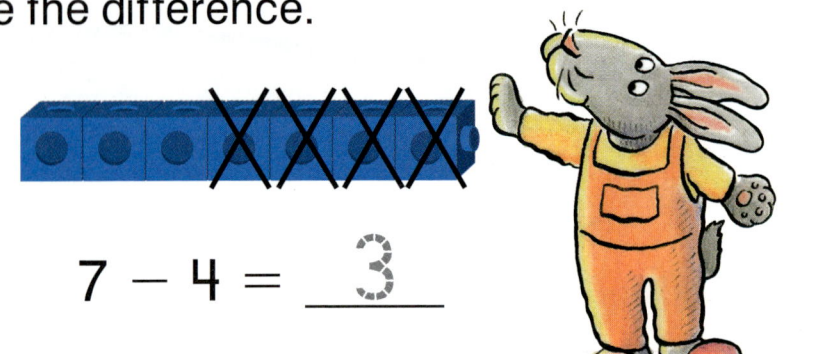

    $7 - 4 = \underline{3}$

2.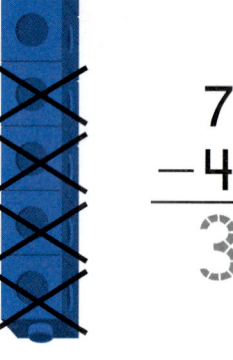

    $\begin{array}{r} 7 \\ -4 \\ \hline 3 \end{array}$

3. $\begin{array}{r} 10 \\ -0 \\ \hline \end{array}$
4. $\begin{array}{r} 6 \\ -3 \\ \hline \end{array}$
5. $\begin{array}{r} 4 \\ -2 \\ \hline \end{array}$
6. $\begin{array}{r} 8 \\ -4 \\ \hline \end{array}$
7. $\begin{array}{r} 9 \\ -2 \\ \hline \end{array}$
8. $\begin{array}{r} 5 \\ -0 \\ \hline \end{array}$

9. $\begin{array}{r} 3 \\ -2 \\ \hline \end{array}$
10. $\begin{array}{r} 8 \\ -6 \\ \hline \end{array}$
11. $\begin{array}{r} 9 \\ -0 \\ \hline \end{array}$
12. $\begin{array}{r} 7 \\ -2 \\ \hline \end{array}$
13. $\begin{array}{r} 5 \\ -4 \\ \hline \end{array}$
14. $\begin{array}{r} 6 \\ -6 \\ \hline \end{array}$

15. $\begin{array}{r} 10 \\ -5 \\ \hline \end{array}$
16. $\begin{array}{r} 4 \\ -0 \\ \hline \end{array}$
17. $\begin{array}{r} 7 \\ -7 \\ \hline \end{array}$
18. $\begin{array}{r} 9 \\ -4 \\ \hline \end{array}$
19. $\begin{array}{r} 8 \\ -0 \\ \hline \end{array}$
20. $\begin{array}{r} 7 \\ -6 \\ \hline \end{array}$

Problem Solving

Logical Reasoning

Solve. Write the number.

21. I am greater than 8.
    I am less than 10.
    What number am I?

    _____

22. I am less than 5.
    I am greater than 3.
    What number am I?

    _____

Write About It • Explain how you solve this riddle. I am greater than 0. I am less than 2. What number am I?

🏠 **HOME ACTIVITY** • Write subtraction sentences that go across, and have your child find the difference for each. Then ask your child to write the same problems going down.

Name _____

Subtract to Compare

Learn

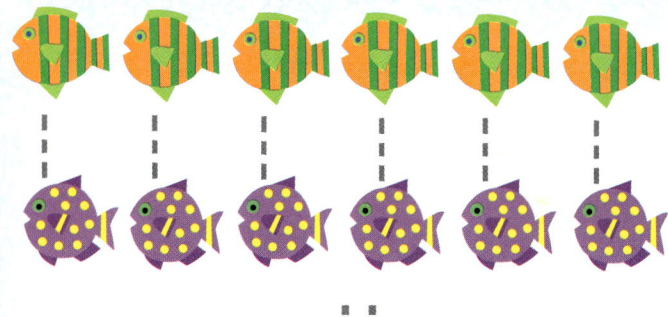

10 − 6 = __4__

There are more 🐟 than 🐟.
You can subtract to find how many more.

Check

Draw lines to match.
Subtract to find how many more.

1.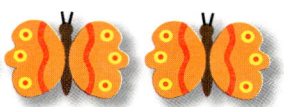

4 − 2 = _____

_____ more 🦋

2.

8 − 5 = _____

_____ more 🐞

3.

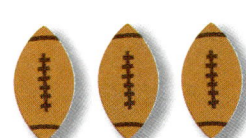

7 − 3 = _____

_____ more ⚽

4.

5 − 4 = _____

_____ more ⛸

Explain It • Daily Reasoning

Why do you subtract to find how many more 🟡 than 🔴 there are?

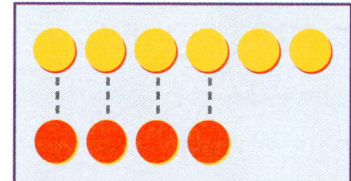

Chapter 4 • Using Subtraction

Practice and Problem Solving

Draw lines to match.
Subtract to find how many more.

1.

    $6 - 3 = \underline{3}$

    $\underline{3}$ more

2.

    $4 - 1 = \underline{}$

    $\underline{}$ more

3.

    $3 - 2 = \underline{}$

    $\underline{}$ more

4.

    $5 - 3 = \underline{}$

    $\underline{}$ more

Problem Solving
Application

Solve.

5. John had 7 stamps.
   Sue had 3 stamps.
   How many more stamps
   did John have?

   $\underline{}$ stamps

6. Jane had 5 pennies.
   Mark had 2 pennies.
   How many more pennies
   did Jane have?

   $\underline{}$ pennies

 Write About It • Look at Exercise 6.
Draw the pennies. Then compare to check
your answer.

🏠 **HOME ACTIVITY** • Have your child make up subtraction stories for you to solve.

Name _____

Problem Solving Strategy
Draw a Picture

Kathy had a box of 8 crayons.
She gave some crayons away.
She has 5 left.
How many crayons did Kathy give away?

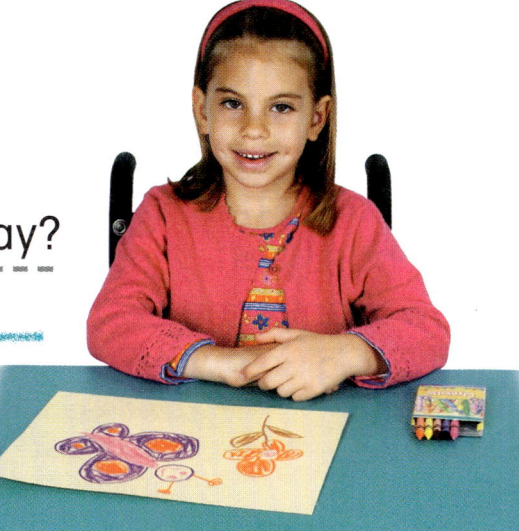

UNDERSTAND

What do you want to find out?
Draw a line under the question.

PLAN

You can draw a picture to solve the problem.

SOLVE

  ___3___ crayons

What number do I add to 5 to get 8?
$8 - \blacksquare = 5$
$5 + \underline{3} = 8$

CHECK

Does your answer make sense?
Explain.

Draw a picture to solve the problem.
Write how many were given away.

What number do I add to 3 to make 10?

1. I had 10 pencils.
   I gave some away.
   I have 3 left. How many pencils did I give away?

   _____ pencils

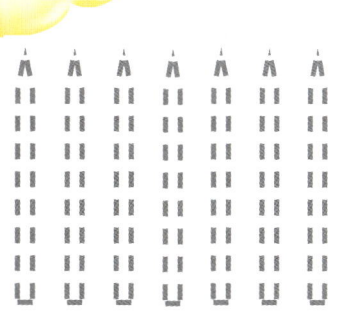

Chapter 4 • Using Subtraction

Problem Solving Practice

Keep in Mind!
Understand
Plan
Solve
Check

Draw a picture to solve the problem.
Write how many were given away.

1. Pat had 9 markers.
   She gave some away.
   She has 4 left.
   How many markers did Pat give away?

   What number do I add to 4 to make 9?

   __5__ markers

2. Dave had 8 stickers.
   He gave some to Joe.
   He has 6 left.
   How many stickers did Dave give to Joe?

   What number do I add to 6 to make 8?

   _____ stickers

3. Ed had 3 erasers.
   He gave some away.
   He has 1 left.
   How many erasers did Ed give away?

   What number do I add to 1 to make 3?

   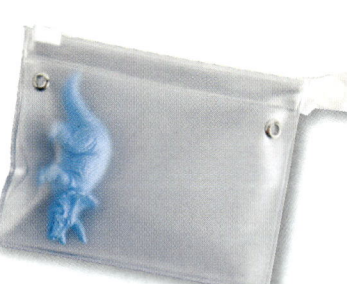

   _____ erasers

HOME ACTIVITY • Tell a math story like those in the problems on this page. Ask your child to draw a picture to solve the problem and then explain the drawing to you.

Name _____

Extra Practice

Complete the subtraction sentences.
Show ways to subtract from 7.

1. 7 – ___ = ___

2. 7 – ___ = ___

Show ways to subtract from 9.

3. 9 – ___ = ___

4. 9 – ___ = ___

Write the difference.

5. 5
   −0
   ___

6. 8
   −8
   ___

7. 7
   −2
   ___

8. 10
   − 7
   ___

9. 9
   −5
   ___

Draw lines to match.
Subtract to find how many more.

10.

4 – 3 = ___

___ more

11.

6 – 2 = ___

___ more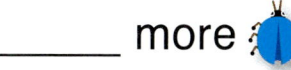

Problem Solving

Draw a picture to solve the problem.

What number do I add to 6 to make 10?

12. Elise had 10 pencils. She gave some away. She has 6 left. How many pencils did Elise give away?

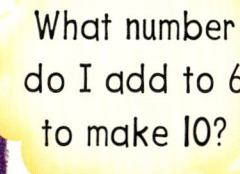

___ pencils

Chapter 4 • Using Subtraction

fifty-nine **59**

Name _____

✅ Review/Test

Concepts and Skills

Complete the subtraction sentences.
Show ways to subtract from 8.

1. 8 – ____ = ____

2. 8 – ____ = ____

Show ways to subtract from 10.

3. 10 – ____ = ____

4. 10 – ____ = ____

Write the difference.

5. 6
   −4
   ___

6. 9
   −6
   ___

7. 8
   −1
   ___

8. 10
   − 9
   ___

9. 3
   −3
   ___

Draw lines to match.
Subtract to find how many more.

10.

6 − 3 = ____

____ more

11.

5 − 2 = ____

____ more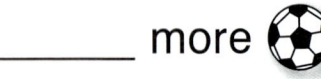

Problem Solving

Draw a picture to solve the problem.

12. Fran had 5 erasers. She gave some to a friend. She has 3 left. How many erasers did Fran give to her friend?

____ erasers

What number do I add to 3 to make 5?

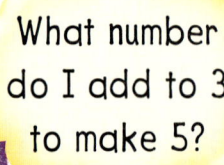

60 sixty

Name _____

⭐Standardized Test Prep
Chapters 1–4

Choose the answer for questions 1–5.

1. Which subtraction sentence tells how many more cats than pandas there are?

   - $8 - 2 = 6$
   - $8 - 3 = 5$
   - $8 - 4 = 4$
   - $8 - 6 = 2$

2. Which is another way to write $6 - 2 = 4$?

   - $\begin{array}{r}8\\-2\\\hline 6\end{array}$
   - $\begin{array}{r}8\\-6\\\hline 2\end{array}$
   - $\begin{array}{r}4\\-2\\\hline 2\end{array}$
   - $\begin{array}{r}6\\-2\\\hline 4\end{array}$

3. $8 - 2 = $ _____

   12   11   6   5

4. $9 - 3 = $ _____

   6   7   12   13

5. Ann has 4 flowers. She gives 2 away. How many are left?

   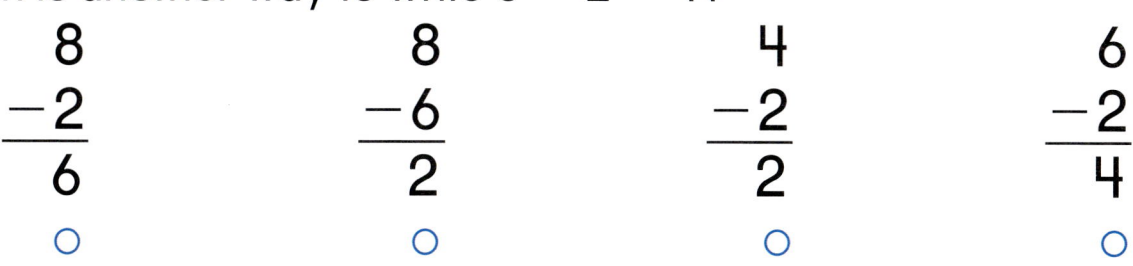

   1   2   4   6

Show What You Know

6. Write a subtraction sentence that equals 10. Use 🎲 to explain your answer. Draw the 🎲 you use.

IT'S IN THE BAG
Cat Pocket-Dots

PROJECT You will make a cat pocket to hold your dot cards to practice your math facts.

You Will Need

- Lunch-size bag
- Blackline patterns
- Crayons
- Glue
- Scissors

Directions

1. Color the cat face. Then cut it out.

2. Lay the bag in front of you. Put the flap at the top facing you. Glue the cat face to the flap.

3. Color the dots on the dot cards. Cut the cards apart.

4. Use dot cards 1 to 6 to make number sentences.

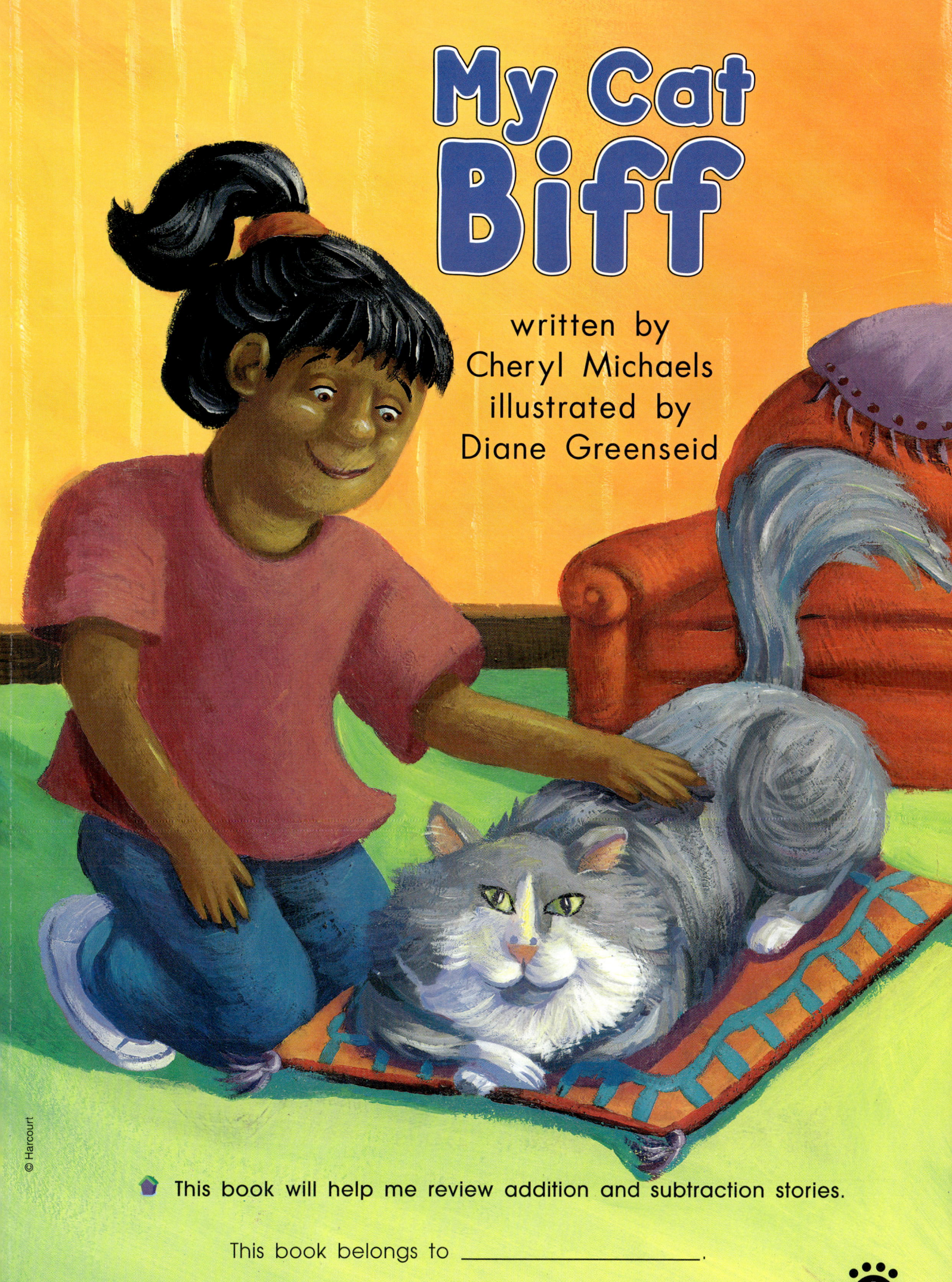

Biff had 3 balls.
I gave him one more.

3 + 1 = ____

Biff had 4 balls.
I gave him two more.

4 + 2 = _____

Biff had 6 balls.
He hit one under the chair.

6 − 1 = ____

Name _____

PROBLEM SOLVING ON LOCATION

At the Petting Zoo

Old MacDonald's Petting Zoo is near Huntsville, Alabama. You can see and pet animals.

Use the pictures to help you write the addition sentence.

1 How many in all?

_____ ◯ _____ = _____ animals

2 How many in all?

_____ ◯ _____ = _____ animals

llama

3 How many in all?

_____ ◯ _____ = _____ animals

emu

Name _____

CHALLENGE

Equals

 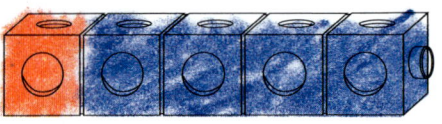

Both sides show 5. They are equal.

__2__ + __3__ = __1__ + __4__

5 = 5

Use different numbers of 🟧 and 🟦.
Show sides that are equal.
Color. Write the numbers.

1.

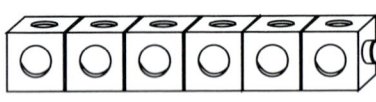 =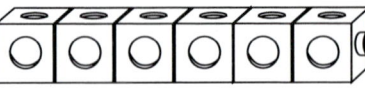

____ + ____ = ____ + ____

2.

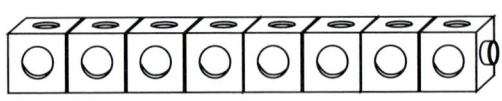 =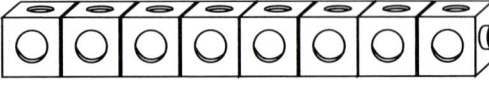

____ + ____ = ____ + ____

3.

=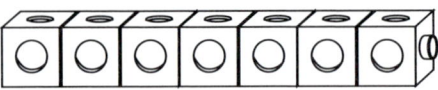

____ + ____ = ____ + ____

4.

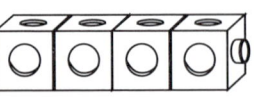 =

____ + ____ = ____ + ____

64 sixty-four

Name _____

✓ Study Guide and Review

Vocabulary

Add. Circle the **sum**.

Subtract. Circle the **difference**.

1.

   5 + 1 = ____

2.

   2 − 0 = ____

Skills and Concepts

Draw circles to show each number.
Write the sum.

3.

   0 + 5 = ____

4.

   2 + 2 = ____

Cross out pictures to subtract. Write the difference.

5.

   5 − 2 = ____

6.

   6 − 5 = ____

Write the subtraction sentence.

7.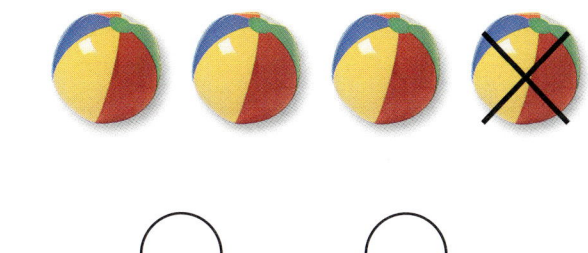

   ____ ◯ ____ ◯ ____

8.

   ____ ◯ ____ ◯ ____

Unit 1 • Study Guide and Review

Complete the addition or subtraction sentence.

9. Show a way to subtract from 9.

9 − ____ = ____

10. Show a way to make 10.

____ + ____ = 10

11. Write the numbers to match the dots. Write the sum.

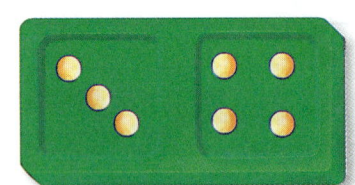

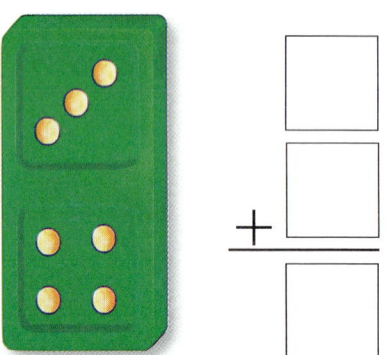

____ + ____ = ____

Draw lines to match.
Subtract to find how many more.

12.

6 − 2 = ____

____ more

13.

5 − 4 = ____

____ more

Problem Solving

Draw a picture. Then write an addition sentence to solve.

14. 2 fish swim.
1 more fish comes.
How many fish
are there in all?

____ fish

66 sixty-six

Name _____

✓ Performance Assessment

Pick Up Jacks

Ann and Jenny were playing with jacks.

- Jenny placed some jacks in a circle.

- Ann picked up 2 jacks from the circle.

- After Ann picked up the 2 jacks, there were fewer than 4 jacks in the circle.

Write a subtraction number sentence that fits this math story. Draw pictures to help you.

Show your work.

Name _____

TECHNOLOGY

The Learning Site • Seashell Search

1. Go to **www.harcourtschool.com**.
2. Click on 🪣.
3. Start. ➡
4. Add to play.

Practice and Problem Solving

Write the sum or difference.

1. 2 + 4 = ____
2. 3 + 1 = ____
3. 6 + 4 = ____

4. 6 − 5 = ____
5. 5 − 1 = ____
6. 7 − 3 = ____

Write two ways to make 7.

7. ____ ◯ ____ ◯ ____
8. ____ ◯ ____ ◯ ____

9. Sara has 2 shells. She finds 4 more. How many shells does she have in all?

   _____ shells

10. Jim has 9 pennies. He gives 2 away. How many pennies does he have left?

    _____ pennies

LOOKING BACK
SCHOOL HOME CONNECTION

Dear Family,

In Unit 1 we learned how to find sums and differences. Here is a game for us to play together. This game will give me a chance to share what I have learned.

Love,

_____

Directions
1. Put a bean on a space.
2. Use pennies to show one way to make that number.
3. Take turns. Your partner uses rocks instead of beans.
4. If you get the same number again, show a new way to make it.
5. The first person to cover 3 spaces in a row wins.

Materials
- 8 beans (or other small objects)
- 8 rocks (or other small objects)
- 10 pennies

Unit 2 • Unit Game

sixty-nine A **69A**

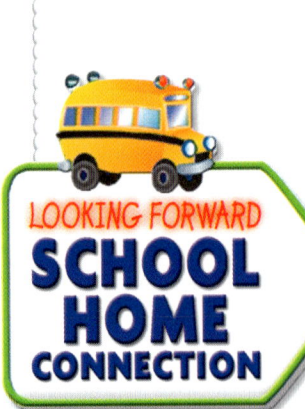

LOOKING FORWARD — SCHOOL HOME CONNECTION

Dear Family,

During the next few weeks, we will learn different ways to memorize addition and subtraction facts. Here is important math vocabulary and a list of books to share.

Love,

_____

Vocabulary
- count on
- count back
- fact family

Vocabulary Power

count on A way to add by counting on from the greater number.

6 + 2 = 8

Say 6. Count on 2.
7, 8

count back A way to subtract by counting backward from the greater number.

5 − 2 = 3

Say 5. Count back 2.
4, 3

A **fact family** includes all the addition and subtraction facts that use the same numbers.

5 + 2 = 7   7 − 2 = 5
2 + 5 = 7   7 − 5 = 2

BOOKS TO SHARE

To read about addition and subtraction with your child, look for these books in your library.

Domino Addition, by Lynette Long Ph.D., Charlesbridge, 1996.

How Many, How Many, How Many, by Rick Walton, Candlewick, 1996.

Ten Sly Piranhas, by William Wise, Penguin Putnam, 1993.

Seven Little Rabbits, by John Becker, Walker, 1994.

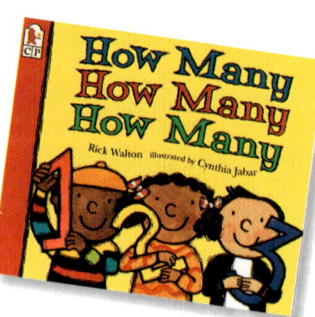

 Visit *The Learning Site* for additional ideas and activities. www.harcourtschool.com

CHAPTER 5 Addition Strategies

FUN FACTS

An octopus has a soft, bag-shaped body and 8 rubbery arms.

Theme: Sea Life

Name _____

✓ Check What You Know

Addition Patterns

Count the 🎈. Draw one more.
Write how many in all.

1.

    1 + 1 = ____

2.

    2 + 1 = ____

3.

    3 + 1 = ____

4.

    4 + 1 = ____

5.

    5 + 1 = ____

6.

    6 + 1 = ____

7. 🎈🎈🎈🎈🎈🎈🎈

    7 + 1 = ____

70 seventy   Use this page to review important skills needed for this chapter.

Name _____

Count On 1 and 2

Vocabulary
count on

Explore

Say 5. Count on 1.

$5 + 1 = \underline{6}$

Say 6. Count on 2.

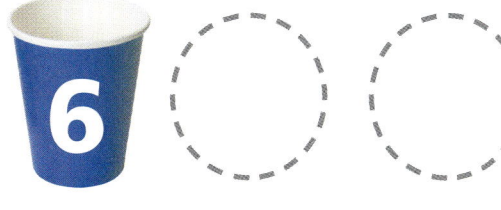

$6 + 2 = \underline{8}$

Connect

Use 🔴. Count on. Write the sum.

1.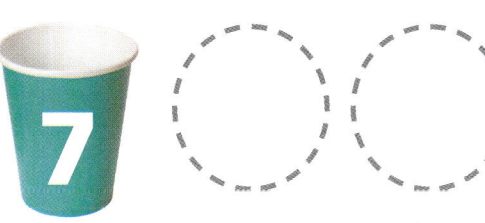

   $7 + 2 = \underline{}$

2.

   $8 + 1 = \underline{}$

3.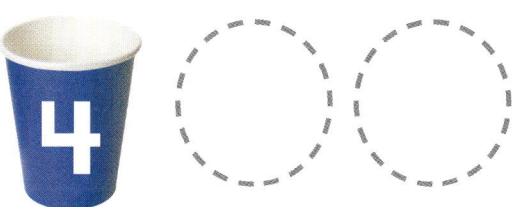

   $4 + 2 = \underline{}$

4.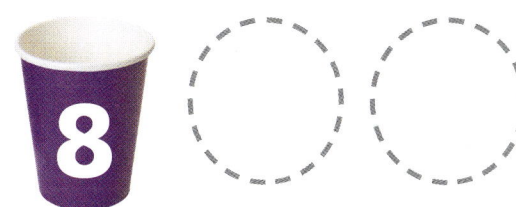

   $8 + 2 = \underline{}$

Explain It • Daily Reasoning

Which number would you start with to find the sum for 2 + 6? Does it matter? Explain.

$2 + 6 = ?$

Chapter 5 • Addition Strategies

Practice and Problem Solving

Use 🔴. Count on. Write the sum.

1.

   $4 + 1 = \underline{5}$

2.

   $4 + 2 = \underline{}$

3. $7 + 2 = \underline{}$

4. $5 + 1 = \underline{}$

5. $5 + 2 = \underline{}$

6. $7 + 1 = \underline{}$

7. $3 + 2 = \underline{}$

8. $8 + 1 = \underline{}$

9. $2 + 1 = \underline{}$

10. $8 + 2 = \underline{}$

11. $3 + 1 = \underline{}$

Problem Solving
Algebra

Complete the addition sentence.

12.  8 in all

    $6 + \blacksquare = 8$

    $\blacksquare = \underline{}$

13.  7 in all

    $6 + \blacksquare = 7$

    $\blacksquare = \underline{}$

 **Write About It** • Look at Exercise 13. Explain how you got your answer.

 HOME ACTIVITY • Choose numbers from 1 to 7, and have your child count on 1 or 2.

Name _____

Use a Number Line to Count On

Learn

You can use a number line to help you count on.

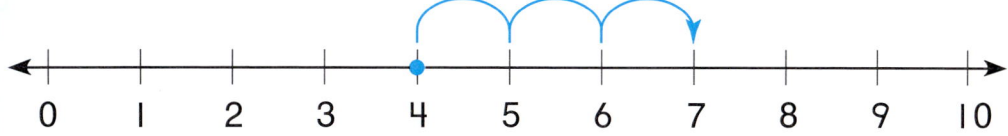

4 + 3 = __7__

Start on 4.
Then move 3 spaces to the right. **5, 6, 7**

Check

Use the number line.
Count on to find the sum.

1.

7 + 3 = ____

2. 6 + 2 = ____

3. 5 + 2 = ____

4. 8 + 1 = ____

5. 9 + 1 = ____

6. 6 + 3 = ____

Explain It • Daily Reasoning

What is the least sum you can get when you count on 3? Why?

Chapter 5 • Addition Strategies

Practice and Problem Solving

Use the number line.
Count on to find the sum.

Start on 5.
Count on 3.
6, 7, 8

$$\begin{array}{r}5\\+3\\\hline 8\end{array}$$

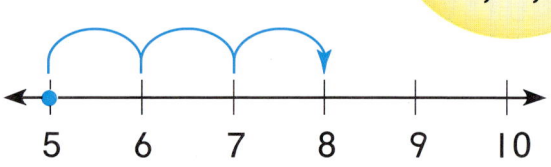

1. 7 +3
2. 8 +2
3. 1 +2
4. 4 +3
5. 3 +1
6. 5 +1

7. 6 +2
8. 4 +1
9. 7 +2
10. 9 +1
11. 6 +3
12. 8 +1

13. 5 +2
14. 4 +2
15. 2 +1
16. 7 +1
17. 3 +2
18. 5 +3

Problem Solving

Mental Math

Solve.

19. Maria is 6 years old.
Ted is 1 year older than Maria.
Ann is 2 years older than Ted.
How old is Ann?

_____ years old

Write About It • Look at Exercise 19.
Explain how you got your answer.

🏠 **HOME ACTIVITY** • Have your child count a group of from 1 to 7 objects, tell you the number, and then count on to add 3.

Name _____

Use Doubles

Explore (Hands On)

Vocabulary
doubles

When you add two numbers that are the same, the sentence is a **doubles** fact.

3 + 3 = 6

Connect

Use 🟦.
Write the addition sentence.

1.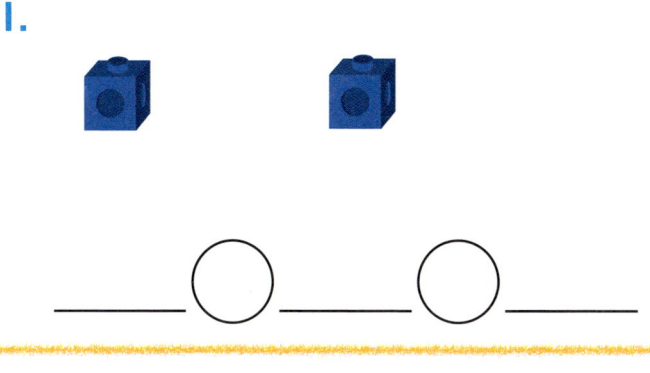

   ___ ◯ ___ ◯ ___

2.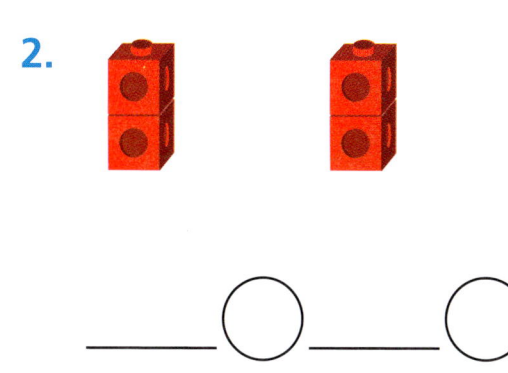

   ___ ◯ ___ ◯ ___

3.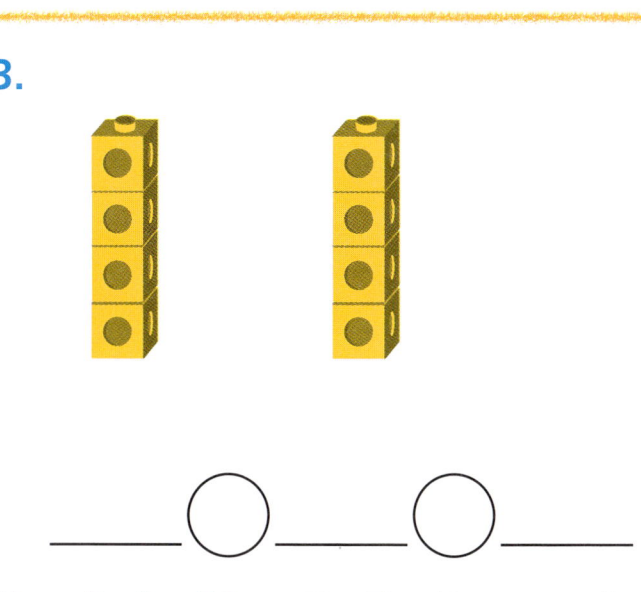

   ___ ◯ ___ ◯ ___

4.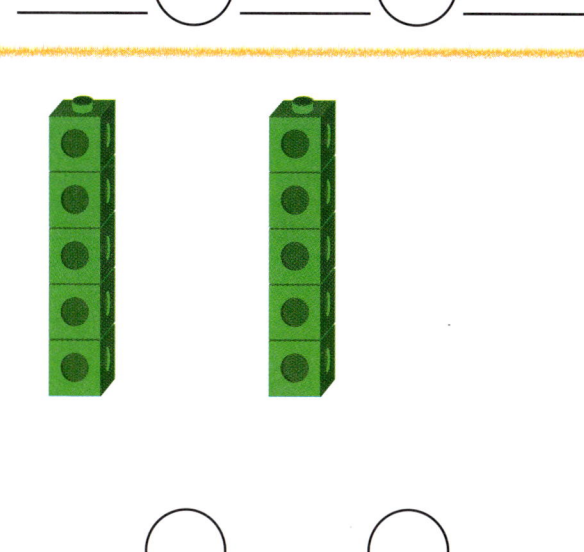

   ___ ◯ ___ ◯ ___

Explain It • Daily Reasoning

Which of these numbers could not be the sum for a doubles fact? Why?

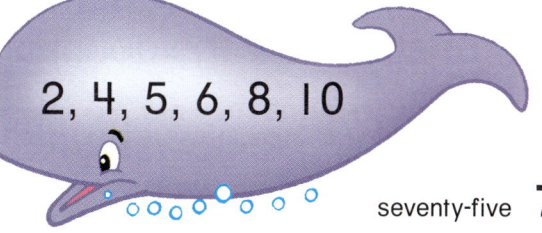
2, 4, 5, 6, 8, 10

Chapter 5 • Addition Strategies

Practice and Problem Solving

$$\begin{array}{r} 5 \\ +5 \\ \hline 10 \end{array}$$

Add. Then circle the doubles facts.

1. 5 +3
2. 1 +1
3. 2 +2
4. 4 +2
5. 3 +2
6. 0 +0

7. 4 +4
8. 6 +1
9. 5 +2
10. 7 +3
11. 8 +1
12. 9 +1

13. 5 +5
14. 6 +3
15. 7 +2
16. 3 +3
17. 4 +3
18. 8 +2

Problem Solving
Visual Thinking

Write a doubles fact for each picture.

19.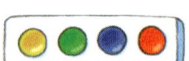

    ___ ◯ ___ ◯ ___

20.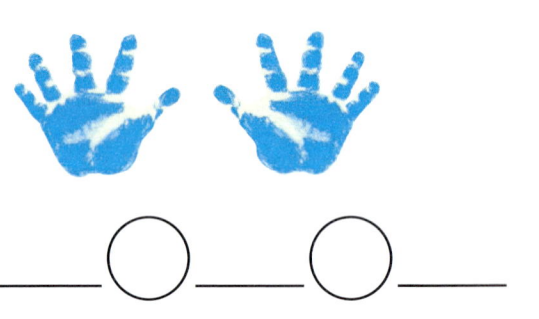

    ___ ◯ ___ ◯ ___

Write About It • Look at Exercise 20. Draw a picture of something else you could use to show the doubles fact.

HOME ACTIVITY • Ask your child to choose a number from 1 to 5 and tell you a doubles fact that uses that number.

Name _____

Problem Solving Strategy
Draw a Picture

There are 2 plates.

5 crackers are on each plate.

How many crackers are there?

UNDERSTAND

What do you want to find out?

Draw a line under the question.
Circle the information you need.

PLAN

You can draw a picture to solve the problem.

SOLVE

Draw 2 plates.
Draw 5 crackers on each plate.

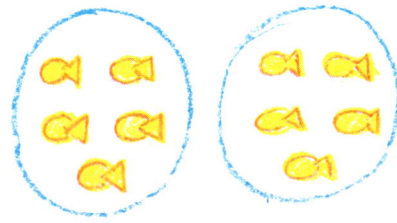

CHECK

Does your answer make sense?

Write an addition sentence to check.

___5___ ⊕ ___5___ ⊜ ___10___ crackers

Draw a picture to solve.
Write an addition sentence to check.

What numbers do I need to solve the problem?

1. There are 4 blue fish.
   There are 4 red fish.
   How many fish are there?

   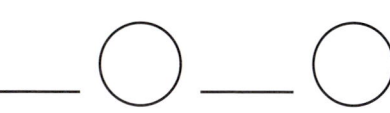
   ____ ◯ ____ ◯ ____ fish

Chapter 5 • Addition Strategies

Problem Solving Practice

Draw a picture to solve. Write an addition sentence to check.

What numbers will help me solve the problem?

Keep in Mind!
Understand
Plan
Solve
Check

1. 4 crabs walk in the sand. 5 more join them. How many crabs are there?

   4 ⊕ 5 ⊟ 9 crabs

2. There are 3 whales. 4 more come. How many whales are there?

   ___ ◯ ___ ◯ ___ whales

3. There are 2 nests. There are 3 turtles in each nest. How many turtles are there?

   ___ ◯ ___ ◯ ___ turtles

4. There are 6 big shells. There are 3 little shells. How many shells are there?

   ___ ◯ ___ ◯ ___ shells

HOME ACTIVITY • Tell your child an addition story. Have him or her draw a picture to solve and then tell you the addition sentence.

Name _____

Extra Practice

Use the number line.
Count on to find the sum.

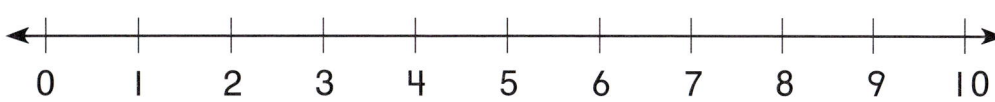

1. $6 + 2 =$ ____   2. $9 + 1 =$ ____

3. $\quad 5$ 4. $\quad 8$ 5. $\quad 4$ 6. $\quad 7$ 7. $\quad 4$ 8. $\quad 5$
   $+2$ $+1$ $+3$ $+1$ $+2$ $+3$

Add. Then circle the doubles facts.

9. $\quad 5$ 10. $\quad 6$ 11. $\quad 4$ 12. $\quad 6$ 13. $\quad 3$ 14. $\quad 2$
   $+5$ $+3$ $+4$ $+1$ $+2$ $+2$

Problem Solving

Draw a picture to solve.
Write an addition sentence to check.

15. There are 4 blue fish.
    There are 3 red fish.
    How many fish are there?

 fish

16. There are 2 pails.
    There are 5 shells in each.
    How many shells are there?

 shells

Chapter 5 • Addition Strategies   seventy-nine **79**

Name _____

✓ Review/Test

Concepts and Skills

Use the number line.
Count on to find the sum.

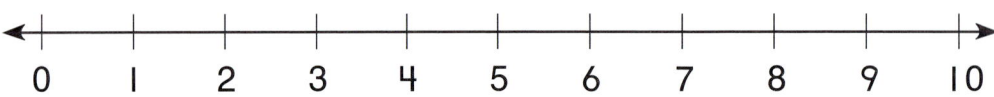

1. 8 + 1 = ____
2. 7 + 3 = ____

3. 7
  +2

4. 8
  +2

5. 6
  +3

6. 6
  +2

7. 9
  +1

8. 5
  +3

Add. Then circle the doubles facts.

9. 3
  +3

10. 4
   +3

11. 5
   +5

12. 4
   +4

13. 2
   +2

14. 3
   +2

Problem Solving

Draw a picture to solve.
Write an addition sentence to check.

15. There are 7 big sand dollars.
    There are 2 little sand dollars.
    How many sand dollars are there?

 sand dollars

16. There are 2 buckets.
    There are 4 starfish in each.
    How many starfish are there?

 starfish

80 eighty

Name _____

⭐Standardized Test Prep
Chapters 1–5

Choose the answer for questions 1–3.

1. Which is the sum for 3 + 2?

   4   5   6   7
   ○   ○   ○   ○

2. Which does the number line show?

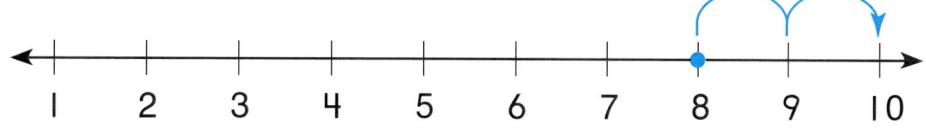

  8 + 1   8 + 2   10 − 1   10 − 2
   ○   ○   ○   ○

3. Which is a way to make 7?

  4 + 1   4 + 3   3 + 3   3 + 2
   ○   ○   ○   ○

Show What You Know

4. Draw a picture of a doubles fact. Write the number sentence to explain your answer.

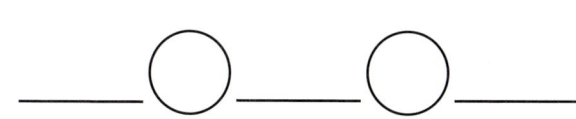

MATH GAME

Doubles Bubbles

Play with a partner.

You will need

1. Put your 🎲 at START.
2. Toss the 🎲.
3. Move your 🎲 that many spaces.
4. If you land on **doubles,** give the doubles fact for the number you tossed.
5. The first player to get to END wins.

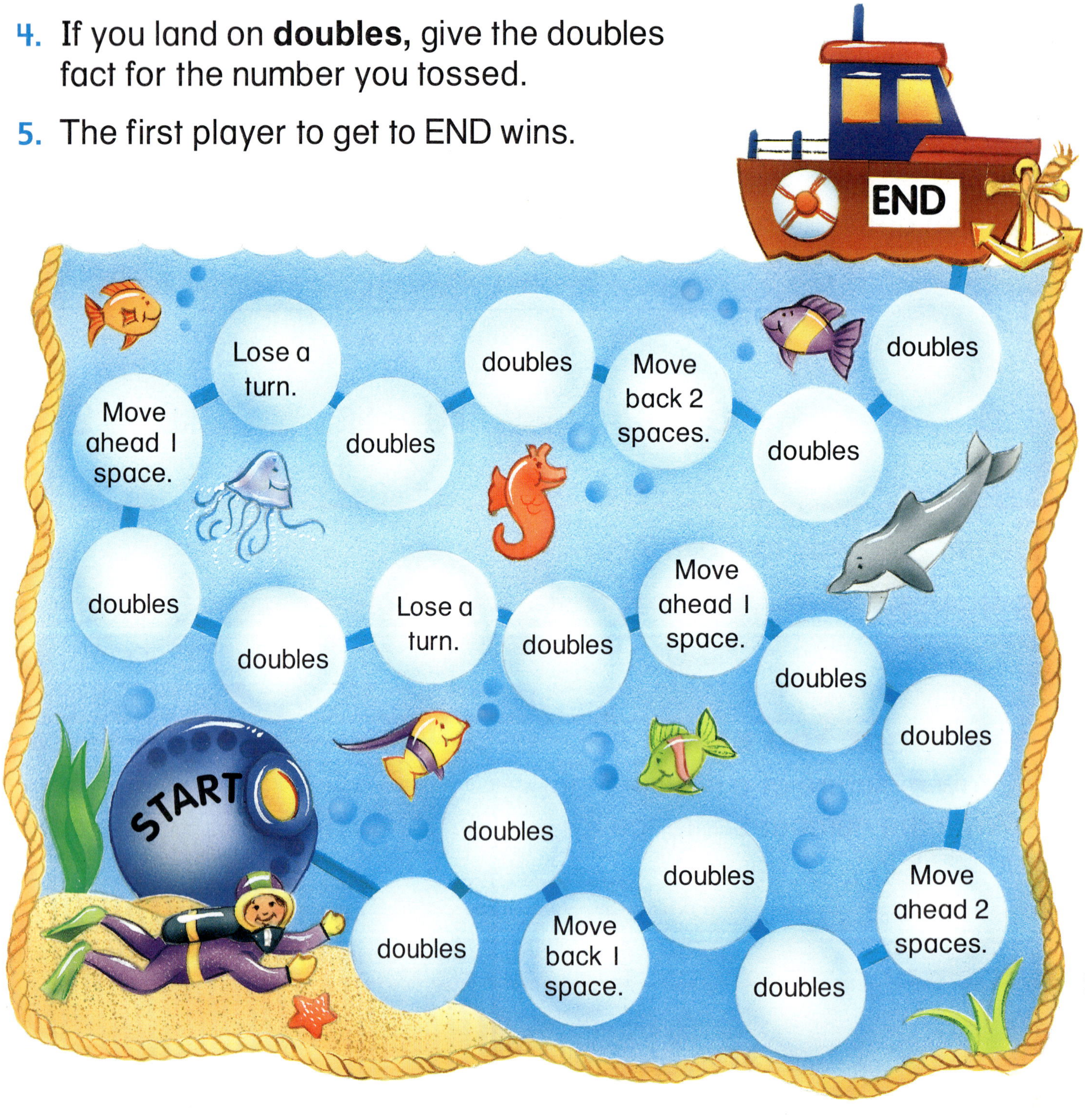

Name _____

✓ Check What You Know

Add in Any Order

Add. Circle the addition sentences in each row that have the same sum.

1. $3 + 1 =$ _____   2. $1 + 3 =$ _____   3. $1 + 2 =$ _____

4. $2 + 5 =$ _____   5. $7 + 1 =$ _____   6. $5 + 2 =$ _____

7. $4 + 2 =$ _____   8. $4 + 1 =$ _____   9. $2 + 4 =$ _____

10. $0 + 3 =$ _____   11. $1 + 3 =$ _____   12. $3 + 0 =$ _____

Use a Number Line to Count On

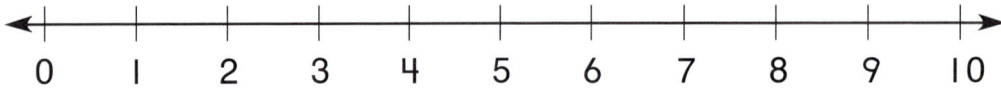

Use the number line. Count on to find the sum.

13. 4
    +2

14. 3
    +2

15. 5
    +1

16. 7
    +2

17. 6
    +2

18. 8
    +2

19. 4
    +3

20. 6
    +3

21. 2
    +1

22. 3
    +1

Use this page to review important skills needed for this chapter.

Name _____

Use the Strategies

Learn

What helps you remember these facts?

$1 + 0 = 0$
$1 + 1 = 2$
$1 + 2 = 3$
$1 + 3 = 4$

I use add 0, doubles, or count on.

Check

Add. Write the sums.

1. **Count On 1**
   $5 + 1 =$ __6__
   $6 + 1 =$ ___
   $7 + 1 =$ ___
   $8 + 1 =$ ___
   $9 + 1 =$ ___

2. **Count On 2**
   $4 + 2 =$ ___
   $5 + 2 =$ ___
   $6 + 2 =$ ___
   $7 + 2 =$ ___
   $8 + 2 =$ ___

3. **Count On 3**
   $4 + 3 =$ ___
   $5 + 3 =$ ___
   $6 + 3 =$ ___
   $7 + 3 =$ ___

4. **Add 0**
   $6 + 0 =$ ___
   $7 + 0 =$ ___
   $8 + 0 =$ ___
   $9 + 0 =$ ___
   $10 + 0 =$ ___

5. **Use Doubles**
   $1 + 1 =$ ___
   $2 + 2 =$ ___
   $3 + 3 =$ ___
   $4 + 4 =$ ___
   $5 + 5 =$ ___

Explain It • Daily Reasoning

Why is $3 + 3 = 6$ a doubles fact?

Chapter 6 • Addition Facts Practice

Practice and Problem Solving

$$\begin{array}{r}4\\+3\\\hline 7\end{array}$$

Add. Write the sum.

1. $\begin{array}{r}4\\+3\\\hline 7\end{array}$
2. $\begin{array}{r}7\\+3\\\hline\end{array}$
3. $\begin{array}{r}5\\+2\\\hline\end{array}$
4. $\begin{array}{r}8\\+1\\\hline\end{array}$
5. $\begin{array}{r}2\\+2\\\hline\end{array}$

6. $\begin{array}{r}5\\+3\\\hline\end{array}$
7. $\begin{array}{r}5\\+1\\\hline\end{array}$
8. $\begin{array}{r}6\\+1\\\hline\end{array}$
9. $\begin{array}{r}4\\+4\\\hline\end{array}$
10. $\begin{array}{r}9\\+1\\\hline\end{array}$

11. $\begin{array}{r}4\\+2\\\hline\end{array}$
12. $\begin{array}{r}4\\+5\\\hline\end{array}$
13. $\begin{array}{r}3\\+3\\\hline\end{array}$
14. $\begin{array}{r}1\\+1\\\hline\end{array}$
15. $\begin{array}{r}3\\+2\\\hline\end{array}$

16. $\begin{array}{r}6\\+3\\\hline\end{array}$
17. $\begin{array}{r}5\\+5\\\hline\end{array}$
18. $\begin{array}{r}9\\+0\\\hline\end{array}$
19. $\begin{array}{r}6\\+2\\\hline\end{array}$
20. $\begin{array}{r}8\\+2\\\hline\end{array}$

Problem Solving

Logical Reasoning

21. There are 9 children in all. 2 are outside the playhouse, and the rest are inside. How many children are inside?

_____ children are inside.

Write About It • Look at Exercise 21. Draw pictures to show how you got your answer.

HOME ACTIVITY • On each day of the week, choose a different number and work with your child to practice the facts that have that sum. For example, on Monday, practice all the facts that have a sum of 5.

Name _____

Sums to 8

Learn

You can change the order of the numbers you add. The sum is the same.

$$\begin{array}{r} 5 \\ +3 \\ \hline 8 \end{array}$$

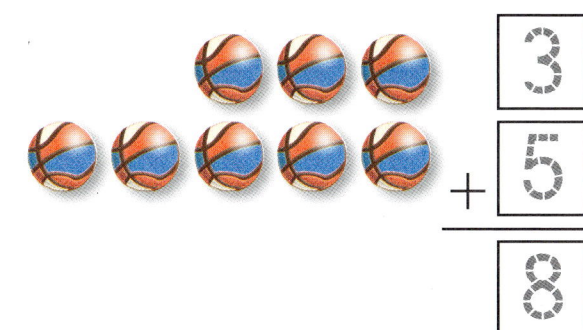

$$\begin{array}{r} 3 \\ +5 \\ \hline 8 \end{array}$$

Check

Add. Change the order.
Write the new fact.

1. $\begin{array}{r} 5 \\ +2 \\ \hline \end{array}$ $\begin{array}{r} \Box \\ +\Box \\ \hline \Box \end{array}$

2. $\begin{array}{r} 4 \\ +3 \\ \hline \end{array}$ $\begin{array}{r} \Box \\ +\Box \\ \hline \Box \end{array}$

3. $\begin{array}{r} 1 \\ +7 \\ \hline \end{array}$ $\begin{array}{r} \Box \\ +\Box \\ \hline \Box \end{array}$

4. $\begin{array}{r} 6 \\ +2 \\ \hline \end{array}$ $\begin{array}{r} \Box \\ +\Box \\ \hline \Box \end{array}$

5. $\begin{array}{r} 7 \\ +0 \\ \hline \end{array}$ $\begin{array}{r} \Box \\ +\Box \\ \hline \Box \end{array}$

6. $\begin{array}{r} 5 \\ +1 \\ \hline \end{array}$ $\begin{array}{r} \Box \\ +\Box \\ \hline \Box \end{array}$

Explain It • Daily Reasoning

Does the sum change when you change the order of the numbers you are adding? Explain.

Chapter 6 • Addition Facts Practice

Practice and Problem Solving

1. Add. Use the key. Color each space by the sum. What patterns do you see?

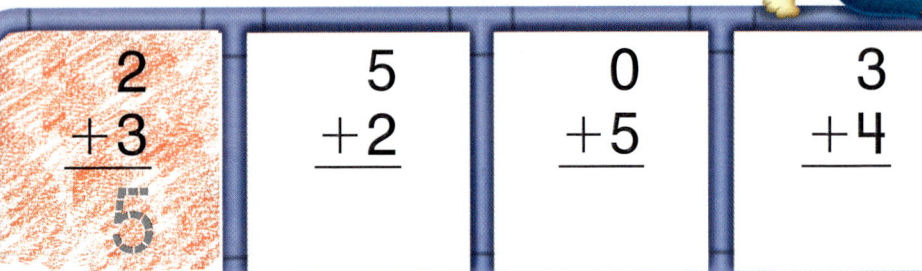

2 +3 **5**	5 +2	0 +5	3 +4	4 +1
3 +3	2 +6	6 +0	3 +5	2 +4
7 +0	1 +4	1 +6	3 +2	2 +5
6 +2	1 +5	7 +1	4 +2	0 +8

Problem Solving
Mental Math

Solve. Draw a picture to check.

2. Eric has 8 flowers in two pots. He has the same number in each pot. How many flowers are in each pot?

_____ flowers

 Write About It • Write a math story about this number sentence. Draw a picture to show your story.

$3 + 3 = 6$

HOME ACTIVITY • Ask your child to see how many addition facts with a sum of 8 he or she can write.

Name _____

Sums to 10

Learn

The order of the numbers changed. The sum is the same.

```
  5      4           6      4
 +4     +5          +4     +6
 ——     ——          ——     ——
  9      9          10     10
```

Check

Add. Write the sums.

1.	9 +0	0 +9	2.	9 +1	1 +9	3.	7 +2	2 +7
4.	7 +3	3 +7	5.	5 +4	4 +5	6.	4 +3	3 +4
7.	10 + 0	0 +10	8.	8 +1	1 +8	9.	6 +2	2 +6
10.	6 +3	3 +6	11.	3 +5	5 +3	12.	5 +2	2 +5
13.	8 +2	2 +8	14.	4 +2	2 +4	15.	1 +7	7 +1

Explain It • Daily Reasoning

When is the sum the same as one of the two numbers you are adding?

Chapter 6 • Addition Facts Practice

Practice and Problem Solving

Add across. Add down.
Write the sums.

1.
2	4	6
5	3	8
7	7	

2.
6	3	
2	7	

3.
4	6	
4	0	

4.
8	2	
1	2	

Problem Solving
Mental Math

Circle two ways to name the same number.

5. 6 + 2   4 + 4   5 + 1   3 + 2

6. 0 + 9   7 + 3   6 + 3   5 + 2

 Write About It • Look at Exercise 6. Write another way to name the same number.

HOME ACTIVITY • Say a number from 1 to 10, and ask your child to tell you an addition fact that has that number as its sum. Repeat the activity for a new sum.

Name _____

Algebra: Follow the Rule

Vocabulary
rule

Learn

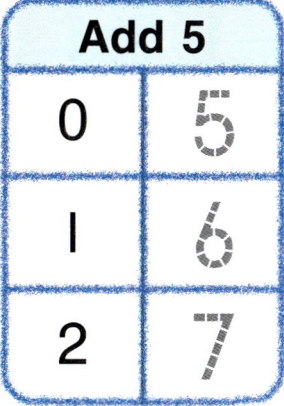

Add 5	
0	5
1	6
2	7

The rule is Add 5. I add 5 each time.

Check

Complete the table. Follow the rule.

1.
Add 2	
4	
6	
8	

2.
Add 3	
4	
3	
2	

3.
Add 4	
4	
5	
6	

4.
Add 1	
9	
8	
7	

5.
Add 2	
1	
2	
3	

6.
Add 0	
8	
9	
10	

Explain It • Daily Reasoning

Does every table on this page have a pattern? Explain.

Chapter 6 • Addition Facts Practice

Practice and Problem Solving

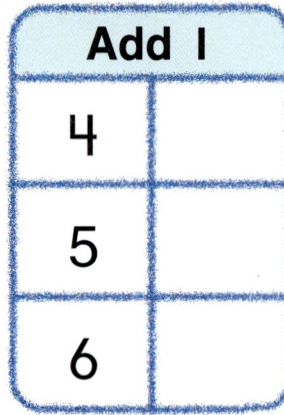

Complete the table. Follow the rule.

1. **Add 3**

5	8
6	9
7	10

2. **Add 5**

5	
4	
3	

3. **Add 1**

4	
5	
6	

4. **Add 2**

3	
5	
7	

5. **Add 4**

3	
2	
1	

6. **Add 6**

3	
2	
1	

Problem Solving
Logical Reasoning

Write the rule.

7. **Add ___**

2	5
4	7
6	9

8. **Add ___**

4	9
2	7
0	5

9. **Add ___**

7	7
8	8
9	9

 **Write About It** • Look at Exercise 9. Explain how you figured out the rule.

HOME ACTIVITY • Ask your child to write an addition rule. Help your child make a table that follows the rule.

Name _____

Problem Solving Strategy
Write a Number Sentence

<u>6 children play.</u>

<u>3 more come.</u>

How many children are there now?

UNDERSTAND

What information do you know?
Underline it.

PLAN

How can you solve this problem?
Write a number sentence.

SOLVE

__6__ children play

__3__ more come

__6__ ⊕ __3__ ⊖ __9__
           children

CHECK

Does your answer make sense?
Explain.

Solve. Write a number sentence.
Draw a picture to check.

1. 3 boys go down the slide.
   3 girls go down the slide.
   How many children in
   all go down the slide?

   ____ ◯ ____ ◯ ____
                    children

THINK:
How can I find out how many children there are in all?

Chapter 6 • Addition Facts Practice

ninety-three **93**

Problem Solving Practice

Solve. Write a number sentence.
Draw a picture to check.

Keep in Mind!
Understand
Plan
Solve
Check

THINK: What do I need to use to solve the problem?

1. There are 8 bean bags. Kendra finds 1 more. How many bean bags are there in all?

   ___ ◯ ___ ◯ ___
   bean bags

2. 6 boys run races. 2 girls join them. How many children run in all?

   ___ ◯ ___ ◯ ___
   children

3. There are 4 soccer balls in one bag. There are 6 in another bag. How many soccer balls are there in all?

   ___ ◯ ___ ◯ ___
   soccer balls

4. 3 girls jump rope. 4 more girls join them. How many girls jump rope?

   ___ ◯ ___ ◯ ___
   girls

HOME ACTIVITY • Tell your child a math story, and ask him or her to write a number sentence to solve it. For example: "A boy has 5 toy cars. Then he finds 3 more. How many toy cars does he have now?" (5 + 3 = 8)

Name _____

Extra Practice

Complete the table. Follow the rule.

Add. Change the order. Write the new fact.

1.
Add 1	
9	
8	
7	

2. 9
   +0
   ___

   ☐
   +☐
   ___
   ☐

3. 6
   +2
   ___

   ☐
   +☐
   ___
   ☐

Add. Write the sum.

4. 4
   +2
   ___

5. 6
   +3
   ___

6. 1
   +1
   ___

7. 8
   +2
   ___

8. 7
   +2
   ___

9. 5
   +3
   ___

10. 5
    +1
    ___

11. 4
    +4
    ___

12. 4
    +3
    ___

13. 6
    +1
    ___

14. 7
    +3
    ___

15. 2
    +2
    ___

Problem Solving

Solve. Write a number sentence. Draw a picture to check.

16. 2 girls are playing catch. 4 more girls join them. How many girls are there in all?

    ____ ◯ ____ ◯ ____
    girls

Chapter 6 • Addition Facts Practice

Name _____

✓ Review/Test

Concepts and Skills

Complete the table. Follow the rule.

Add. Change the order. Write the new fact.

1.
Add 3	
4	
5	
6	

2.
$$\begin{array}{r}2\\+8\\\hline\end{array}\quad\begin{array}{r}\square\\+\square\\\hline\square\end{array}$$

3.
$$\begin{array}{r}4\\+5\\\hline\end{array}\quad\begin{array}{r}\square\\+\square\\\hline\square\end{array}$$

Add. Write the sum.

4. $\begin{array}{r}9\\+1\\\hline\end{array}$
5. $\begin{array}{r}5\\+2\\\hline\end{array}$
6. $\begin{array}{r}4\\+4\\\hline\end{array}$
7. $\begin{array}{r}7\\+2\\\hline\end{array}$
8. $\begin{array}{r}6\\+3\\\hline\end{array}$
9. $\begin{array}{r}4\\+2\\\hline\end{array}$

10. $\begin{array}{r}3\\+3\\\hline\end{array}$
11. $\begin{array}{r}7\\+1\\\hline\end{array}$
12. $\begin{array}{r}6\\+2\\\hline\end{array}$
13. $\begin{array}{r}8\\+1\\\hline\end{array}$
14. $\begin{array}{r}5\\+5\\\hline\end{array}$
15. $\begin{array}{r}7\\+3\\\hline\end{array}$

Problem Solving

Solve. Write a number sentence. Draw a picture to check.

16. 5 boys play kickball. 4 more boys join them. How many boys are playing in all?

____ ◯ ____ ◯ ____ boys

Name _____

Standardized Test Prep
Chapters 1–6

Choose the answer for questions 1–6.

1. 2 + 3 = ____

   ○ 1   ○ 5   ○ 7   ○ 8

2. 7 + 1 = ____

   ○ 6   ○ 8   ○ 10   ○ 13

3. 5 + 2 = ____

   ○ 1   ○ 2   ○ 7   ○ 9

4. 5 + 5 = ____

   ○ 0   ○ 6   ○ 10   ○ 16

5. Which is a way to make 10?

   ○ 7 + 2   ○ 6 + 1   ○ 5 + 3   ○ 8 + 2

6. Kathy has 9 goldfish. She buys 1 more. How many goldfish does she have in all?

   ○ 12   ○ 10   ○ 7   ○ 6

Show What You Know

7. Write a rule.
   Write numbers in the table that explain the rule.

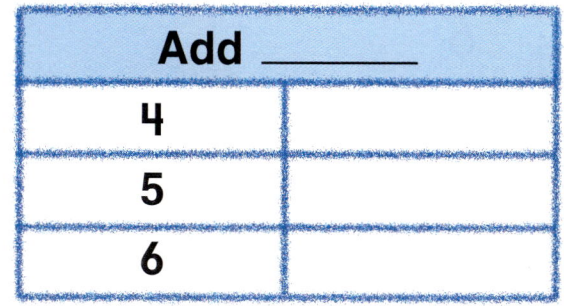

Add ____	
4	
5	
6	

Chapter 6 — ninety-seven 97

Name _____

Building Numbers

Play with a partner.
Fill in your chart.

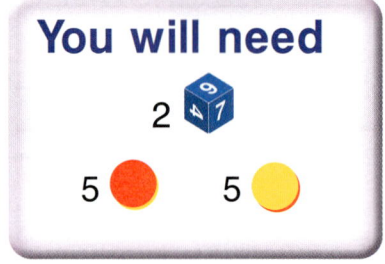

You will need

2 🎲

5 🔴   5 🟡

1. One player uses 🔴. The other player uses 🟡.

2. Toss the 🎲 and 🎲.

3. Find an answer in your chart that matches one of the numbers you tossed. Cover that answer with a 🔴.

4. Your turn is over if there is no match.

5. The first player to cover all the answers wins.

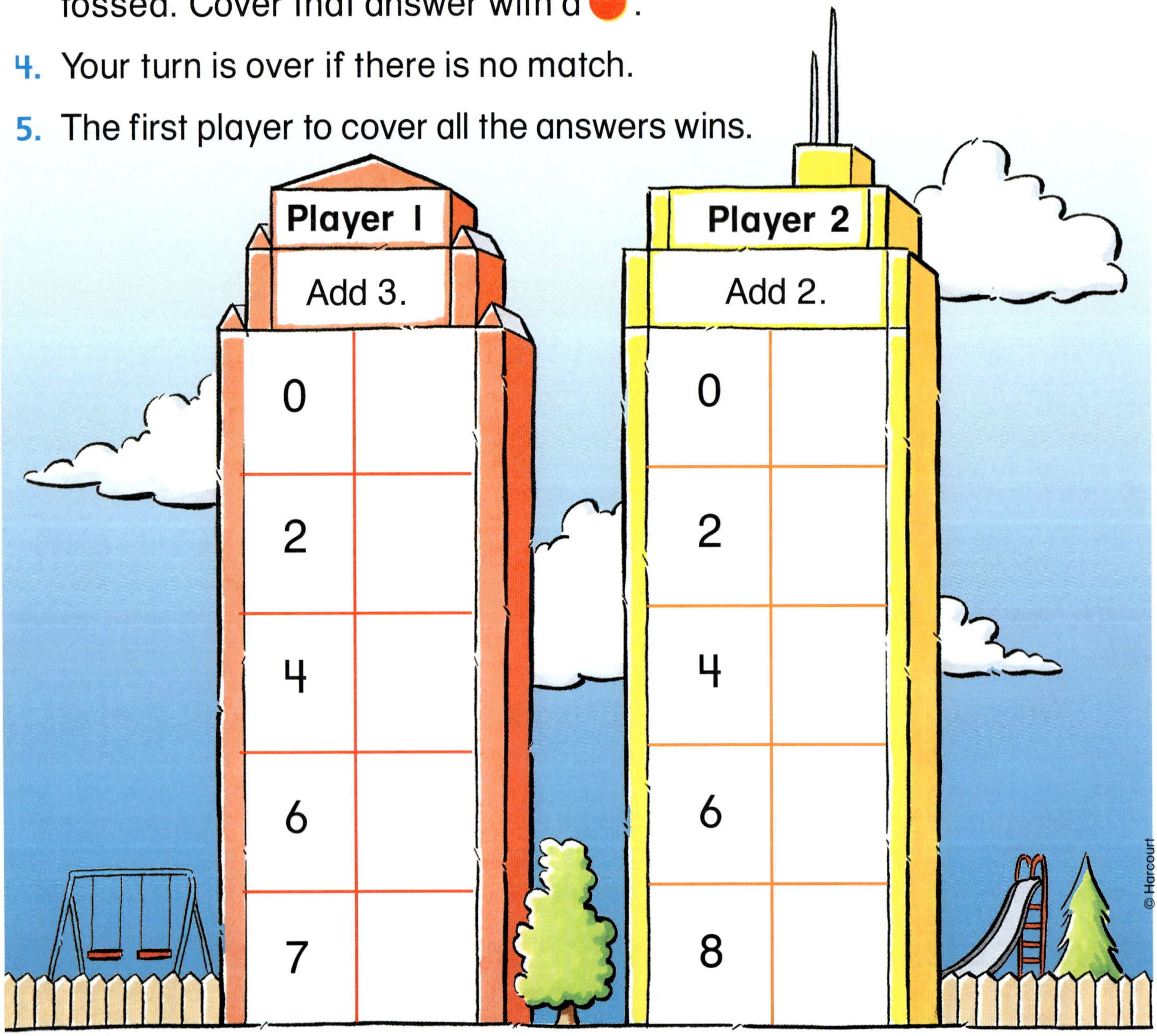

Player 1	Player 2
Add 3.	Add 2.
0	0
2	2
4	4
6	6
7	8

98 ninety-eight

CHAPTER 7
Subtraction Strategies

FUN FACTS

A good mixture for making bubbles is 2 parts dishwashing liquid, 4 parts glycerine, and 1 part light corn syrup.

Theme: Things in the Air

✓ Check What You Know

Count Back on a Number Line

Start at 9.
Count back.
Circle the number you are on.

1. Count back 1.

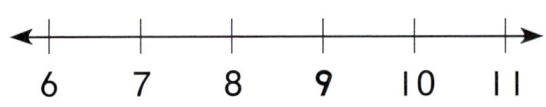

2. Count back 2.

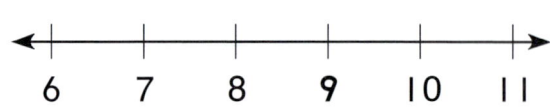

Subtraction Patterns

Count the birds.
Mark an X on the bird that is flying away.
Write how many birds are left.

3.

8 − 1 = _____

4.

7 − 1 = _____

5.

6 − 1 = _____

6.

5 − 1 = _____

100 one hundred   Use this page to review important skills needed for this chapter.

Name _____

Use a Number Line to Count Back 1 and 2

Vocabulary
number line
count back

Learn

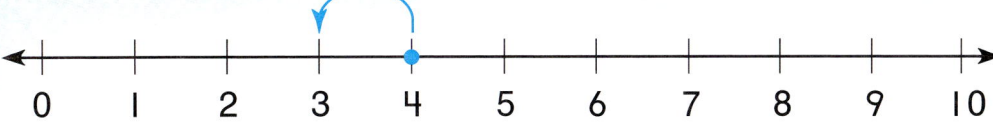

4 − 1 = __3__   Start at 4 on the number line. Count back 1. You are on 3.

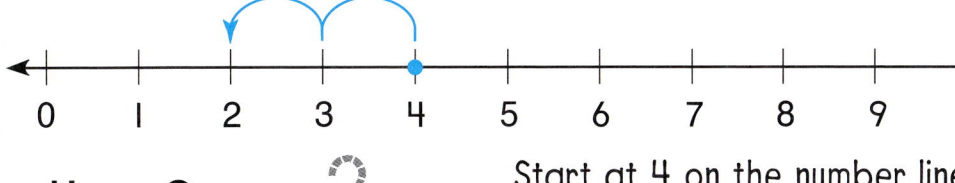

4 − 2 = __2__   Start at 4 on the number line. Count back 2. You are on 2.

Check

Use the number line.
Count back to subtract.

1.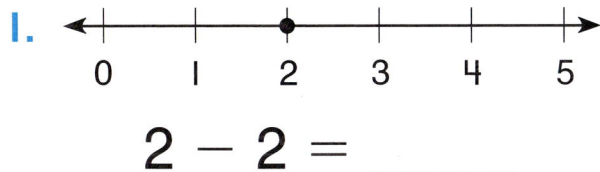

    2 − 2 = _____

2.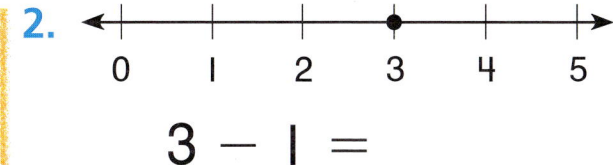

    3 − 1 = _____

3.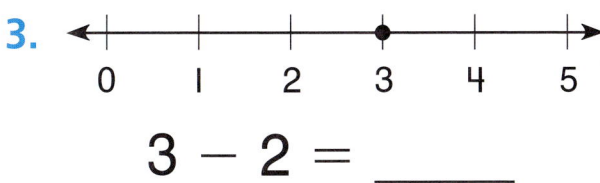

    3 − 2 = _____

4.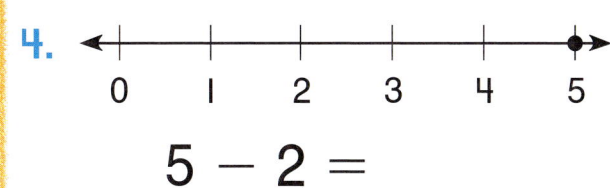

    5 − 2 = _____

5.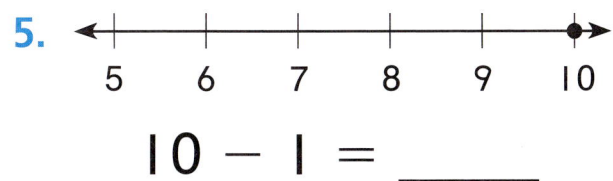

    10 − 1 = _____

6.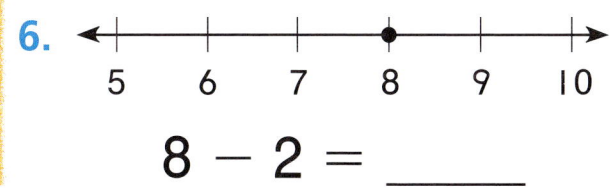

    8 − 2 = _____

Explain It • Daily Reasoning

When you use a number line to help you subtract, why do you move to the left?

Chapter 7 • Subtraction Strategies

Practice and Problem Solving

Use the number line.
Count back to subtract.

Start at 7.
Count back 2.
You are on 5.

1.

   7 − 2 = 5

2.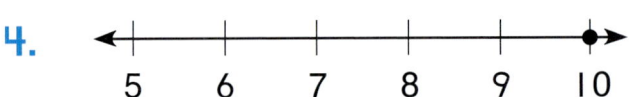

   5 − 1 = ___

3.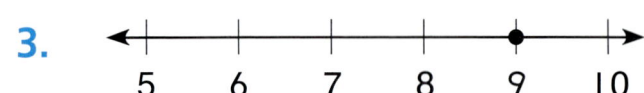

   9 − 1 = ___

4.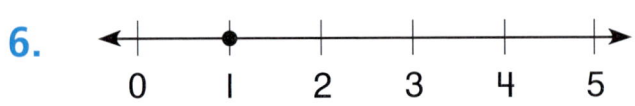

   10 − 2 = ___

5.
   5 − 1 = ___

   8 − 1 = ___

6.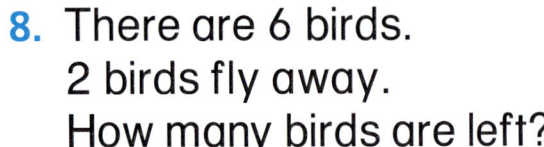

   1 − 1 = ___

7.

   9 − 2 = ___

Problem Solving

Application

Use the number line to solve.
Write the number sentence.

8. There are 6 birds.
   2 birds fly away.
   How many birds are left?   ___ ◯ ___ ◯ ___ birds

 **Write About It** • Explain how you used the number line in Exercise 8 to find your answer.

🏠 **HOME ACTIVITY** • Have your child show counting back to subtract on the number line. Ask him or her to find 8 − 2.

102 one hundred two

Name _____

Use a Number Line to Count Back 3

Learn

Start at 6.
Count back 3.
You are on 3.

$6 - 3 = \underline{3}$

Check

Use the number line. Count back to subtract.

1. $7 - 3 = \underline{}$

2. $8 - 3 = \underline{}$

3. $10 - 3 = \underline{}$

4. $4 - 3 = \underline{}$

5. $5 - 3 = \underline{}$

6. $9 - 3 = \underline{}$

Explain It • Daily Reasoning

How could you count back to subtract without using a number line?

Chapter 7 • Subtraction Strategies

Practice and Problem Solving

Count back to subtract. Use the key.
Color each part by the difference.

5 or less: GREEN
6 or greater: YELLOW

7
−3
___

6
−3
3

4 − 3 = ___

10
− 2
___

8 − 3 = ___

10
− 3
___

4 − 1 = ___

9 − 3 = ___

7
−2
___

8
−2
___

9
−2
___

6 − 2 = ___

5
−2
___

5 − 3 = ___

HOME ACTIVITY • Have your child explain how to count back to find the difference for 9 − 3.

104 one hundred four

Name _____

Algebra: Relate Addition and Subtraction

Vocabulary
related facts

 **Explore**

These addition and subtraction sentences are related facts.

$7 + 3 = 10$

$10 - 3 = 7$

These facts use the same numbers!

Connect

Use 🟥 and 🟦 to add and to subtract. Complete the chart.

	Use 🟥	Add 🟦	Write the sum.	Take away	Write the difference.
1.	4	2	$4 + 2 = \underline{6}$	2	$6 - 2 = \underline{4}$
2.	5	3	$5 + 3 = \underline{}$	3	$8 - 3 = \underline{}$
3.	2	5	$2 + 5 = \underline{}$	5	$7 - 5 = \underline{}$
4.	7	2	$7 + 2 = \underline{}$	2	$9 - 2 = \underline{}$
5.	8	0	$8 + 0 = \underline{}$	0	$8 - 0 = \underline{}$

Explain It • Daily Reasoning

How are $6 + 3 = 9$ and $9 - 3 = 6$ alike? How are they different? Why are they called related facts?

Practice and Problem Solving

Add. Then subtract.

1.

   $5 + 4 = \underline{9}$

   $9 - 4 = \underline{5}$

2.

   $7 + 1 = \underline{}$

   $8 - 1 = \underline{}$

3.

   $4 + 3 = \underline{}$

   $7 - 3 = \underline{}$

4. 8   9   5. 4   8   6. 6   10
   +1   -1   +4   -4   +4   - 4
   ——   ——   ——   ——   ——   ——

Problem Solving
Application

Solve. Write the addition or subtraction sentence.

7. 5 bugs are on a leaf. 3 more join them. Now how many bugs are there?

8. 8 bugs are on a leaf. 3 bugs fly away. Now how many bugs are there?

Write About It • Make up a subtraction story that uses the number 10. Draw to show your story. Write the number sentence.

 HOME ACTIVITY • Have your child use 10 small objects to show an addition problem and then the related subtraction problem. Ask him or her to tell the addition or subtraction sentence each time.

Name _____

Problem Solving Strategy
Draw a Picture

6 ladybugs were flying.

Some landed on a leaf.

4 ladybugs are still in the air.

How many ladybugs landed?

UNDERSTAND

What do you want to find out?

Draw a line under the question.

PLAN

You can draw a picture to solve the problem.

SOLVE

6 − ☐ = 4

What number do I add to 4 to get 6?

4 + __2__ = 6

__2__ ladybugs landed.

CHECK

Does your answer make sense? Explain.

Draw a picture to solve the problem.

What number do I add to 5 to make 7?

1. 7 birds were flying.
   Some landed on a tree.
   5 birds are still in the air.
   How many birds landed?

   _____ birds

Chapter 7 • Subtraction Strategies   one hundred seven **107**

Problem Solving Practice

Keep in Mind!
Understand
Plan
Solve
Check

Draw a picture to solve the problem.

1. 9 butterflies were flying. Some butterflies landed on a bush. 6 butterflies are still in the air. How many butterflies landed?

   What number do I add to 6 to make 9?

   _____ butterflies

2. 8 kites were flying. Some kites came down. 4 kites are still in the air. How many kites came down?

   What number do I add to 4 to make 8?

   _____ kites

3. 10 bees were flying. Some went into a hive. 7 bees are still in the air. How many bees went into the hive?

   What number do I add to 7 to make 10?

   _____ bees

HOME ACTIVITY • Tell a math story like these in the problems on this page. Ask your child to draw a picture to solve the problem and then explain his or her drawing to you.

108 one hundred eight

Name _____

Extra Practice

Use the number line.
Count back to subtract.

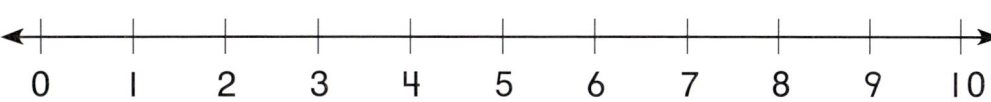

1. $4 - 1 = $ ____

2. $3 - 2 = $ ____

3. $7 - 3 = $ ____

4. $8 - 1 = $ ____

5. $2 - 2 = $ ____

6. $10 - 3 = $ ____

7. $5 - 1 = $ ____

8. $5 - 2 = $ ____

Add. Then subtract.

9.   6   8
      +2   −2

10.   5   6
      +1   −1

11.   4   6
      +2   −2

Problem Solving

Draw a picture to solve the problem.

12. 5 birds were flying.
Some landed on a tree.
2 are still in the air.
How many birds landed?

What number do I add to 2 to make 5?

_____ birds

Chapter 7 • Subtraction Strategies

Name _____

✓ Review/Test

Concepts and Skills

Use the number line.
Count back to subtract.

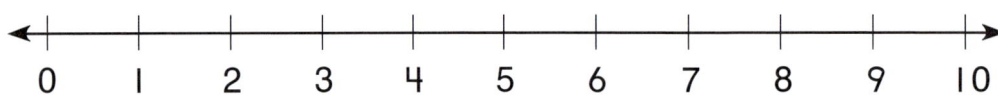

1. 7 − 1 = ___
2. 4 − 3 = ___
3. 8 − 2 = ___
4. 10 − 1 = ___
5. 3 − 3 = ___
6. 9 − 2 = ___
7. 6 − 2 = ___
8. 9 − 1 = ___

Add. Then subtract.

9. 7   10
   +3   − 3

10. 6   9
   +3   − 3

11. 2   9
   +7   − 7

Problem Solving

Draw a picture to solve the problem.

12. 8 bees were flying. Some went into a hive. 6 bees are still flying. How many bees went into the hive?

What number do I add to 6 to make 8?

_____ bees

Name _____

★Standardized Test Prep
Chapters 1–7

Choose the answer for questions 1–4.

1. Which does the number line show?

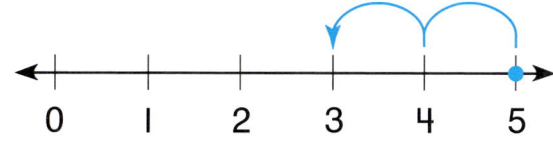

5 − 3 = __   5 − 2 = __   3 + 2 = __   2 + 3 = __
  ○   ○   ○   ○

2. Which fact is related to 8 + 2 = 10?

6 + 2 = 8   7 + 1 = 8   8 − 2 = 6   10 − 8 = 2
  ○   ○   ○   ○

3. Which does the number line show?

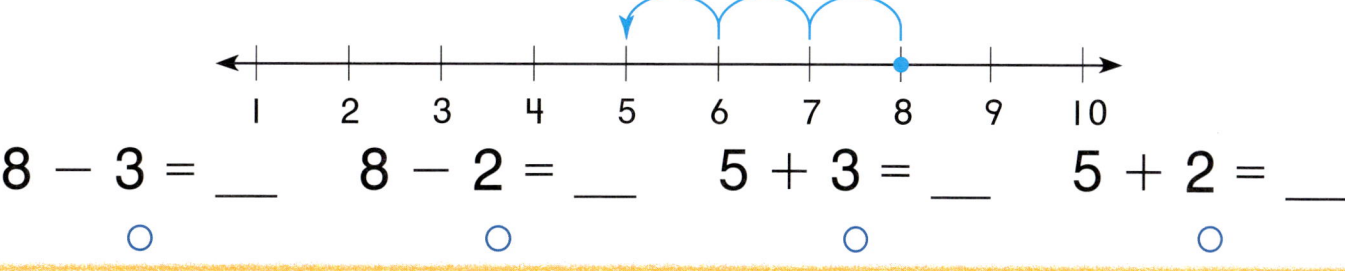

8 − 3 = __   8 − 2 = __   5 + 3 = __   5 + 2 = __
  ○   ○   ○   ○

4. Which does the number line show?

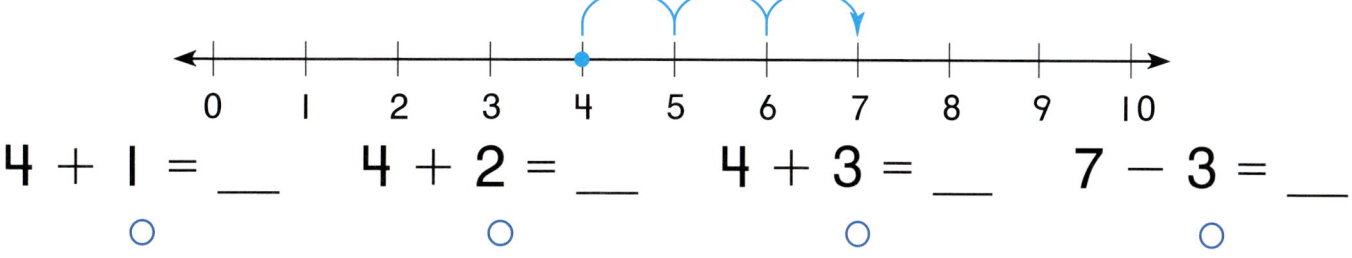

4 + 1 = __   4 + 2 = __   4 + 3 = __   7 − 3 = __
  ○   ○   ○   ○

Show What You Know

5. Write numbers on the number line.
Draw arrows to show subtraction.
Write the subtraction sentence to explain.

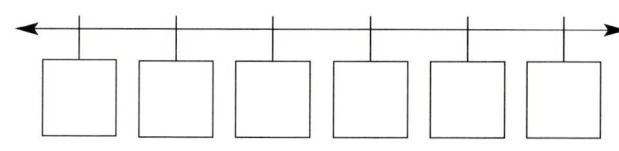   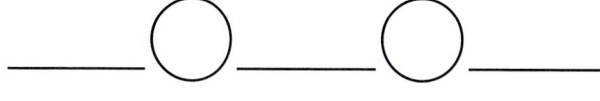

Name ______________________________

MATH GAME

Up, Up, and Away

Play with a partner.

1. Put your ♟ at START.
2. Stack the subtraction cards face down.
3. Take a card, and find the difference.
4. Move your ♟ that many spaces.
5. The first player to get to END wins.

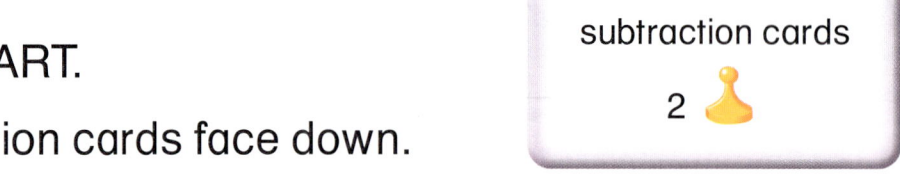

You will need

subtraction cards

2 ♟

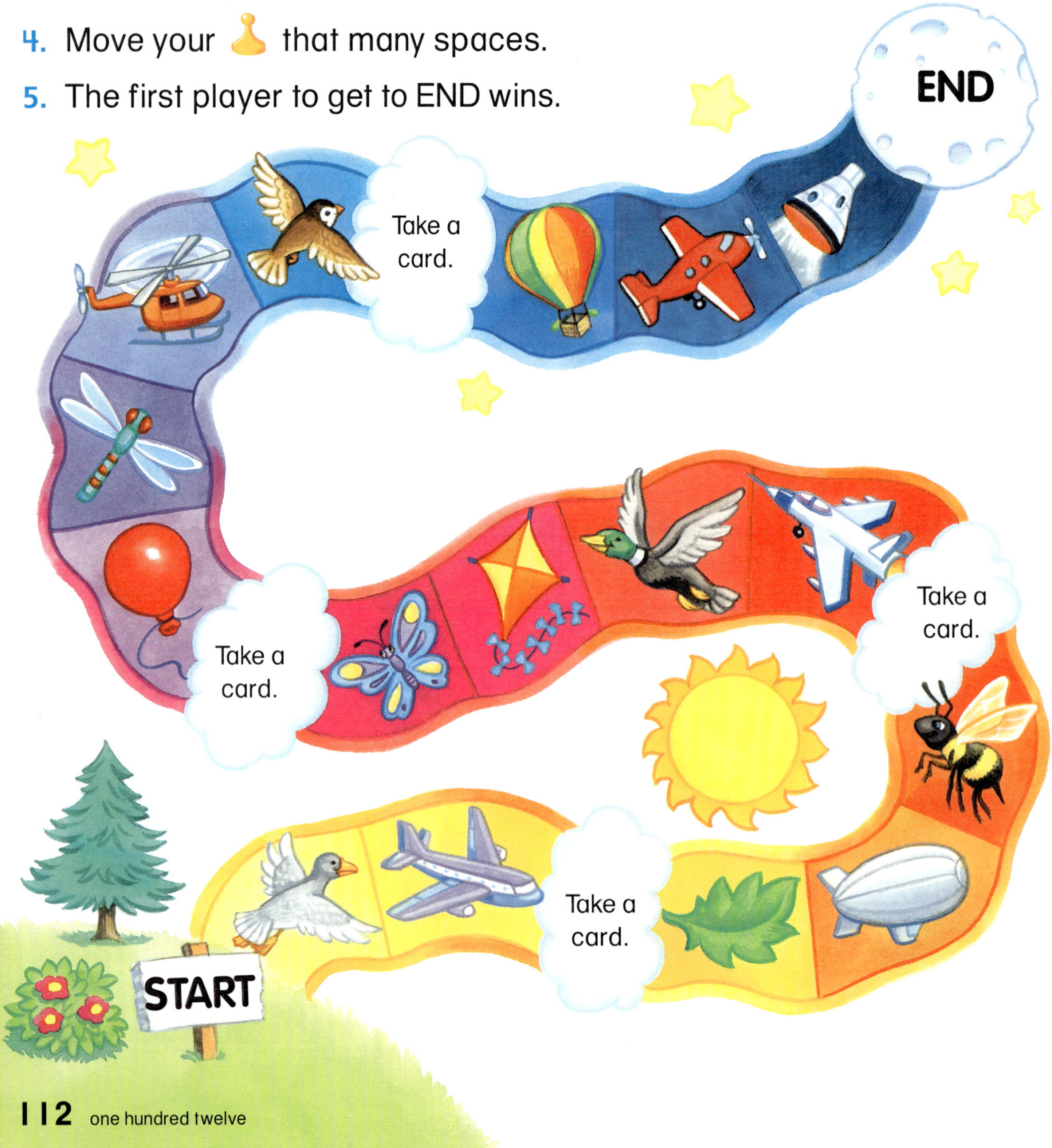

CHAPTER 8
Subtraction Facts Practice

FUN FACTS

The starfruit is star-shaped when cut. It has 6 points.

Theme: Fun Food

Name _____

✓ Check What You Know

Count Back to Subtract: Facts to 10

Use the number line. Count back to subtract.

1. (number line 0–5, dot at 4)

    4 − 1 = ____

2. (number line 0–5, dot at 3)

    3 − 2 = ____

3. (number line 0–5, dot at 5)

    5 − 1 = ____

4. (number line 5–10, dot at 7)

    7 − 2 = ____

5. (number line 5–10, dot at 8)

    8 − 2 = ____

6. (number line 5–10, dot at 10)

    10 − 1 = ____

Relate Addition and Subtraction

Add. Then subtract.

7.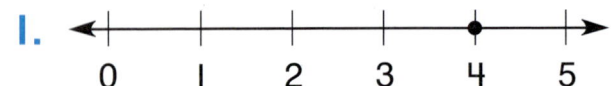

    6 + 3 = ____

    9 − 3 = ____

8.

    5 + 2 = ____

    7 − 5 = ____

9. 3   5
   +2   −3
   ___   ___

10. 8   10
    +2   − 8
    ___   ___

11. 3   7
    +4   −3
    ___   ___

114 one hundred fourteen   Use this page to review important skills needed for this chapter.

Name _____

Use the Strategies

Learn

You can count back, subtract 0, or subtract all.

10 − 1
10 − 2
10 − 3
10 − 0
10 − 10

Check

Subtract. Write the difference.

1. **Count Back 1**

   10 − 1 = __9__

   9 − 1 = ___

   8 − 1 = ___

   7 − 1 = ___

2. **Count Back 2**

   10 − 2 = __8__

   9 − 2 = ___

   8 − 2 = ___

   7 − 2 = ___

3. **Count Back 3**

   10 − 3 = __7__

   9 − 3 = ___

   8 − 3 = ___

   7 − 3 = ___

4. **Subtract 0**

   10 − 0 = __10__

   9 − 0 = ___

   8 − 0 = ___

5. **Subtract All**

   10 − 10 = __0__

   9 − 9 = ___

   8 − 8 = ___

Explain It • Daily Reasoning

How can knowing that 10 − 3 = 7 help you find the difference for 10 − 4?

Chapter 8 • Subtraction Facts Practice

Practice and Problem Solving

Subtract. Circle the facts for **subtract 0** and for **subtract all**.

1. (9 − 9 = 0)
2. (8 − 0 = 8)
3. 7 − 2
4. 8 − 3
5. 6 − 3
6. 10 − 1

7. 7 − 3
8. 9 − 2
9. 10 − 2
10. 4 − 0
11. 6 − 1
12. 8 − 8

13. 7 − 1
14. 10 − 0
15. 9 − 3
16. 5 − 3
17. 4 − 2
18. 10 − 10

19. 6 − 0
20. 8 − 1
21. 7 − 7
22. 9 − 1
23. 8 − 2
24. 10 − 3

Problem Solving
Visual Thinking

25. Cross out some of the apples. Write a subtraction sentence to tell about the picture.

    ____ ◯ ____ ◯ ____

 **Write About It** • Why is 0 the answer when you subtract all?

HOME ACTIVITY • Make subtraction flash cards with your child. Have your child find all the facts that have a difference of 1, for example, 4 − 3 = 1.

Name _____

Subtraction to 10

Learn

These facts use the same numbers.

```
  10        10
-  2      -  8
----      ----
   8         2
```

10 − 2 = 8, so
10 − 8 = 2.

Check

Subtract. Circle the pair of facts if they use the same numbers.

1. 9   9
   −1   −8
   ──   ──
    8   1

2. 7   7
   −7   −0
   ──   ──

3. 10   10
   − 5 − 9
   ──   ──

4. 10   10
   − 6 − 4
   ──   ──

5. 8   8
   −3   −7
   ──   ──

6. 9   9
   −5   −4
   ──   ──

7. 8   8
   −5   −4
   ──   ──

8. 10   10
   − 7 − 3
   ──   ──

9. 9   9
   −2   −7
   ──   ──

10. 9   9
   −6   −3
   ──   ──

11. 8   8
   −2   −6
   ──   ──

12. 7   7
   −5   −1
   ──   ──

Explain It • Daily Reasoning

If you know that 10 − 1 = 9, what other subtraction fact do you know? Explain.

10 − 1 = 9

Chapter 8 • Subtraction Facts Practice

Practice and Problem Solving

Subtract across. Subtract down.

1.
5	4	1
3	2	1
2	2	0

2.
6	3	
4	3	

3.
7	1	
6	0	

4.
8	4	
7	4	

Problem Solving

Logical Reasoning

Solve the riddle. Write the number.

5. If you count back 2 from me, the answer is 3. What number am I?

_____

6. If you count back 3 from me, the answer is 4. What number am I?

_____

 Write About It • Look at Exercise 6. Explain how you got your answer.

 HOME ACTIVITY • Have your child tell you all the subtraction facts from 8 − 0 through 8 − 8.

118 one hundred eighteen

Name _____

Algebra: Follow the Rule

Vocabulary
rule

Learn

Subtract 2	
10	8
8	6
6	4

The rule is subtract 2, so I subtract 2 from each number.

Check

Complete the table. Follow the rule.

1.
Subtract 1	
7	
5	
3	

2.
Subtract 5	
10	
9	
8	

3.
Subtract 3	
5	
6	
7	

4.
Subtract 0	
5	
7	
9	

5.
Subtract 4	
7	
8	
9	

6.
Subtract 2	
2	
4	
6	

Explain It • Daily Reasoning

What patterns do you see? Explain.

Chapter 8 • Subtraction Facts Practice

Practice and Problem Solving

Complete the table. Follow the rule.

1. **Subtract 2**

5	3
4	
3	

2. **Subtract 0**

2	
4	
6	

3. **Subtract 3**

10	
9	
8	

4. **Subtract 1**

10	
8	
6	

5. **Subtract 5**

5	
6	
7	

6. **Subtract 4**

4	
5	
6	

Problem Solving
Logical Reasoning

Write the rule.

7. **Subtract _____**

7	5
5	3
3	1

8. **Subtract _____**

6	5
4	3
2	1

Write About It • Look at Exercise 8. Explain how you got your answer.

HOME ACTIVITY • Ask your child to write a subtraction rule and make a table that follows the rule. Have him or her explain how to use the table.

Name _____

Fact Families to 10

Vocabulary
fact family

Explore (Hands On)

4 + 2 = __6__

2 + 4 = __6__

6 − 2 = __4__

6 − 4 = __2__

The numbers in this **fact family** are 2, 4, and 6.

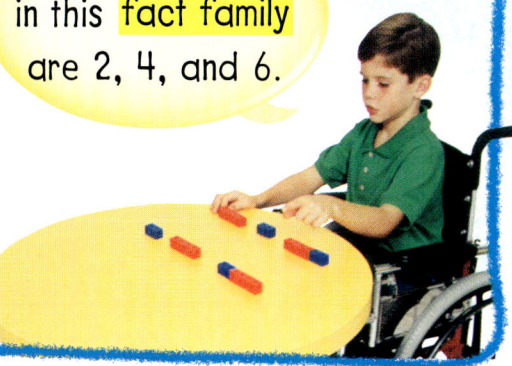

Connect

Use  and ■ to add or subtract.
Write the numbers in the fact family.

1. 8 + 2 = ___
    2 + 8 = ___
    10 − 2 = ___
    10 − 8 = ___

    | 2 | 8 | 10 |

2. 4 + 1 = ___
    1 + 4 = ___
    5 − 1 = ___
    5 − 4 = ___

    | ☐ | ☐ | ☐ |

3. 7 + 2 = ___
    2 + 7 = ___
    9 − 2 = ___
    9 − 7 = ___

    | ☐ | ☐ | ☐ |

4. 8 + 1 = ___
    1 + 8 = ___
    9 − 1 = ___
    9 − 8 = ___

    | ☐ | ☐ | ☐ |

Explain It • Daily Reasoning

How many addition and subtraction facts are in the fact family for these numbers? Use ■ and ■ to prove your answer.

 4  4  8

Practice and Problem Solving

Add or subtract. Write the numbers in the fact family.

1.

    $\begin{array}{r}6\\+2\\\hline 8\end{array}$ $\quad$ $\begin{array}{r}2\\+6\\\hline 8\end{array}$ $\quad$ $\begin{array}{r}8\\-2\\\hline 6\end{array}$ $\quad$ $\begin{array}{r}8\\-6\\\hline 2\end{array}$

2	6	8

2.

    $\begin{array}{r}4\\+3\\\hline\end{array}$ $\quad$ $\begin{array}{r}3\\+4\\\hline\end{array}$ $\quad$ $\begin{array}{r}7\\-3\\\hline\end{array}$ $\quad$ $\begin{array}{r}7\\-4\\\hline\end{array}$

3.

    $\begin{array}{r}5\\+1\\\hline\end{array}$ $\quad$ $\begin{array}{r}1\\+5\\\hline\end{array}$ $\quad$ $\begin{array}{r}6\\-1\\\hline\end{array}$ $\quad$ $\begin{array}{r}6\\-5\\\hline\end{array}$

Problem Solving
Algebra

4. Write the missing numbers.

    $\begin{array}{r}6\\+\ \square\\\hline 9\end{array}$ $\quad$ $\begin{array}{r}\square\\+\ 6\\\hline 9\end{array}$ $\quad$ $\begin{array}{r}9\\-\ \square\\\hline 6\end{array}$ $\quad$ $\begin{array}{r}9\\-\ 6\\\hline \square\end{array}$

Write About It • Look at Exercise 4. Explain why the number facts belong in a fact family.

HOME ACTIVITY • Have your child write the facts in a fact family and then explain to you why those number sentences belong in that family.

122 one hundred twenty-two

Name _____

Problem Solving Skill
Choose the Operation

Jessie has 6 apples.
She gives 4 away.
How many apples does
she have left?

Some apples are taken away. I need to subtract.

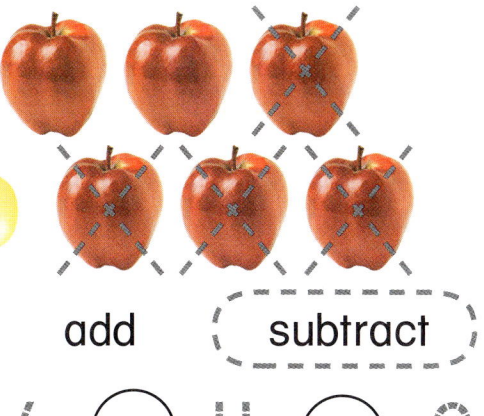

add   (subtract)

6 ⊖ 4 ⊜ 2

__2__ apples

There are 3 forks on a table.
Ida brings 2 more.
How many are there now?

More forks are added. I need to add.

(add)   subtract

3 ⊕ 2 ⊜ 5

__5__ forks

Circle **add** or **subtract**.
Write the number sentence.

THINK: Do I add or subtract?

1. There are 7 pretzels.
   Children eat 4 of them.
   How many are left?

   _____ pretzels

   add   subtract

   ___ ◯ ___ ◯ ___

2. There are 9 carrots.
   Bunnies eat 5 of them.
   How many carrots
   are left?

   _____ carrots

   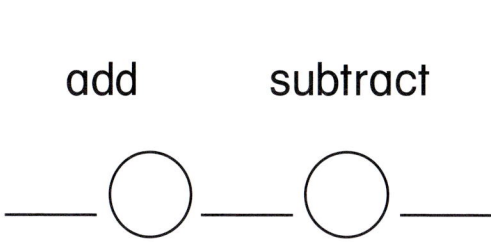

   add   subtract

   ___ ◯ ___ ◯ ___

Chapter 8 • Subtraction Facts Practice   one hundred twenty-three **123**

Problem Solving Practice

Circle **add** or **subtract**.
Write the number sentence.

THINK: Do I add or subtract?

1. There are 5 muffins.
   Zoe brings 2 more.
   How many are there now?

   _7_ muffins

   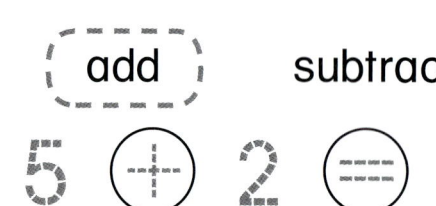
   (add)   subtract

   _5_ ⊕ _2_ ⊜ _7_

2. There are 6 apples.
   Children eat 2 of them.
   How many are left?

   ____ apples

   add   subtract
   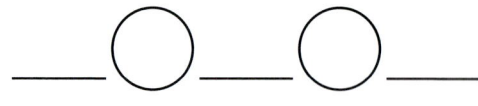

3. There are 7 pears.
   John brings 3 more.
   How many are there now?

   ____ pears

   add   subtract

4. There are 8 sandwiches.
   Children eat 3 of them.
   How many are left?

   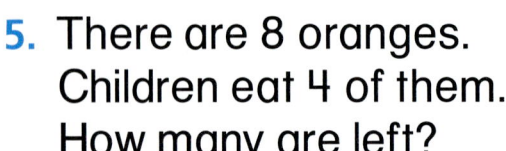
   ____ sandwiches

   add   subtract

5. There are 8 oranges.
   Children eat 4 of them.
   How many are left?

   ____ oranges

   add   subtract
   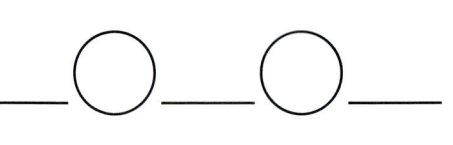

HOME ACTIVITY • For each problem, ask your child to tell how he or she decided whether to add or subtract.

Name _____

Extra Practice

Subtract. Circle the pair of facts if they use the same numbers.

1. 6   6   2. 7   7   3. 8   8
  −2 −4   −5 −3   −3 −5

Add or subtract.
Write the numbers in the fact family.

4.

   3   2   5   5
  +2   +3   −3   −2

   ☐ ☐ ☐

Complete the table. Follow the rule.

5. **Subtract 1**

9	
8	
7	

6. **Subtract 0**

5	
4	
3	

7. **Subtract 3**

3	
4	
5	

Problem Solving

Circle **add** or **subtract**.
Write the number sentence.

8. There are 6 acorns under a tree.
   A squirrel eats 3 of them.
   How many acorns are left?

   _____ acorns

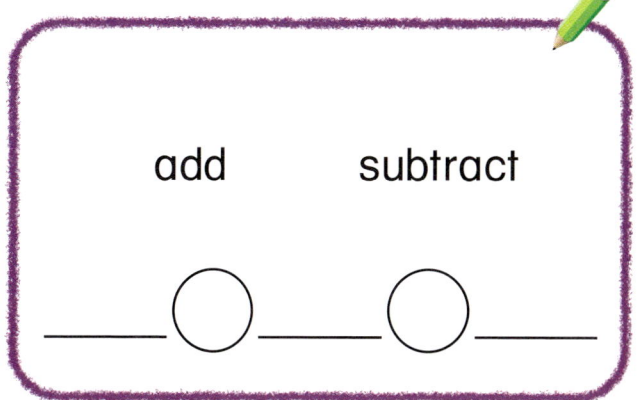

add   subtract

Name _____

✓ Review/Test

Concepts and Skills

Subtract. Circle the pair of facts if they use the same numbers.

1. 9   9
   −5 −4

2. 10   10
   − 8 − 1

3. 7   7
   −4 −3

Add or subtract.
Write the numbers in the fact family.

4.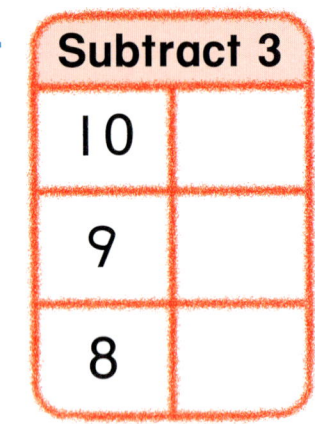

   4   2   6   6
   +2   +4   −2   −4

   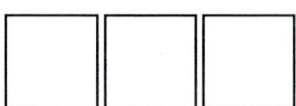

Complete the table. Follow the rule.

5. **Subtract 3**

10	
9	
8	

6. **Subtract 2**

8	
9	
10	

7. **Subtract 5**

5	
7	
9	

Problem Solving

Circle **add** or **subtract**.
Write the number sentence.

8. There are 10 grapes. Meg eats 2 of them. How many are left?

   _____ grapes

   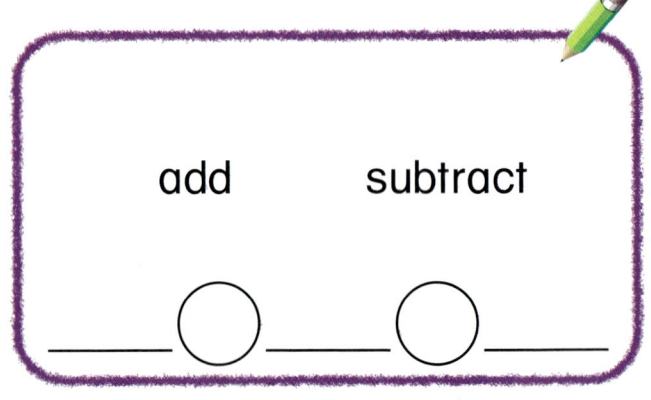

   add   subtract

   ___ ◯ ___ ◯ ___

126 one hundred twenty-six

Name _____

Standardized Test Prep
Chapters 1–8

Choose the answer for questions 1–6.

1. Which number completes the table?

Count Back 2
8 − 2 = 6
9 − 2 = 7
10 − 2 = ?

   4 ○ 6 ○ 8 ○ 10 ○

2. Which number completes the table?

Subtract 4	
4	0
5	1
6	?

   1 ○ 2 ○ 9 ○ 10 ○

3. 10 − 1 = ____

   9 ○ 10 ○ 11 ○ 13 ○

4. 9 − 2 = ____

   6 ○ 7 ○ 10 ○ 11 ○

5. Which subtraction fact is related to 4 + 3 = 7?

   7 − 5 = 2 ○   8 − 4 = 4 ○   7 − 3 = 4 ○   10 − 3 = 7 ○

6. 3 pickles are in a bowl. 2 more are added. Which number sentence tells how many pickles are in the bowl now?

   3 − 2 = 1 ○   3 − 3 = 0 ○   3 + 2 = 5 ○   2 + 2 = 4 ○

Show What You Know

7. Use 3, 7, and 10. Write the four number sentences that explain the fact family.

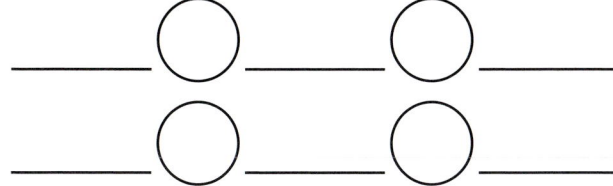
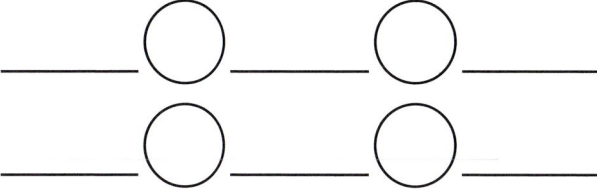

IT'S IN THE BAG
Math Under the Sea

PROJECT Create your own snorkel mask to practice your math facts.

You Will Need
- Blackline patterns
- Crayons
- Scissors

Directions

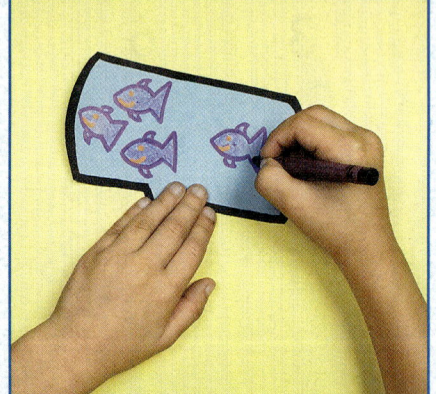

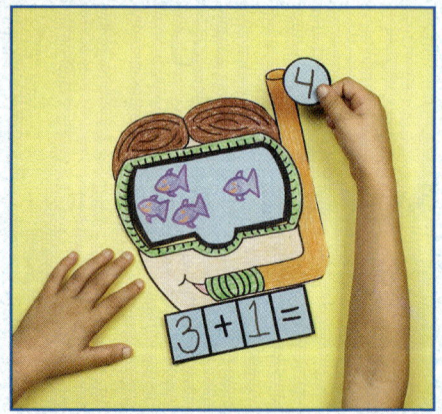

1. Color the snorkel person.
2. Cut out the snorkel person.
3. Draw an addition or subtraction problem. Use turtles, fish, or shells in your problem.
4. Write the addition or subtraction sentence. Then write the answer on a bubble.
5. Draw other problems. Write the number sentences and answers.

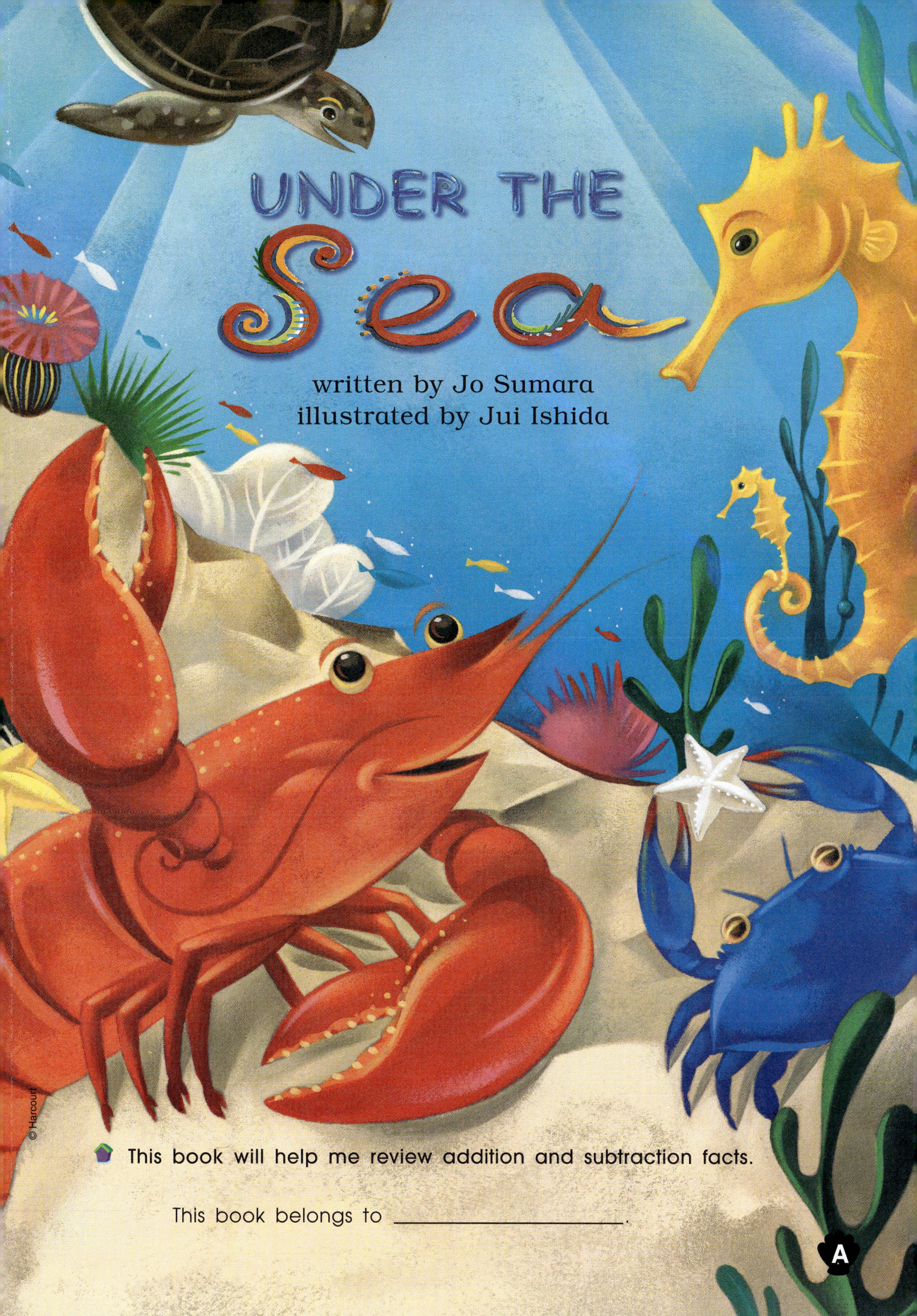

1 lobster sits on the sand in the sea.

2 more come along,
so now there are ____.

6 dolphins jump up,

do a flip, and then dive.

1 swims away,

so now there are ____.

1 sea horse floats by.
He looks like a hero.

Soon he is gone,
and then there are ___.

Name _____

PROBLEM SOLVING ON LOCATION

At the Aquarium

You can see clown fish and sea horses at the Tennessee Aquarium.

Each tank has  and .

Draw a picture and write a number sentence to solve.

Tennessee Aquarium

1 There are 5 animals in the tank.
3 are clown fish.
How many are sea horses?

5 ⊖ 3 = 2

2 sea horses

2 There are 8 animals in the tank.
4 are sea horses.
How many are clown fish?

____ ◯ ____ = ____

____ clown fish

3 There are 9 animals in the tank.
8 are sea horses.
How many are not sea horses?

____ ◯ ____ = ____

____ not sea horses

Unit 2 • Chapters 5–8

one hundred twenty-nine **129**

Name _____

CHALLENGE

Missing Parts

6 = __8__ − 2   6 = 8 − __2__

Add or subtract.
Write the missing numbers.

1.

   10 = ____ + 4   10 = 6 + ____

2.

   4 = ____ − 3   4 = 7 − ____

3.

   5 = ____ − 4   5 = 9 − ____

4.

   8 = ____ + 3   8 = 5 + ____

130 one hundred thirty

Name _____

✓ Study Guide and Review

Skills and Concepts

Use the number line. Circle the number you use to **count on**. Add.

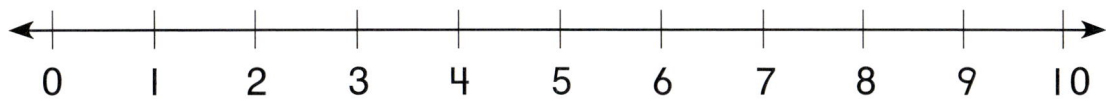

1. 6 + 2 = ____
2. 7 + 3 = ____

Use the number line. Circle the number you use to **count back**. Subtract.

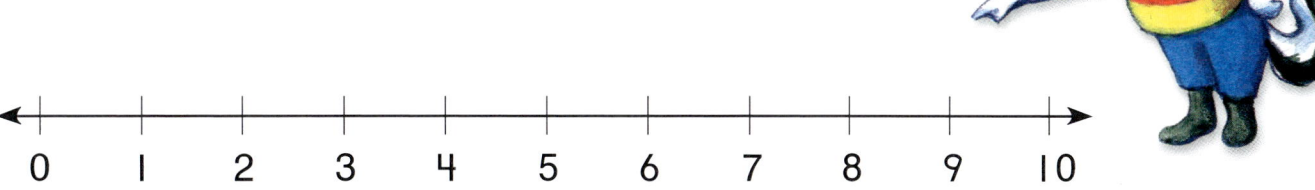

3. 8 − 2 = ____
4. 9 − 3 = ____

Add. Then circle the doubles facts.

5.	6.	7.	8.	9.	10.
2 + 2	8 + 2	2 + 5	4 + 4	3 + 3	7 + 2

Add. Then subtract.

11.		12.		13.	
5 + 4	9 − 4	7 + 3	10 − 7	4 + 4	8 − 4

Unit 2 • Study Guide and Review

Add. Change the order. Write the new fact.

14. 4
    + 2

15. 1
    + 6

16. 3
    + 5

Add or subtract.
Write the numbers in the fact family.

17. 4 + 6 = _____   10 − 6 = _____

    6 + 4 = _____   10 − 4 = _____

Complete the table. Follow the rule.

18. | Add 3 | |
|---|---|
| 0 | |
| 2 | |
| 4 | |

19. | Subtract 2 | |
|---|---|
| 6 | |
| 5 | |
| 4 | |

20. | Subtract 1 | |
|---|---|
| 10 | |
| 9 | |
| 8 | |

Problem Solving

Circle **add** or **subtract**. Write the number sentence.

21. Max has 5 apples.
    Meg has 3 apples.
    How many do they have in all?

_____ apples

add   subtract

_____ ◯ _____ ◯ _____

132 one hundred thirty-two

Name _____

✓ Performance Assessment

Little Lambs

Maria went inside the barn.
Little lambs were in two stalls.

- She counted 3 little lambs in one stall.
- She counted some more little lambs in the other stall.
- Maria counted fewer than 7 little lambs in all.

Write a number sentence that fits this math story. Write the other number sentences in that fact family.

Show your work.

Name _____

TECHNOLOGY

Calculator • Add and Subtract

Use a .
Write the answers.
Press ON/C 2 + 3 = __5__ − 1 = __4__

Practice and Problem Solving

1. Press ON/C 6 + 4 = _____ − 1 = _____

2. Press ON/C 6 − 4 = _____ + 4 = _____

3. Press ON/C 3 + 0 = _____ + 7 = _____

4. Press ON/C 3 − 0 = _____ + 6 = _____

5. Press ON/C 7 + 2 = _____ + 1 = _____

6. Press ON/C 7 − 2 = _____ + 1 = _____

7. Press ON/C 6 − 3 = _____

Explain your answer.
Use 🔴.

134 one hundred thirty-four

Dear Family,

In Unit 2 we learned addition and subtraction facts to 10. Here is a game for us to play together. This game will give me a chance to share what I have learned.

Love,

_____

Directions
1. Put your game piece on START.
2. Use a paper clip and a pencil to make the spinner. Spin. Move that many spaces.
3. Add or subtract the number you spin and the number your game piece is on.
4. Move forward 1 if you added. Move forward 2 if you subtracted.
5. Take turns. The first person to get to END wins.

Materials
- 2 game pieces or beans
- pencil
- paper clip

Get Those Numbers

Unit 3 • Unit Game

one hundred thirty-five A   135A

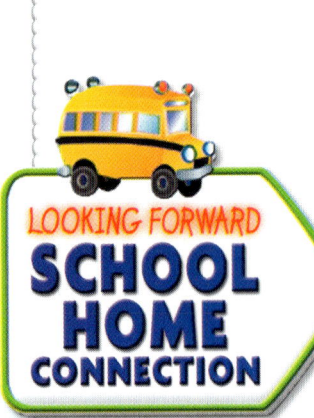

LOOKING FORWARD SCHOOL HOME CONNECTION

Dear Family,

During the next few weeks, we will learn about graphs and about numbers to 100. Here is important math vocabulary and a list of books to share.

Love,

_____

Vocabulary
picture graph
bar graph
is greater than
is less than
is equal to

Vocabulary Power

picture graph

Favorite Fruits	
apples	🍎🍎🍎🍎🍎
oranges	🍊

bar graph

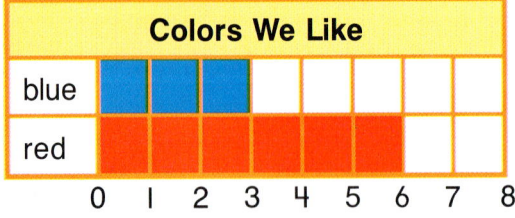

26 > 24
26 is greater than 24.

24 < 26
24 is less than 26.

24 = 24
24 is equal to 24.

BOOKS TO SHARE

To read about graphs and about numbers to 100 with your child, look for these books in your library.

Is It Rough? Is It Smooth? Is It Shiny?
by Tana Hoban, Greenwillow, 1990.

Pancakes for Breakfast,
by Tomie dePaola, Harcourt, 1990.

Two of Everything,
by Lily Toy Hong, Albert Whitman, 1993.

Splash,
by Ann Jonas, Greenwillow, 1995.

GO ON-LINE Visit *The Learning Site* for additional ideas and activities. www.harcourtschool.com

CHAPTER 9
Graphs and Tables

FUN FACTS

You see ten fingers when you make handprint paintings.

Theme: Favorites

Name _____

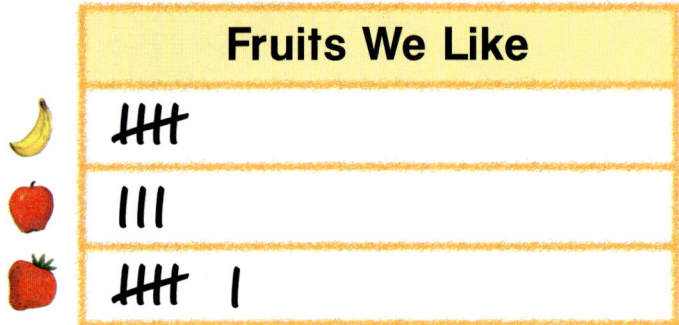

Read a Tally Table

Fruits We Like	
🍌	⳾⳾⳾⳾⳾
🍎	|||
🍓	⳾⳾⳾⳾⳾	

Write how many.

1.  _____
2.  _____
3.  _____

4. Circle the fruit the most children chose.

Make Picture Graphs

5. Look at the picture.
   Make a graph about pennies and nickels.

Pennies and Nickels

Write how many of each coin.
Circle the number that shows fewer.

6.  _____

7.  _____

136 one hundred thirty-six

Name _____

Algebra: Sort and Classify

Vocabulary
sort

Explore

You can sort these shapes.

All of these are triangles. **All of these are green.**

These are both triangles and green.

Connect

Sort your shapes a different way.
Draw each group. Tell how you sorted.

Explain It • Daily Reasoning

How could you sort your shapes into four different groups? Show one way.

Chapter 9 • Graphs and Tables
one hundred thirty-seven **137**

Practice and Problem Solving

Draw a line from each shape to the group where it belongs.

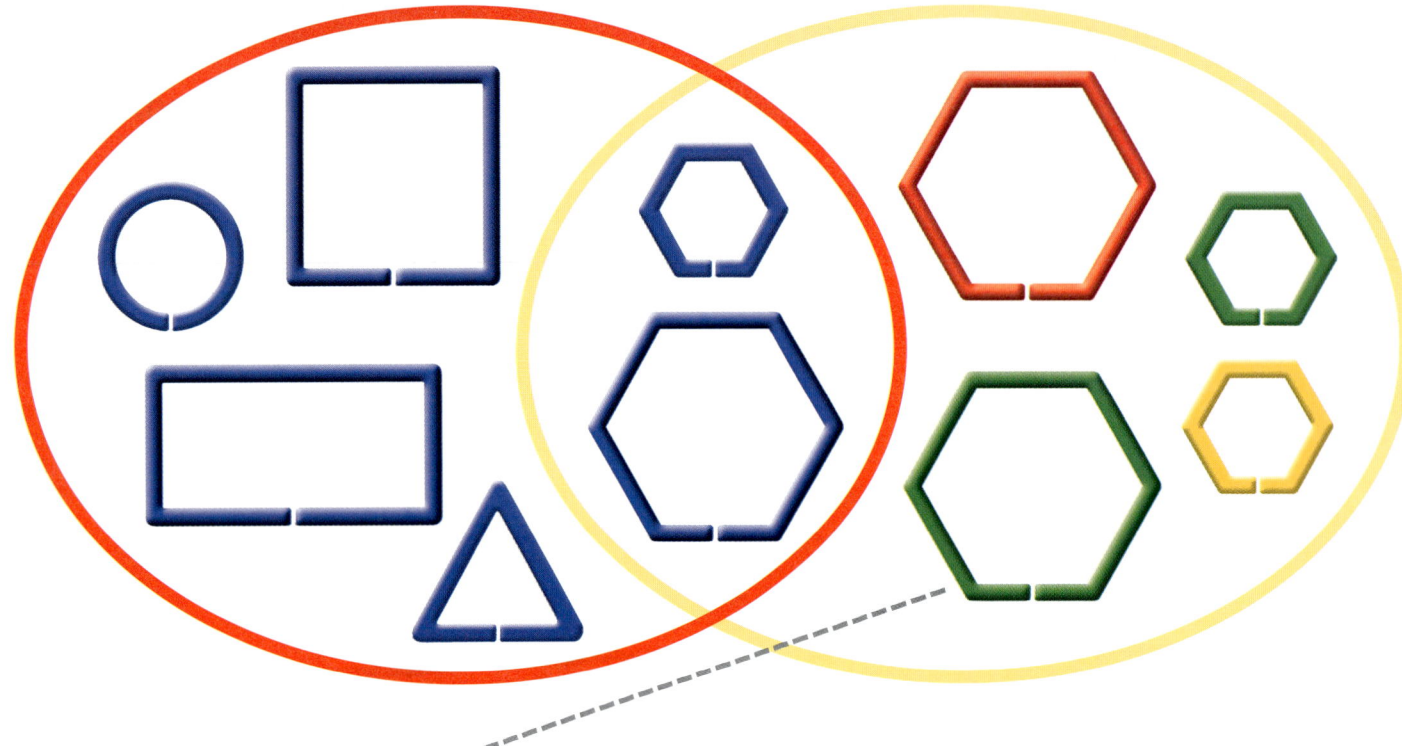

1.
2.
3. (circle)
4. (red hexagon)

Problem Solving
Application

5. Draw how you could sort these buttons.

 **Write About It** • Draw how you could sort these buttons.

HOME ACTIVITY • Ask your child to explain how he or she sorted in Exercises 1–4.

138 one hundred thirty-eight

Name _____

Make Concrete Graphs

Vocabulary
concrete graph

 **Explore**

This concrete graph shows how many crayons there are of each color.

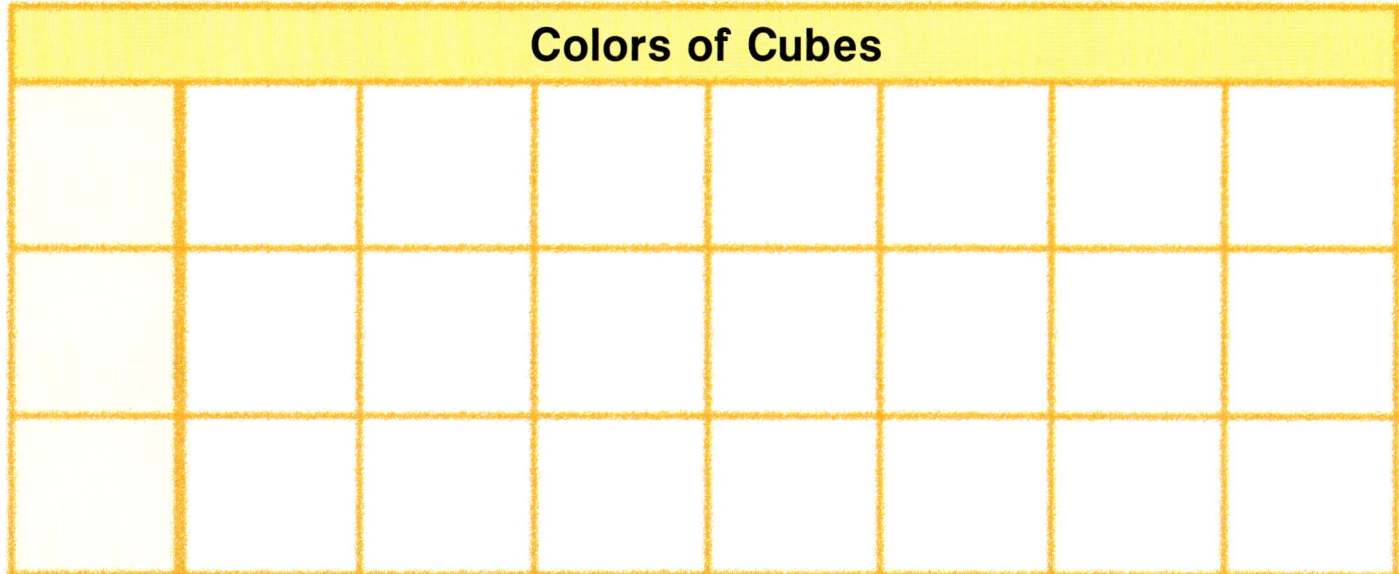

Connect

Sort 🟥, 🟦, and 🟩. Make a graph.

Colors of Cubes

1. How many 🟥 are there? _____

2. How many 🟦 are there? _____

3. How many 🟩 are there? _____

Explain It • Daily Reasoning

Which color cube did you have the most of? How do you know?

Chapter 9 • Graphs and Tables

Practice and Problem Solving

Use the graph to answer the questions.

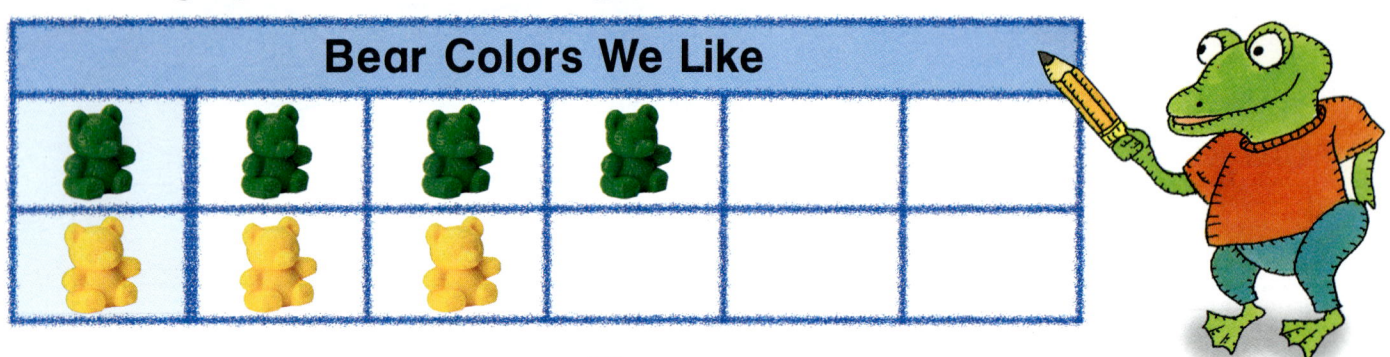

1. How many children chose 🐻? _____

2. How many children chose 🐻? _____

3. Which color did more children choose? _____

4. Which color did fewer children choose? _____

5. How many children in all chose colors? _____

Problem Solving
Application

6. Ask six classmates what their favorite bear color is. Use 🐻, 🐻, 🐻, 🐻 to show each choice.

Favorite Bear Colors

Write About It • Which is the favorite bear color of the most classmates? Explain how you know.

HOME ACTIVITY • Give your child a collection of pots and lids. Have him or her line them up in two rows. Ask how many are in each row, which row has more, and which has fewer.

Name _____

Make Picture Graphs

Vocabulary
picture graph

Learn

This picture graph uses pictures to show how many children chose each fruit.

Fruits We Like

🍎 apples	🍎	🍎	🍎			
🍊 oranges	🍊	🍊				
🍌 bananas	🍌	🍌	🍌	🍌		

The most children chose bananas.

Check

1. Some children drew pictures of their favorite fruits. Sort. Draw to complete the picture graph.

Fruits We Like

🍓 strawberries	🍓					
🍇 grapes	🍇					
🍒 cherries	🍒					

2. How many children drew  ? _____

3. Which fruit did the most children draw? _____

4. Which fruit did the fewest children draw? _____

Explain It • Daily Reasoning

What would you ask to find out your classmates' favorite fruits?

Chapter 9 • Graphs and Tables

Practice and Problem Solving

Vegetables We Like									
potatoes	🥔	🥔	🥔						
peas	🟢								
carrots	🥕	🥕	🥕	🥕	🥕				
beans	🌱	🌱							

Use the picture graph to answer the questions.

1. How many children chose carrots? _____

2. Did more choose beans or peas? _____

3. Did fewer choose potatoes or carrots? _____

4. How many more chose carrots than beans? _____

Problem Solving
Logical Reasoning

5. Complete the graph.

   There are 3 fewer oranges than apples. There are 2 more pears than oranges.

Fruits in the Bowl

 **Write About It** • Look at Exercise 5. How did you know how many oranges to draw?

HOME ACTIVITY • Have your child collect 10 to 15 stuffed animals or other toys. Have him or her sort them into groups and tell how many are in the group that has the most.

Name _____

Read a Tally Table

Vocabulary
tally table
tally mark

Learn

Which snack do you like better?

Snacks We Like		Total
pretzels	|||| ||	7
carrots	|||| ||||	9

This tally table shows how many children chose each snack.

Each tally mark | stands for one child.
|||| stands for five children.
More children chose carrots than pretzels.

Check

Choose two kinds of juice from the pictures.
Ask eight children the question.
Then fill in the tally table.

Which juice do you like better?

Juices We Like		Total

orange   grape   apple

Use the tally table to answer these questions.

1. How many children chose _____ ? _____

2. How many children chose _____ ? _____

3. Which juice did more children choose? _____

Explain It • Daily Reasoning

What would happen if you added more choices of juice?

Chapter 9 • Graphs and Tables

Practice and Problem Solving

Choose two bird colors from the pictures.
Ask eight children the question.
Then fill in the tally table.

Which bird color do you like better?

Bird Colors We Like		Total

𝄁𝄁𝄁𝄁𝄁 stands for 5.

Use the tally table to answer these questions.

1. How many children chose _____ ? _____

2. How many children chose _____ ? _____

3. Did fewer children choose _____ or _____ ?
   Circle the color word.

4. How many fewer? _____

Problem Solving
Application

5. How many more children chose 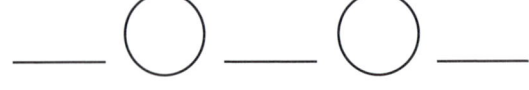 than 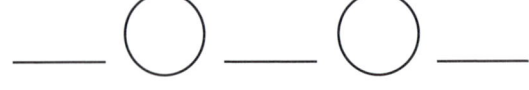 ?
   Use the tally table. Write the number sentence.

   ___ ◯ ___ ◯ ___

   ____ more children

Birds We Like		Total
🐦	𝄁𝄁𝄁𝄁𝄁 |||	
🐦	||||	

 Write About It • Look at Exercise 5.
Explain how you got your answer.

🏠 **HOME ACTIVITY** • Give your child 10 to 12 objects of two kinds, such as forks and spoons. Have him or her make a tally table to show how many there are of each kind.

Name _____

Make Bar Graphs

Vocabulary
bar graph

Learn

Make a bar graph by coloring one box for each tally mark.

More children ride than walk.

How We Go to School		Total
walk 🚶	IIII	4
ride 🚌	IIII I	6

How We Go to School
walk 🚶
ride 🚌
0 1 2 3 4 5 6

Check

1. Write how many tally marks.

Things We Like to Do		Total
read 📘	IIII III	8
paint 🖌	IIII	
play sports ⚾	IIII	

2. What is the question for this graph?

_____

3. Color the bar graph to match the tally marks.

Explain It • Daily Reasoning

How does writing how many tally marks help you make a bar graph?

Chapter 9 • Graphs and Tables

Practice and Problem Solving

1. Write how many tally marks.

2. Color the bar graph to match.

Our Pets		Total
cat	🐱	𝍲 𝍲
dog	🐶	𝍲𝍲𝍲𝍲𝍲 𝍲𝍲𝍲𝍲𝍲
fish	🐟	||||

Use the graph to answer the questions.

3. How many children have cats? _____

4. How many more children have cats than fish? _____

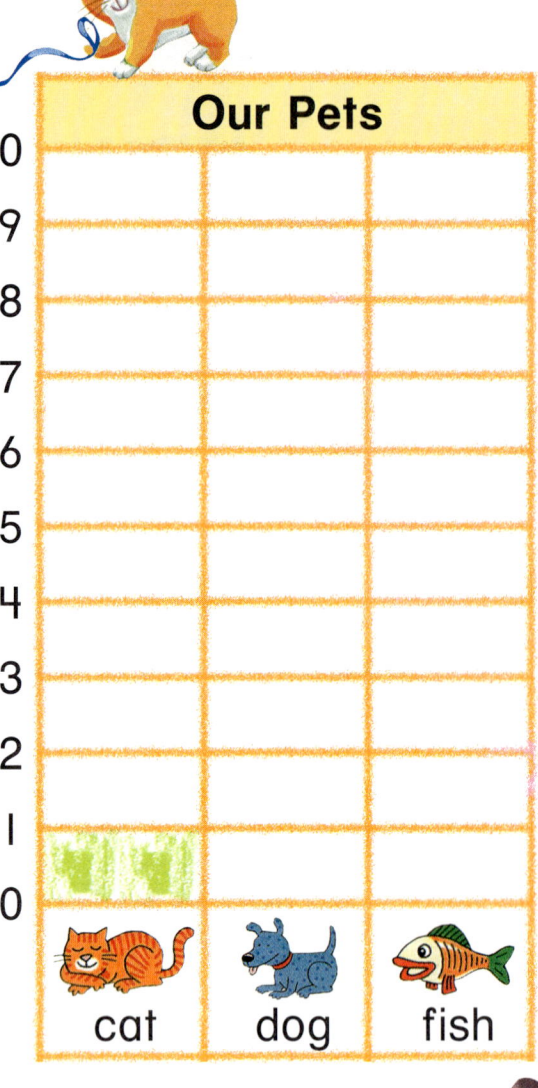

Problem Solving
Logical Reasoning

5. Use these clues to make a bar graph.
   More children have bears than cars.
   The fewest children have dolls.

Our Toys

car 🚗										
bear 🧸										
doll 👧										

0 1 2 3 4 5 6 7 8 9 10

 Write About It • How is the bar graph in Exercise 5 different from the first bar graph on this page?

🏠 **HOME ACTIVITY** • Cover the tally table. Ask your child how many children have each kind of pet.

Name _____

Problem Solving Skill
Use Data from a Graph

Use the bar graph to answer the questions.

THINK: Each box equals one child's choice.

Subjects We Like

	0	1	2	3	4	5	6	7	8	9	10
math											
reading											
science											
social studies											

1. How many children chose math or reading?

    _____ children

    THINK: You can add to solve a problem.

    $7 \oplus 3 \ominus 10$

2. How many more children chose social studies than science?

    _____ children

    THINK: You can subtract to solve a problem.

    ___ ___ ___

3. Did more children choose science or reading?

    _____

4. How many more children chose science than reading?

    _____ children chose science.

    _____ children chose reading.

    _____ more child

    ___  ___ ◯ ___

Chapter 9 • Graphs and Tables

one hundred forty-seven **147**

Problem Solving Practice

Use the bar graph to answer the questions.

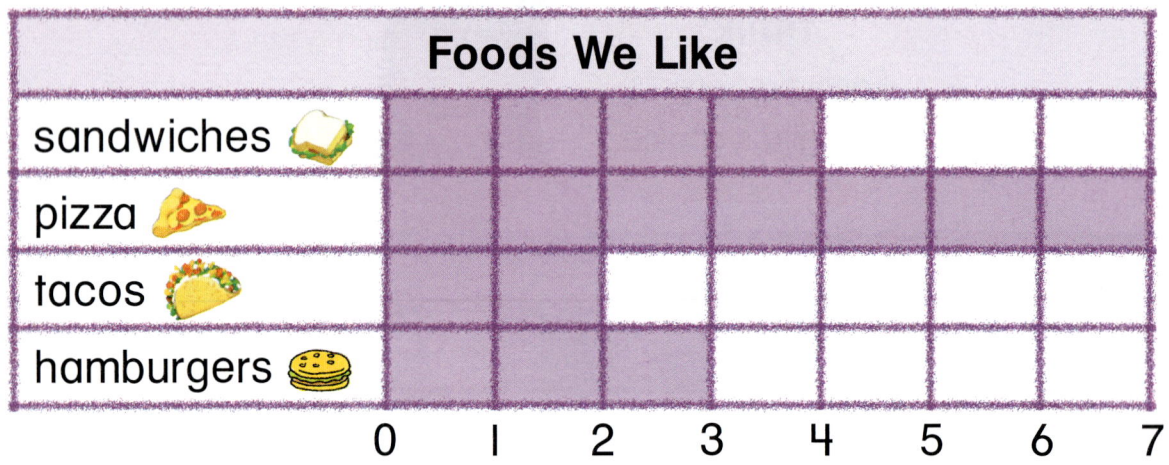

1. How many children chose pizza or tacos?

   _____ children

   THINK: You can add to solve a problem.

   _7_ ⊕ _2_ ⊖ _9_

2. How many more children chose sandwiches than tacos?

   _____ children

   THINK: You can subtract to solve a problem.

   ____ ◯ ____ ◯ ____

3. Did more children choose pizza or hamburgers?

   _____

4. How many more children chose pizza than hamburgers?

   _____ children chose pizza.

   _____ children chose hamburgers.

   _____ more children

   ____ ◯ ____ ◯ ____

HOME ACTIVITY • Ask your child to use the bar graph to tell which food the fewest children chose and which food the most children chose.

Name _____

Interpret Graphs

Learn

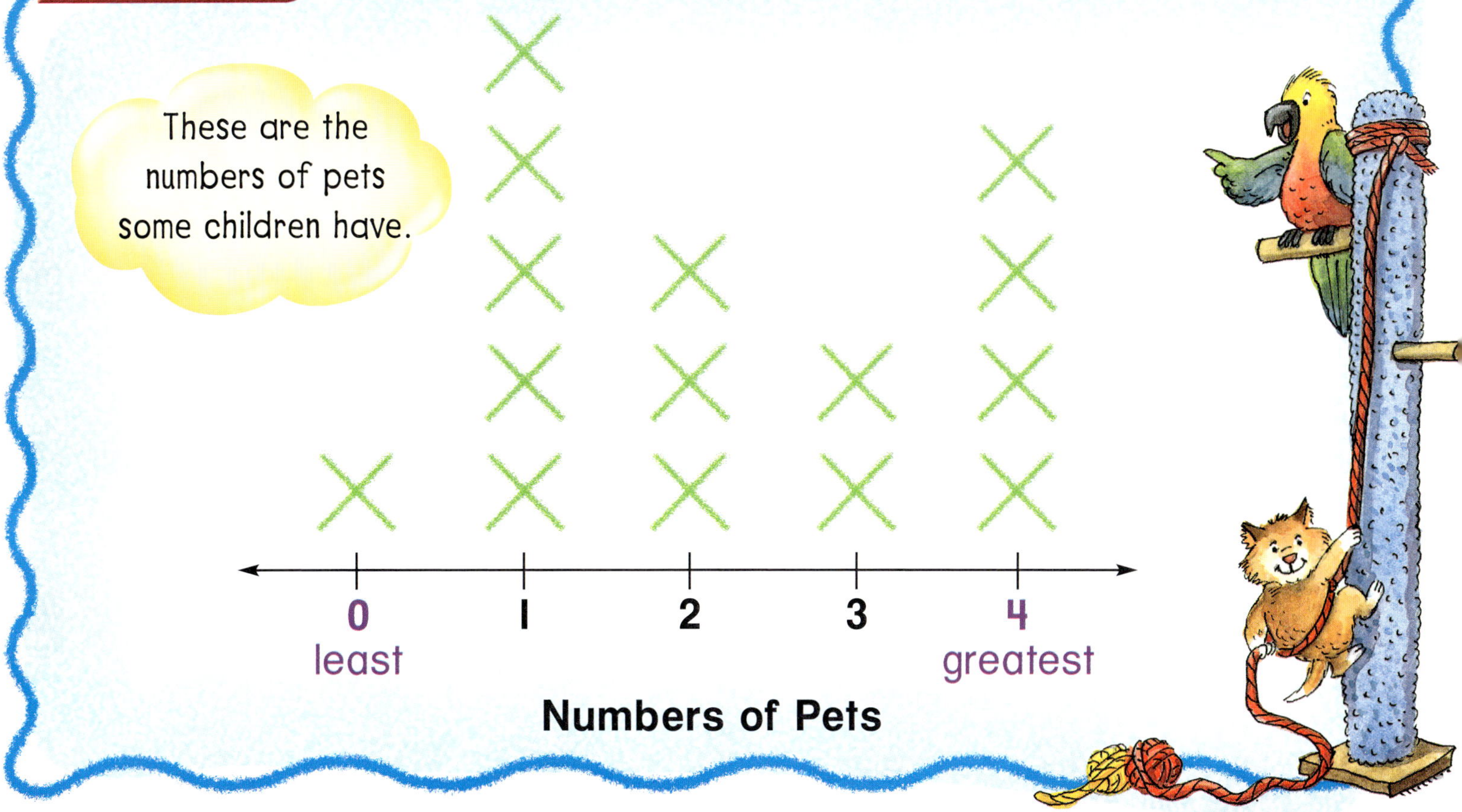

These are the numbers of pets some children have.

```
            X
            X           X
            X   X       X
        X   X   X   X   X
    X   X   X   X   X
←———+———+———+———+———+———→
    0   1   2   3   4
  least               greatest
        Numbers of Pets
```

Check

Use the graph to answer the questions.

1. How many pets do the most children have? _____

2. What is the least number of pets children have? _____

3. What is the greatest number of pets children have? _____

4. What is the difference between the greatest number of pets and the least number of pets?

Explain It • Daily Reasoning

How many children were asked about their pets? How do you know?

Chapter 9 • Graphs and Tables

Practice and Problem Solving

Use the graph to answer the questions.

1. How many hours do the most children play? _____

2. What is the greatest number of hours children play? _____

3. What is the least number of hours children play? _____

4. What is the difference between the greatest number of hours and the least number of hours?

Numbers of Hours Children Play Each Day

Problem Solving

Application

Solve.

5. Two more children play 2 hours each day. How many children play 2 hours each day now?   _____ children

6. Two more children play 4 hours each day. How many children play 4 hours each day now?   _____ children

 Write About It • Look at Exercise 6. Draw a picture of how the graph would look.

HOME ACTIVITY • Help your child make a graph like the one on this page to show how many hours family members watch television on weekdays.

150 one hundred fifty

Name _____

Extra Practice

Children chose from three sports.

1. Write how many tally marks.

   Which sport do you like the best?

Sports We Like		Total
soccer	|||||	
baseball	||	
basketball	||||	

2. Color the bar graph to match the tally table.

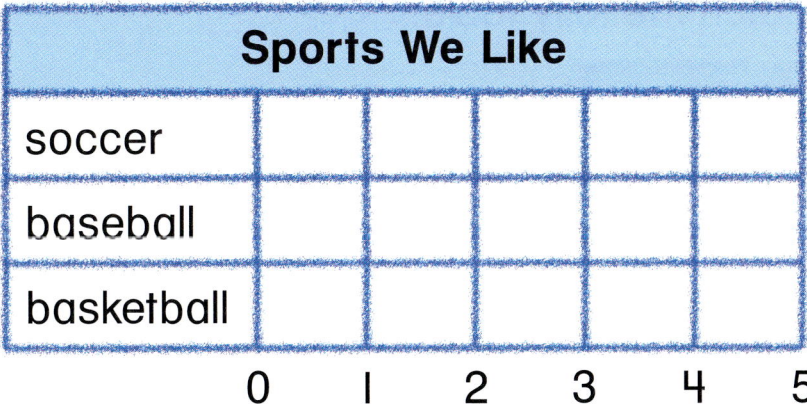

Problem Solving

Use the bar graph to answer the questions.

3. How many children chose basketball?

   _____

4. Which game did the most children choose?

   _____

5. How many children chose soccer? _____

Chapter 9 • Graphs and Tables

one hundred fifty-one **151**

Name _____

✓ Review/Test

Concepts and Skills

Children chose from three shirt colors.

  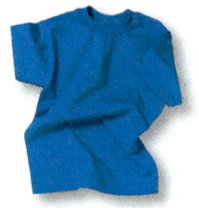

1. Write how many tally marks.

   Which shirt color do you like the best?

Shirt Colors We Like		Total
red	|||||	
yellow	||||	
blue	|||||		

2. Color the bar graph to match the tally table.

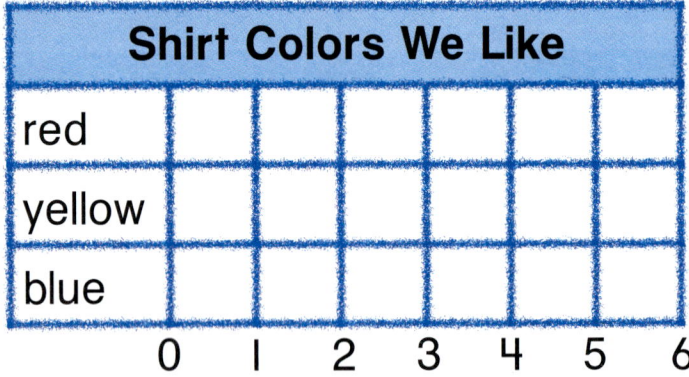

Problem Solving

Use the bar graph to answer the questions.

3. How many children chose red?

   _____

4. Which color did the most children choose?

   _____

5. How many children chose blue? _____

152 one hundred fifty-two

Name _____

⭐ Standardized Test Prep
Chapters 1–9

Choose the answer for questions 1–3.
Use the graph to answer questions 1 and 2.

Our Pets					
dog	🐕	🐕	🐕	🐕	🐕
cat	🐈	🐈	🐈		
rabbit	🐇	🐇			

1. How many children have ?

   2   3   5   7
   ○   ○   ○   ○

2. Which pet do the fewest children have?

   ○   ○   ○

3. Which subtraction fact is related to $4 + 2 = 6$?

   $4 - 1 = 3$ $6 - 5 = 1$ $4 - 3 = 1$ $6 - 2 = 4$
   ○   ○   ○   ○

Show What You Know

4. Sort. Fill in the tally table to explain how you sorted. Color the bar graph to match the tally marks.

5. How many more children chose apples than bananas?

   1   3   4   5
   ○   ○   ○   ○

Chapter 9   one hundred fifty-three **153**

Name _____

MATH GAME

Graph Game

Play with a partner.

1. Spin the 🎯.
2. Put 1 cube of that color in your graph.
3. Take turns until one player fills a row.
4. That player tosses the 🎲.
5. The player who has a row with that many cubes wins. If no player has a row with that many, toss again.

You will need

10 🟥
10 🟦
10 🟨

Player 1

Player 2

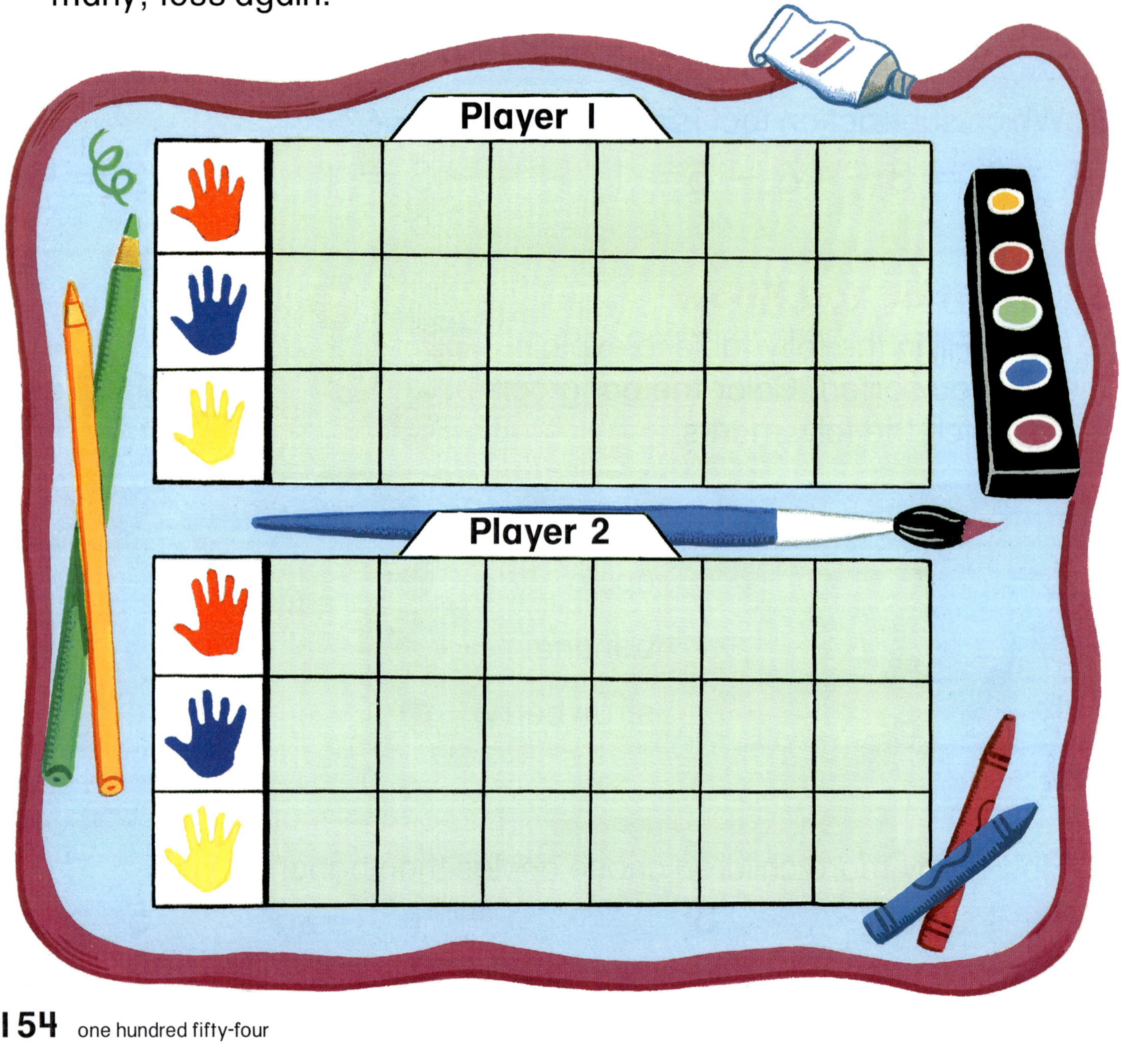

CHAPTER 10
Place Value to 100

FUN FACTS
SOCIAL STUDIES

A medium size piñata can hold about 100 pieces of hard candy and small toys.

Theme: Time for a Party

Name _____

✓ Check What You Know

Make Groups of 10

Count. Draw more to make a group of 10.

1.

2.

3.

4.

11 to 20: Using Ten Frames

Count. Circle the number that tells how many.
Write the number.

5. 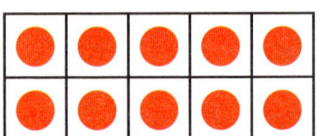   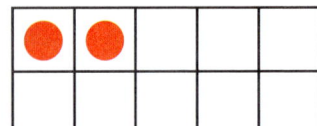   11   12   13   ____

6. 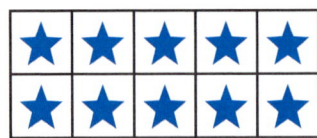   13   14   15   ____

7.       17   18   19   ____

8.       18   19   20   ____

Name _____

Teen Numbers

Vocabulary
ten
ones

Explore

You use 1 ten and ones to show teen numbers.

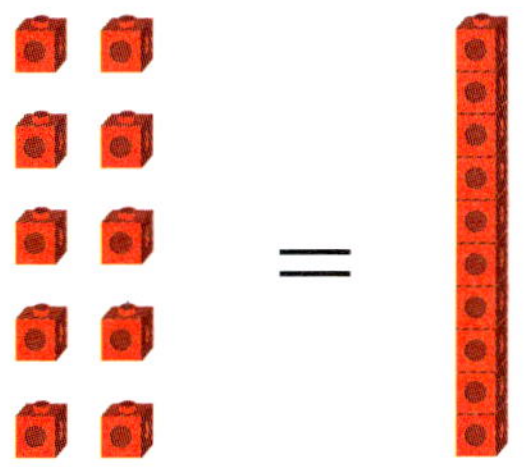

10 ones = 1 ten

10 ones can be grouped into 1 ten.

10 ten

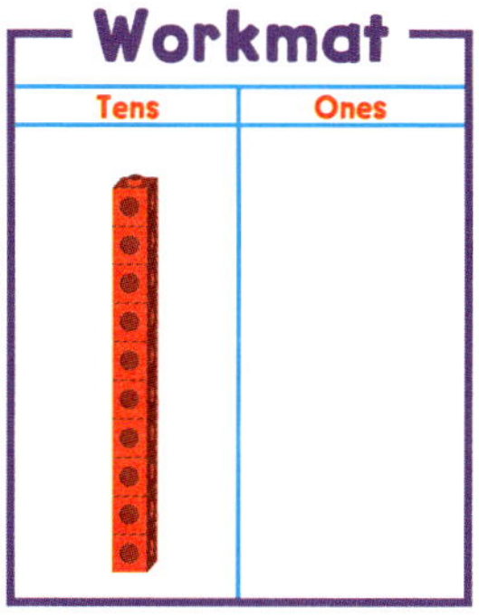

Workmat
Tens	Ones

1 ten   ones

10 is 1 group of ten. There are 0 ones.

Connect

Use Workmat 3 and ▢. Show the teen number. Draw the tens and ones. Write how many tens and ones.

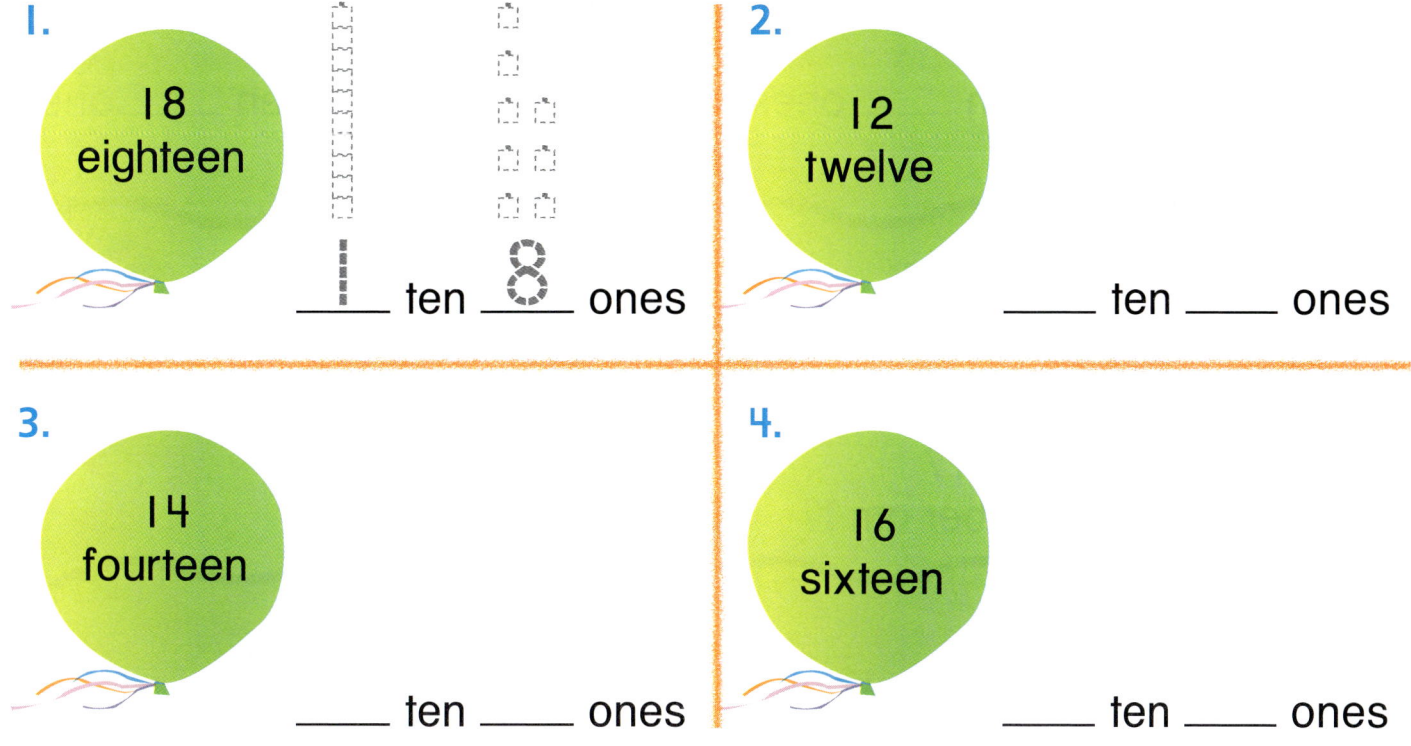

1. 18 eighteen — __1__ ten __8__ ones

2. 12 twelve — ____ ten ____ ones

3. 14 fourteen — ____ ten ____ ones

4. 16 sixteen — ____ ten ____ ones

Explain It • Daily Reasoning

What number comes before the first teen number?

Chapter 10 • Place Value to 100

Practice and Problem Solving

Draw the tens and ones.
Write how many tens and ones.

1. 14 fourteen
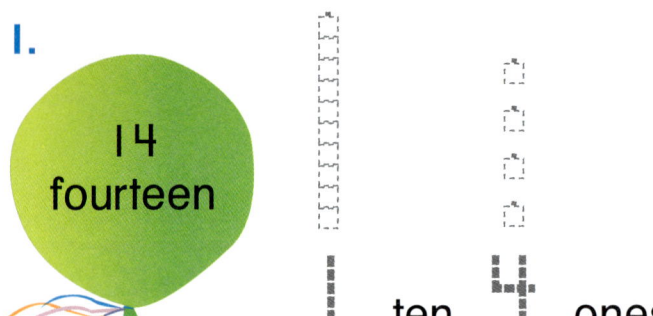
__1__ ten __4__ ones

2. 19 nineteen
____ ten ____ ones

3. 13 thirteen
____ ten ____ ones

4. 11 eleven
____ ten ____ ones

5. 17 seventeen
____ ten ____ ones

6. 15 fifteen
____ ten ____ ones

Problem Solving

Logical Reasoning

Write the teen number that solves the riddle.

7. I am less than 19.
I am more than 17.
What teen number am I? _____

 Write About It • Look at Exercise 7.
Draw the tens and ones to show your answer.

🏠 **HOME ACTIVITY** • Have your child use small objects to show teen numbers between 10 and 20. Ask him or her to make groups of tens and ones, tell how many are in each group, and say the number.

Name _____

Tens

Explore

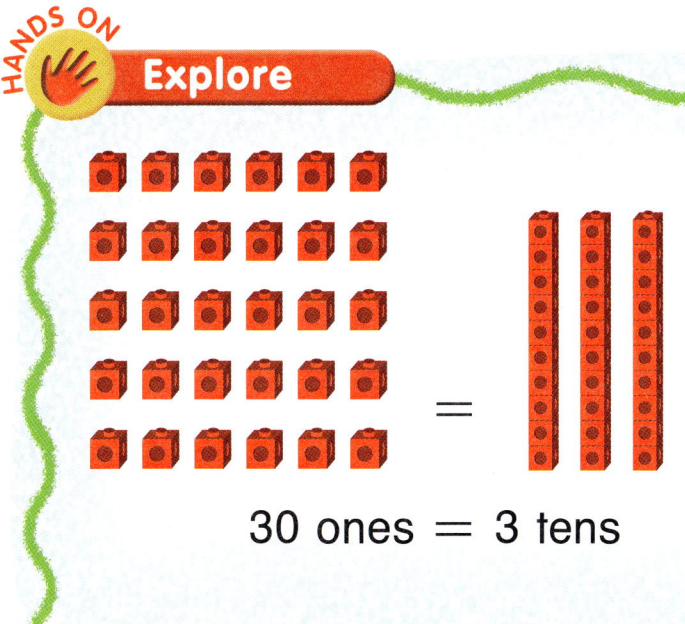

30 ones = 3 tens

3 tens = $\underline{30}$
thirty

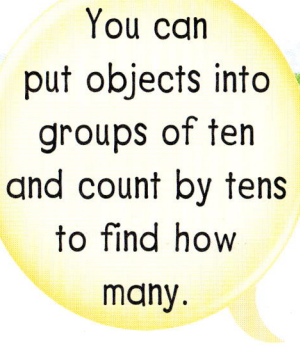

You can put objects into groups of ten and count by tens to find how many.

Connect

Use  to make tens. Draw the tens.
Count by tens. Write the number.

1. Make 2 tens.

   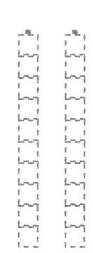

   $\underline{20}$
   twenty

2. Make 4 tens.

   _____
   forty

3. Make 5 tens.

   _____
   fifty

Explain It • Daily Reasoning

How many tens equal 100? How do you know?

Chapter 10 • Place Value to 100

Practice and Problem Solving

Count by tens. Write the number.

1.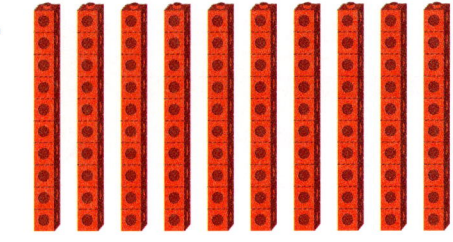

   __10__ = __100__
   tens   one hundred

2.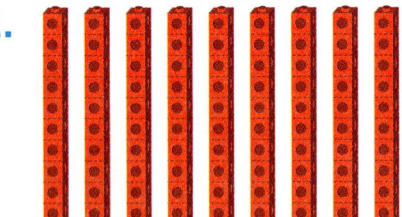

   _____ = _____
   tens   ninety

3.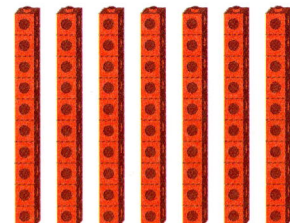

   _____ = _____
   tens   seventy

4.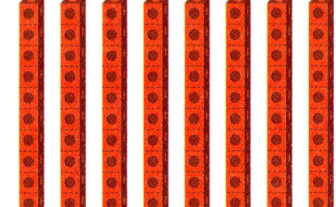

   _____ = _____
   tens   eighty

Problem Solving
Application

Draw to show the story. Write the answer.

5. Jon gave 6 friends marbles. He gave each friend 10 marbles. How many marbles did he give his friends?

   _____ marbles

 Write About It • Look at Exercise 5. Explain how you got your answer.

🏠 **HOME ACTIVITY** • Have your child group objects into tens and tell how many there are in all.

Name _____

Tens and Ones to 50

 **Explore**

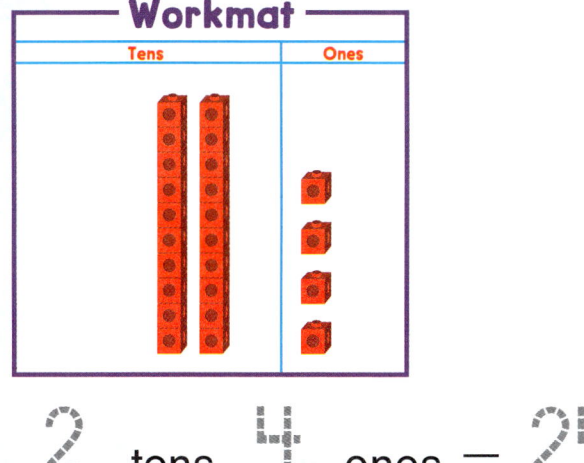

24 is 2 groups of ten and 4 ones.

__2__ tens __4__ ones = __24__

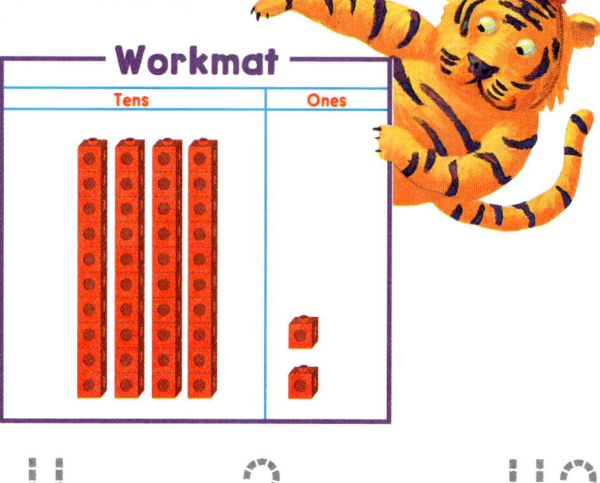

42 is 4 groups of ten and 2 ones.

__4__ tens __2__ ones = __42__

Connect

Use Workmat 3 and 🟥.
Show the groups of ten. Show the ones.
Write how many tens and ones. Write the number.

1. _____ tens _____ one = _____

2. _____ ten _____ ones = _____

3. _____ tens _____ ones = _____

4. _____ tens _____ ones = _____

Explain It • Daily Reasoning

What does the zero mean in the number **30**?
Use 🟥 to prove your answer.

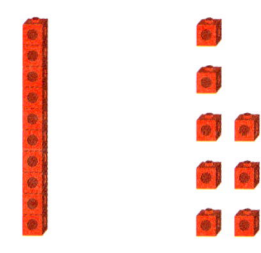

Chapter 10 • Place Value to 100

one hundred sixty-one **161**

Practice and Problem Solving

Write how many tens and ones. Write the number.

1.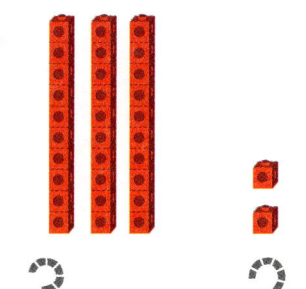

   __3__ tens __2__ ones = __32__

2.

   ____ tens ____ ones = ____

3.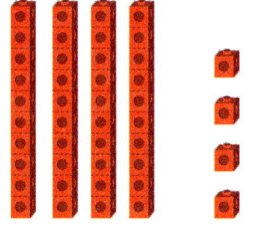

   ____ tens ____ ones = ____

4.

   ____ tens ____ ones = ____

5.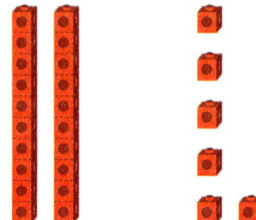

   ____ tens ____ ones = ____

6.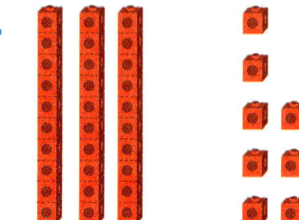

   ____ tens ____ ones = ____

Problem Solving
Visual Thinking

7. Show the same number using only tens. Write how many tens and ones.

   ____ tens ____ ones   ____ tens ____ ones

 Write About It • Look at Exercise 7. Explain what happens to the tens and ones when you use only tens.

HOME ACTIVITY • Say numbers up to 50. Have your child draw cubes to show them. Ask him or her to write how many tens and ones are shown in each drawing and then to write the number.

Name _____

Tens and Ones to 50

 **Explore**

24 is 2 groups of ten and 4 ones.

42 is 4 groups of ten and 2 ones.

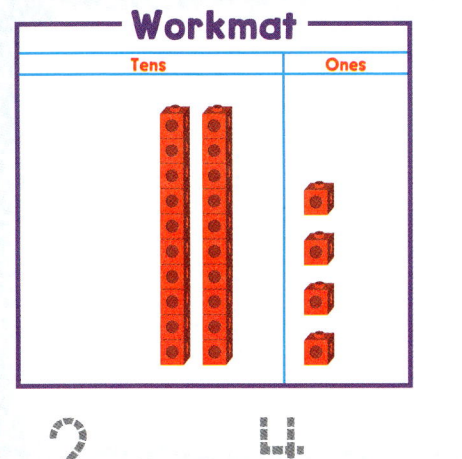

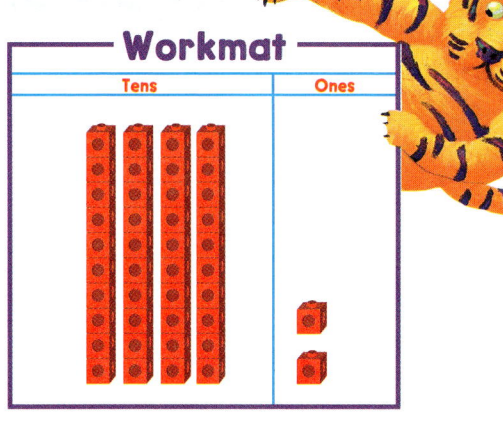

__2__ tens __4__ ones = __24__

__4__ tens __2__ ones = __42__

Connect

Use Workmat 3 and 🟥.
Show the groups of ten. Show the ones.
Write how many tens and ones. Write the number.

1.

____ tens ____ one = ____

2.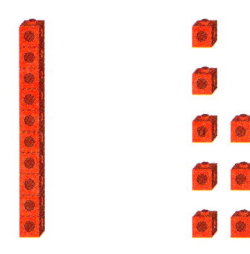

____ ten ____ ones = ____

3.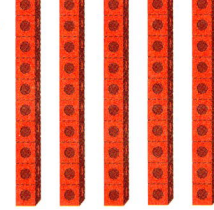

____ tens ____ ones = ____

4.

____ tens ____ ones = ____

Explain It • Daily Reasoning

What does the zero mean in the number **30**?
Use 🟥 to prove your answer.

Chapter 10 • Place Value to 100

Practice and Problem Solving

Write how many tens and ones. Write the number.

1.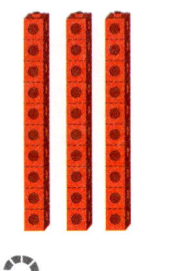

   __3__ tens __2__ ones = __32__

2.

   ____ tens ____ ones = ____

3.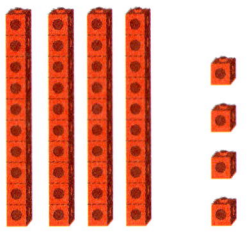

   ____ tens ____ ones = ____

4.

   ____ tens ____ ones = ____

5.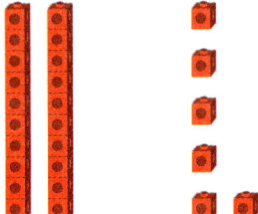

   ____ tens ____ ones = ____

6.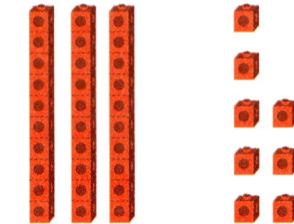

   ____ tens ____ ones = ____

Problem Solving
Visual Thinking

7. Show the same number using only tens. Write how many tens and ones.

   ____ tens ____ ones | ____ tens ____ ones

Write About It • Look at Exercise 7. Explain what happens to the tens and ones when you use only tens.

▲ **HOME ACTIVITY** • Say numbers up to 50. Have your child draw cubes to show them. Ask him or her to write how many tens and ones are shown in each drawing and then to write the number.

Name _____

Tens and Ones to 100

Vocabulary
hundred

Explore

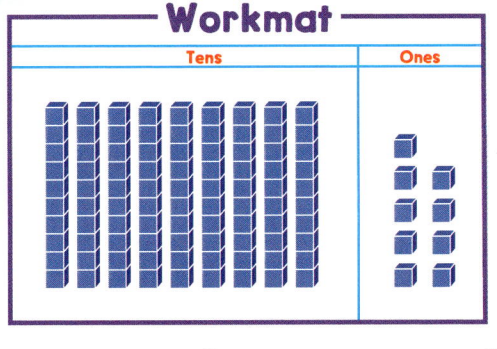

__9__ tens __9__ ones = __99__   __10__ tens __0__ ones = __100__

99 is 9 groups of ten and 9 ones.

100 is 10 groups of ten.
100 is 1 hundred.

Connect

Use Workmat 3 and .
Write how many tens and ones.
Write the number.

1.

____ tens ____ ones = ____

2.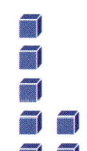

____ tens ____ ones = ____

3.

____ tens ____ ones = ____

4.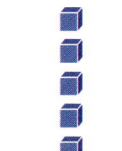

____ tens ____ ones = ____

Explain It • Daily Reasoning

What number would you write for 9 tens 1 one?
What number would you write for 9 tens 8 ones?

Practice and Problem Solving

Write how many tens and ones.
Write the number.

1.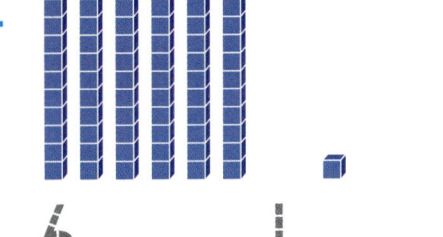

   _6_ tens _1_ one = _61_

2.

   ____ tens ____ ones = ____

3.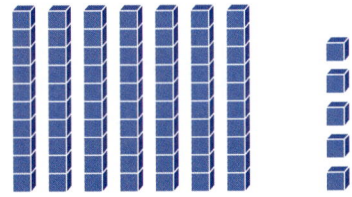

   ____ tens ____ ones = ____

4.

   ____ tens ____ ones = ____

5.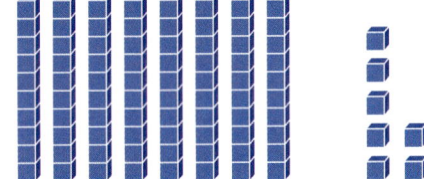

   ____ tens ____ ones = ____

6.

   ____ tens ____ ones = ____

Problem Solving

Application

Is the line under tens or ones?
Circle your answer.

7. 2<u>3</u>   tens   ones

8. 2<u>5</u>   tens   ones

9. <u>4</u>7   tens   ones

10. 3<u>0</u>   tens   ones

 **Write About It** • What does the **2** in **27** stand for?

 HOME ACTIVITY • Say a number between 50 and 100. Have your child draw cubes to show the number, tell how many tens and ones there are, and then write the number.

Name _____

Algebra: Different Ways to Make Numbers

Learn

Here are some different ways to think about a number.

__9__ tens __5__ ones = __95__

__90__ + __5__

9 tens 5 ones = 95
90 + 5

Check

Write how many tens and ones.
Write the number in a different way.

1.

____ tens ____ ones = ____

____ + ____

2.

____ tens ____ ones = ____

____ + ____

3.

____ tens ____ ones = ____

____ + ____

4.

____ tens ____ ones = ____

____ + ____

Explain It • Daily Reasoning

What does the **8** mean in each of these numbers? Use  to prove your answer.

84   48

Chapter 10 • Place Value to 100

Practice and Problem Solving

Write how many tens and ones.
Write the number in a different way.

1.

    __8__ tens __8__ ones = __88__

    __80__ + __8__

2.

    ____ tens ____ ones = ____

    ____ + ____

3.

    ____ tens ____ ones = ____

    ____ + ____

4.

    ____ tens ____ ones = ____

    ____ + ____

Problem Solving
Application

Solve.

5. Jesse puts 97 stickers in his book. Each page holds 10 stickers. How many pages does he fill? _____ pages

6. How many stickers are left over to start a new page? _____ stickers

Write About It • Explain how you found the answer to Exercise 6.

HOME ACTIVITY • Say a number between 10 and 100. Ask your child to write it first as tens and ones and then as addition. For example, 34 is 3 tens 4 ones and 30 + 4.

Name _____

Problem Solving Skill
Make Reasonable Estimates

Vocabulary
estimate

About how many books can you carry?

When I don't need to know the exact number, I can estimate.

about 5

about 50

about 500

50 and 500 are too many.
5 is a good estimate.

Circle the closest estimate.
Tell how you know.

1. About how many 🧍 would ride on one bus?

   about 3

   about 30

   about 300

2. About how many 📕 would fill up one book bag?

   about 5

   about 50

   about 500

3. About how many 👟 are in the classroom?

   about 4

   about 40

   about 400

4. About how many would fill two hands?

   about 1

   about 10

   about 100

Chapter 10 • Place Value to 100

Problem Solving Practice

Circle the closest estimate.

THINK: Which number makes the most sense?

1. About how many  are in your classroom?

   about 3

    (about 30)

   about 300

2. About how many could fill a lunch box?

   about 1

   about 10

   about 100

3. About how many  could you hold in one hand?

   about 5

   about 50

   about 500

4. About how many would fill a cup?

   about 1

   about 10

   about 100

5. About how many sheets of  would cover your desk?

   about 4

   about 40

   about 400

6. About how many  are in your classroom?

   about 3

   about 30

   about 300

HOME ACTIVITY • Ask your child to choose the closest estimate for the number of pennies he or she can hold in one hand: about 10 pennies or about 100 pennies. Then have him or her check.

168 one hundred sixty-eight

Name _____

Extra Practice

Write how many tens. Write the number.

1.

   ____ tens = ____

2.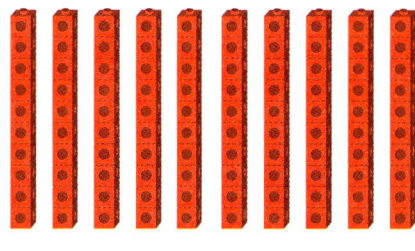

   ____ tens = ____

Write how many tens and ones. Write the number.

3.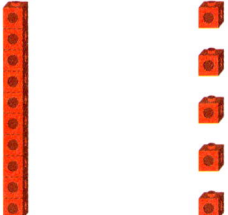

   ____ ten ____ ones = ____

4.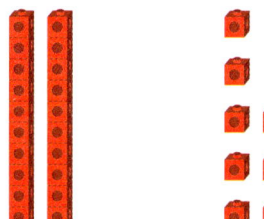

   ____ tens ____ ones = ____

Write how many tens and ones. Write the number in a different way.

5.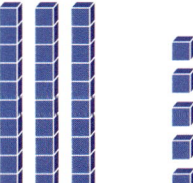

   ____ tens ____ ones = ____

   ____ + ____

6.

   ____ tens ____ ones = ____

   ____ + ____

Problem Solving

Circle the closest estimate.

7. About how many would fill the bag?

   about 2

   about 20

   about 200

Chapter 10 • Place Value to 100

Name _____

✓ Review/Test

Concepts and Skills

Write how many tens. Write the number.

1.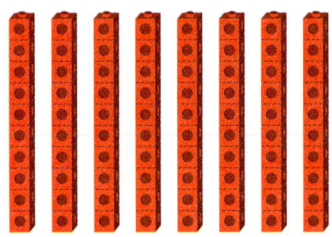

   ____ tens = ____

2.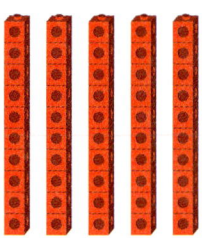

   ____ tens = ____

Write how many tens and ones. Write the number.

3.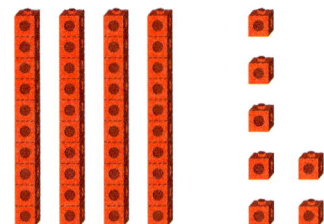

   ____ tens ____ ones = ____

4.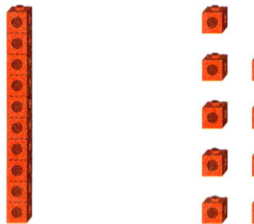

   ____ ten ____ ones = ____

Write how many tens and ones. Write the number in a different way.

5.

   ____ tens ____ one = ____

   ____ + ____

6.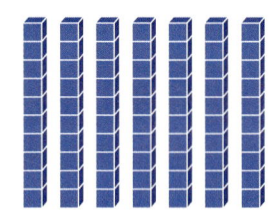

   ____ tens ____ ones = ____

   ____ + ____

Problem Solving

Circle the closest estimate.

7. About how many  would fill the cup?

   about 1

   about 10

   about 100

170 one hundred seventy

Name _____

★Standardized Test Prep
Chapters 1–10

Choose the answer for questions 1–4.

1. Which is another way to write the number?

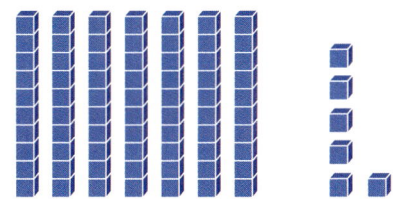

7 tens + 6 ones = 76

60 + 7   70 + 3
○   ○

70 + 2   70 + 6
○   ○

2. Which does the picture show?

3 tens   5 tens
○   ○

7 tens   9 tens
○   ○

3. Which is the closest estimate?
   About how many 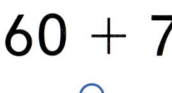 are in your classroom?

about 3   about 30   about 300
○   ○   ○

4. Which fact is related to 5 − 2 = 3?

1 + 4 = 5   5 + 3 = 8   3 + 2 = 5   3 − 2 = 1
○   ○   ○   ○

Show What You Know

5. Choose a number. Draw to explain how many tens and ones. Write the number two ways.

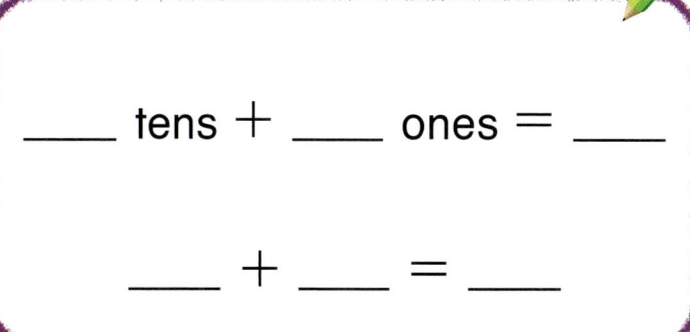

___ tens + ___ ones = ___

___ + ___ = ___

Name _____

MATH GAME

Teen Spin

Play with a partner.

1. Put all the  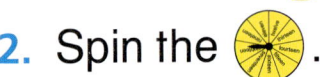 in the penny pile.
2. Spin the 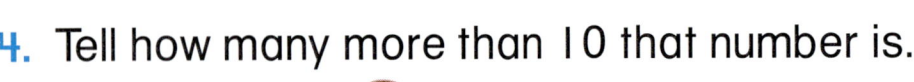.
3. Read the teen number word.
4. Tell how many more than 10 that number is.
5. Put that many  in your bank.
6. Take turns until the penny pile is gone.
7. The player with more  wins.

Penny Pile

172 one hundred seventy-two

CHAPTER 11

Comparing and Ordering Numbers

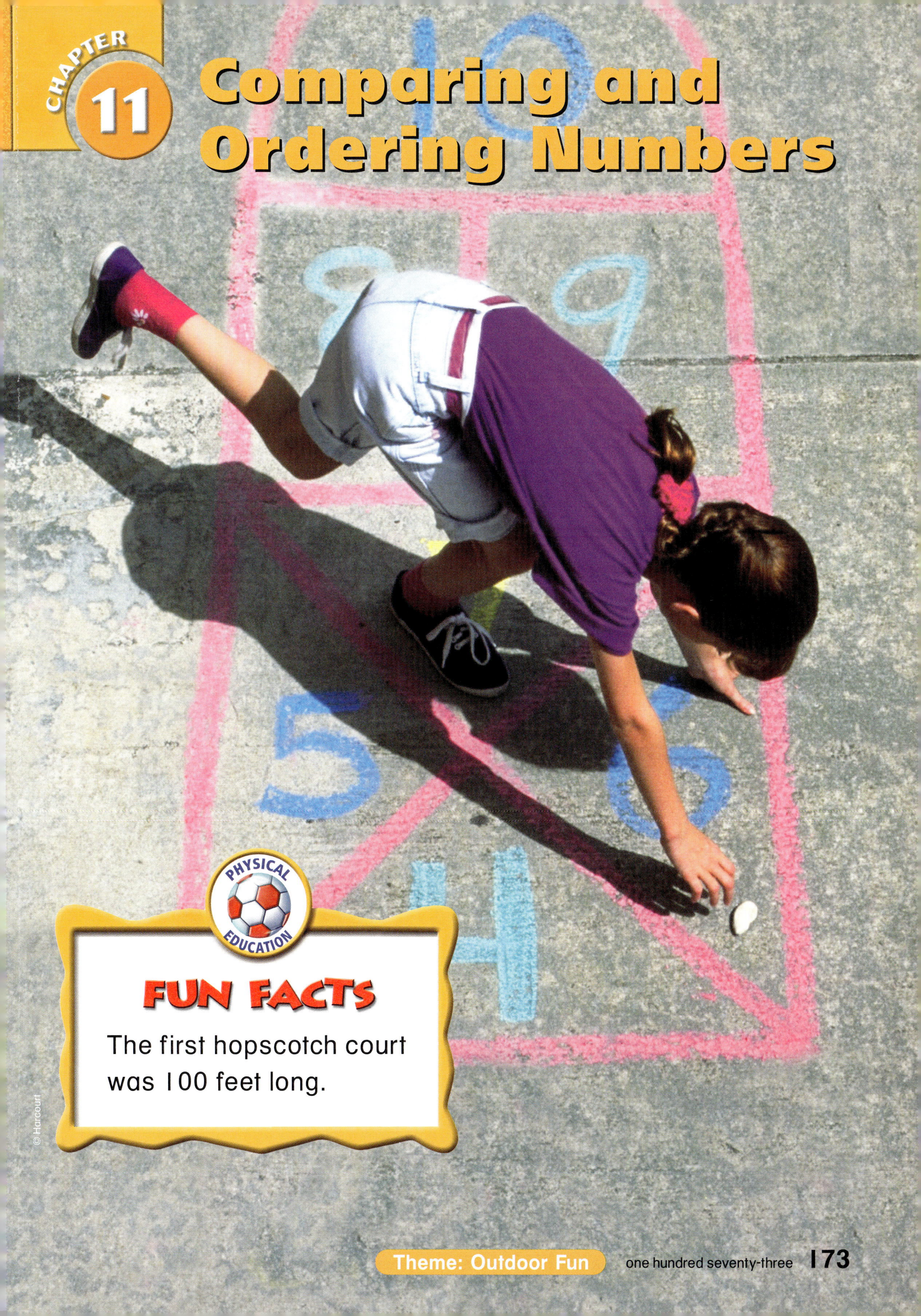

FUN FACTS

The first hopscotch court was 100 feet long.

Theme: Outdoor Fun

✓ Check What You Know

More, Less, Same
Count. Write the number.

1. Circle the number that is less.

_____   _____

2. Circle the number that is more.

_____   _____

3. Circle the 2 numbers that are the same.

_____   _____   _____

Order Numbers on a Number Line
Write the missing numbers.

4.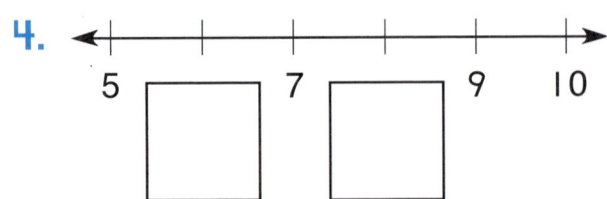

5.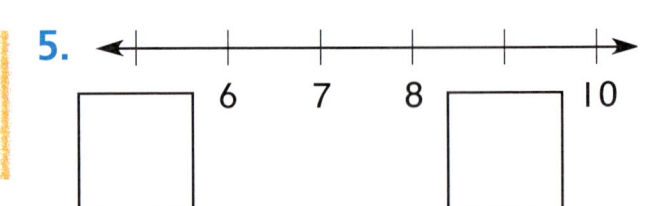

Name _____

Algebra: Greater Than

Vocabulary
is greater than >

Explore

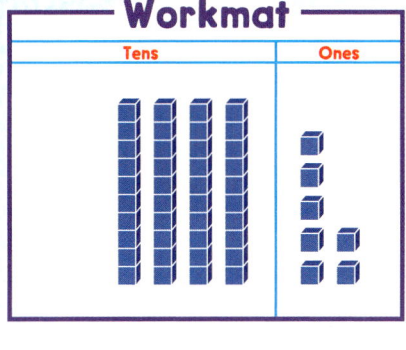
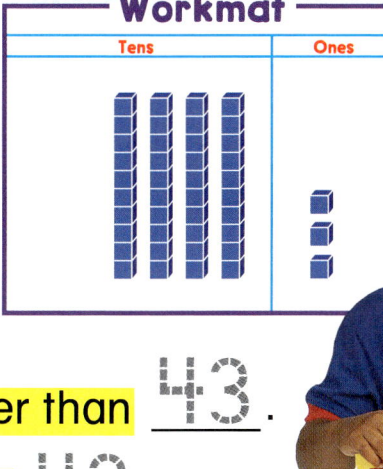

43 and 47 have the same number of tens, but 47 has more ones.

__47__ is greater than __43__.

__47__ > __43__

Connect

Use  to show each number.
Circle the greater number. Write the numbers.

1. 35   (53)

   __53__ is greater than __35__.

   __53__ > __35__

2. 56   46

   _____ is greater than _____.

   _____ > _____

3.  13   30

   _____ is greater than _____.

   _____ > _____

4.  66   69

   _____ is greater than _____.

   _____ > _____

Explain It • Daily Reasoning

To find the greater number, should you look first at the ones or at the tens? Why?

Practice and Problem Solving

Circle the greater number.
Write the numbers.
You can use .

THINK: Look at the tens place first.

1.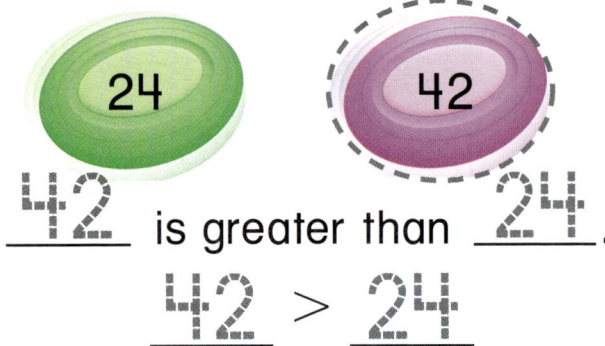

   42 is greater than 24.

   42 > 24

2.

   _____ is greater than _____.

   _____ > _____

3.

   _____ is greater than _____.

   _____ > _____

4.

   _____ is greater than _____.

   _____ > _____

5.

   _____ is greater than _____.

   _____ > _____

6.

   _____ is greater than _____.

   _____ > _____

Problem Solving
Application

7. Circle the numbers that are greater than 50.

   14   83   94   44   62   70

Write About It • Use one of the numbers you circled in Exercise 7 to complete ☐ > 50.

HOME ACTIVITY • Say two numbers that are less than 100. Ask your child which is greater. Then have him or her write the two numbers, using the *greater than* symbol (>).

176 one hundred seventy-six

Name _____

Algebra: Less Than

Vocabulary
is less than <

Explore

"25 has fewer tens than 35."

__25__ is less than __35__.

__25__ < __35__

Connect

Use ▬ ▪ to show each number.
Circle the number that is less. Write the numbers.

1. 66   **(65)**

   __65__ is less than __66__.

   __65__ < __66__

2. 82   91

   ____ is less than ____.

   ____ < ____

3.  19    16

   ____ is less than ____.

   ____ < ____

4.  73    48

   ____ is less than ____.

   ____ < ____

Explain It • Daily Reasoning

How could you find out which number is less without using ▬ ▪ ?

Chapter 11 • Comparing and Ordering Numbers

Practice and Problem Solving

Circle the number that is less.
Write the numbers. You can use ▬ ▪ .

1.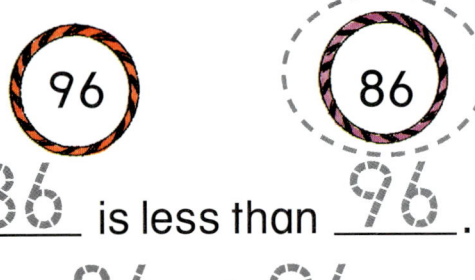
   96   (86)
   _86_ is less than _96_.
   _86_ < _96_

2. 88   68
   ____ is less than ____.
   ____ < ____

3. 49   50
   ____ is less than ____.
   ____ < ____

4. 19   17
   ____ is less than ____.
   ____ < ____

5. 27   28
   ____ is less than ____.
   ____ < ____

6. 34   43
   ____ is less than ____.
   ____ < ____

Problem Solving
Application

7. Circle the numbers that are less than 50.

   49   65   80   11   33   51

Write About It • Use words to compare 50 and one of the numbers you circled in Exercise 7.

🏠 **HOME ACTIVITY** • Say two numbers that are less than 100. Ask your child which number is less. Then have him or her write the two numbers, using the *less than* symbol (<).

Name _____

Algebra: Use Symbols to Compare

Explore

Compare the two numbers.

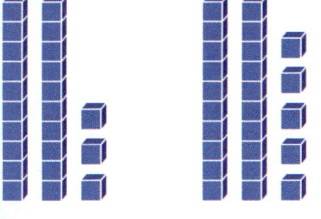  

23 ⓛ 25   25 ⓔ 25   26 ⓖ 25

23 is less than 25.   25 is equal to 25.   26 is greater than 25.

Connect

Compare the numbers.
Use  to show each number.
Draw the .
Write <, >, or = in the circle.

1.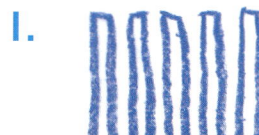

   52 ⓛ 56

2. 56 ◯ 51

3. 17 ◯ 71

4. 37 ◯ 37

Explain It • Daily Reasoning

How can you show 71 in two ways? Explain.

Practice and Problem Solving

Compare the numbers.
Use ▭▭▭▭▭ ▫ to show each number.
Draw the ▭▭▭▭▭ ▫.

Write <, >, or = in the circle.

REMEMBER
< means is less than.
> means is greater than.
= means is equal to.

1. 21 ◯ 12

2. 46 ◯ 49

3. 38 ◯ 38

4. 55 ◯ 59

Problem Solving
Algebra

Write <, >, or = in the circle.

5. 6 tens 4 ones ◯ 60 + 4

6. 30 + 5 ◯ 2 tens 5 ones

7. 9 tens 8 ones ◯ 90 + 9

8. 40 + 3 ◯ 4 tens 3 ones

 **Write About It** • What is the same about 91 and 99? What is different?

HOME ACTIVITY • Say two numbers that are less than 100. Ask your child to compare the numbers by writing them, using the symbols he or she learned in this lesson.

180 one hundred eighty

Name _____

Order on a Number Line

Vocabulary
before
between
after

Learn

30 31 32 33 34 **35** 36 **37** 38 39 40

35 is just **before** 36.
36 is **between** 35 and 37.
37 is just **after** 36.

Check

Write the number that is just before, between, or just after.

1. 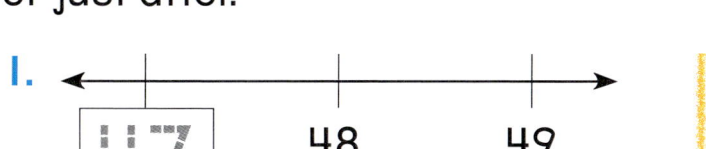 **47** 48 49

2. 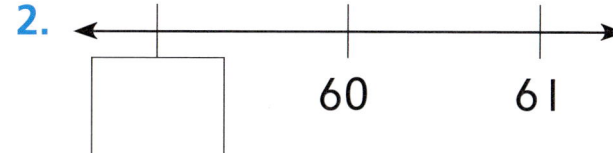 ___ 60 61

3. 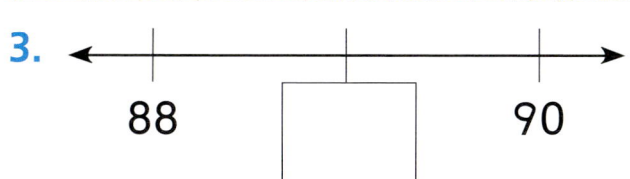 88 ___ 90

4. 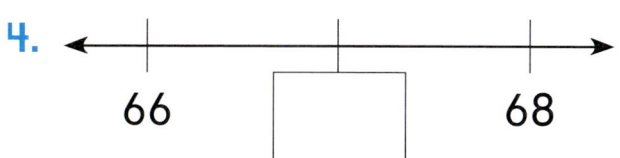 66 ___ 68

5. 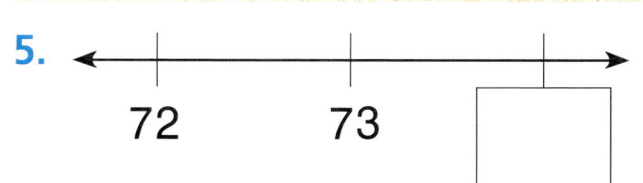 72 73 ___

6. 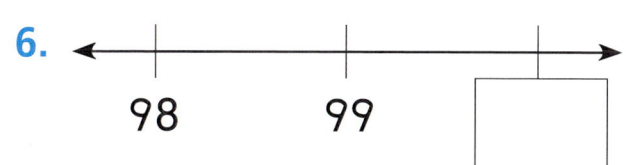 98 99 ___

Explain It • Daily Reasoning

What number comes just after 100? Explain how you know.

Chapter 11 • Comparing and Ordering Numbers

Practice and Problem Solving

Write the number that is just before, between, or just after.

1. 98 | 99 | 100

2. 11 | ☐ | 13

3. 39 | ☐ | 41

4. 54 | ☐ | 56

5. ☐ | 31

6. 44 | ☐

7. ☐ | 20

8. 79 | ☐

9. ☐ | 58

10. 28 | ☐

Problem Solving
Visual Thinking

11. Write the missing numbers on the number line.

☐ | 94 | ☐ | 96 | ☐ | ☐ | ☐ | 100 | ☐

Write About It • Explain how you found the missing numbers in Exercise 11.

HOME ACTIVITY • Say a two-digit number. Ask your child to tell you the number that is just before it and the number that is just after it. Then ask your child to use the word *between* to tell about your number.

182 one hundred eighty-two

Name _____

Count Forward and Backward

Vocabulary
count forward
count backward

Learn

52, 53, 54 | 52, 51, 50

Count forward from 52. | Count backward from 52.

Check

Write the numbers.

Count forward.
1. 11, ____, ____
2. 17, ____, ____
3. 68, ____, ____
4. 27, ____, ____
5. 89, ____, ____
6. 57, ____, ____

Count backward.
7. 13, ____, ____
8. 16, ____, ____
9. 99, ____, ____
10. 41, ____, ____
11. 71, ____, ____
12. 50, ____, ____

Explain It • Daily Reasoning

What number do you say when you count backward from 1? Explain.

Chapter 11 • Comparing and Ordering Numbers

Practice and Problem Solving

10, 11, 12, 13, 14, 15

Write the numbers.

Count forward.

1. 21, 22, ___, ___, ___, ___, ___, ___, ___

2. 45, ___, ___, ___, ___, ___, ___, ___, ___

3. 77, ___, ___, ___, ___, ___, ___, ___, ___

Count backward.

4. 20, 19, ___, ___, ___, ___, ___, ___, ___

5. 42, ___, ___, ___, ___, ___, ___, ___, ___

6. 67, ___, ___, ___, ___, ___, ___, ___, ___

Problem Solving
Application

7. These are lockers. Start on 27. Count forward. Write the number on each locker.

8. Tom's locker is 31. Circle Tom's locker.

 **Write About It** • Write a story telling how you get from locker 27 to Tom's locker.

HOME ACTIVITY • Say a two-digit number. Have your child count forward. Say a different two-digit number. Have your child count backward.

184 one hundred eighty-four

Name _____

Problem Solving Skill
Use a Model

Use the model .
Find 10 more or 10 less.
Write the number.

To find 10 more, draw 1 more ten.

1. Tara has 65 marbles.
   Dave has 10 more than Tara.
   How many marbles does
   Dave have?

   __75__ marbles

2. Chen has 13 toy cars.
   Anna has 10 less.
   How many toy cars does
   Anna have?

   To find 10 less, cross out 1 ten.

   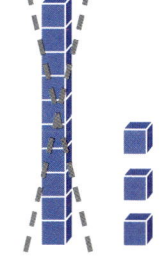

   _____ toy cars

3. Dan counted 25 children
   on the playground.
   Chris counted 10 more
   than Dan. How many
   children did Chris count?

   _____ children

Chapter 11 • Comparing and Ordering Numbers

Problem Solving Practice

Use the model .
Find 10 more or 10 less.
Write the number.

THINK: Do I need to find 10 more or 10 less?

1. Pat has 60 toy trucks. Fred has 10 less. How many toy trucks does Fred have?

   _____ toy trucks

2. Music class has 35 children. Art class has 10 less. How many children are in art class?

   _____ children

3. Craig has 60 jacks. Brooke has 10 more than Craig. How many jacks does Brooke have?

   _____ jacks

4. Dave has 42 baseball cards. Kim has 10 more than Dave. How many baseball cards does Kim have?

   _____ baseball cards

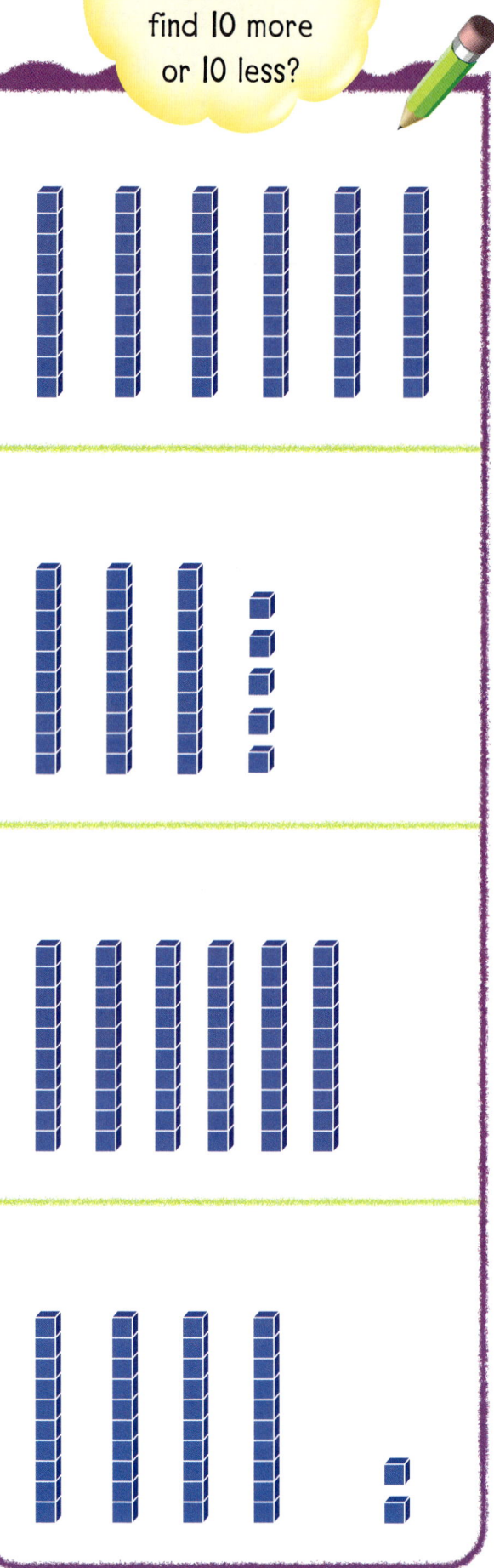

🏠 **HOME ACTIVITY** • Have your child tell how he or she used each model to solve the problem.

186 one hundred eighty-six

Name _____

Extra Practice

Circle the greater number.
Write the numbers.

1.    ____ > ____

Circle the number that is less.
Write the numbers.

2. 95 96   ____ < ____

3. Count forward.   68, ____, ____

4. Count backward.   41, ____, ____

Write the number that is just before, between,
or just after.

5.
   29 [ ] 31

6.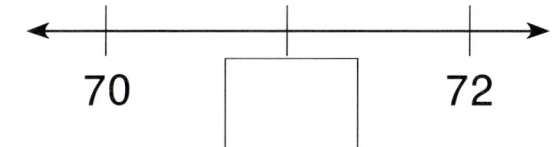
   70 [ ] 72

7.
   12 [ ]

8.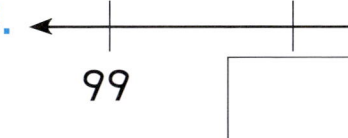
   99 [ ]

9.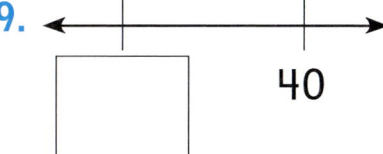
   [ ] 40

Problem Solving

Use the model ▬ ▪ . Find 10
more or 10 less. Write the number.

10. Brad has 23 toy cars. Ken
    has 10 less. How many toy
    cars does Ken have?

    ____ toy cars

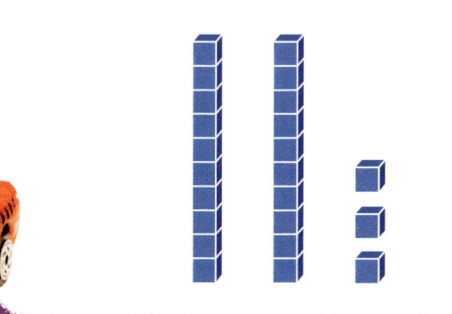

Chapter 11 • Comparing and Ordering Numbers   one hundred eighty-seven **187**

Name _____

✓ Review/Test

Concepts and Skills

Circle the greater number.
Write the numbers.

1.     _____ > _____

Circle the number that is less.
Write the numbers.

2.    _____ < _____

3. Count forward.   90, _____, _____

4. Count backward.   63, _____, _____

Write the number that is just before, between,
or just after.

5.    6.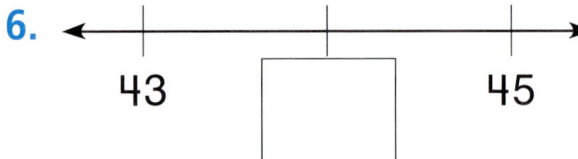

7. 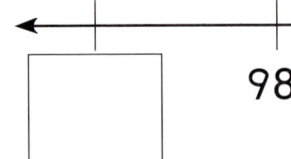   8. 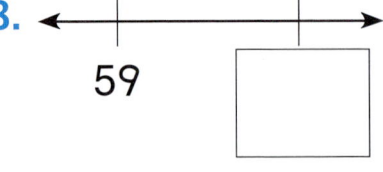   9.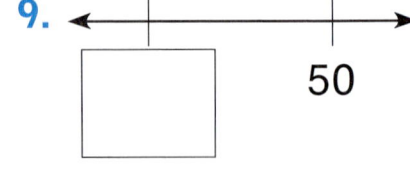

Problem Solving

Use the model ▬ ▪. Find 10 more or 10 less. Write the number.

10. Jose has 65 jacks. Elsa has 10 more. How many jacks does Elsa have?

    _____ jacks

188 one hundred eighty-eight

Name _____

Standardized Test Prep
Chapters 1–11

Choose the answer for questions 1–4.

1. Which number is between 33 and 35?

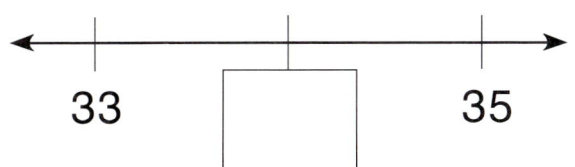

| 32 | 34 | 36 | 37 |
| ○ | ○ | ○ | ○ |

2. Which number is less than 24?

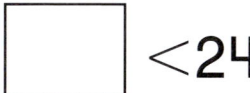

| 19 | 27 | 30 | 41 |
| ○ | ○ | ○ | ○ |

3. Which numbers are missing?

__20__, __19__, _____, _____, _____

| 18, 17, 16 | 19, 20, 21 | 21, 22, 23 | 21, 20, 19 |
| ○ | ○ | ○ | ○ |

4. Which is another way to write 9 − 3 = 6?

$$\begin{array}{r}9\\-4\\\hline 5\end{array} \qquad \begin{array}{r}9\\-3\\\hline 6\end{array} \qquad \begin{array}{r}9\\-2\\\hline 7\end{array} \qquad \begin{array}{r}9\\-1\\\hline 8\end{array}$$

○ ○ ○ ○

Show What You Know

5. Find 10 less. Use the model to explain your answer.

April has 37 marbles.
Molly has 10 less.
How many marbles does Molly have?

_____ marbles

Chapter 11

Name _____

Greater Steps

Play with a partner.

You will need
2 🪀
2 🎲

1. Put your 🪀 at START.
2. Toss the 🎲 and the 🎲.
3. Use one number as tens and one number as ones. Can you make a number that solves the problem on your next step?
4. If you can, move your 🪀 up to that step.
5. If you can not, your turn is over.
6. The first player to get to END wins.

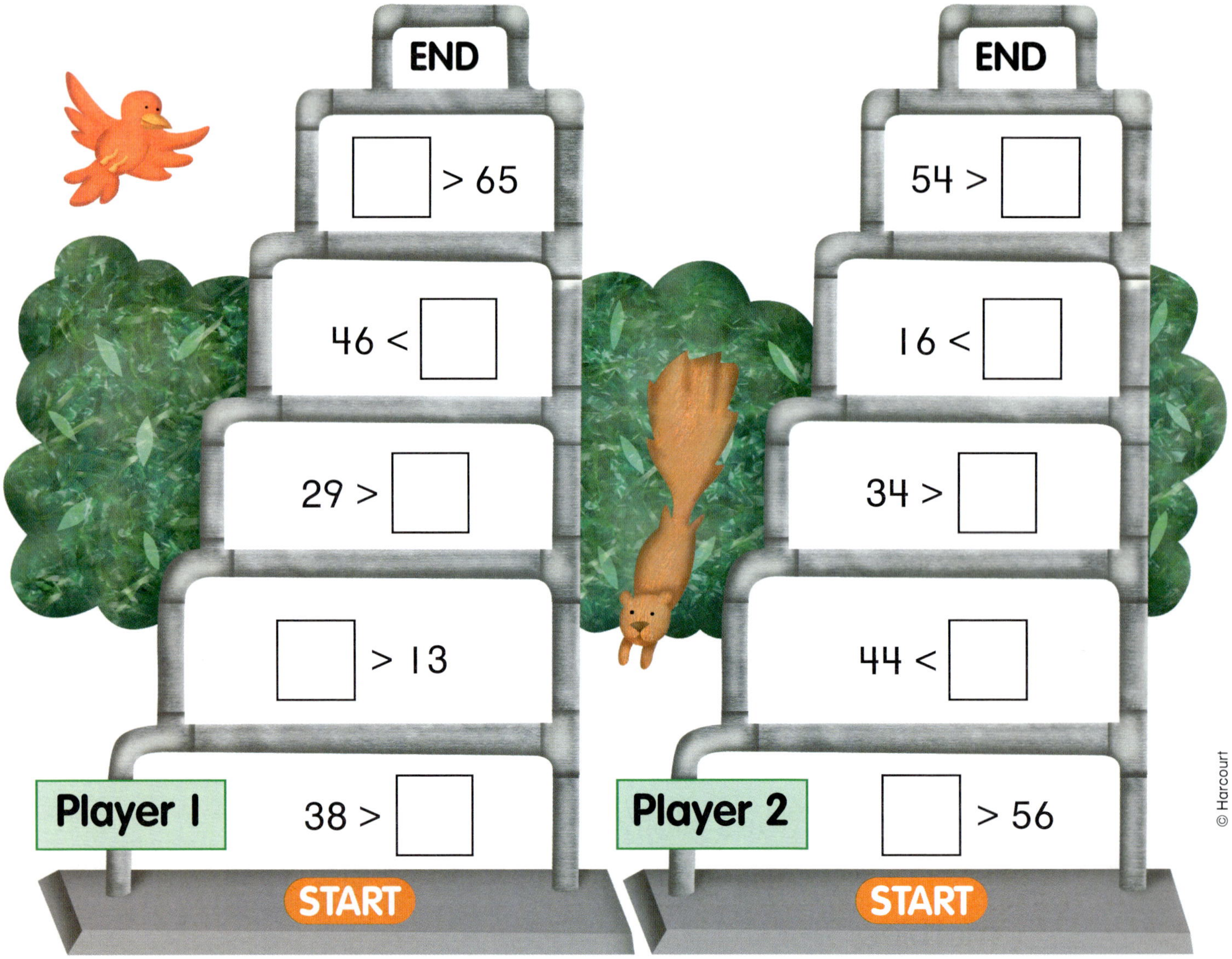

Player 1

END
☐ > 65
46 < ☐
29 > ☐
☐ > 13
38 > ☐
START

Player 2

END
54 > ☐
16 < ☐
34 > ☐
44 < ☐
☐ > 56
START

190 one hundred ninety

CHAPTER 12

Number Patterns

FUN FACTS

The number of crayons in some boxes are all even numbers: 8, 16, 24, 32, 48, 64, and 96.

Theme: Art Class

Name _____

✓ Check What You Know

Count Orally Using a Hundred Chart

Touch and count. Color the last number counted.

1. Start at 1 and count to 30.
2. Start at 40 and count to 53.
3. Start at 92 and count to 98.

1	2	3	4	5	6	7	8	9	10
11	12	13	14	15	16	17	18	19	20
21	22	23	24	25	26	27	28	29	30
31	32	33	34	35	36	37	38	39	40
41	42	43	44	45	46	47	48	49	50
51	52	53	54	55	56	57	58	59	60
61	62	63	64	65	66	67	68	69	70
71	72	73	74	75	76	77	78	79	80
81	82	83	84	85	86	87	88	89	90
91	92	93	94	95	96	97	98	99	100

Ordinal Numbers

4. Circle the second cat.
5. Mark an X on the fifth cat.
6. Draw a line under the first cat.

Name _____

Skip Count by 2s, 5s, and 10s

Learn

Skip count. Count the jars of paint by twos. Write how many.

  2   4   6   ____   ____

 12   ____   ____   ____   ____   ____ jars of paint

Check

Skip count. Count the fingers by fives. Write how many.

1.

   5   10   ____   ____   ____   ____

   35   ____   ____   ____   ____   ____ fingers

Skip count. Count the toes by tens. Write how many.

2.

   10   20   ____   ____   ____

    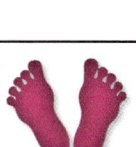 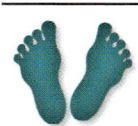 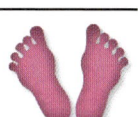

   ____   ____   ____   ____   ____ toes

Explain It • Daily Reasoning

What number comes after 100 when you skip count by tens? Explain.

Chapter 12 • Number Patterns

Practice and Problem Solving

Skip count. Write how many.

1.

   2 , ____ , ____ , ____ , ____ , ____ , ____

2.

   5 , ____ , ____ , ____ , ____ , ____ , ____

3.

   10 , ____ , ____ , ____ , ____ , ____ , ____

Skip count. Write the missing numbers.

4. 2, 4, 6, ____ , ____ , ____ , 14, ____ , 18

5. 10, ____ , 30, ____ , ____ , 60, 70, ____ , 90

Problem Solving
Visual Thinking

6. Skip count.
   Each hand has 5 fingers.
   How many fingers are there in all?

   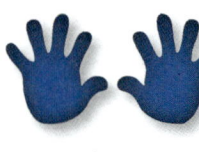  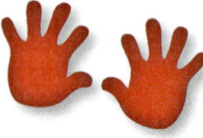

   ____ fingers

 **Write About It** • Draw a picture to show skip counting by twos. Write the numbers.

HOME ACTIVITY • Draw 20 stars. Have your child circle groups of 2 and then count by twos to find the total. Repeat the activity for groups of 5.

Name _____

Algebra: Patterns on a Hundred Chart

Learn

> Start on 2. Count forward by tens.

1	2	3	4	5	6	7	8	9	10
11	12	13	14	15	16	17	18	19	20
21	22	23	24	25	26	27	28	29	30
31	32	33	34	35	36	37	38	39	40
41	42	43	44	45	46	47	48	49	50
51	52	53	54	55	56	57	58	59	60
61	62	63	64	65	66	67	68	69	70
71	72	73	74	75	76	77	78	79	80
81	82	83	84	85	86	87	88	89	90
91	92	93	94	95	96	97	98	99	100

Check

Start on the given number. Count forward by tens. Write the numbers you say.

1. Start on 1.

   11, 21, ____, ____, ____, ____, ____, ____, ____

Explain It • Daily Reasoning

What pattern do you see? Explain.

Chapter 12 • Number Patterns

one hundred ninety-seven **197**

Practice and Problem Solving

Start on the given number. Count forward by tens. Write the numbers you say. Use a hundred chart if you need to.

1. Start on 7.

   17, 27, ____, ____, ____, ____, ____, ____, ____

2. Start on 9.

   19, ____, ____, ____, ____, ____, ____, ____, ____

3. Start on 5.

   ____, ____, ____, ____, ____, ____, ____, ____, ____

4. Start on 3.

   ____, ____, ____, ____, ____, ____, ____, ____, ____

5. Start on 6.

   ____, ____, ____, ____, ____, ____, ____, ____, ____

Problem Solving

Logical Reasoning

6. Write the missing numbers.

   94, 84, 74, 64, ____, 44, ____, ____, 14, ____

7. Write the missing numbers.

   98, 88, ____, 68, ____, ____, ____, 28, ____, ____

Write About It • What pattern can help you count forward by tens from any number?

HOME ACTIVITY • Say any number less than 10. Ask your child to start on that number and count forward by tens.

Name _____

Even and Odd

Vocabulary
even
odd

Learn

What pattern can you find in even and odd numbers?

An **even** number of objects can be grouped into pairs.

4

5

An **odd** number of objects has one left over.

Check

Use  to show each number.
Circle **even** or **odd**.

1.	1	even	(odd)	2.	2	even odd
3.	3	even odd		4.	4	even odd
5.	5	even odd		6.	6	even odd
7.	7	even odd		8.	8	even odd
9.	9	even odd		10.	10	even odd

Explain It • Daily Reasoning

Color the numbers. odd 🖍   even 🖍

1	2	3	4	5	6	7	8	9	10

What pattern do even and odd numbers make?

Practice and Problem Solving

Color  or to continue the pattern.

1.

1	2	3	4	5	6	7	8	9	10
11	12	13	14	15	16	17	18	19	20
21	22	23	24	25	26	27	28	29	30
31	32	33	34	35	36	37	38	39	40
41	42	43	44	45	46	47	48	49	50

Write **even** or **odd**.
You can use to help.

2. Are the red numbers even or odd? _____

3. Are the blue numbers even or odd? _____

Problem Solving
Application

4. Start with 2. Skip count by twos.
   Do you say even or odd numbers? _____

5. Start with 10. Skip count by tens.
   Do you say even or odd numbers? _____

 Write About It • Skip count by fives to 50.
Write the numbers. Circle the odd numbers.
What pattern do you see?

HOME ACTIVITY • Give your child a group of 20 small objects, such as beans. Have him or her count the objects and tell how many. Then have your child pair the objects and tell whether the number is even or odd.

Name _____

Problem Solving Strategy
Find a Pattern

Find a pattern to solve.

1 star has 5 points.

How many points do 5 stars have?

UNDERSTAND

What do you want to find out?
Circle the question.

PLAN

Make a chart to find the pattern.

SOLVE

Use the chart. Count by fives.

number of stars	1	2	3	4	5
number of points	5	10	15		

5 stars have __25__ points.

CHECK

Does your answer make sense? Explain.

Find a pattern to solve. Write how many.

1. 1 dog has two ears.
   How many ears do 5 dogs have?

number of dogs	1	2	3	4	5
number of ears	2	4			

5 dogs have _____ ears.

Chapter 12 • Number Patterns

Problem Solving Practice

Keep in Mind!
Understand
Plan
Solve
Check

Find a pattern to solve.
Write how many.

1. 1 flower has 10 petals.
   How many petals do 5 flowers have?

number of flowers	1	2	3	4	5
number of petals	10	20			

   5 flowers have _____ petals.

2. 1 bunny has 2 ears.
   How many ears do 7 bunnies have?

number of bunnies	1	2	3	4	5	6	7
number of ears	2						

   7 bunnies have _____ ears.

3. 1 starfish has 5 arms.
   How many arms do 6 starfish have?

number of starfish	1	2	3	4	5	6
number of arms	5					

   6 starfish have _____ arms.

HOME ACTIVITY • Ask your child to continue the patterns in the charts to tell how many ears 8 bunnies have, how many petals 6 flowers have, and so on.

Ordinal Numbers

Learn

first second third fourth fifth sixth seventh eighth ninth tenth

Check

Circle to show order.

1. 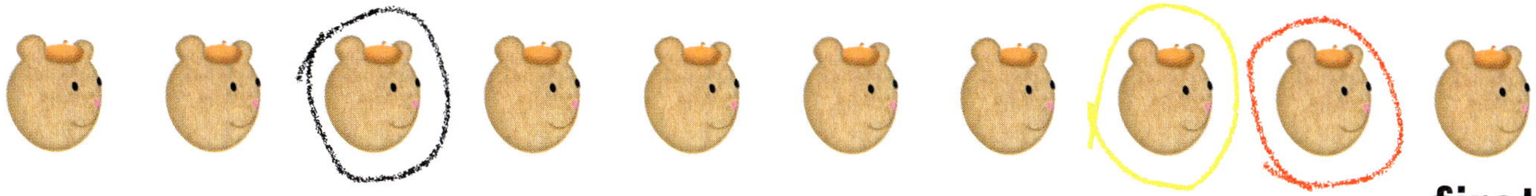 second 🖍 third 🖍 eighth 🖍 **first**

2. 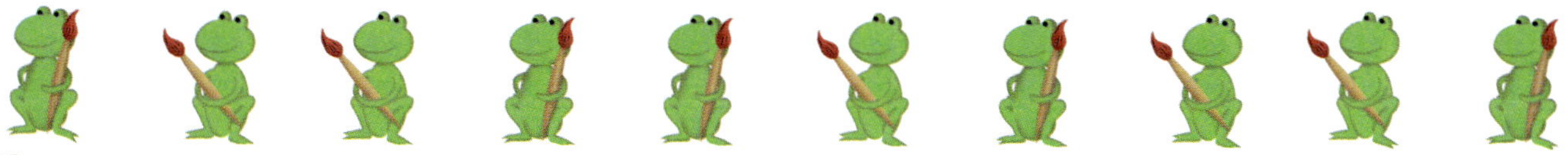 **first** first 🖍 fourth 🖍 tenth 🖍

3. 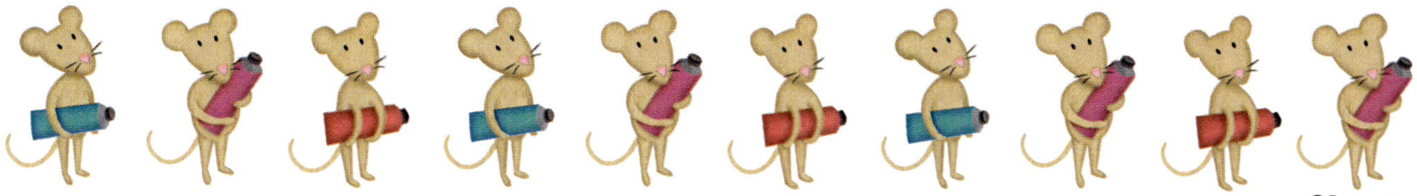 third 🖍 sixth 🖍 ninth 🖍 **first**

4. 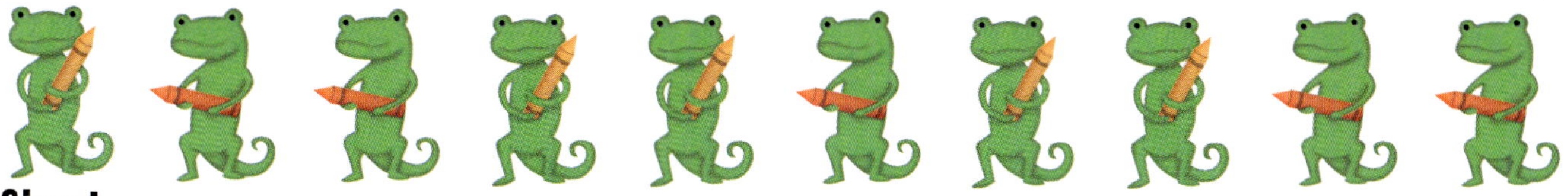 **first** second 🖍 fifth 🖍 ninth 🖍

Explain It • Daily Reasoning

If you are eighth in line, how many people are in front of you? Explain.

Practice and Problem Solving

1. Color to show order.

first   second   third   fifth   seventh   tenth

Problem Solving
Application

2. Color the bee that is second from the hive ✏️. 
   Color the bee that is fourth from the hive ✏️.

 Write About It • Draw 10 flowers in a row. Label one **first**. Circle the flower that is eighth. Tell how you know.

🏠 **HOME ACTIVITY** • Ask your child to show you which butterfly in the picture is fourth in line.

204   two hundred four

Name _____

Extra Practice

1. Write the missing numbers. Count by twos.
   Use 🖍 to color the numbers you say.

21			24		26		28		30
	32			35				39	

2. Count again. Count by fives.
   Use 🖍 to color the numbers you say.

3. Count again. Count by tens.
   Use 🖍 to circle the numbers you say.

4. Color the numbers.
   odd 🖍   even 🖍

5. Circle to show order.

fourth 🖍   sixth 🖍   eighth 🖍   ninth 🖍   first

Problem Solving

Find a pattern to solve. Write how many.

6. 1 box has 10 crayons.
   How many crayons do 6 boxes have?

number of boxes	1	2	3	4	5	6
number of crayons	10					

6 boxes have _____ crayons.

Chapter 12 • Number Patterns

Name _____

✓ Review/Test

Concepts and Skills

1. Write the missing numbers. Count by twos.
   Use 🖍 to color the numbers you say.

1	2	3	4				8	9	10
	12			15	16	17			

2. Count again. Count by fives.
   Use 🖍 to color the numbers you say.

3. Count again. Count by tens.
   Use 🖍 to circle the numbers you say.

4. Color the numbers.
   odd 🖍   even 🖍

41	42	43	44	45	46	47	48	49	50

5. Circle to show order.

   first

   second 🖍   fifth 🖍   ninth 🖍   tenth 🖍

Problem Solving

Find a pattern to solve.
Write how many.

6. 1 face has 2 eyes.
   How many eyes do
   5 faces have?

number of faces	1	2	3	4	5
number of eyes	2				

5 faces have _____ eyes.

206 two hundred six

Name _____

⭐ Standardized Test Prep
Chapters 1–12

1. Count by fives. Which number is missing?

   5, 10, 15, 20, ___, 30

   25　　35　　40　　45
   ○　　○　　○　　○

2. Count by twos. Which number is missing?

   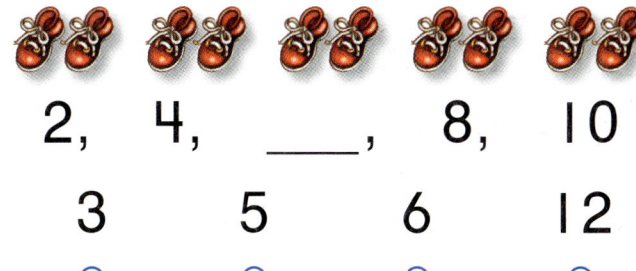

   2,　4,　___,　8,　10

   3　　5　　6　　12
   ○　　○　　○　　○

3. Which number is even?

   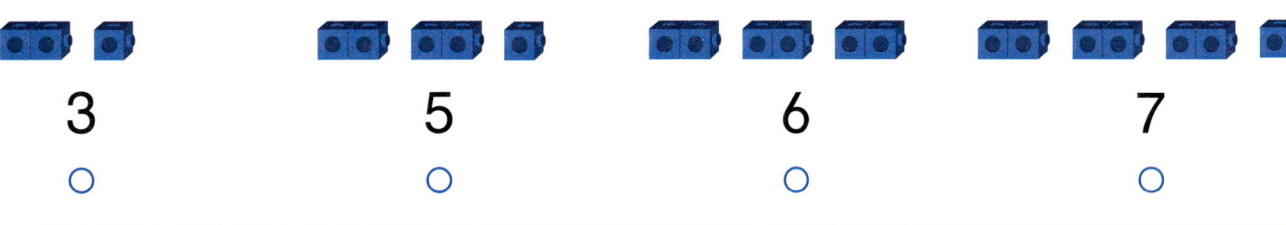

   3　　　　5　　　　6　　　　7
   ○　　　　○　　　　○　　　　○

4. Which is fourth?

   first

   ○　　○　　○　　○

5. Which number is just before 28?

   27　　28　　29　　36
   ○　　○　　○　　○

Show What You Know

6. How many ears are on 3 cats? Draw a picture to explain your answer.

Number of Cats	1	2	3
Number of Ears	2	4	

Chapter 12　　　　　　　　　　　　　　　two hundred seven **207**

Name _____

MATH GAME

Even Skips

Play with a partner.

You will need

1. Put your 🟡 on START.
2. Toss the 🎲.
3. Move your 🟡 that many spaces.
4. If you land on an odd number, your turn is over.
5. If you land on an even number, skip-count on by twos 3 times. Move to that number.
6. The first player to get to END wins.

208 two hundred eight

CHAPTER 13

Addition and Subtraction Facts to 12

FUN FACTS

You can walk through an outdoor rocket garden and see many rockets set on the ground in rows.

Theme: Ways To Travel

Name _____

✅ Check What You Know

Use a Number Line to Count On

Use the number line. Count on to find the sum.

1. 2	2. 4	3. 6	4. 5	5. 8	6. 7
+2	+1	+3	+2	+1	+3

Use Doubles

Add. Then circle the doubles facts.

7. 4	8. 4	9. 2	10. 5	11. 2	12. 3
+3	+4	+3	+5	+4	+3

Use a Number Line to Count Back

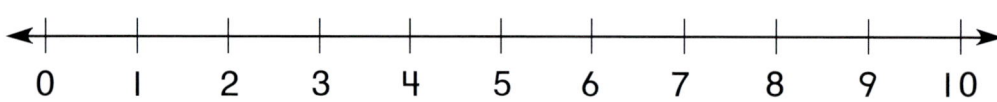

Use the number line. Count back to subtract.

13. 9	14. 6	15. 10	16. 8	17. 4	18. 10
−3	−3	− 2	−3	−2	− 1

210 two hundred ten   Use this page to review important skills needed for this chapter.

Name _____

Count On to Add

Vocabulary
count on

Learn

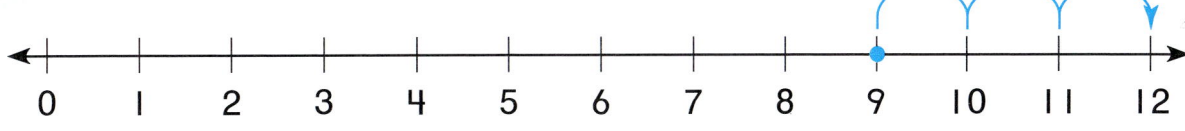

⑨
+3
___
12

Start on 9. Then move 3 spaces to the right.
10, 11, 12

Start with the greater number.
Count on to add.

Check

Circle the greater number.
Use the number line. Count on to add.

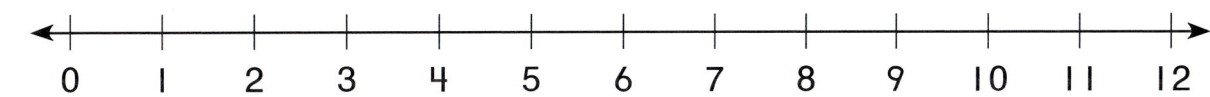

1. ⑤   2. 2   3. 3   4. 9   5. 3   6. 7
   +3   +7   +8   +1   +9   +3

7. 8   8. 2   9. 9   10. 8   11. 1   12. 4
   +1   +9   +2   +2   +7   +3

13. 3   14. 5   15. 3   16. 8   17. 6   18. 2
    +7   +2   +6   +3   +2   +8

Explain It • Daily Reasoning

Why is it easier to start with the greater number when you count on?

Chapter 13 • Addition and Subtraction Facts to 12

Practice and Problem Solving

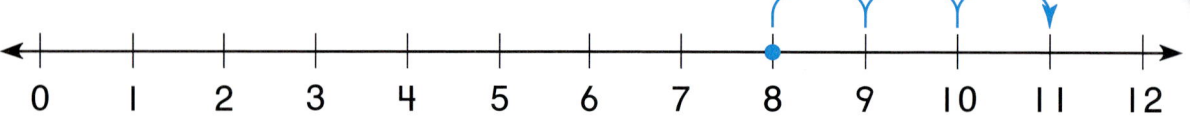

3 + ⑧ = 11

Start on 8. Move 3 spaces to the right.
9, 10, 11

Circle the greater number.
Use the number line. Count on to add.

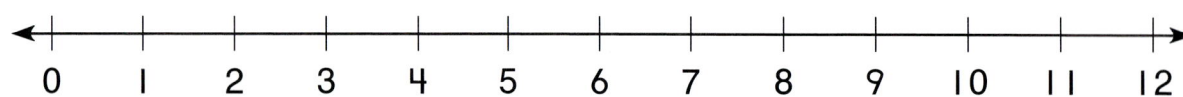

1. ⑥ + 2 = ___
2. 3 + 7 = ___
3. 9 + 3 = ___
4. 1 + 8 = ___
5. 6 + 3 = ___
6. 8 + 2 = ___
7. 2 + 9 = ___
8. 3 + 5 = ___
9. 7 + 2 = ___
10. 3 + 4 = ___
11. 9 + 1 = ___
12. 5 + 2 = ___

Problem Solving
Application

Count on to solve. Draw a picture to check.

13. Ann Lee saved 6¢.
Carol saved 3¢.
How much did
they save in all? ___ ¢

Write About It • Make up an addition story about this picture. Then write the number sentence.

HOME ACTIVITY • With your child, make flash cards for the addition facts for sums through 12. Practice the facts together.

Name _____

Doubles and Doubles Plus 1

Vocabulary
doubles
doubles plus one

Learn

5
+5
—
10

5
+6
—
11

"6 + 5 = 11 is a doubles plus one fact, too."

5 + 5 = 10 is a **doubles** fact.

5 + 6 = 11 is a **doubles plus one** fact.

Check

Write the three sums.
Then circle the doubles fact.

1. (3 +3 = 6)   3 +4   4 +3
2. 4 +4   4 +5   5 +4
3. 2 +2   2 +3   3 +2
4. 1 +1   1 +2   2 +1
5. 0 +0   0 +1   1 +0
6. 5 +5   5 +6   6 +5

Explain It • Daily Reasoning

How does knowing the sum for 4 + 4 help you find the sums for 4 + 5 and 5 + 4?

Chapter 13 • Addition and Subtraction Facts to 12

Practice and Problem Solving

Write the sums.

1. $2 + 2 = \underline{4}$, so $2 + 3 = \underline{5}$

2. $1 + 1 = \underline{}$, so $2 + 1 = \underline{}$

3. $5 + 5 = \underline{}$, so $5 + 6 = \underline{}$

4. $4 + 4 = \underline{}$, so $5 + 4 = \underline{}$

5. $0 + 0 = \underline{}$, so $0 + 1 = \underline{}$

6. $3 + 3 = \underline{}$, so $3 + 4 = \underline{}$

Problem Solving

Logical Reasoning

Solve. Draw a picture to check.

7. Pat has 3 🪙.
   Bob has double that many.
   Sue has double what Bob has.

   How many 🪙 does each person have?

   Pat   Bob   Sue

 Write About It • Look at Exercise 7.
Explain how you got your answers.

🏠 **HOME ACTIVITY** • Have your child tell you the doubles facts and the doubles plus one facts for 2, 3, 4, and 5. For example, 2 + 2 = 4, so 2 + 3 = 5.

Name _____

Algebra: Add 3 Numbers

Explore

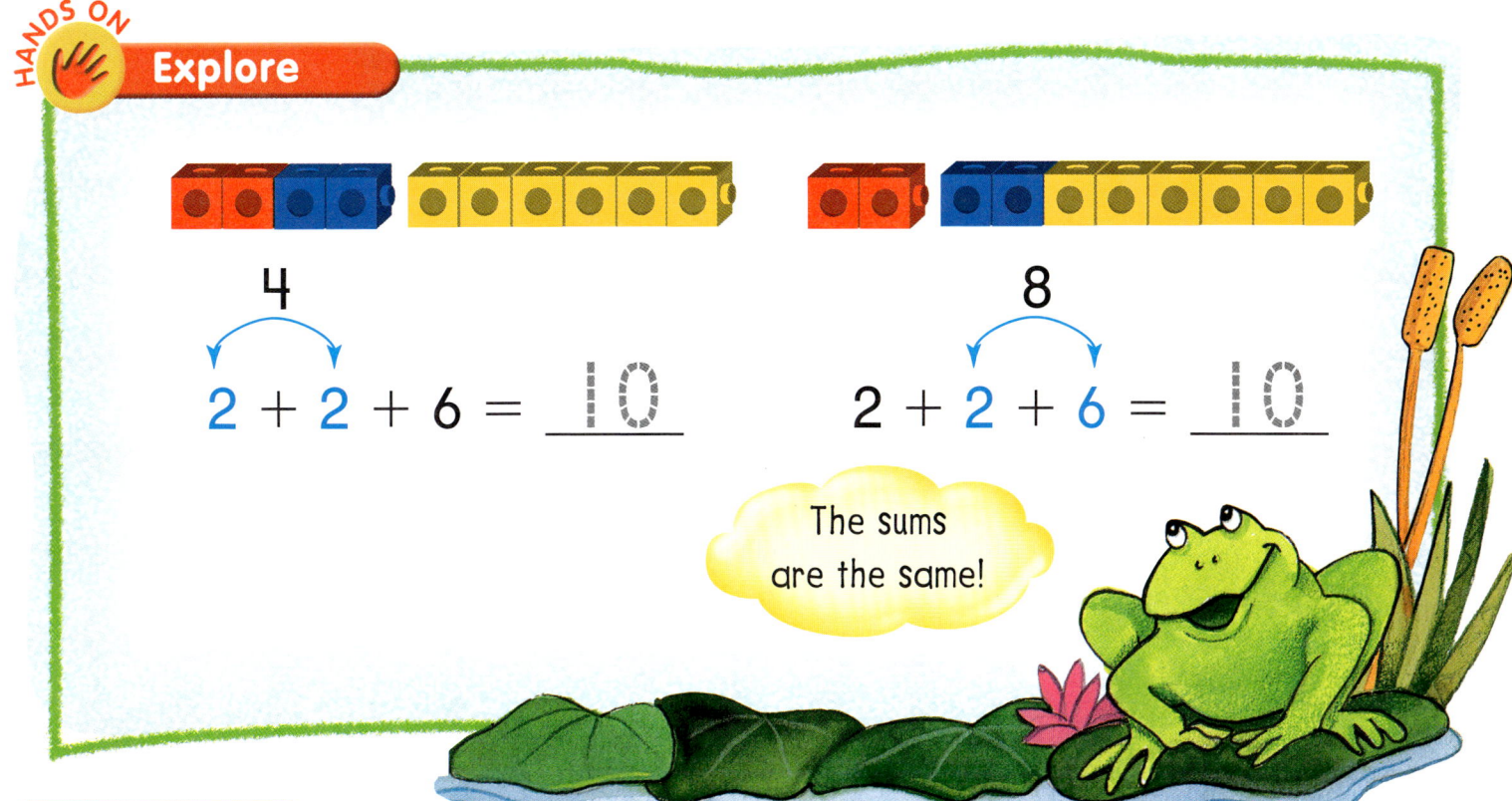

4
2 + 2 + 6 = 10

8
2 + 2 + 6 = 10

The sums are the same!

Connect

Use 🟥 🟦 🟨. Add the blue numbers first.
Write the sums.

1. 3 + 2 + 5 = ____   3 + 2 + 5 = ____

2. 5 + 2 + 2 = ____   5 + 2 + 2 = ____

3. 9 + 0 + 3 = ____   9 + 0 + 3 = ____

4. 3 + 3 + 2 = ____   3 + 3 + 2 = ____

5. 1 + 5 + 3 = ____   1 + 5 + 3 = ____

6. 3 + 6 + 2 = ____   3 + 6 + 2 = ____

Explain It • Daily Reasoning

The numbers to be added are 6, 2, and 1.
Which numbers will you add first? Why?

Chapter 13 • Addition and Subtraction Facts to 12

Practice and Problem Solving

Circle the two numbers you add first. Write the sum.

1.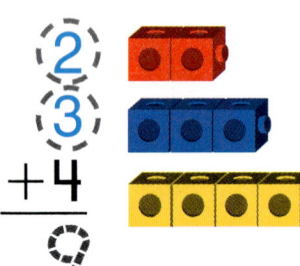
   ②
   ③
   +4
   ——
   9

   5
   +4
   ——
   9

2.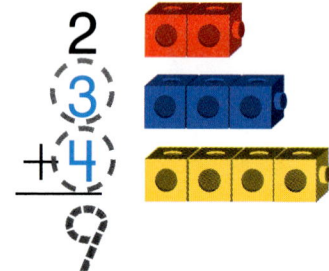
   2
   ③
   +④
   ——
   9

   2
   +7
   ——
   9

3. 2
   5
   +1
   ——

4. 3
   4
   +3
   ——

5. 1
   1
   +6
   ——

6. 7
   2
   +1
   ——

7. 2
   1
   +6
   ——

8. 6
   1
   +4
   ——

9. 3
   5
   +2
   ——

10. 2
    5
    +5
    ——

11. 3
    2
    +3
    ——

12. 4
    5
    +0
    ——

Problem Solving
Mental Math

Add in your head. Draw to check.

13. Tim has 2 dogs. Steve has 3 cats. Greg has 6 fish. How many pets do the boys have in all?

    _____ pets

Write About It • Look at Exercise 13. Which numbers did you decide to add first? Tell why.

HOME ACTIVITY • Have your child use small objects to show how he or she found the sum for each exercise on this page.

Name _____

Problem Solving Strategy
Write a Number Sentence

5 children ride bicycles.

4 children join them.

(How many children are riding bicycles now?)

UNDERSTAND

What do you want to find out?
Circle the question.

PLAN

What facts do you need?
Underline them.

SOLVE

Write a number sentence to solve.

__5__ ⊕ __4__ ⊖ __9__ children

CHECK

Does your answer make sense?
Draw a picture to check.

Write a number sentence.
Draw a picture to check.

THINK: Where do I put the numbers in my sentence?

1. Jim saw 4 boats. Then he saw 3 more. How many boats did he see in all?

____ ◯ ____ ◯ ____ boats

Chapter 13 • Addition and Subtraction Facts to 12

two hundred seventeen **217**

Problem Solving Practice

Write a number sentence.
Draw a picture to check.

Keep in Mind!
Understand
Plan
Solve
Check

THINK: Where do I put the numbers in my sentence?

1. 5 children run.
   6 more join them.
   How many children are running now?

   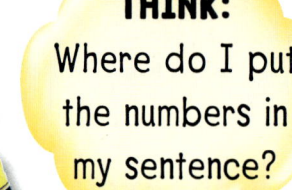

   ___◯___◯___ children

2. Lilly sees 7 cars.
   Then she sees 3 more.
   How many cars does she see in all?

   ___◯___◯___ cars

3. 9 children go for a walk.
   3 more children join them.
   How many children are walking now?

   ___◯___◯___ children

4. Ross has 2 toy rockets.
   Ida gives him 7 more.
   How many toy rockets does Ross have now?

   ___◯___◯___ toy rockets

HOME ACTIVITY • Give your child 1 to 9 small objects all alike, such as paper clips. Then add several more, to a total of no more than 12. Have your child write an addition sentence about them. Repeat, using different numbers.

Name _____

Count Back to Subtract

Vocabulary
count back

Learn

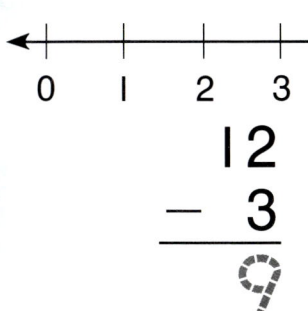

12
− 3
───
9

Start at 12. Then move 3 spaces to the left.
11, 10, 9

Start at 12. **Count back** to subtract.

Check

Use the number line to count back.
Write the difference.

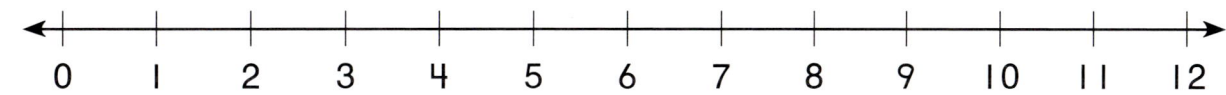

1. 10   2. 8   3. 6   4. 9   5. 7   6. 8
   − 2   −1   −2   −2   −2   −2

7. 11   8. 10   9. 9   10. 6   11. 8   12. 7
   − 3   − 3   −3   −1   −3   −1

13. 10   14. 11   15. 9   16. 7   17. 6   18. 5
   − 1   − 2   −1   −3   −3   −3

Explain It • Daily Reasoning

How can you find the difference for 10 − 3 without using a number line?

10 − 3

Chapter 13 • Addition and Subtraction Facts to 12
two hundred nineteen **219**

Practice and Problem Solving

Count back to subtract.

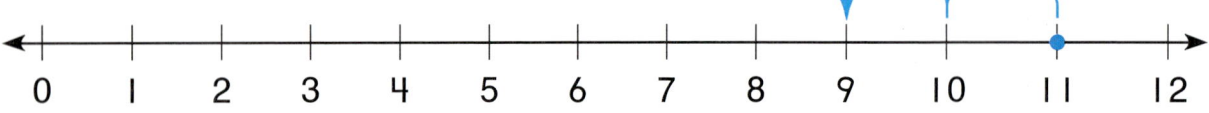

11 − 2 = __9__

Start at 11.
Then move 2 spaces to the left.
10, 9

Count back to subtract. Write the difference.
You can use the number line to help.

1. 12 − 3 = ___
2. 9 − 3 = ___
3. 10 − 2 = ___
4. 9 − 2 = ___
5. 10 − 3 = ___
6. 11 − 3 = ___
7. 10 − 1 = ___
8. 11 − 2 = ___
9. 6 − 3 = ___
10. 7 − 3 = ___
11. 9 − 1 = ___
12. 8 − 3 = ___

Problem Solving
Application

Write a number sentence to solve.
Use the number line to help.

13. There are 12 cars in the parking lot. 2 cars leave. How many cars are still in the parking lot?

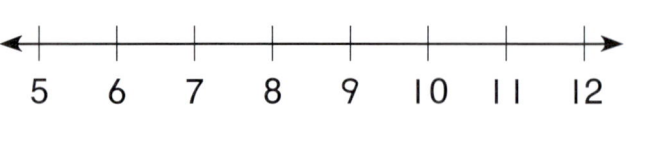

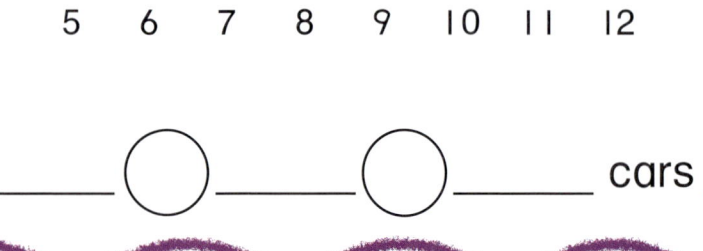 cars

 Write About It • Look at Exercise 13. Explain how you used the number line to subtract.

HOME ACTIVITY • Help your child use the number line on this page to practice any subtraction facts he or she missed in this lesson.

Name _____

Subtract to Compare

Learn

How many more red cars than blue cars are there?

There are 2 more red cars than blue cars.

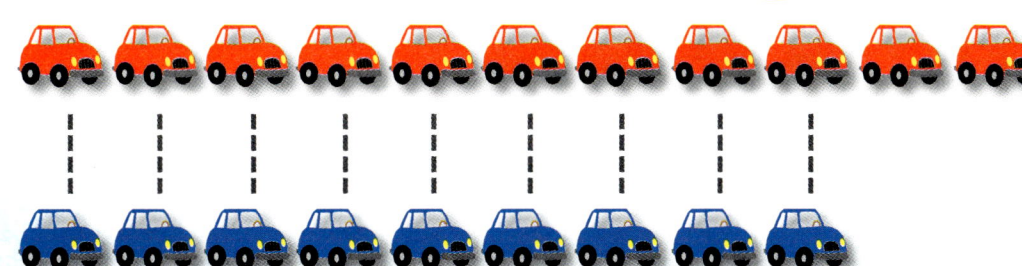

$$\begin{array}{r} 11 \\ -9 \\ \hline 2 \end{array}$$

Check

Draw lines to match. Write the difference.

1. How many fewer small boats than big boats are there?

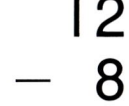

$$\begin{array}{r} 12 \\ -8 \\ \hline \end{array}$$

2. How many more green bikes than yellow bikes are there?

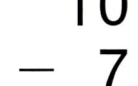

$$\begin{array}{r} 10 \\ -7 \\ \hline \end{array}$$

Explain It • Daily Reasoning

Which group in the picture has more? How can you prove your answer?

Chapter 13 • Addition and Subtraction Facts to 12

two hundred twenty-one **221**

Practice and Problem Solving

Draw lines to match.
Write the difference.

1.  10 − 8 = 2

2.  11 − 7

3.  12 − 9

4.  12 − 7

Problem Solving
Application

Solve. Draw a picture to check.

5. Margie has 10 cars.
   Jake has 6 cars.
   How many more cars
   does Margie have?

   _____ more cars

 **Write About It** • Look at Exercise 5.
Explain how you got your answer.

HOME ACTIVITY • Set out two groups of objects, one with more objects than the other. Have your child show how to use matching to subtract to find out how many more are in the larger group.

Name _____

Extra Practice

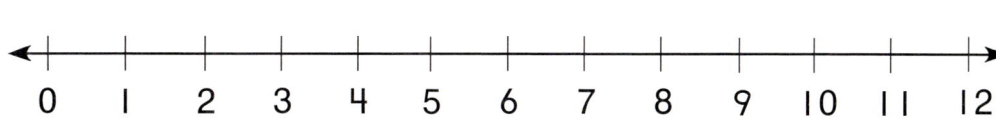

Circle the greater number. Count on to add.

Count back to subtract. Write the difference.

1. 8
  +3

2. 8
  +2

3. 2
  +5

4. 9
  −2

5. 8
  −3

6. 10
  − 3

Write all the sums. Then circle the doubles facts.

7. 2 + 2 = ___
8. 4 + 3 = ___
9. 5 + 5 = ___

Circle the two numbers you added first. Write the sum.

10. 3 + 2 + 1 = ____
11. 7 + 1 + 2 = ____

Draw lines to match. Write the difference.

12.

10
− 6

Problem Solving

Write a number sentence. Draw a picture to check.

13. 6 children are on the bus. 2 more children get on. How many children are on the bus?

 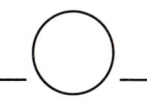 _____ children

Chapter 13 • Addition and Subtraction Facts to 12

two hundred twenty-three **223**

Name _____

✓ Review/Test

Concepts and Skills

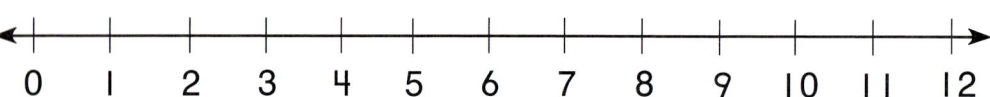

Circle the greater number. Count on to add.

Count back to subtract. Write the difference.

1. 9 +3
2. 9 +2
3. 3 +6
4. 11 − 2
5. 10 − 3
6. 12 − 3

Write all the sums. Then circle the doubles facts.

7. 4 + 4 = ___
8. 5 + 4 = ___
9. 3 + 3 = ___

Circle the two numbers you add first. Write the sum.

10. 5 + 5 + 2 = ____
11. 4 + 4 + 2 = ____

Draw lines to match. Write the difference.

10 − 4

12.

Problem Solving

Write a number sentence. Draw a picture to check.

13. 7 children run. 3 more children join them. How many children are running now?

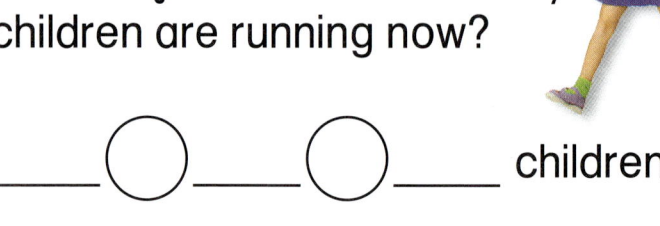 children

224 two hundred twenty-four

Name _____

⭐Standardized Test Prep
Chapters 1–13

1.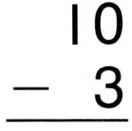
      5   7   13   15
   ○   ○   ○   ○

2. Which does the number line show?

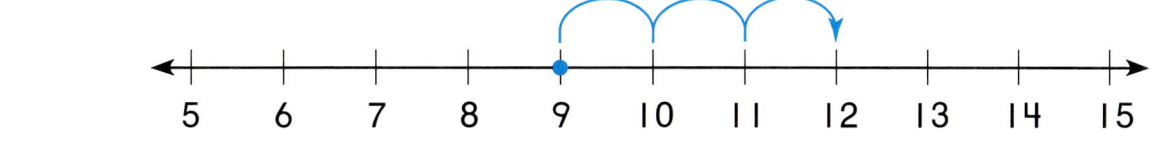

   $9 - 2 = 7$ $9 - 3 = 6$ $2 + 9 = 11$ $3 + 9 = 12$
   ○   ○   ○   ○

3. Which is a doubles plus 1 fact?

   $3 + 3 = 6$ $3 + 4 = 7$ $5 + 5 = 10$ $7 + 4 = 11$
   ○   ○   ○   ○

4. Which is the sum?

   $3 + 4 + 2 = $ _____
       8   9   10   11
       ○   ○   ○   ○

5. Which tells how many more apples than pears there are?

   $7 - 5 = 2$ $8 - 5 = 3$
   ○   ○

   $5 + 2 = 7$ $5 + 3 = 8$
   ○   ○

Show What You Know

6. Write the number sentence. Draw a picture to explain your answer.

   Kate picks 4 pumpkins. Edna picks 5 pumpkins. How many pumpkins do they pick in all?

   ___ ◯ ___ ◯ ___ pumpkins

Chapter 13   two hundred twenty-five **225**

Name _____

MATH GAME

Boats Full of Facts

Play with a partner.

1. Put your 🨅 at START.
2. Spin the 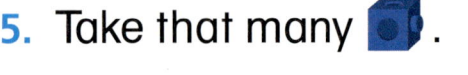.
3. Move your 🨅 that many boats.
4. Find the sum or difference.
5. Take that many 🟦.
6. When the first player gets to END, count 🟦. 
7. The player with more 🟦 wins.

You will need

2 🨅 🟦

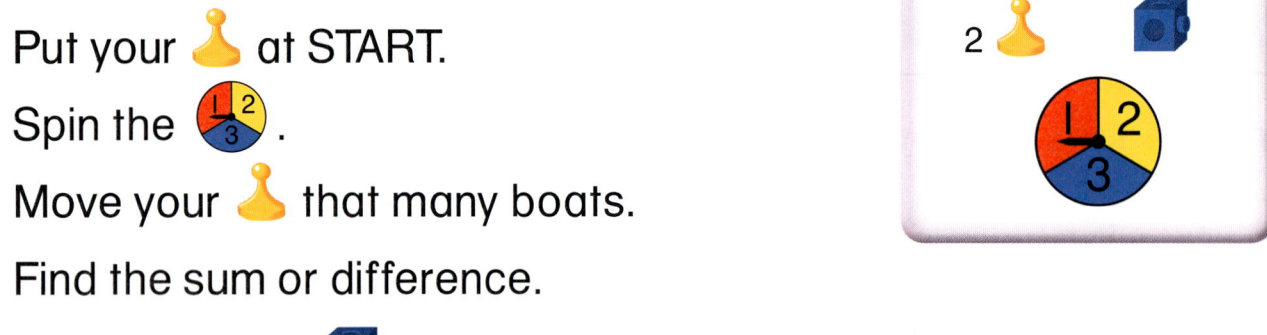

226 two hundred twenty-six

Name _____

✓ Check What You Know

Sums to 10

Add. Write the sums.

1.	2 +8	8 +2	2. 6 +3	3 +6	3. 7 +1	1 +7
4.	4 +5	5 +4	5. 3 +7	7 +3	6. 8 +0	0 +8

Subtraction to 10

Subtract. Circle the pair of facts if they use the same numbers.

7.	9 −2	9 −7	8. 8 −0	8 −8	9. 10 − 4	10 − 5
10.	7 −6	7 −2	11. 8 −2	8 −6	12. 10 − 3	10 − 7

Subtract across. Subtract down.

13.

9	4	
6	2	

14.

10	3	
8	2	

228 two hundred twenty-eight   Use this page to review important skills needed for this chapter.

Name _____

Algebra: Related Addition and Subtraction Facts

Vocabulary
related facts

Explore (HANDS ON)

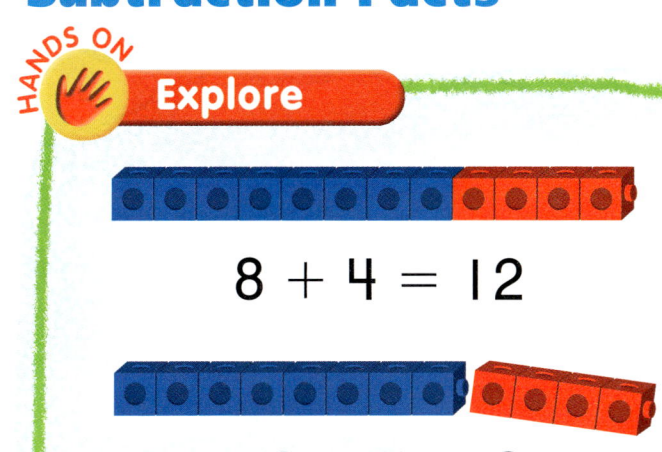

$8 + 4 = 12$

$12 - 4 = 8$

Related facts use the same numbers.

Connect

Use 🟦 🟥 to show related facts. Complete the chart.

Use 🟦	Add 🟥	Write the sum.	Take away	Write the subtraction sentence.
1. 6	3	$6 + 3 = \underline{9}$	3	$\underline{9} \bigcirc \underline{3} \bigcirc \underline{6}$
2. 7	5	$7 + 5 = \underline{}$	7	$\underline{} \bigcirc \underline{} \bigcirc \underline{}$
3. 4	6	$4 + 6 = \underline{}$	4	$\underline{} \bigcirc \underline{} \bigcirc \underline{}$
4. 3	8	$3 + 8 = \underline{}$	8	$\underline{} \bigcirc \underline{} \bigcirc \underline{}$
5. 6	6	$6 + 6 = \underline{}$	6	$\underline{} \bigcirc \underline{} \bigcirc \underline{}$

Explain It • Daily Reasoning

How can knowing an addition fact help you remember a subtraction fact?

Chapter 14 • Practice Addition and Subtraction

Practice and Problem Solving

Write each sum or difference.
Circle the related facts in each row.

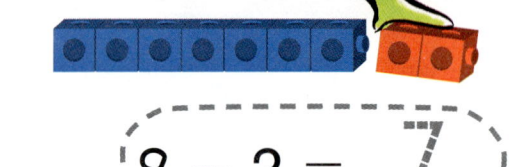

1. (7 + 2 = 9)   5 + 2 = 7   (9 − 2 = 7)

2. 8 + 4 = ___   12 − 4 = ___   10 − 4 = ___

3. 11 − 4 = ___   9 + 1 = ___   10 − 1 = ___

4. 10 − 7 = ___   3 + 7 = ___   7 + 4 = ___

5. 6 + 5 = ___   12 − 5 = ___   11 − 5 = ___

6. 9 + 3 = ___   8 − 4 = ___   12 − 3 = ___

Problem Solving
Algebra

7. Circle three numbers that you can use to write a pair of related facts. Write the number sentences.

___ ◯ ___ ◯ ___   ___ ◯ ___ ◯ ___

Write About It • Look at Exercise 7. Write the other related addition and subtraction sentences.

 HOME ACTIVITY • Give your child an addition problem, such as 4 + 5, and ask him or her to tell you the sum (9). Then ask your child to tell you a related subtraction fact (9 − 5 = 4 or 9 − 4 = 5).

Name _____

Fact Families to 12

Vocabulary: fact family

Explore

8, 3, and 11 are the numbers in this fact family.

8 + 3 = 11

3 + 8 = 11

11 − 3 = 8

11 − 8 = 3

Connect

Use . Add or subtract.
Write the numbers in the fact family.

1. 7 + 4 = 11
    4 + 7 = 11
    11 − 4 = 7
    11 − 7 = 4

    | 7 | 4 | 11 |

2. 8 + 4 = ___
    4 + 8 = ___
    12 − 4 = ___
    12 − 8 = ___

3. 5 + 4 = ___
    4 + 5 = ___
    9 − 4 = ___
    9 − 5 = ___

4. 6 + 5 = ___
    5 + 6 = ___
    11 − 5 = ___
    11 − 6 = ___

Explain It • Daily Reasoning

How many facts are in the fact family for 12, 6, and 6?
Use  to prove your answer.

Chapter 14 • Practice Addition and Subtraction

Practice and Problem Solving

Add or subtract.
Write the numbers in the fact family.

1.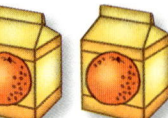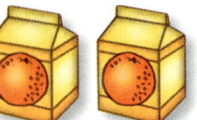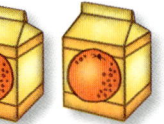

7	5	12	12
+5	+7	− 5	− 7
12			

2.

6	4	10	10
+4	+6	− 4	− 6

3.

9	3	12	12
+3	+9	− 9	− 3

Problem Solving
Logical Reasoning

Solve the riddle. Write the number.

4. When I am added to 4, we make 10.
   What number am I? _____

Write About It • Write a number sentence that shows your answer for Exercise 4. Then write the rest of the fact family.

HOME ACTIVITY • Tell your child an addition fact with a sum of 12 or less. Have your child tell the other number sentences in the fact family.

Name _____

Sums and Differences to 12

Learn

These are some ways to find sums and differences.

count on
7 + 2 = 9

count back
10 − 2 = 8

doubles
5 + 5 = 10

related facts
5 + 3 = 8 and 8 − 3 = 5

Check

Write the sum or difference.

1. 7 + 2 = __9__

2. 11 − 3 = ___
3. 6 − 0 = ___
4. 7 + 3 = ___

5. 10 − 2 = ___
6. 12 − 6 = ___
7. 5 + 3 = ___

8. 9 + 0 = ___
9. 9 − 2 = ___
10. 11 − 2 = ___

11. 8 − 4 = ___
12. 10 + 2 = ___
13. 6 + 3 = ___

14. 9 − 5 = ___
15. 8 − 8 = ___
16. 4 + 3 = ___

17. 11 − 5 = ___
18. 6 + 6 = ___
19. 4 + 5 = ___

Explain It • Daily Reasoning

How could knowing 12 − 3 = 9 help you find the difference for 12 − 4?

12 − 4

Chapter 14 • Practice Addition and Subtraction

Practice and Problem Solving

Write the sum or difference.

1. 8 + 4 = 12
2. 10 − 3
3. 6 + 6
4. 12 − 7
5. 3 + 8
6. 8 − 5

7. 9 − 4
8. 11 − 2
9. 3 + 5
10. 12 − 4
11. 5 + 5
12. 7 − 3

13. 6 + 2
14. 10 − 6
15. 4 + 3
16. 11 − 8
17. 3 + 7
18. 9 + 1

19. 5 + 7
20. 11 − 6
21. 6 + 3
22. 10 − 5
23. 7 + 4
24. 6 + 5

Problem Solving

Visual Thinking

25. Write the fact family that tells about the picture.

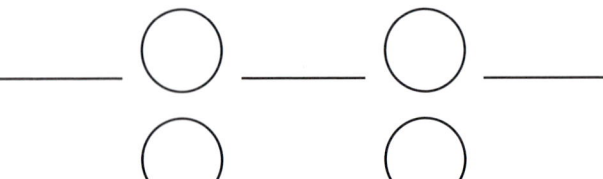
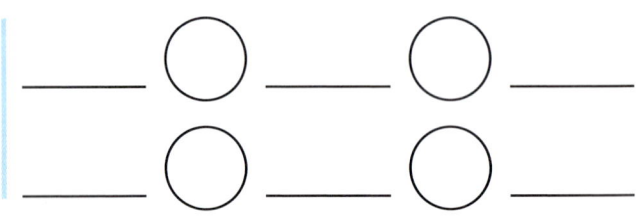

 **Write About It** • How would your fact family be different if there were 1 more cherry in the second row?

HOME ACTIVITY • With your child, make flash cards for the addition and subtraction facts through 12. Practice the facts each day.

Name _____

Algebra: Missing Numbers

Learn

What is the missing number?

3 + ☐ = 9   9 − 3 = ☐

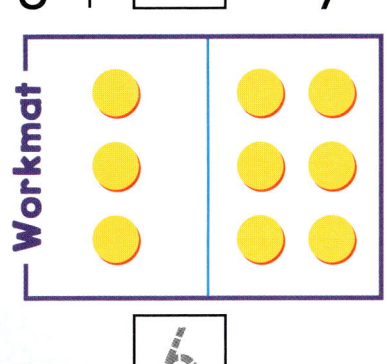

3 + 6 = 9   9 − 3 = 6

Check

Write the missing number.
Use 🟡 if you need to.

Use a related fact to help you.

1. 6 + ☐ = 10   10 − 6 = ☐

2. ☐ + 3 = 6   6 − 3 = ☐

3. 8 + ☐ = 12   12 − 8 = ☐

4. ☐ + 5 = 11   11 − 5 = ☐

5. 5 + ☐ = 12   12 − 5 = ☐

Explain It • Daily Reasoning

Use 🟡 to show why you can solve ☐ + 5 = 9 by using subtraction.

Chapter 14 • Practice Addition and Subtraction   two hundred thirty-five **235**

Practice and Problem Solving

Write the missing number.
Use 🟡 if you need to.

1. $2 + \boxed{5} = 7$ $7 - 2 = \boxed{5}$

2. $\boxed{} + 3 = 9$ $9 - 3 = \boxed{}$

3. $7 + \boxed{} = 10$ $10 - 7 = \boxed{}$

4. $\boxed{} + 7 = 8$ $8 - 7 = \boxed{}$

5. $8 + \boxed{} = 9$ $9 - 8 = \boxed{}$

6. $\boxed{} + 5 = 8$ $8 - 5 = \boxed{}$

7. $3 + \boxed{} = 11$ $11 - 3 = \boxed{}$

Problem Solving
Algebra

8. What is the missing number?

$$\begin{array}{r} 9 \\ + \blacksquare \\ \hline 11 \end{array} \quad \begin{array}{r} \blacksquare \\ + 9 \\ \hline 11 \end{array} \quad \begin{array}{r} 11 \\ - 9 \\ \hline \blacksquare \end{array} \quad \begin{array}{r} 11 \\ - \blacksquare \\ \hline 9 \end{array}$$

■ = _____

Write About It • Look at Exercise 8. Write the numbers that are in the fact family. Explain how you know.

HOME ACTIVITY • Put 12 small items in a bag. Have your child remove some, count them, and tell how many are left in the bag. Repeat.

Name _____

Problem Solving
Choose a Strategy

You can use different ways to solve a problem.

Scott ate 4 hot dogs.
Tal also ate 4 hot dogs.
How many hot dogs did they eat in all?

Make a model.	Draw a picture.	Write a number sentence.
		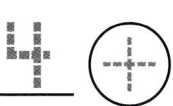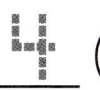
 8 hot dogs	 8 hot dogs	8 hot dogs

Choose a way to solve each problem.
Make a model 🎲, draw a picture 🖍,
or write a number sentence ✏️.
Show your work.

THINK: Which way do I want to solve this problem?

1. 8 ants are on the picnic table.
   3 go away.
   How many ants are there now?

    ants

2. The basket has 11 apples.
   Jose takes 2 apples.
   How many apples are there now?

   _____ apples

Chapter 14 • Practice Addition and Subtraction

Problem Solving Practice

Choose a way to solve each problem. Make a model 🎲, draw a picture 🖍, or write a number sentence ✏️. Show your work.

THINK: What is another way to solve the problem?

1. Meg's mom makes 12 muffins.
   Her family eats 9 muffins.
   How many muffins are left?

   _____ muffins

2. Sara sets out 9 plates.
   Children take 3 plates.
   How many plates are left?

   _____ plates

3. There are 4 pretzels.
   Hans brings 3 more pretzels.
   How many pretzels are there now?

   _____ pretzels

4. Rick eats 4 cherries.
   Peter eats 6 cherries.
   How many do they eat in all?

   _____ cherries

HOME ACTIVITY • Ask your child to explain how he or she solved each problem on this page. Then ask him or her to show a different way to solve each problem.

Name _____

Extra Practice

Write each sum or difference.
Circle the related facts.

1. 10 − 2 = ___   9 + 3 = ___   12 − 3 = ___

Add or subtract. Write the numbers in the fact family.

2. 7 + 4 = ___
   4 + 7 = ___
   11 − 4 = ___
   11 − 7 = ___

3. 6 + 3 = ___
   3 + 6 = ___
   9 − 3 = ___
   9 − 6 = ___
   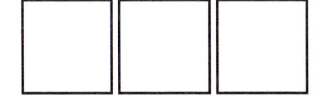

Write the sum or difference.

4. 8   5. 11   6. 12   7. 6   8. 3   9. 10
   +1   − 5   − 4   +4   +4   − 2

Write the missing number.

10. 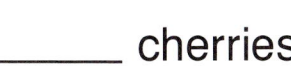 + 5 = 11   11 − 5 =

Problem Solving

Choose a way to solve the problem.

11. Lily has 8 cherries.
    Her friend gives her 3 cherries.
    How many does Lily have now?

    _____ cherries

Name _____

✓ Review/Test

Concepts and Skills

Write each sum or difference.
Circle the related facts.

1. 4 + 7 = ___   11 − 7 = ___   11 − 2 = ___

Add or subtract. Write the numbers in the fact family.

2. 4 + 8 = ___
   8 + 4 = ___
   12 − 8 = ___
   12 − 4 = ___
   ☐ ☐ ☐

3. 6 + 5 = ___
   5 + 6 = ___
   11 − 5 = ___
   11 − 6 = ___
   ☐ ☐ ☐

Write the sum or difference.

4. 9
   +1
   ___

5. 12
   − 6
   ___

6. 10
   − 4
   ___

7. 7
   +5
   ___

8. 4
   +5
   ___

9. 11
   − 3
   ___

Write the missing number.

10. 8 + ☐ = 12   12 − 8 = ☐

Problem Solving

Choose a way to solve the problem.

11. Alex has 12 pretzels.
    He gives 4 pretzels to friends.
    How many pretzels are left?

    _____ pretzels

Name _____

⭐Standardized Test Prep
Chapters 1–14

Choose the answer for questions 1–5.

1. 12   18   17
   − 5   ○   ○
   ___   8   7
          ○   ○

2. 5   1   2
   +6   ○   ○
   ___   10   11
         ○   ○

3. Which is the missing number?

   6 + ☐ = 10   2   4   6   8
                 ○   ○   ○   ○

4. Gabe had 11 berries. He ate 4. Which number sentence tells how many berries Gabe has left?

   11 − 7 = 4   11 − 4 = 7   7 + 4 = 11   4 + 7 = 11
       ○   ○   ○   ○

5. Which is a way to make 9?

   4 + 2   5 + 4   4 + 1   4 + 3
     ○   ○   ○   ○

Show What You Know

6. Write four number sentences that are in the same fact family. Draw a picture of each number sentence to explain.

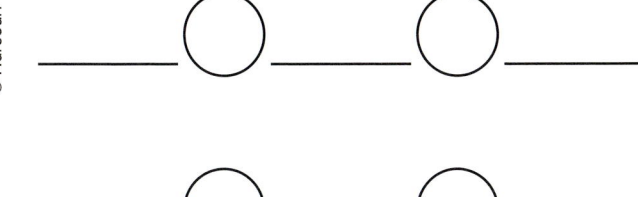

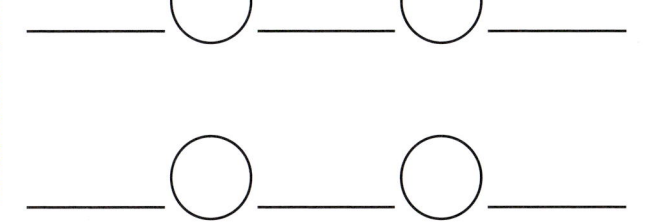

IT'S IN THE BAG
Animals' Picnic Basket

PROJECT Create a slide-through picnic basket of addition and subtraction facts.

You Will Need

- Large brown bag
- Pattern tracer
- Cardboard facts strip
- Scissors
- Crayons

Directions

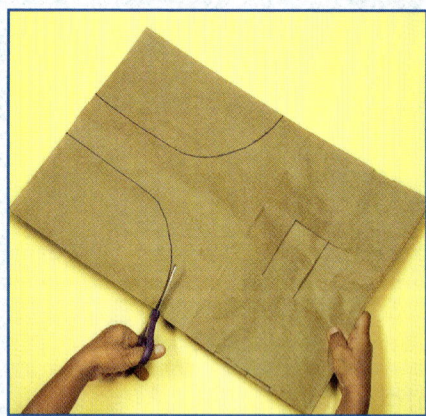

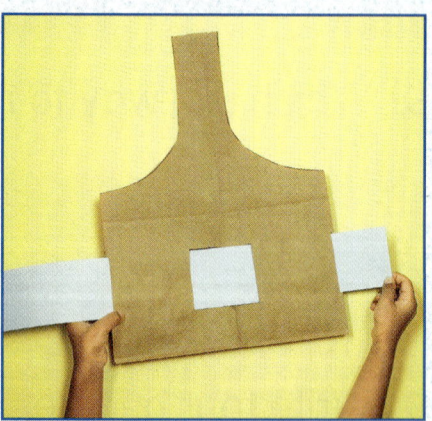

1. Put the bag flat in front of you. Place the pattern at the top of the bag. Trace around the pattern.

2. Cut on the lines you drew.

3. Put the end of the facts strip in the left side. Push it through to the other side.

4. Decorate your picnic basket. Draw and write addition and subtraction facts on the strip so they show in the basket's window.

242 two hundred forty-two

Unit 3

The Animals' Picnic

BY DAVID MCPHAIL

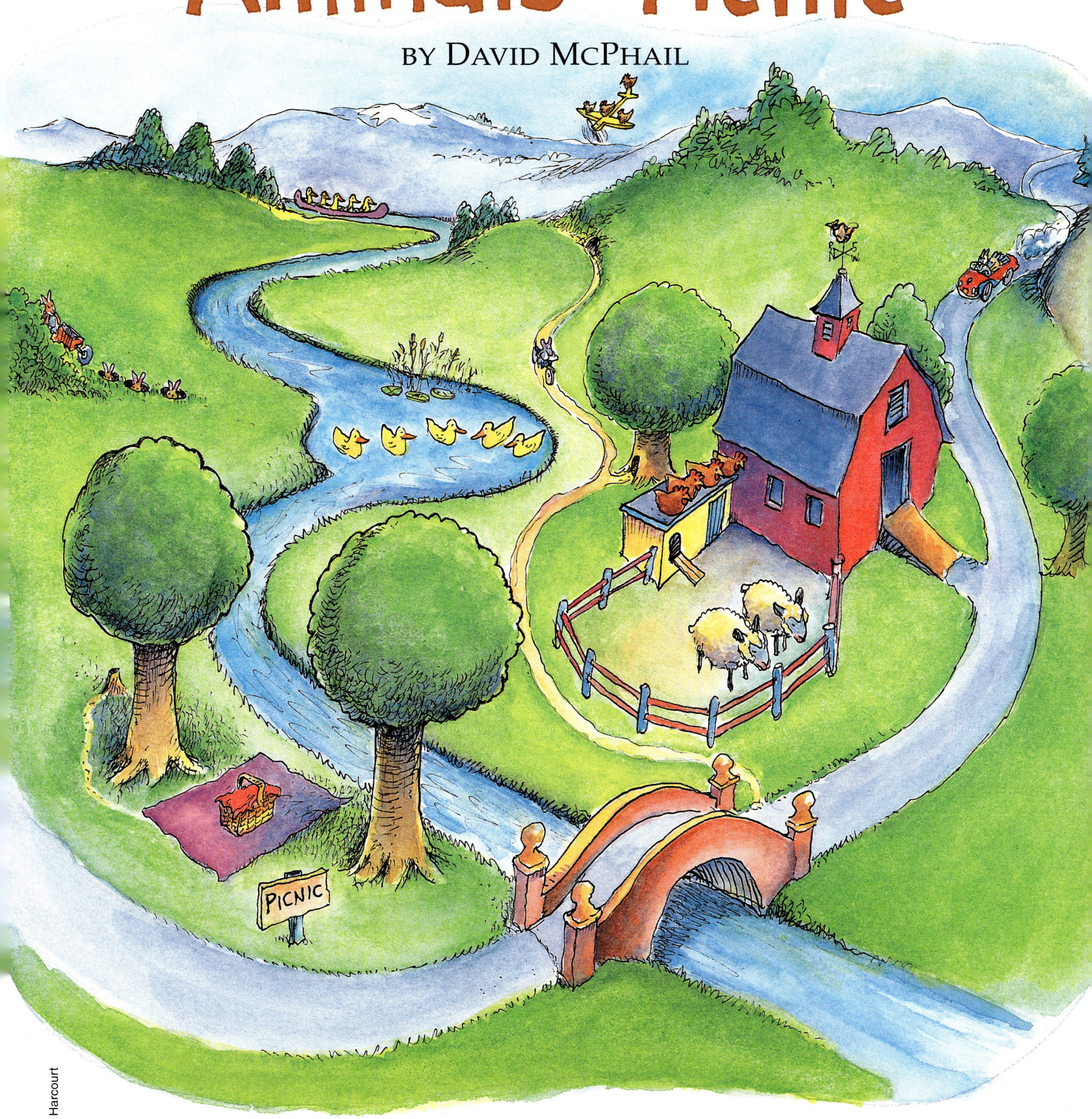

This book will help me review doubles.

This book belongs to _____.

All the animals were having a picnic.

One mouse invited one mouse.

They went by bike.

Two sheep invited two sheep.

They went by car.

Three rabbits invited three rabbits.

They went by wheelbarrow.

Four ants invited four ants.

They walked.

The ants got there first.

PROBLEM SOLVING ON LOCATION

In Turkey Run State Park

You can canoe, hike, and camp outdoors at Turkey Run State Park in Indiana.

1 These tents hold 2 people. Skip count by twos. Write how many people the tents can hold.

_2_, _4_, _____, _____, _____, _____ people

2 These tents hold 5 people. Skip count by fives. Write how many people the tents can hold.

_5_, _____, _____, _____, _____, _____, _____, _____ people

3 These tents hold 10 people. Skip count by tens. Write how many people the tents can hold.

_10_, _____, _____, _____, _____, _____, _____ people

Name _____

CHALLENGE

Represent Numbers in Different Ways

This number is shown in three different ways.

11      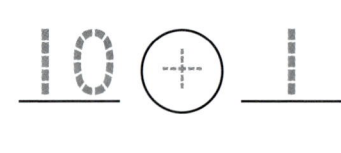   10 ⊕ 1

Show each number three different ways.

Number	Use 🟥. Draw to show.	Draw a picture.	Write a name for the number.
1. 7			___ ◯ ___
2. 10			___ ◯ ___
3. 8			___ ◯ ___
4. 12			___ ◯ ___

Name _____

✓ Study Guide and Review

Vocabulary

Write how many **tens** and **ones**.
Write the number in a different way.

1.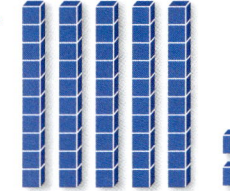

   _____ tens _____ ones = _____

   _____ + _____

2.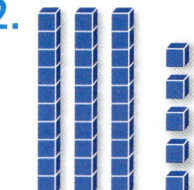

   _____ tens _____ ones = _____

   _____ + _____

Skills and Concepts

Circle the number that is greater.
Write the numbers.

3.

   _____ is greater than _____.

   _____ > _____

4.

   _____ is greater than _____.

   _____ > _____

Circle the number that is less.
Write the numbers.

5.

   _____ is less than _____.

   _____ < _____

6.

   _____ is less than _____.

   _____ < _____

Unit 3 • Study Guide and Review

Sort. Draw to complete the picture graph.

7.

Lunches We Like						
hot dog						
pizza						
soup						

Count by fives. Write the missing numbers.

8. 5, 10, ____, ____, 25, ____, ____, 40

Add or subtract. Think of a related fact to help.

9. 8   10. 10   11. 9   12. 5   13. 6   14. 11
   +4   −5   +3   −5   +6   −2

Problem Solving

Write the number sentence.
Draw a picture to check.

15. There are 12 eggs.
    Dad cooks 6 of them.
    How many eggs are left?

____ ◯ ____ ◯ ____ eggs

Name _____

✓ Performance Assessment

Buying Fish

Megan and her sister Erin bought some fish at the pet store.

- Erin bought 1 more fish than Megan.
- Megan bought fewer than 7 fish.

Write a doubles-plus-one sentence that fits this math story.

Show your work.

Unit 3 • Performance Assessment

two hundred forty-seven **247**

Name _____

TECHNOLOGY

Calculator • Skip Counting

You can use a to skip count.

Skip count by twos.

Press   .

Read the number 2.

Press =.

Read the number 4.

Press =.

Read the number 6.

So, count 2, 4, 6 to count by twos.

Practice and Problem Solving

Use a calculator.

1. Skip count by threes.

    Press ON/C + 3 = = = = = =
    □ □ □ □ □ □

2. Count by adding the next larger number each time.

    Press ON/C 1 + 2 = + 3 = + 4 =
    □ □ □

248 two hundred forty-eight

LOOKING BACK
SCHOOL HOME CONNECTION

Dear Family,

In Unit 3 we learned about graphs, numbers to 100, and facts to 12. Here is a game for us to play together. This game will give me a chance to share what I have learned.

Love,

_____

Directions
1. Cover each apple with a penny.
2. Pick up 1 penny.
3. Use the number on that apple. Tell an addition or subtraction fact that uses doubles or doubles plus one.
4. Put the penny on the graph to show the kind of fact you made.
5. Take turns until a row is full. Look at the graph. Count the number of doubles facts and doubles plus one facts.
6. Tell which kind of fact you made more of. Play again.

Materials
21 pennies or beans

Double the Apples

How We Doubled the Apples

doubles					
doubles plus 1					

Unit 4 • Unit Game

LOOKING FORWARD
SCHOOL HOME CONNECTION

Dear Family,

During the next few weeks, we will learn about solid figures, plane shapes, and patterns. We will also learn more about addition and subtraction to 20. Here is important math vocabulary and a list of books to share.

Love,

_____

Vocabulary

- rectangle
- square
- circle
- triangle
- sphere
- cone
- cylinder
- pyramid
- cube
- rectangular prism

Vocabulary Power

Solid Figures:

rectangular prism   sphere

cone   cylinder

pyramid   cube

Plane Shapes:

rectangle   square   circle   triangle

BOOKS TO SHARE

To read about geometry and patterns with your child, look for these books in your library.

When a Line Bends... A Shape Begins,
by Rhonda Gowler Greene, Houghton Mifflin, 2001.

Circus Shapes,
by Stuart J. Murphy, HarperCollins, 1998.

The Very Busy Spider,
by Eric Carle, Penguin Putnam, 1999.

A Fair Bear Share,
by Stuart J. Murphy, HarperCollins, 1998.

 Visit *The Learning Site* for additional ideas and activities. www.harcourtschool.com

CHAPTER 15

Solid Figures and Plane Shapes

FUN FACTS

Most sand castles are built from a pile of sand that has been packed down. Then molds can be placed on top.

Theme: Shapes in Our World

Name _____

✓ Check What You Know

Sort Solid Figures

Color the 🔵 shape blue.

Color the 🔺 shape red.

Color the 🟫 shape yellow.

Color the 🟡 shape green.

1.
2.
3.

4.
5.
6.

Sort Plane Shapes

Circle the same shape.

7.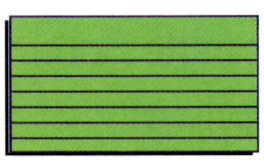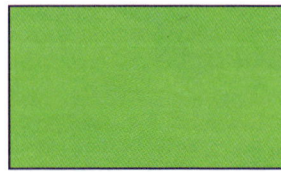

8.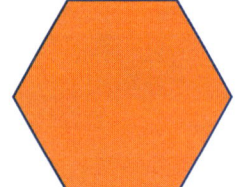

250 two hundred fifty   Use this page to review important skills needed for this chapter.

Name _____

Solid Figures

Explore (Hands On)

Vocabulary
cylinder   sphere
pyramid   cone
rectangular prism   cube

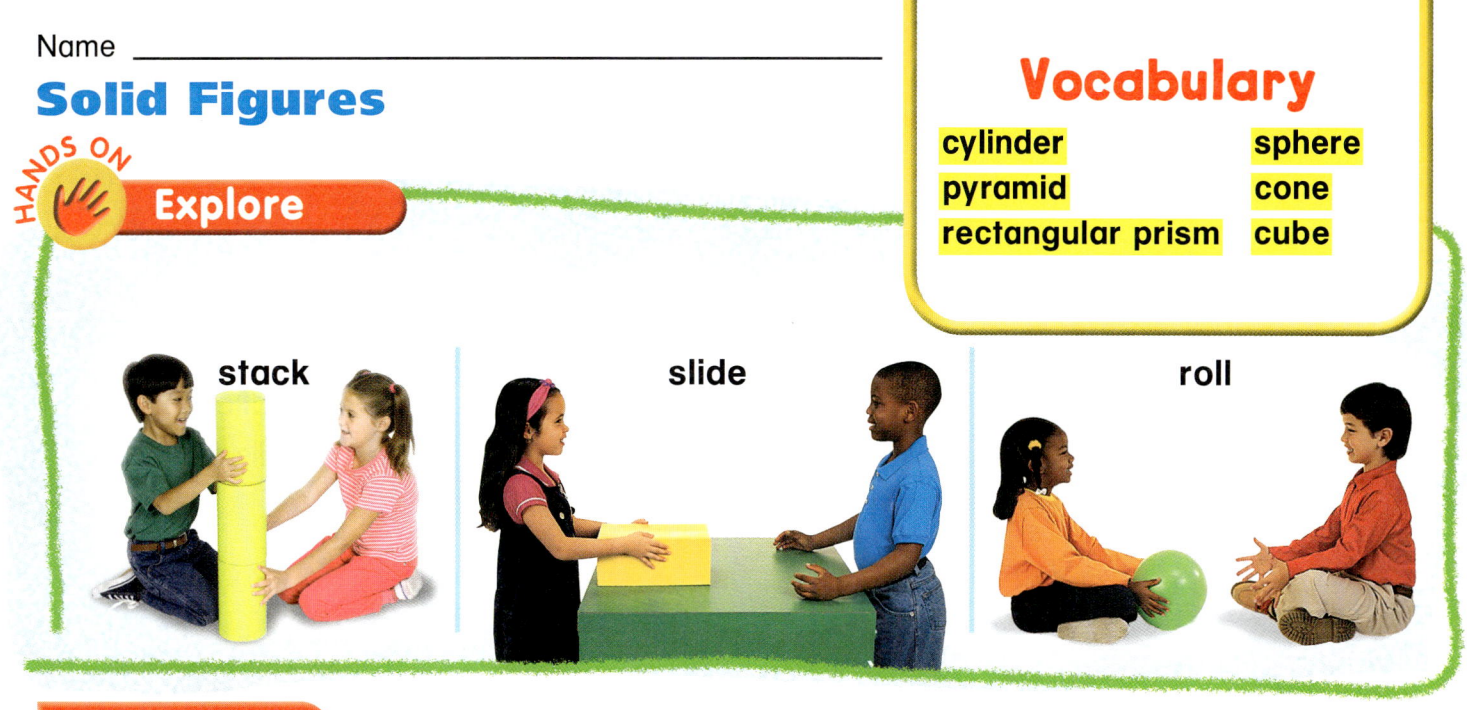

stack   slide   roll

Connect

Use solids. Sort. Write **yes** or **no**.

	Does it stack?	roll?	slide?
1. sphere	no		
2. cone			
3. cube			
4. cylinder			
5. pyramid			
6. rectangular prism			

Explain It • Daily Reasoning

Which solids roll? Tell why.

Chapter 15 • Solid Figures and Plane Shapes

Practice and Problem Solving

cube pyramid rectangular prism

These can slide.

sphere

This is round and curved. It rolls.

Use solids.

1. Color each solid that will stack.

2. Color each solid that will roll.

3. Color each solid that will slide.

Problem Solving
Logical Reasoning

4. Cross out the solid that does not belong. Circle the sentence that tells why.

   It will not stack.

   It will not roll.

Write About It • Draw something in your classroom that will roll. Tell why.

 **HOME ACTIVITY** • Find objects that are shaped like the solids on this page. Work with your child to find out which ones will stack, roll, and slide.

252 two hundred fifty-two

Name _____

Faces and Vertices

Vocabulary
vertex
vertices
face

Explore

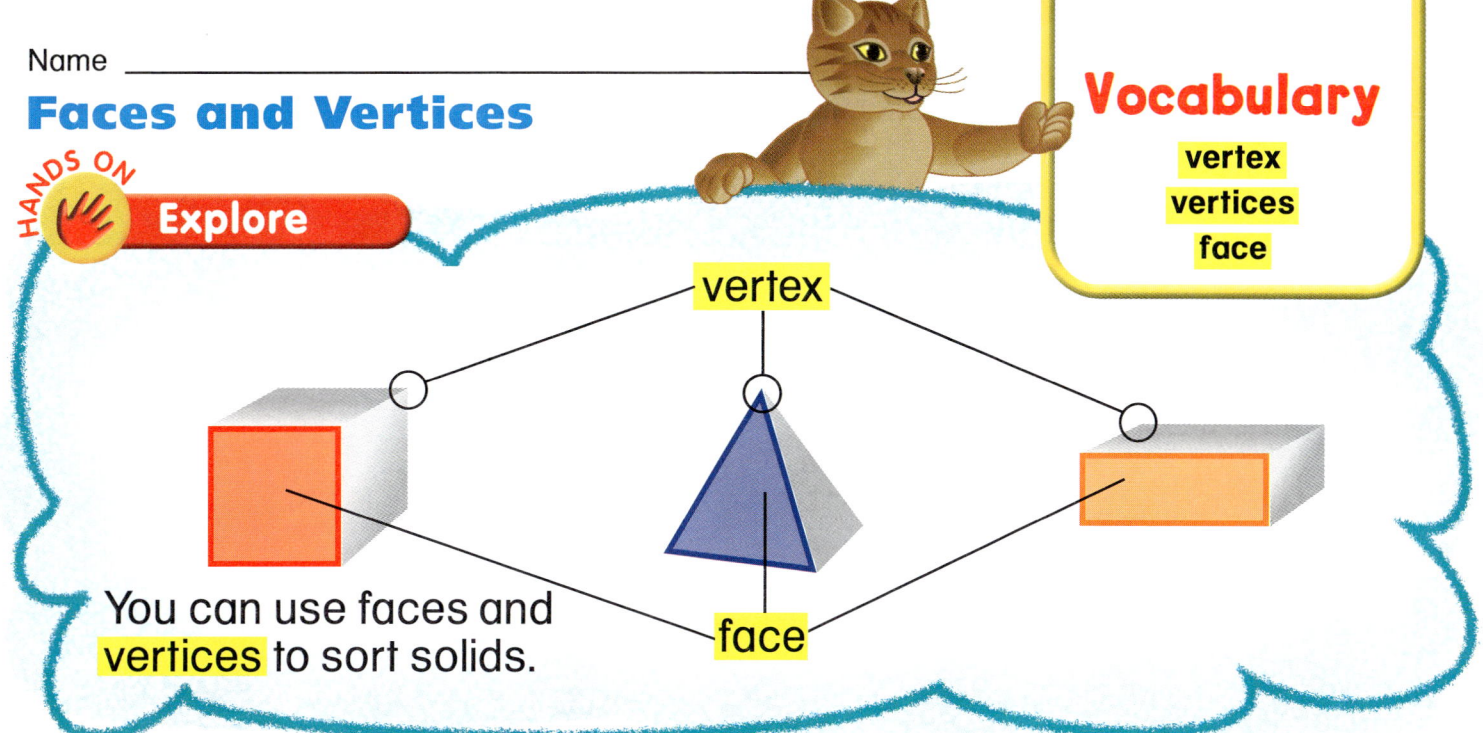

You can use faces and **vertices** to sort solids.

Connect

Sort solids by the number of faces or vertices.
Color the pictures that match the sentence.

1. I have 6 faces.

    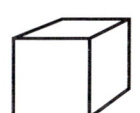

2. I have 5 faces.

    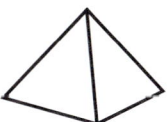

3. I have 8 vertices.

    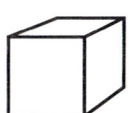

   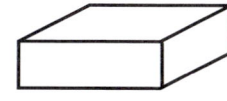 

4. I have 5 vertices.

Explain It • Daily Reasoning

How are a sphere and a rectangular prism different?

Practice and Problem Solving

Use solids.
Circle the pictures that match the sentence.

1. These solids have 6 faces.

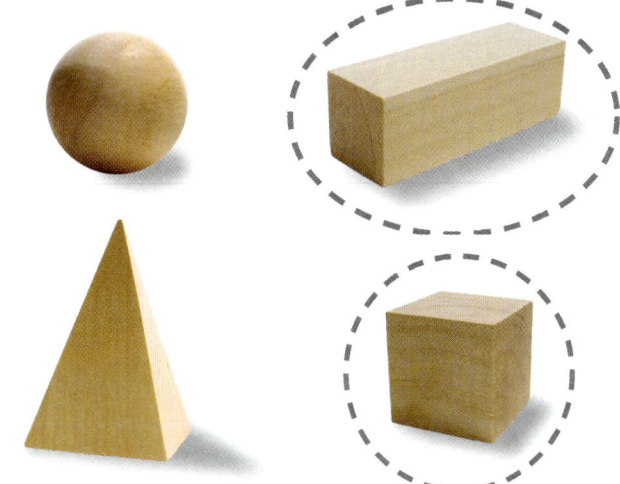

2. This solid has 5 vertices.

3. These solids have 8 vertices.

4. This solid has 5 faces.

Problem Solving

Logical Reasoning

5. Draw the solid that solves the riddle.

I am curved.

I am shaped like a beach ball.

 **Write About It** • Find 5 cubes in the classroom. Describe them.

HOME ACTIVITY • Find objects that are shaped like the solids on this page. Have your child count the faces of each object.

Name _____

Plane Shapes on Solid Figures

Vocabulary
circle
square
triangle
rectangle

Explore

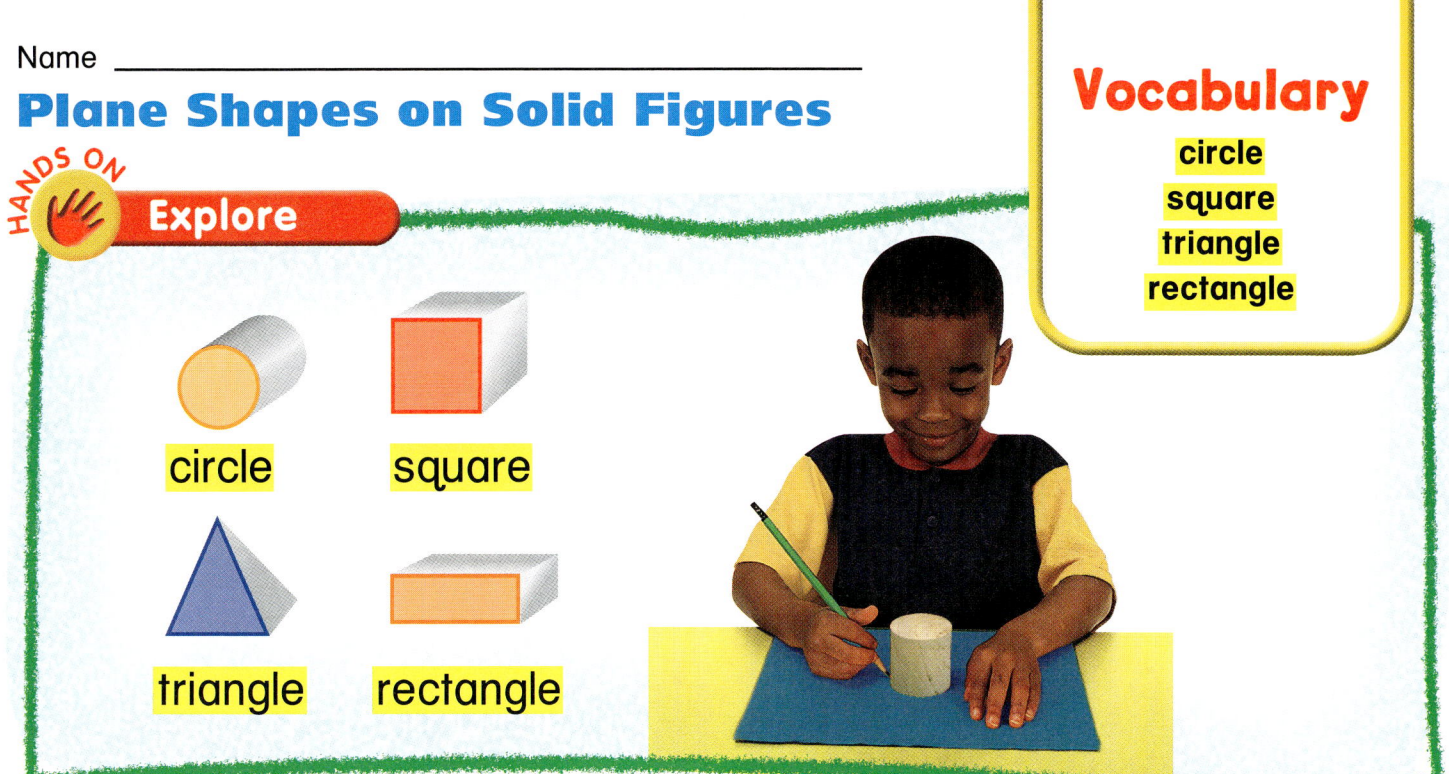

Connect

Use solids. Trace around each one.
Write the name of the shape you drew.

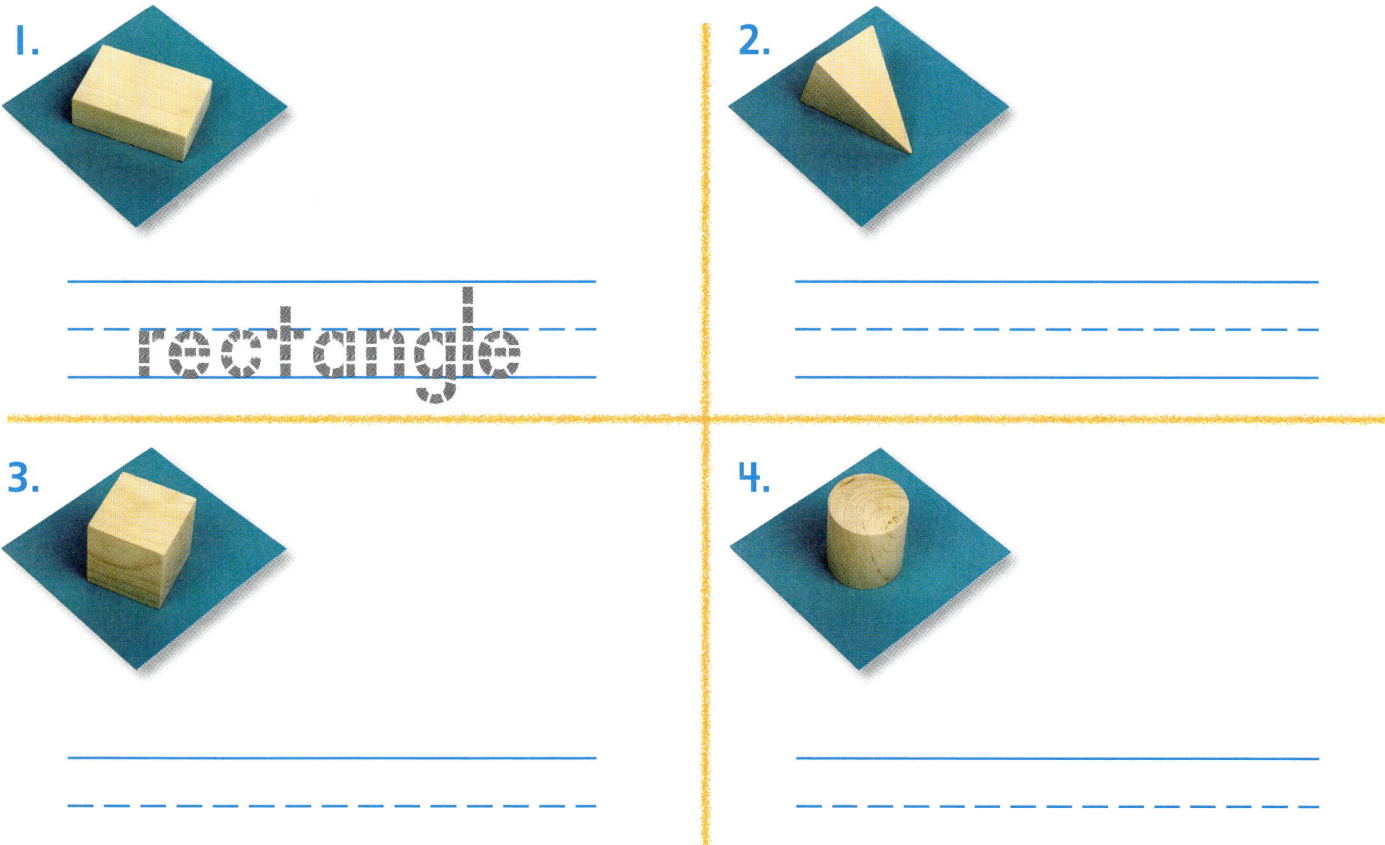

1. rectangle
2. _____
3. _____
4. _____

Explain It • Daily Reasoning

What two shapes can you trace from this pyramid?

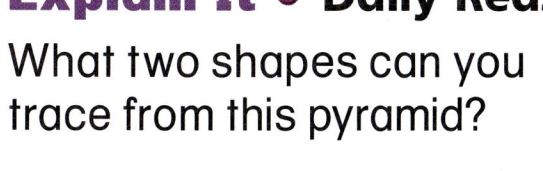

Chapter 15 • Solid Figures and Plane Shapes

two hundred fifty-five **255**

Practice and Problem Solving

Draw a house.
Use at least one ▭, one ◯, one △, and one ☐.

1. Color ▭ 🖍️(orange).
2. Color ◯ 🖍️(yellow).
3. Color △ 🖍️(blue).
4. Color ☐ 🖍️(green).

Problem Solving
Visual Thinking

5. Draw a small rectangle.

6. Draw a large triangle.

 Write About It • Find objects in the classroom that have faces shaped like triangles, circles, squares, and rectangles. Trace and label the faces.

HOME ACTIVITY • Gather some objects that are solid figures, such as a box and a can. Have your child place each on a sheet of paper, trace the faces and name the shape he or she drew.

Name _____

Sort and Identify Plane Shapes

Explore — HANDS ON

Vocabulary
side
vertex
vertices

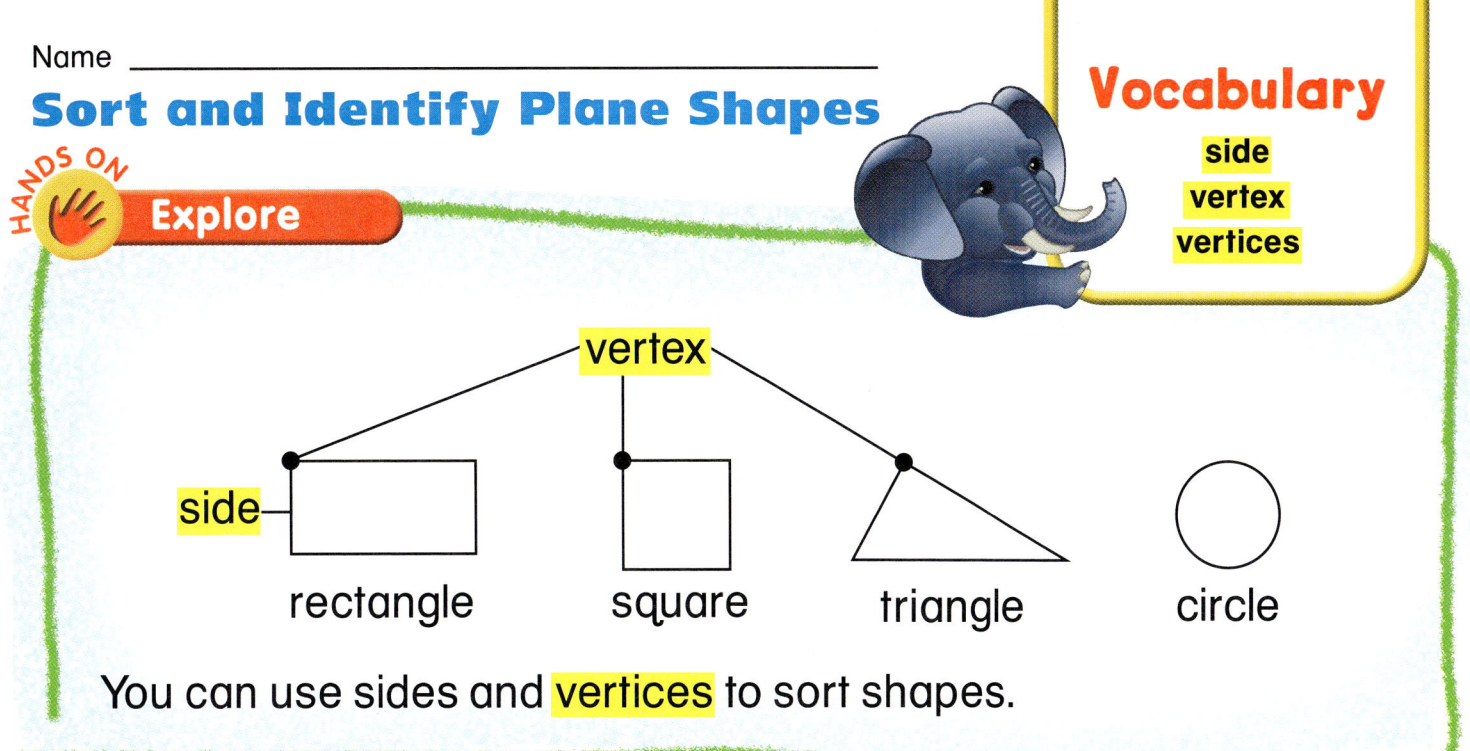

You can use sides and vertices to sort shapes.

Connect

Use shapes. Sort by the number of sides and vertices. Draw the shapes. Write the names.

1. Find a shape with 4 sides and 4 vertices.

   rectangle

2. Find a different shape with 4 sides and 4 vertices.

   _____

3. Find a shape with 0 vertices.

   _____

4. Find a shape with 3 sides and 3 vertices.

   _____

Explain It • Daily Reasoning

How are a rectangle and a square alike?

Chapter 15 • Solid Figures and Plane Shapes

Practice and Problem Solving

Use to trace each side.
Use 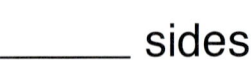 to circle each vertex.
Write how many sides and vertices there are.

1.
   _4_ sides
   _4_ vertices
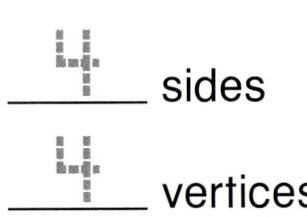

2.
   ____ sides
   ____ vertices

3.
   ____ sides
   ____ vertices
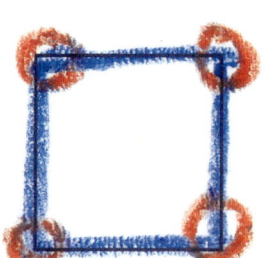

4.
   ____ sides
   ____ vertices
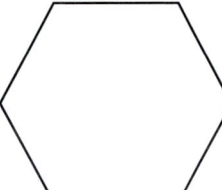

5.
   ____ sides
   ____ vertices

6.
   ____ sides
   ____ vertices
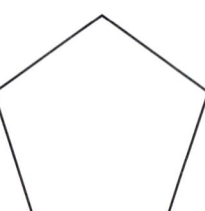

Problem Solving
Visual Thinking

7. Draw one line inside each shape to make 2 triangles.

   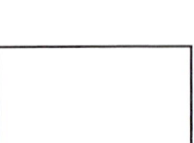 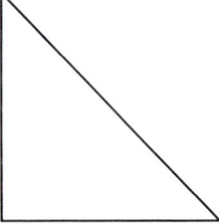

Write About It • Draw a shape that has 4 vertices. Draw two lines inside the shape to make 4 triangles.

 **HOME ACTIVITY** • Ask your child to draw a shape that has 3 sides and 3 vertices (triangle). Ask your child to draw a shape that has 4 sides and 4 vertices (rectangle or square).

Name _____

Problem Solving Strategy
Make a Model

How many make a ?

UNDERSTAND

What do you need to find out?

Read the question again.

PLAN

How can you solve the problem?

Use pattern blocks to make a model.

SOLVE

Write how many you use.

  make a  .

CHECK

How do you know that your answer is correct?

Cover the with to check.

Use pattern blocks to make a model.
Draw to show your model.
Write how many pattern blocks you use.

1. How many make a  ?

_____

Chapter 15 • Solid Figures and Plane Shapes

two hundred fifty-nine **259**

Problem Solving Practice

Use pattern blocks to make a model.
Draw to show your model.
Write how many pattern blocks you use.

Keep in Mind!
Understand
Plan
Solve
Check

1. How many 🔷 make a ⬡ ?

   _____ 🔷

2. How many  🔺 make a 🔷 ?

   _____ 🔺

3. How many  🔺 make a ⬢ ?

   _____ 🔺

4. How many 🔺 and 🔷 make a ⬡ ?

   _____ 🔺 and _____ 🔷

HOME ACTIVITY • Have your child explain how he or she figured out Exercises 1–4.

Name _____

Extra Practice

Use solids to sort.

1. Color each solid that will roll.
   Circle the solids that have 6 faces.
   Draw a line under the solid that has 5 vertices.

2. Use 🖍️ to color the rectangle.
   Use 🖍️ to color the triangle.

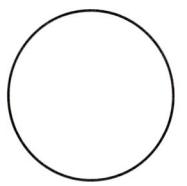 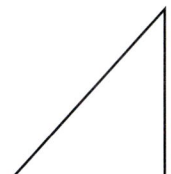 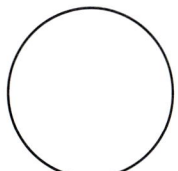 

Write how many sides and vertices there are.

3. _____ sides

   _____ vertices

4. _____ vertices

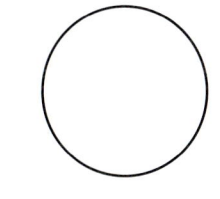

Problem Solving

Use pattern blocks to make a model.
Draw to show your model.
Write how many pattern blocks you use.

5. How many ▲ make a ♦ ?

   _____ ▲

Chapter 15 • Solid Figures and Plane Shapes

two hundred sixty-one **261**

Name _____

✓ Review/Test

Concepts and Skills

Use solids to sort.

1. Color each solid that will stack.
   Circle the solid that has 5 faces.
   Draw a line under the solids that
   have 8 vertices.

2. Use  to color the circle.
   Use  to color the square.

 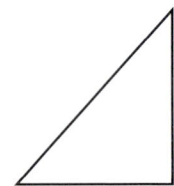 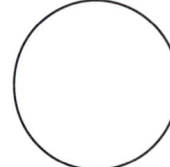 

Write how many sides and vertices there are.

3. _____ sides

   _____ vertices

4. _____ sides

   _____ vertices

   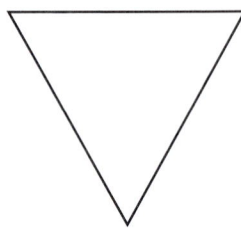

Problem Solving

Use pattern blocks to make a model.
Draw to show your model. Write how
many pattern blocks you use.

5. How many ◆ and ▲ make ?

   _____ ◆ and _____ ▲

262 two hundred sixty-two

Name _____

Standardized Test Prep
Chapters 1–15

Choose the answer for questions 1–5.

1. Which did the fewest children choose?

Fruits We Like				
🍎 apples	🍎	🍎	🍎	
🍌 bananas	🍌	🍌		
🍒 cherries	🍒	🍒	🍒	🍒

○ apples   ○ cherries

○ bananas   ○ grapes

2. Which solid has 6 faces and stacks?

○   ○   ○   ○

3. How many faces are on a ?

○ 1   ○ 6
○ 4   ○ 8

4. Which shape is a circle?

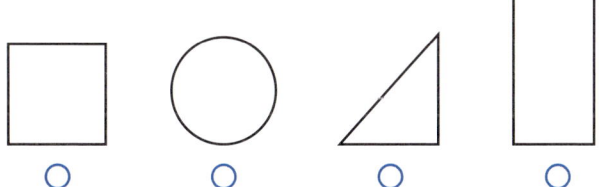
○   ○   ○   ○

5. Which shape has 3 sides and 3 vertices?

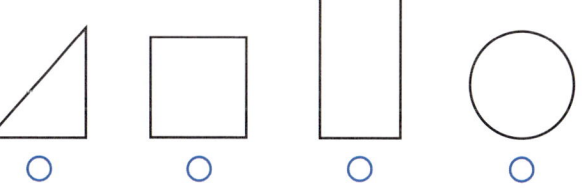
○   ○   ○   ○

Show What You Know

6. Use  and .

How many ▲ make a ▰?

Draw a picture to explain.

____ ▲

Chapter 15   two hundred sixty-three **263**

Name _____

MATH GAME

Make That Shape

Play with a partner.

You will need

6 ⬡   6 ♦
12 ▲   4 ⬠

1. Each player puts 3 ⬡ in a row.
2. Spin the 🎯. 
3. Take 1 pattern block of that shape.
4. If you can, fit it on a ⬡. If you can not fit it, put it back.
5. The first player to cover all 3 ⬡ wins.

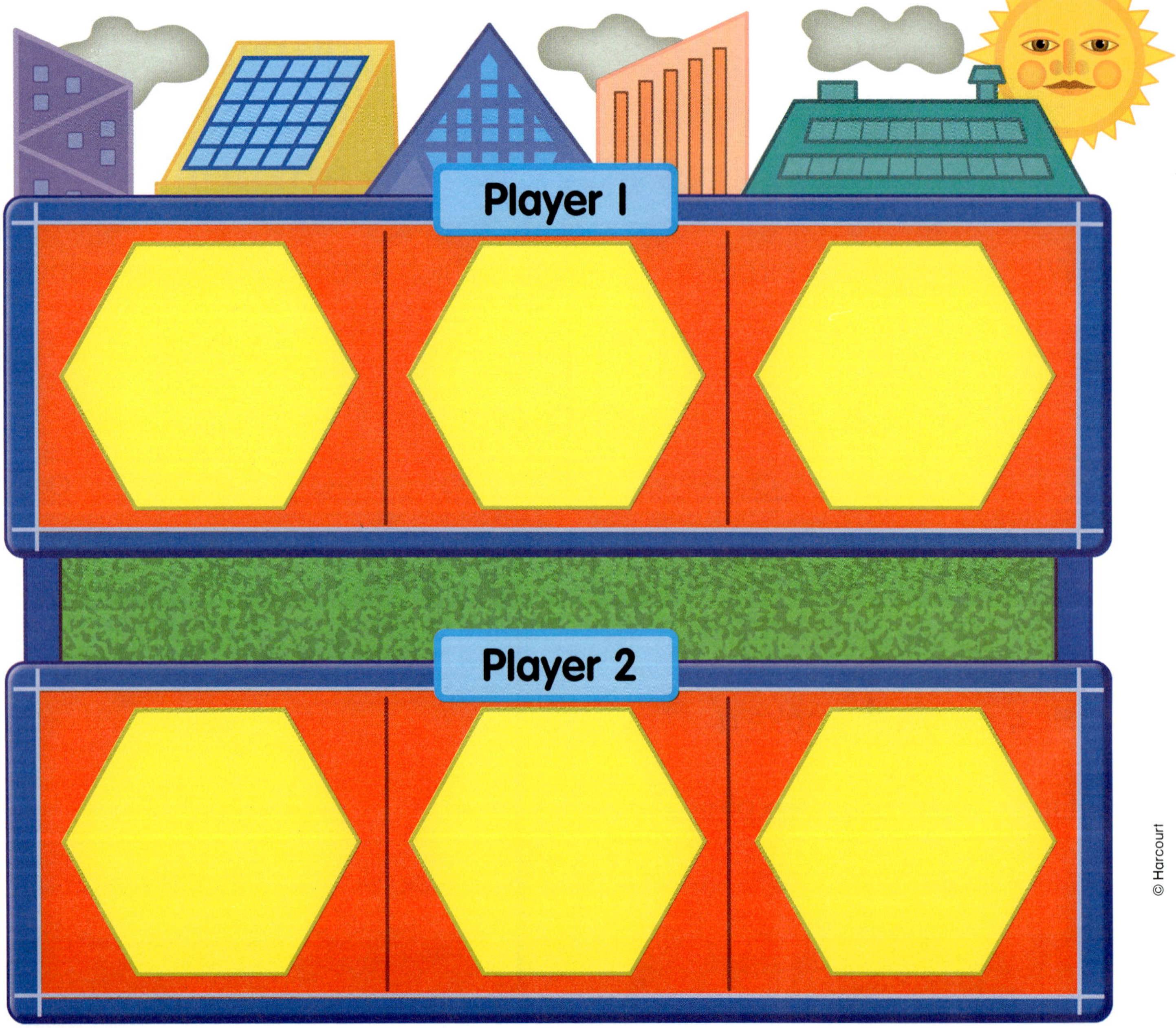

Player 1

Player 2

264 two hundred sixty-four

CHAPTER 16 Spatial Sense

FUN FACTS

Butterflies have two sides that look alike.

Theme: On the Move

Name _____

✓ Check What You Know

Plane Shapes in Different Positions

Color the triangles blue. Color the squares red. Color the rectangles orange.

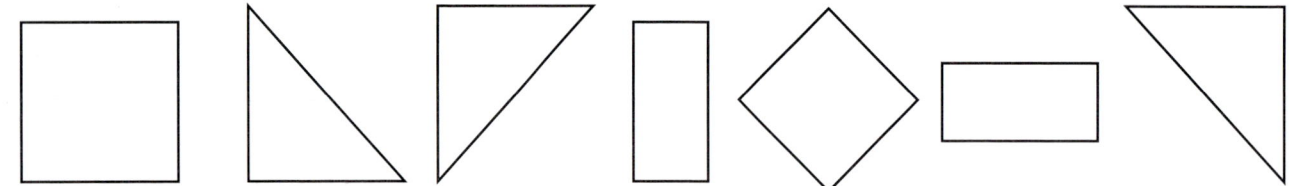

Above, Below, Over, Under

Circle the bird that is above the plane. Mark an X on the bird that is below the plane. Draw the sun over the plane. Draw a cloud under the plane.

Read Simple Patterns

Copy the pattern. Use 2 colors.

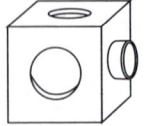 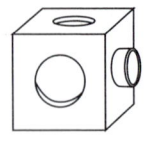 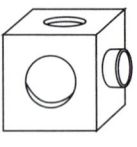 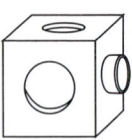 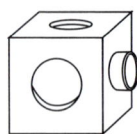 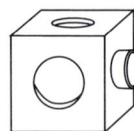 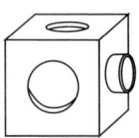 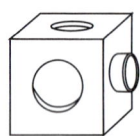

Name _____

Open and Closed

Vocabulary
open figure
closed figure

Learn

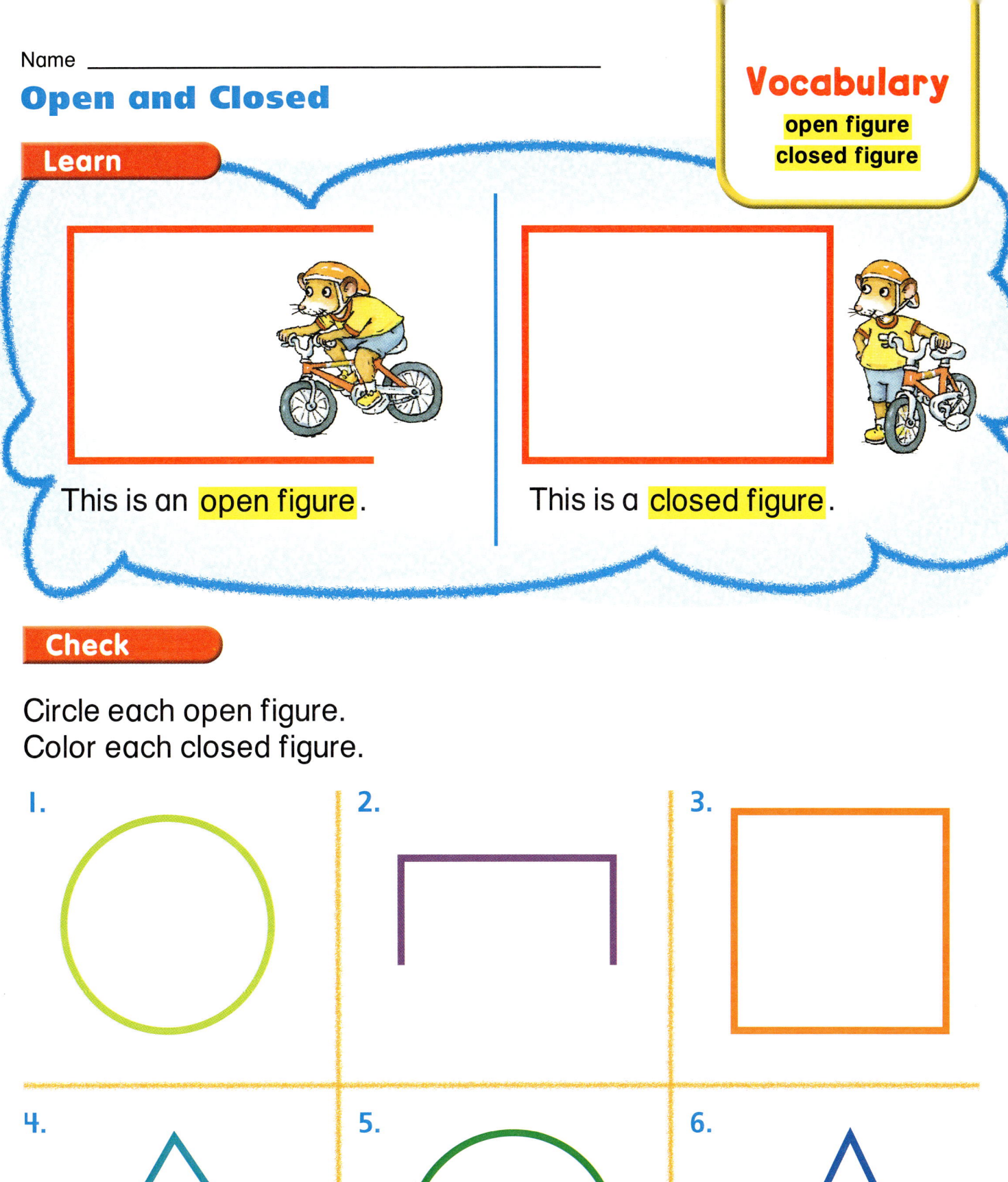

This is an **open figure**.

This is a **closed figure**.

Check

Circle each open figure.
Color each closed figure.

1.
2.
3.
4.
5.
6.

Explain It • Daily Reasoning

How are open and closed figures different?

Chapter 16 • Spatial Sense

two hundred sixty-seven **267**

Practice and Problem Solving

Circle each open figure.
Color each closed figure.

1.
2.
3.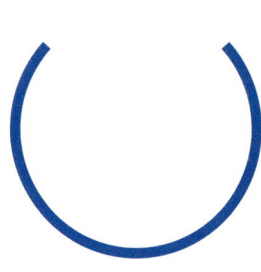
4.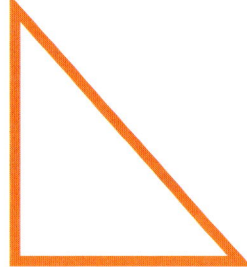
5.
6.
7.
8.

Problem Solving
Application

10. Draw a face. Use only closed figures.

 Write About It • Look at Exercise 10. Which closed figures did you use? Write about the face you drew.

HOME ACTIVITY • Have your child find three objects at home whose outlines are closed figures, for example, the outline of a window.

268 two hundred sixty-eight

Name _____

**Problem Solving Skill
Use a Picture**

Vocabulary
above   below
close by over
near   far
next to   beside
to the left of
to the right of

Follow the directions.

1. The is **above** the .

   Draw a ☀ above the .

2. The ⚽ is **below** the 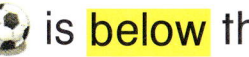.

   Draw a 🌷 below the .

3. The 🇺🇸 is **close by** the .

   Draw a 🚗 close by the .

4. The 🦋 is **over** the .

   Draw a 🐦 over the .

Chapter 16 • Spatial Sense

Problem Solving Practice

Follow the directions.

1. The is near the .

   Draw a  near the .

2. The  is far from the .

   Draw a far from the .

3. The is next to the .

   Draw a next to the .

4. The is beside the .

   Draw a  beside the .

5. The is to the left of the .

   Draw a to the left of the .

6. The  is to the right of the .

   Draw a to the right of the .

HOME ACTIVITY • Have your child use the words *far, next to,* and *beside* to describe the positions of objects in a room in your home. Then have your child use *above, below, over,* and *near*.

Name _____

Give and Follow Directions

Vocabulary
up   left
down   right

Learn

From **Start**, go right 3.
Go up 2.
Where are you?

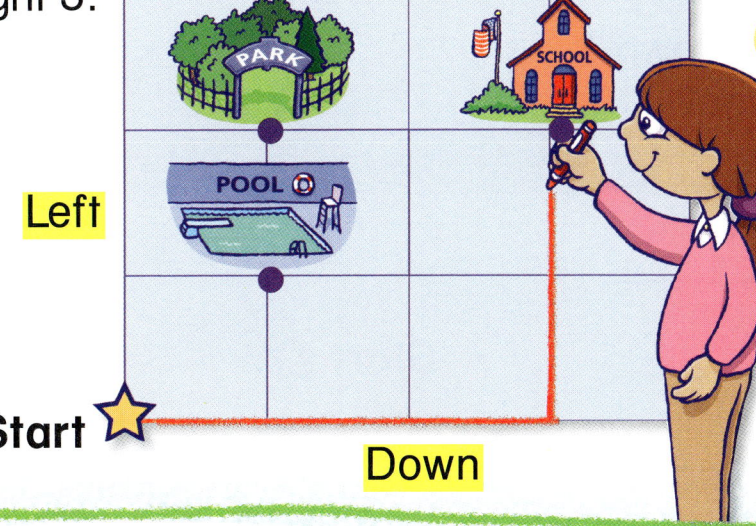

Check

Follow the directions in order.
Draw the path. Write the place.

1. Go down 1. Go left 4.
   Where are you?

   _____
   _____
   _____

2. Go right 2. Go up 1. Go right 2.
   Go up 1. Where are you?

   _____
   _____
   _____

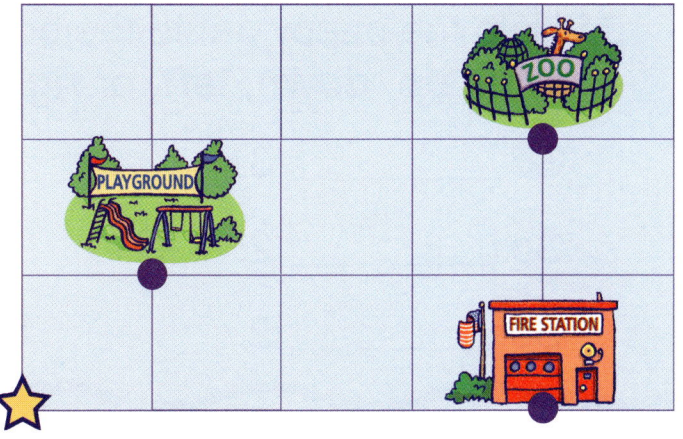

Explain It • Daily Reasoning

How could you go from the
playground to the zoo? Is there
more than one way? Explain.

Chapter 16 • Spatial Sense two hundred seventy-one **271**

Practice and Problem Solving

Follow the directions in order.
Draw the path. Write the place.

1. Go right 3. Go up 2.
   Go left 1. Go down 1.
   Where are you?

   _____

2. Go left 4. Go down 1.
   Go right 3. Go down 1.
   Where are you?

   _____

Problem Solving
Visual Thinking

3. Help the puppy get to the bones.
   Write **up**, **down**, **left**, or **right**.

   Go _____ 3.

   Go _____ 2.

   Go _____ 2.

 Write About It • Choose a place in your school. Make a map. Tell how to get there. Then draw the path.

🏠 **HOME ACTIVITY** • Ask your child to tell another way the puppy could get to the bones in Exercise 3.

Name _____

Symmetry

Vocabulary
line of symmetry

 **Explore**

1. Fold your paper.

2. Start at the fold. Draw a shape.

3. Cut along the line.

4. Open your shape.

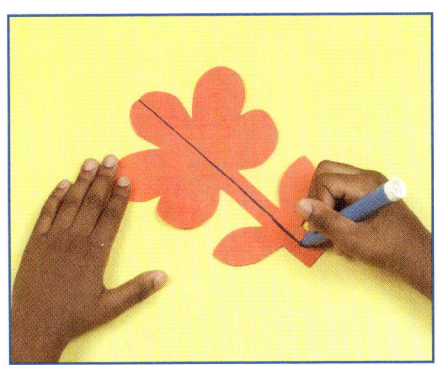
5. Draw a line down the middle.

The line down the middle is called a **line of symmetry**. It shows two parts that match.

Connect

Draw a line of symmetry to show two matching parts.

1.

2.

Explain It • Daily Reasoning

Fold a shape on the line of symmetry. How can you tell if the two parts match?

Chapter 16 • Spatial Sense

two hundred seventy-three **273**

Practice and Problem Solving

Draw a line of symmetry to show two matching parts.

1.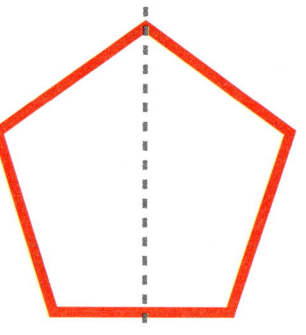

2.

3.

4.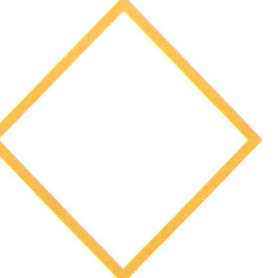

5.

6.

7.

8.

9.

Problem Solving
Visual Thinking

10. Draw a different line of symmetry on each square.

Write About It • Look at Exercise 10. Hold a mirror on each line of symmetry. Write about what you see.

 HOME ACTIVITY • Find objects that are symmetrical. Have your child trace the line of symmetry of each with a finger.

274 two hundred seventy-four

Name _____

Slides and Turns

Vocabulary: slide, turn

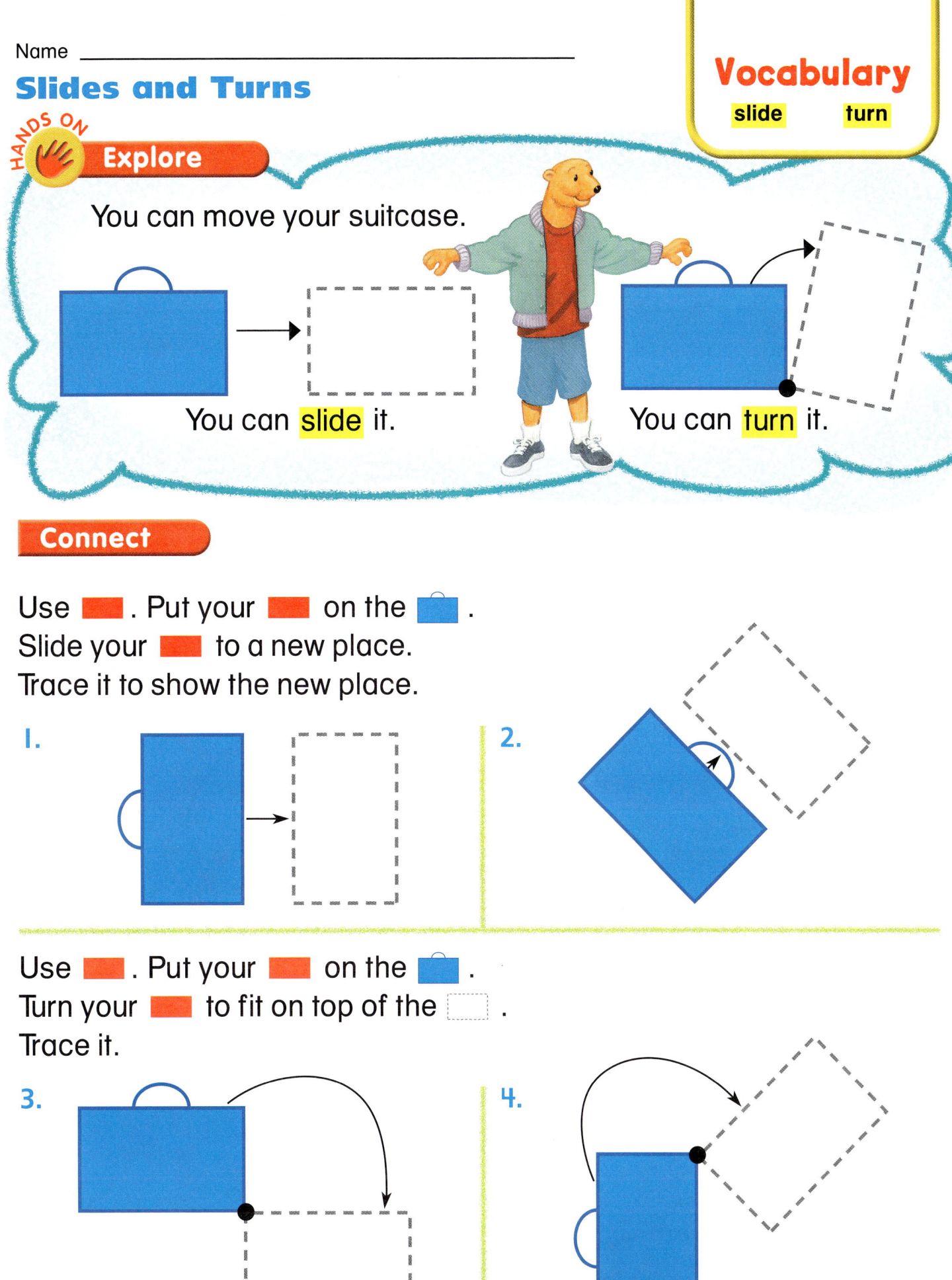

Explore

You can move your suitcase.

You can **slide** it.   You can **turn** it.

Connect

Use ▬. Put your ▬ on the ▬.
Slide your ▬ to a new place.
Trace it to show the new place.

1.
2.

Use ▬. Put your ▬ on the ▬.
Turn your ▬ to fit on top of the ☐.
Trace it.

3.
4.

Explain It • Daily Reasoning

How is a slide different from a turn?

Chapter 16 • Spatial Sense   two hundred seventy-five **275**

Practice and Problem Solving

Circle **slide** or **turn** to name the move.

1.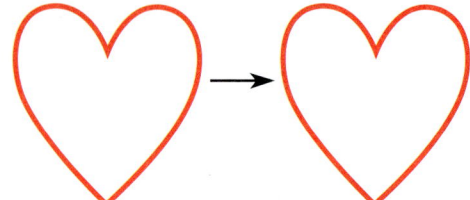

   slide   turn

2.

   slide   turn

3.

   slide   turn

4.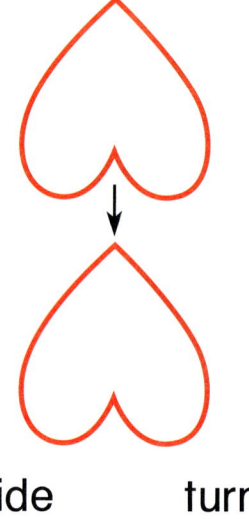

   slide   turn

Problem Solving
Application

5. Marie drew this train. Draw what it looks like to slide the train to the right.

Write About It • Look at Exercise 5. Write about how you moved the train. Use the word **slide**.

 HOME ACTIVITY • Gather items with simple shapes, such as boxes and pot lids. Ask your child to slide a certain item. Then ask your child to turn a different item. Repeat.

Name _____

Extra Practice

Draw the path. Draw the shape.

1. Go down 2. Go right 1.

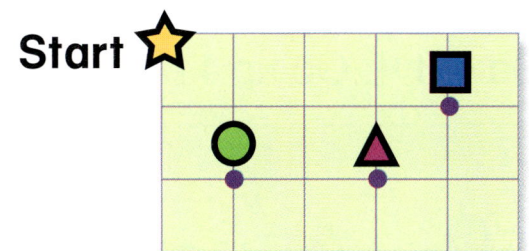

Where are you? _____

2. Go left 2. Go up 1.

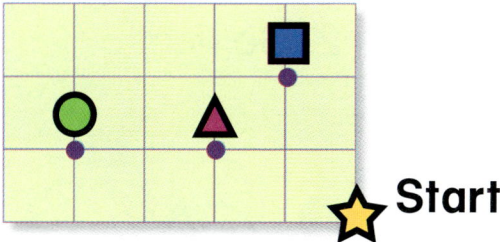

Where are you? _____

Draw a line of symmetry to show two matching parts.

3.

4.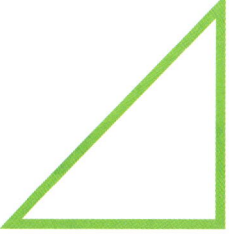

Circle **slide** or **turn** to name the move.

5.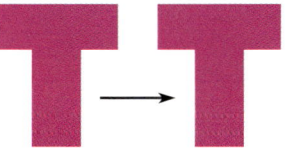

slide   turn

6.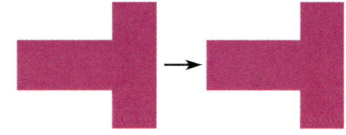

slide   turn

7.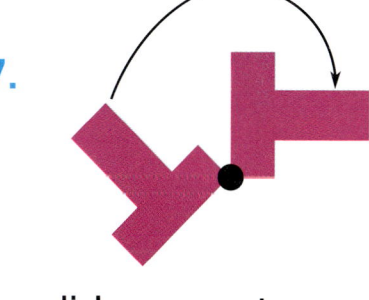

slide   turn

Problem Solving

Follow the directions.

8. Draw a above the .

9. Draw a beside the .

10. Draw a near the .

Chapter 16 • Spatial Sense   two hundred seventy-seven **277**

Name _____

✓ Review/Test

Concepts and Skills

Draw the path. Draw the shape.

1. Go down 2. Go right 3.

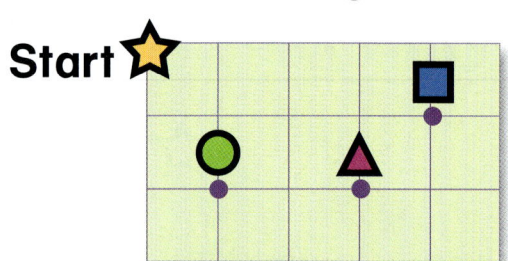

Where are you? _____

2. Go left 4. Go up 1.

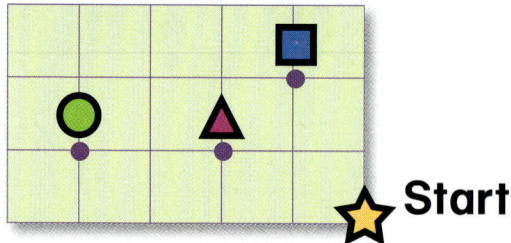

Where are you? _____

Draw a line of symmetry to show two matching parts.

3.

4.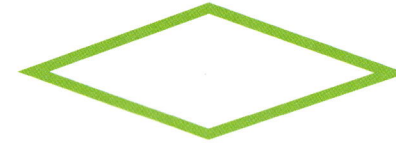

Circle **slide** or **turn** to name the move.

5.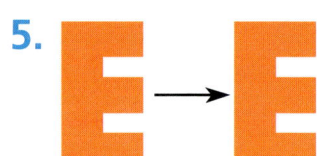

slide   turn

6.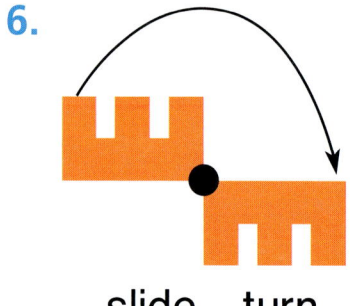

slide   turn

7.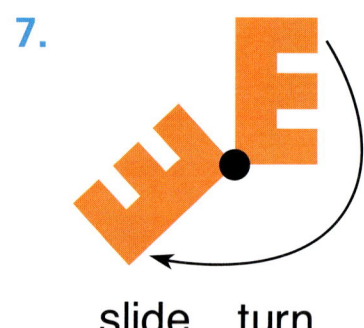

slide   turn

Problem Solving

Follow the directions.

8. Draw ⭐ over the 🚢.

9. Draw a 🐟 below the 🚢.

10. Draw a 🛟 to the left of the 🚢.

278 two hundred seventy-eight

Name _____

Standardized Test Prep
Chapters 1–16

1.

Go left 1. Go down 3.
Where are you?

○   ○   ○   ○

2. Which shows a slide?

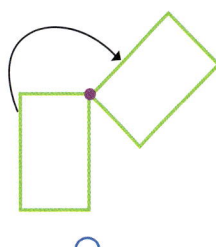   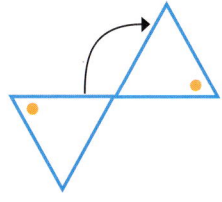
○   ○

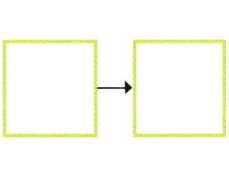   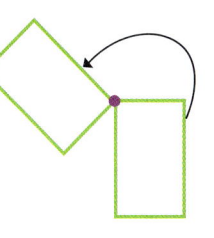
○   ○

3. Which shape does not have a line of symmetry?

   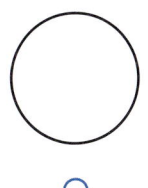   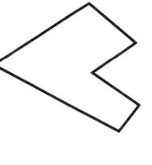   
○   ○   ○   ○

Show What You Know

4.

Draw a 🔴 next to the 🛝 .
Draw a 🐦 over the ⛓ .
Draw a 🌼 close by the 🛒 .
Draw a 🧒 to the left of the 🧑 .

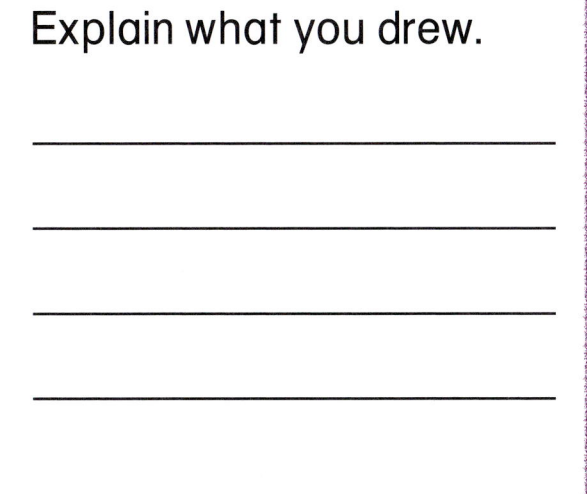

Explain what you drew.

_____
_____
_____
_____

Name _____

MATH GAME

On the Map

Play with a partner.

You will need

2

1. Put your 🎯 on HOME.
2. Spin the 🎡.
3. Move 1 or 2 spaces in that direction.
4. If you can not move 1 or 2 spaces in that direction, your turn is over.
5. The first player to get to SCHOOL wins.

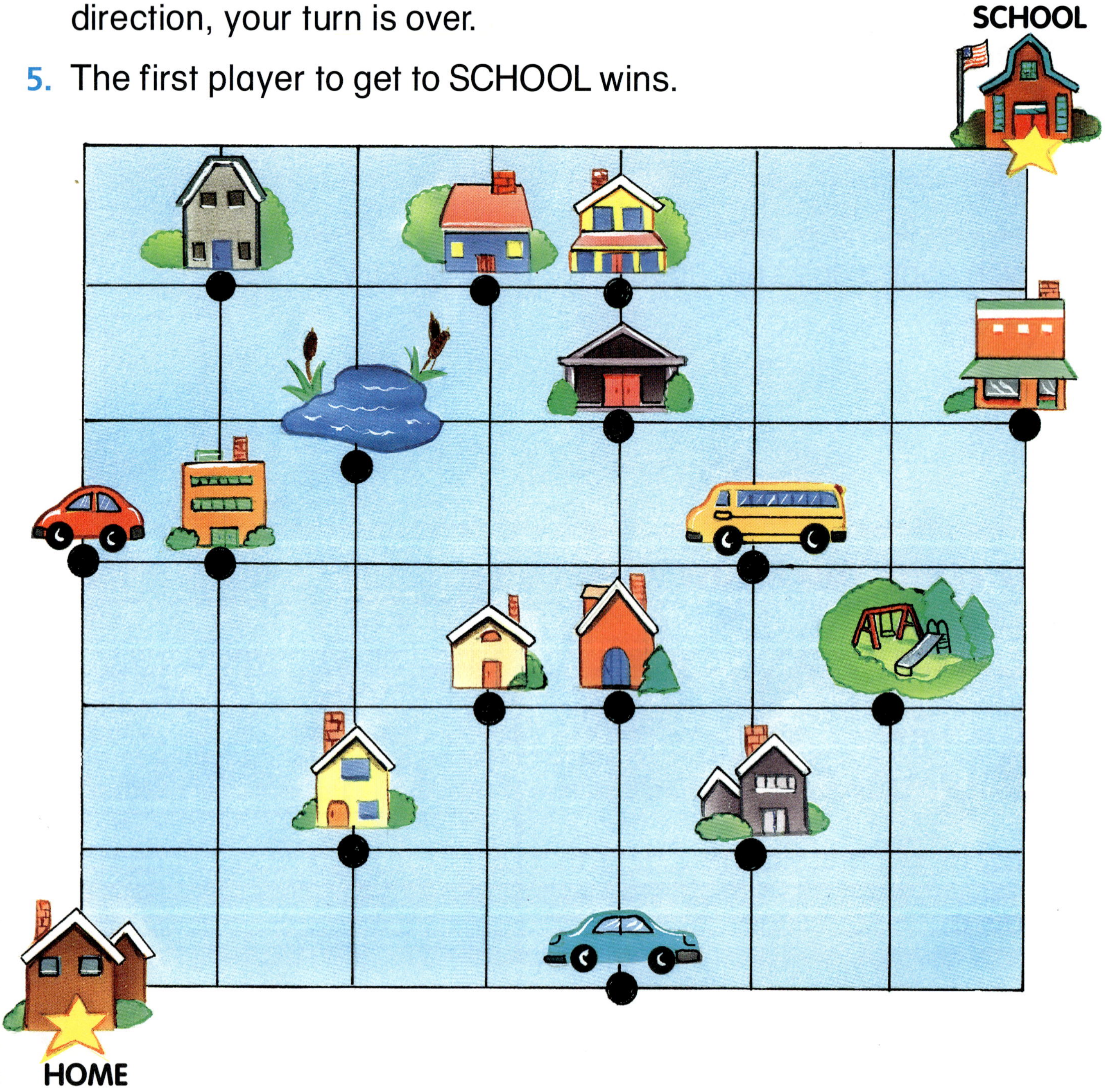

Name _____

Algebra: Make New Patterns

HANDS ON Explore

Use the same shapes to make a different pattern. Draw your new pattern.

Connect

1.

2.

3.

Explain It • Daily Reasoning

How are your patterns the same as the ones shown? How are they different?

Chapter 17 • Patterns

Practice and Problem Solving

Use the same shapes to make a different pattern. Draw your new pattern.

1.

2.

3.

Problem Solving
Logical Reasoning

4. Find the pattern. Draw what comes next.

 **Write About It** • Use ➡ →. Make your own pattern.

🏠 **HOME ACTIVITY** • Have your child arrange objects in a pattern and then explain the pattern to you.

288 two hundred eighty-eight

Name _____

Problem Solving Skill
Correct a Pattern

Find the mistake in the pattern.

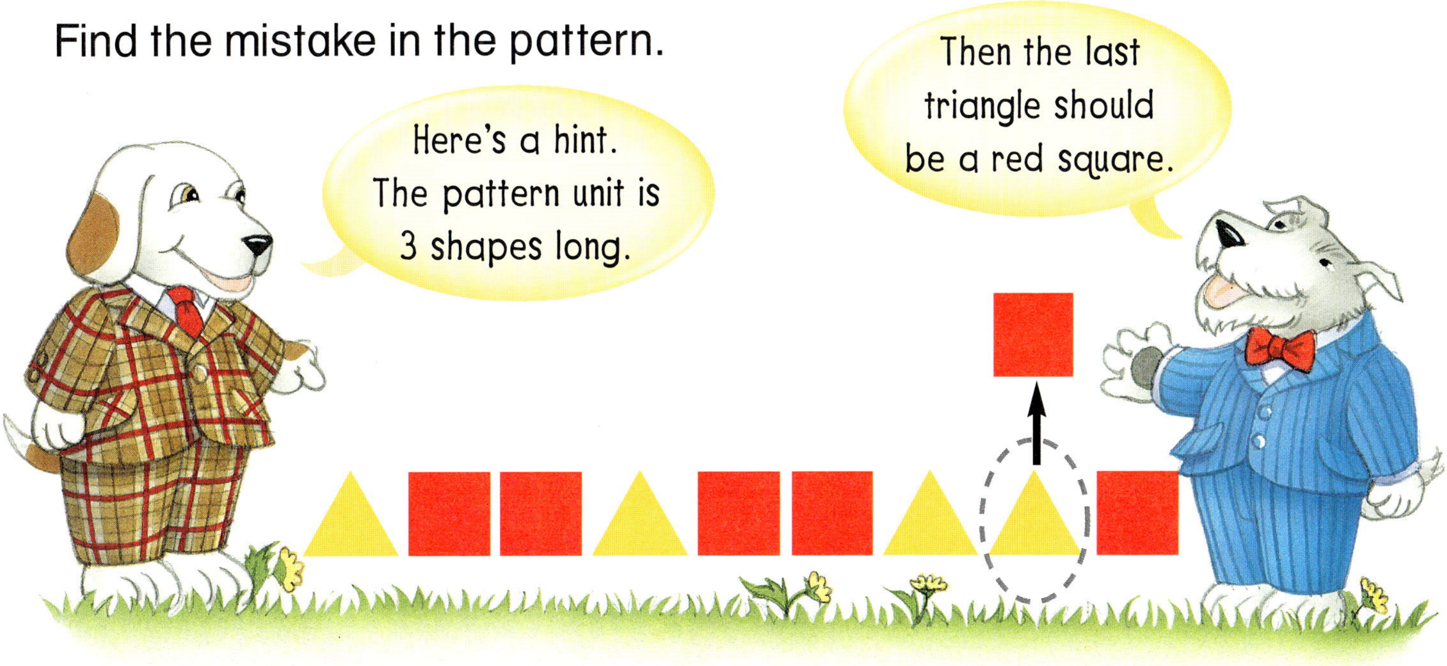

Each pattern unit is 3 shapes long.
Find the pattern.
Circle the mistake. Draw the correct shape.

1. 
2. 
3. 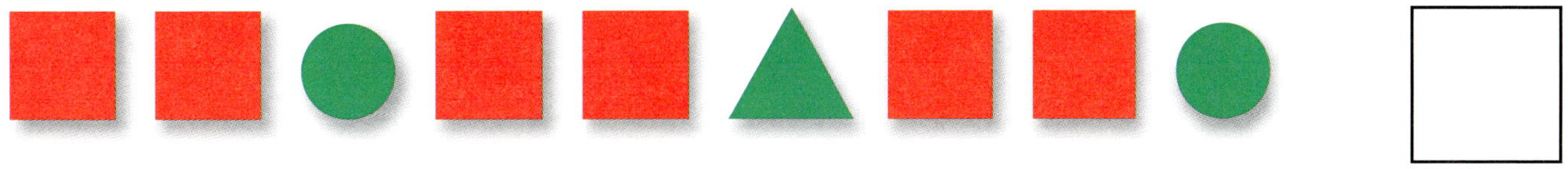
4. 
5.

Chapter 17 • Patterns

Problem Solving Practice

Find the pattern.
Circle the mistake.
Draw the correct shape.

Each pattern unit is 3 shapes long.

1.
2. 
3. 
4. 
5. 
6. 
7. 
8.

HOME ACTIVITY • Arrange objects in a pattern. Change one of the objects so that there is a mistake in the pattern. Have your child find and correct the mistake.

290 two hundred ninety

Name _____

Problem Solving Skill
Transfer Patterns

You can show the same pattern in a different way.

Use shapes to show the same pattern.
Draw the shapes.

1.

2.

3.

Chapter 17 • Patterns

Problem Solving Practice

Use shapes to show the same pattern.
Draw the shapes.

1.

2.

3.

4.

HOME ACTIVITY • Arrange objects in a pattern. Have your child use different objects to show the same pattern.

292 two hundred ninety-two

Name _____

Extra Practice

Find the pattern. Then color to continue it.

1.    2.    3.

4. Circle the pattern unit.

5. Use the same shapes to make a different pattern. Draw your new pattern.

Problem Solving

Find the pattern.
Circle the mistake. Draw the correct shape.

Each pattern unit is 3 shapes long.

6.

7.

Chapter 17 • Patterns

two hundred ninety-three **293**

Review/Test

Concepts and Skills

Find the pattern. Then color to continue it.

1.
2.
3.

4. Circle the pattern unit.

5. Use the same shapes to make a different pattern. Draw your new pattern.

Problem Solving

6. Use shapes to show the same pattern. Draw the shapes.

Name _____

⭐ Standardized Test Prep
Chapters 1–17

Choose the answer for questions 1–3.

1. Which shows the right way to continue the pattern?

2. Find the pattern unit. Then find the mistake. Which shape will correct the mistake?

3. How many faces are on a 🟨 ?

    2   5   6   7
    ○   ○   ○   ○

Show What You Know

4. Use different shapes to show the same pattern. Draw and explain your new pattern.

Chapter 17   two hundred ninety-five **295**

MATH GAME

Pattern Play

Play with a partner.

1. Spin the 🎡. Take any Attribute Links that match that shape or color.

2. Take turns until each player has three links.

3. Use these to make a pattern unit of shapes or colors. Draw your pattern unit. You will make your pattern on the table.

4. Spin again. If that shape or color is in your unit, use it in your pattern where you can.

5. The first player to repeat his or her pattern unit two times wins.

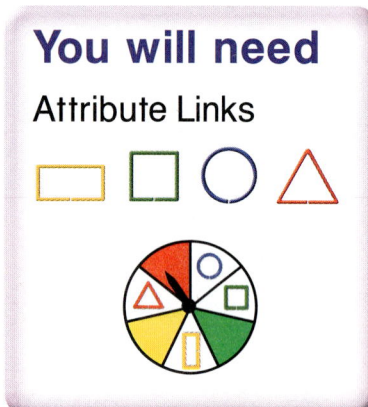

You will need

Attribute Links

Player 1's Pattern Unit

Player 2's Pattern Unit

CHAPTER 18
Addition Facts and Strategies

FUN FACTS

Each paw has 5 toes and 5 claws.

Theme: Wildlife

Name _____

✓ Check What You Know

Count On to Add

Circle the greater number.
Use the number line. Count on to add.

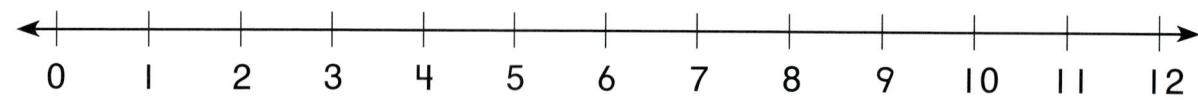

| 1. 8
+2 | 2. 3
+6 | 3. 1
+6 | 4. 7
+3 | 5. 2
+9 | 6. 2
+7 |

Doubles and Doubles Plus 1

Write the three sums.
Then circle the doubles fact.

| 7. 2
+2 | 2
+3 | 3
+2 | 8. 4
+4 | 4
+5 | 5
+4 |

Add 3 Numbers

Circle the two numbers you add first.
Write the sum.

| 9. 2
4
+4 | 10. 3
1
+6 | 11. 4
3
+4 | 12. 3
0
+5 | 13. 6
2
+1 | 14. 5
5
+2 |

298 two hundred ninety-eight   Use this page to review important skills needed for this chapter.

Name _____

Doubles and Doubles Plus 1

Vocabulary
doubles
doubles plus one

Explore

$$\begin{array}{r}8\\+8\\\hline 16\end{array}$$

8 + 8 = 16 is a **doubles** fact.
8 + 9 = 17 is a **doubles plus one** fact.

$$\begin{array}{r}8\\+9\\\hline 17\end{array}$$

Connect

Use 🟡. Write the sums.

1. $\begin{array}{r}5\\+5\\\hline\end{array}$ $\begin{array}{r}5\\+6\\\hline\end{array}$
2. $\begin{array}{r}2\\+2\\\hline\end{array}$ $\begin{array}{r}3\\+2\\\hline\end{array}$
3. $\begin{array}{r}7\\+7\\\hline\end{array}$ $\begin{array}{r}7\\+8\\\hline\end{array}$

4. $\begin{array}{r}0\\+0\\\hline\end{array}$ $\begin{array}{r}0\\+1\\\hline\end{array}$
5. $\begin{array}{r}6\\+6\\\hline\end{array}$ $\begin{array}{r}7\\+6\\\hline\end{array}$
6. $\begin{array}{r}3\\+3\\\hline\end{array}$ $\begin{array}{r}3\\+4\\\hline\end{array}$

7. $\begin{array}{r}4\\+4\\\hline\end{array}$ $\begin{array}{r}4\\+5\\\hline\end{array}$
8. $\begin{array}{r}8\\+8\\\hline\end{array}$ $\begin{array}{r}9\\+8\\\hline\end{array}$
9. $\begin{array}{r}9\\+9\\\hline\end{array}$ $\begin{array}{r}9\\+10\\\hline\end{array}$

Explain It • Daily Reasoning

What are two ways you could find the sum for 10 + 10?

Chapter 18 • Addition Facts and Strategies

Practice and Problem Solving

Write the sums.

1. $4 + 4 = \underline{8}$, so $5 + 4 = \underline{9}$

2. $7 + 7 = \underline{}$, so $7 + 8 = \underline{}$

3. $5 + 5 = \underline{}$, so $6 + 5 = \underline{}$

4. $9 + 9 = \underline{}$, so $9 + 10 = \underline{}$

5. $1 + 1 = \underline{}$, so $1 + 2 = \underline{}$

6. $3 + 3 = \underline{}$, so $4 + 3 = \underline{}$

7. $8 + 8 = \underline{}$, so $8 + 9 = \underline{}$

Problem Solving

Algebra

Write the missing numbers.

8. $5 + \square = 10$ $5 + \square = 11$

9. $2 + \square = 4$ $2 + \square = 5$

10. $6 + \square = 12$ $6 + \square = 13$

 Write About It • Look at Exercises 8, 9, and 10. Explain the pattern you see.

HOME ACTIVITY • Have your child tell you the doubles facts and the doubles plus one facts for 6, 7, 8, and 9 (6 + 6 = 12, 6 + 7 = 13; 7 + 7 = 14, 7 + 8 = 15; and so on).

Name _____

10 and More

Explore

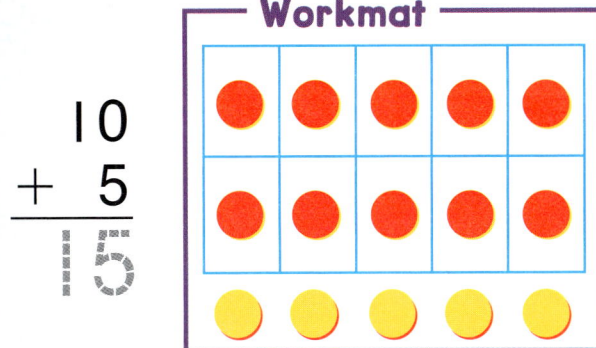

10
+ 5

15

"I can use a ten frame to show 10 + 5."

Connect

Use 🟡 and Workmat 7 to add.
Draw the 🟡. Write the sum.

1. 10
   + 7

   17

2. 10
   + 3

3. 10
   + 8

4. 10
   + 4

5. 10
   + 6

6. 10
   + 2

Explain It • Daily Reasoning

What happens when you add 10 to any number less than 10?

Chapter 18 • Addition Facts and Strategies

three hundred one **301**

Practice and Problem Solving

Write the sum.

1. 10 + 9 = 19

2. 10 + 4 =

3. 10 + 1 =

4. 10 + 6 =

5. 10 + 2 =

6. 10 + 7 =

7. 10 + 3 =

8. 10 + 5 =

9. 10 + 8 =

10. 10 + 0 =

Problem Solving
Logical Reasoning

Choose a way to solve.

11. Jan plants 18 flowers in two rows. She plants 10 in the first row. How many are in the second row?

_____ flowers

Write About It • Look at Exercise 11. Explain how a row of 10 helped you.

HOME ACTIVITY • Ask your child to tell the sums for 10 + 1 through 10 + 9 (10 + 1 = 11, 10 + 2 = 12, and so on).

Name _____

Make 10 to Add

Vocabulary
make a ten

 **Explore**   Find the sum for 9 + 5.

Show 9.
Then show 5.

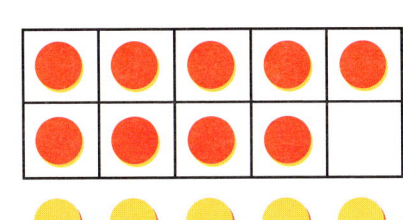

$\begin{array}{r}9\\+5\\\hline 14\end{array}$

Make a ten.
Move 1 counter into the ten frame.

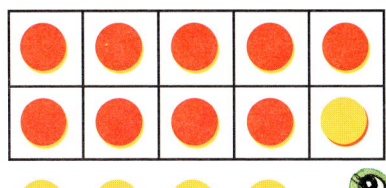

$\begin{array}{r}10\\+4\\\hline 14\end{array}$

Connect

Use 🟡 and Workmat 7.
Show the numbers and add. Then make a ten and add.

1. $\begin{array}{r}9\\+7\\\hline\end{array}$ 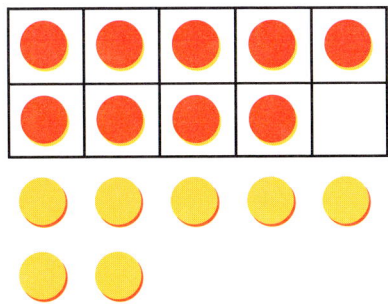 $\begin{array}{r}10\\+\ 6\\\hline\end{array}$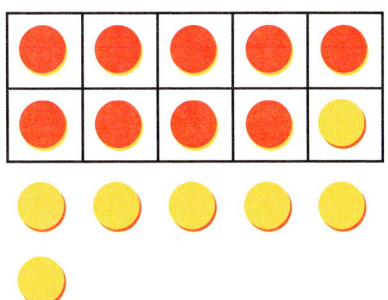

2. $\begin{array}{r}9\\+4\\\hline\end{array}$ 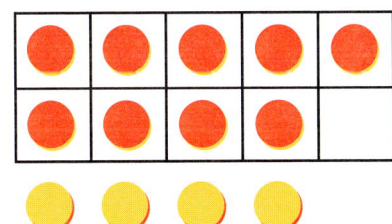 $\begin{array}{r}10\\+\ 3\\\hline\end{array}$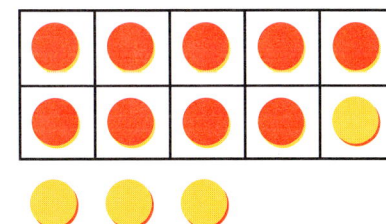

3. $\begin{array}{r}9\\+6\\\hline\end{array}$ 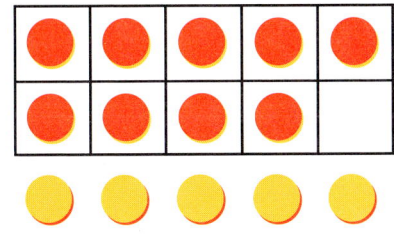 $\begin{array}{r}10\\+\ 5\\\hline\end{array}$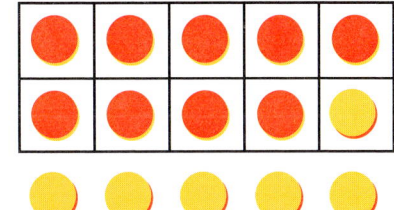

Explain It • Daily Reasoning

How do you know that 9 + 3 = 10 + 2?
Use 🟡 to prove your answer.

Chapter 18 • Addition Facts and Strategies

Practice and Problem Solving

Use 🟡 and Workmat 7.
Show the numbers and add. Then make a ten and add.

1. 9
   +9
   ──
   18

    10
   + 8
   ──
    18

2. 9
   +2

    10
   + 1

3. 9
   +8

    10
   + 7

Problem Solving
Mental Math

Solve in your head.
Draw a picture to check.

4. There were 9 pine cones on the ground. Then 5 more pine cones fell. How many pine cones were on the ground then?

_____ pine cones

Write About It • Look at Exercise 4.
Explain how to make a ten to add 9 + 5.

HOME ACTIVITY • Ask your child to tell the sums for 9 + 1 through 9 + 9 (9 + 1 = 10, 9 + 2 = 11, and so on).

Name _____

Use Make a 10

Explore (Hands On)

Find the sum for 7 + 4.

First show 7. Then show 4.
Fill up the ten frame to add.

```
  7
+ 4
----
 11
```

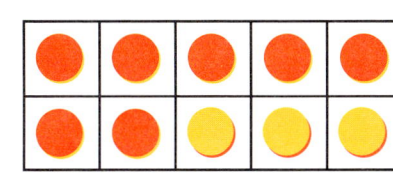

You made a ten and have 1 extra.
10 + 1 = 11

Connect

Use 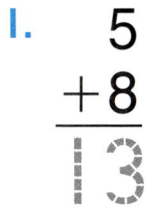 and Workmat 7 to add.
Start with the greater number.
Draw the 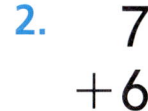. Write the sum.

1.
```
  5
+ 8
----
 13
```
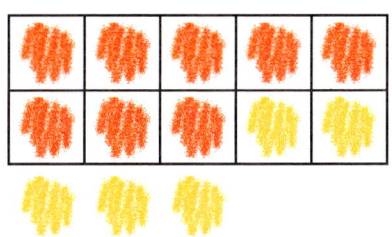

2.
```
  7
+ 6
```
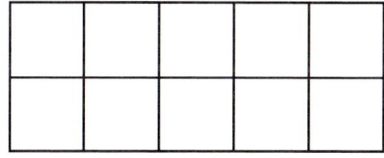

3.
```
  8
+ 4
```
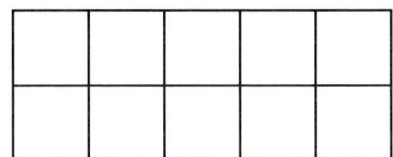

4.
```
  5
+ 6
```
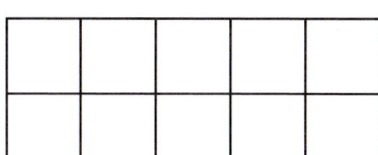

5.
```
  8
+ 7
```
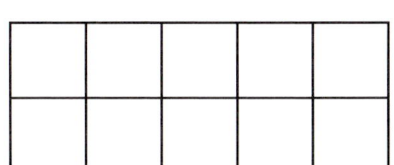

6.
```
  7
+ 5
```
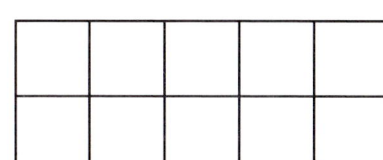

Explain It • Daily Reasoning

How do you make a ten to add two numbers?

Chapter 18 • Addition Facts and Strategies

Practice and Problem Solving

Use 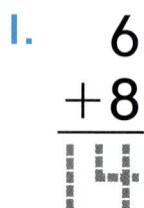 and Workmat 7 to add. Start with the greater number.

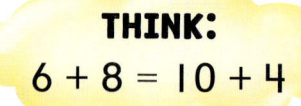
THINK:
6 + 8 = 10 + 4

1. 6
   +8
   ───
   14

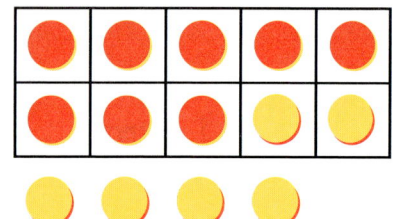

2. 9
  +6

3. 3
  +8

4. 5
  +7

5. 8
  +9

6. 8
  +5

7. 9
  +7

8. 4
  +7

9. 8
  +6

10. 3
   +9

11. 4
   +8

12. 5
   +9

13. 9
   +4

14. 6
   +7

15. 7
   +8

16. 7
   +9

17. 2
   +9

18. 6
   +5

19. 6
   +8

Problem Solving

Logical Reasoning

Choose a way to solve.

20. Josh needs to plant 15 seeds. He has 8 seeds. How many more seeds does he need?

    _____ more seeds

 **Write About It** • Look at Exercise 20. Complete the number sentence. 8 + ☐ = 10 + 5

🏠 **HOME ACTIVITY** • Ask your child to read a problem on this page and tell how to solve it by making a ten. For example, solve 8 + 4 by making it 10 + 2.

Name _____

Algebra: Add 3 Numbers

Learn

You can add three numbers in any order.

⑦
③
+ 4
___
14

7
③
+④
___
14

You can make a ten.
7 + 3 = 10
10 + 4 = 14

You can use doubles.
3 + 4 = 7
7 + 7 = 14

Check

Circle the numbers you add first.
Write the sum.

1. 2   2. 8   3. 9   4. 8   5. 4   6. 6
    7   4   3   3   7   5
   +3   +4   +1   +3   +3   +4
   ___   ___   ___   ___   ___   ___

7. 2   8. 2   9. 4   10. 8   11. 8   12. 4
    2   5   2   8   2   3
   +7   +5   +6   +1   +7   +4
   ___   ___   ___   ___   ___   ___

Explain It • Daily Reasoning

Look at Exercise 1. Add two different numbers first.
Did the sum change? Why or why not?

Chapter 18 • Addition Facts and Strategies

Practice and Problem Solving

Circle the numbers you add first. Write the sum.

1. 1
    (5)
   +(5)

    11

2. 8
    2
   +1
   ---

3. 6
    3
   +7
   ---

4. 1
    2
   +9
   ---

5. 8
    2
   +6
   ---

6. 1
    7
   +7
   ---

7. 4
    9
   +6
   ---

8. 9
    6
   +1
   ---

9. 3
    6
   +3
   ---

10. 4
    4
   +2
   ---

11. 8
    4
   +2
   ---

12. 3
    5
   +5
   ---

13. 6
    1
   +6
   ---

14. 8
    1
   +9
   ---

15. 5
    7
   +3

Problem Solving
Application

Draw a picture to solve.

16. Kim picks 3 pink flowers. Tod picks 7 yellow flowers. Chris picks 5 purple flowers. How many flowers in all do the children pick?

    _____ flowers

 Write About It • Look at Exercise 16. Explain how you could make a ten. How could that help you solve the problem?

 HOME ACTIVITY • Have your child use pennies to show how to add three numbers.

Name _____

Problem Solving Skill
Use Data from a Table

This table tells how many animals children saw at camp.

Animals	Number
chipmunks	6
rabbits	2
squirrels	4
deer	3

Use the table to answer the questions. Write a number sentence to solve.

1. How many deer and squirrels did they see?

   __7__ deer and squirrels   __3__ ⊕ __4__ ⊜ __7__

2. How many more chipmunks than deer did they see?

   _____ more chipmunks   ___ ◯ ___ ◯ ___

3. How many more deer than rabbits did they see?

   _____ more deer   ___ ◯ ___ ◯ ___

4. How many chipmunks and rabbits did they see?

   _____ chipmunks and rabbits   ___ ◯ ___ ◯ ___

5. How many small animals did they see in all?

   Find the numbers for small animals.

   _____ small animals   ___ ◯ ___ ◯ ___ ◯ ___

Chapter 18 • Addition Facts and Strategies   three hundred nine **309**

Problem Solving Practice

This table tells how many birds children saw at camp.

Birds	Number
owl	1
robins	5
blue jays	4
blackbirds	7

Use the table to answer the questions. Write a number sentence to solve.

1. How many robins and blue jays did they see in all?

   _____ robins and blue jays

2. How many more robins than owls did they see?

   _____ more robins

3. How many blackbirds and owls did they see in all?

   _____ blackbirds and owls

4. How many more blackbirds than robins did they see?

   _____ more blackbirds

5. How many birds did they see that were not blue?

   Find the numbers for birds that are not blue.

   _____ birds

HOME ACTIVITY • Ask your child to explain how he or she solved each problem.

Name _____

Extra Practice

Write the sum.

1. 3   3   2. 6   6   3. 5   5
  +3   +4   +6   +7   +5   +6

4. 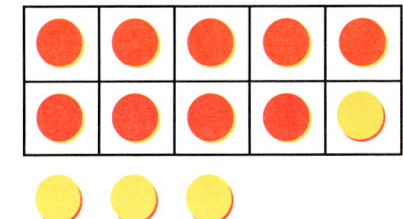   9
            +4

5. 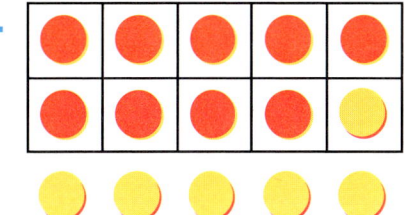   9
            +6

6. 8   7. 8   8. 2   9. 7   10. 6   11. 4
  +4   +8   +7   +7   +4   +5

12. 4   13. 7   14. 2   15. 4   16. 8   17. 3
   +4   +8   7   2   6   7
                  +3   +6   +1   +3

Problem Solving

This table tells how many animals children saw.
Use the table to answer the question.

18. How many animals did the children see in all?

_____ animals

Animals	Number
rabbits	3
deer	7
squirrels	4

Chapter 18 • Addition Facts and Strategies

Name _____

✓ Review/Test

Concepts and Skills

Write the sum.

1. 4   4
  +4 +5

2. 8   8
  +8 +9

3. 7   8
  +7 +7

4. 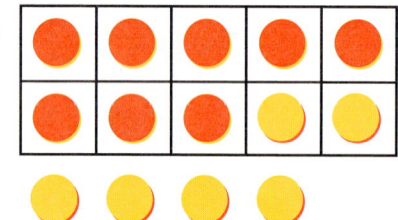   8
              +6

5. 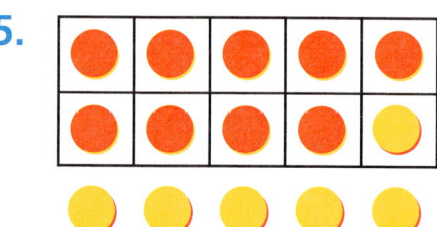   9
              +7

6. 9   7. 6   8. 5   9. 9   10. 7   11. 5
  +5   +6   +5   +9   +5   +6

12. 6   13. 6   14. 7   15. 3   16. 9   17. 4
   +7   +9   2   4   7   8
                  +2   +7   +1   +4

Problem Solving

This table tells how many animals children saw.
Use the table to answer the question.

18. How many animals did the children see in all?

___ ◯ ___ ◯ ___ ◯ ___

_____ animals

Animals	Number
chipmunks	6
rabbits	6
squirrels	4

Name _____

Standardized Test Prep
Chapters 1–18

Choose the answer for questions 1–5.

1. $7 + 7 = 14$, so $7 + 8 =$ ___?___

   14 ○   15 ○   16 ○   17 ○

2. Which shows the sum of $10 + 9$?

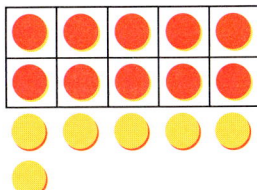 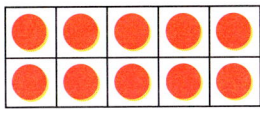 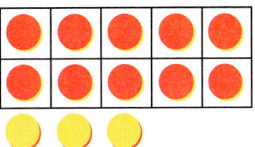 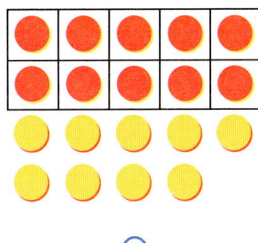

   ○   ○   ○   ○

3. The table shows how many vegetables the children picked.

   How many more cucumbers than beans did they pick?

   2 ○   4 ○   5 ○   8 ○

Vegetables Picked	
beans	8
cucumbers	12
tomatoes	5

4. $\begin{array}{r} 9 \\ 1 \\ +3 \\ \hline \end{array}$

    10 ○   12 ○   13 ○   15 ○

5. Which is the missing number?

   $8 + \square = 13$

   3 ○   5 ○   7 ○   8 ○

Show What You Know

6. Use the ten frame. Draw counters to explain how to make a ten to find the sum.

   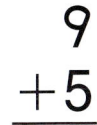 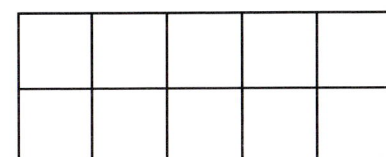

Chapter 18   three hundred thirteen **313**

MATH GAME

Ten Plus

Play with a partner.

1. Put your 🎮 at START.
2. Stack the [2] face down.
3. Start with 9. Take one number card.
4. Find the sum by making 10 first.
5. Say the number you add to 10 to get the sum.
6. Move your 🎮 that many spaces.
7. The first player to get to END wins.

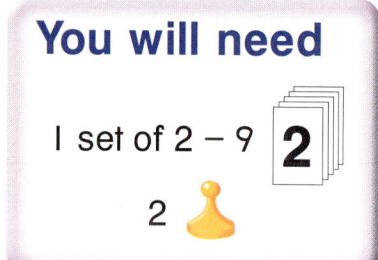

You will need

1 set of 2 – 9

2 🎮

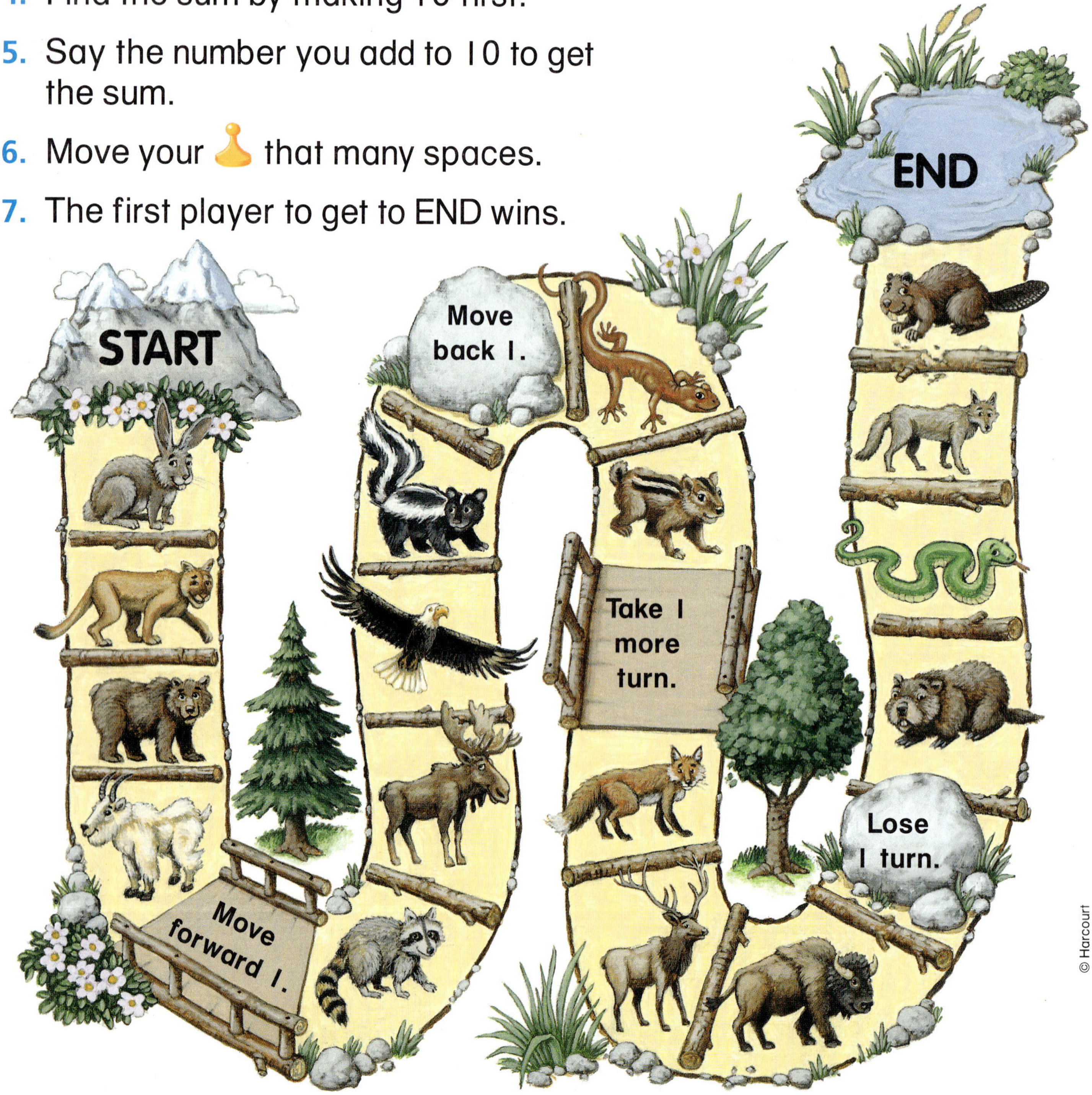

CHAPTER 19

Subtraction Facts and Strategies

FUN FACTS

Hibiscus grows in many shades of its 7 basic colors: red, yellow, blue, pink, white, purple, and orange.

Theme: In the Garden

Name _____

✓ Check What You Know

Count Back to Subtract

Count back to subtract. Write the difference.
You can use the number line to help.

1. 8 − 2
2. 9 − 1
3. 11 − 3
4. 7 − 1
5. 6 − 2
6. 11 − 2

7. 12 − 3
8. 10 − 1
9. 9 − 2
10. 8 − 3
11. 7 − 3
12. 6 − 1

13. 10 − 2
14. 6 − 3
15. 8 − 1
16. 7 − 2
17. 10 − 3
18. 9 − 3

Related Addition and Subtraction Facts to 12

Write each sum or difference.
Circle the related facts in each row.

19. 12 − 4 = ___
20. 12 − 6 = ___
21. 8 + 4 = ___

22. 5 + 7 = ___
23. 11 − 7 = ___
24. 12 − 5 = ___

25. 9 − 6 = ___
26. 9 − 3 = ___
27. 5 + 3 = ___

316 three hundred sixteen   Use this page to review important skills needed for this chapter.

Name _____

Use a Number Line to Count Back

Vocabulary
count back

Learn

You can use the number line to help you count back.

Start at 12.
Count back 3 spaces.
11, 10, 9

Find the difference for 12 − 3.

12 − 3 = __9__

Check

Count back to subtract. Write the difference.
Use the number line to help.

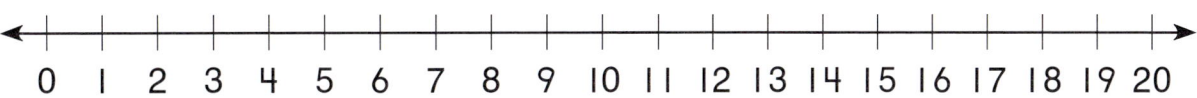

1. 9 − 2 = ____
2. 10 − 1 = ____
3. 8 − 3 = ____
4. 11 − 3 = ____
5. 7 − 1 = ____
6. 6 − 3 = ____
7. 8 − 2 = ____
8. 11 − 2 = ____
9. 10 − 3 = ____
10. 9 − 1 = ____

Explain It • Daily Reasoning

Pat drew this number line to find 10 − 2 and got 12. What mistake did she make?

Chapter 19 • Subtraction Facts and Strategies

three hundred seventeen **317**

Practice and Problem Solving

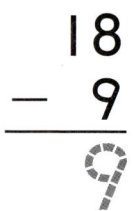
$$\begin{array}{r} 18 \\ -9 \\ \hline 9 \end{array}$$

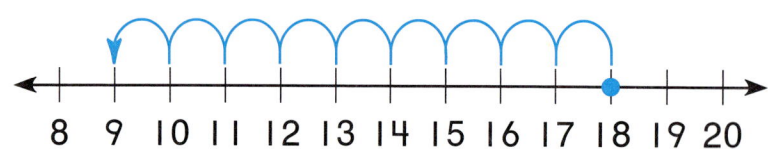

Use the number line to subtract.

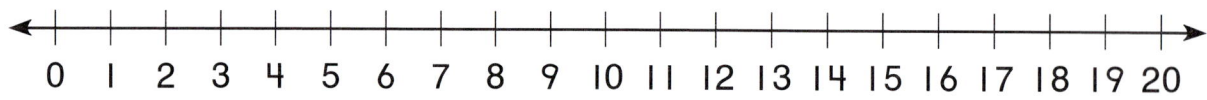

1. $20 - 10$
2. $13 - 6$
3. $17 - 9$
4. $14 - 5$
5. $11 - 3$
6. $16 - 9$

---

7. $15 - 8$
8. $18 - 9$
9. $11 - 2$
10. $12 - 4$
11. $14 - 6$
12. $13 - 5$

---

13. $16 - 7$
14. $10 - 2$
15. $12 - 3$
16. $16 - 8$
17. $15 - 9$
18. $17 - 8$

Problem Solving
Visual Thinking

19. Write the number sentence that tells about the number line.

    ___ ◯ ___ ◯ ___

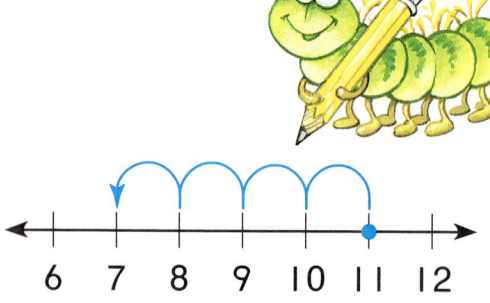

 Write About It • Look at Exercise 19. Explain how you counted on the number line.

🏠 **HOME ACTIVITY** • Ask your child to show how to subtract $18 - 9$ on the number line.

Name _____

Doubles Fact Families

Vocabulary
fact family

Learn

These facts use the same two numbers. Together, they make a doubles fact family.

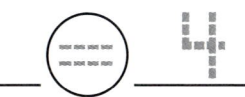

4 + 4 = __8__   __8__ ◯ __4__ ◯ __4__

Check

Write the sum for the doubles addition fact.
Write the subtraction fact that is in the same family.

1. 6 + 6 = ____   ____ ◯ ____ ◯ ____

2. 3 + 3 = ____   ____ ◯ ____ ◯ ____

3. 8 + 8 = ____   ____ ◯ ____ ◯ ____

4. 5 + 5 = ____   ____ ◯ ____ ◯ ____

5. 9 + 9 = ____   ____ ◯ ____ ◯ ____

6. 7 + 7 = ____   ____ ◯ ____ ◯ ____

Explain It • Daily Reasoning

Why are there only two facts in doubles fact families?

Practice and Problem Solving

```
 9              18
+9             − 9
---            ---
18              9
```

Write the sum and difference for each pair.

1. 8   16
   +8   − 8

2. 5   10
   +5   − 5

3. 6   12
   +6   − 6

4. 1   2
   +1   − 1

5. 4   8
   +4   − 4

6. 3   6
   +3   − 3

7. 4   2
   −2   +2

8. 18   9
   − 9   +9

9. 14   7
   − 7   +7

Problem Solving

Logical Reasoning

Solve.

10. 16 children eat 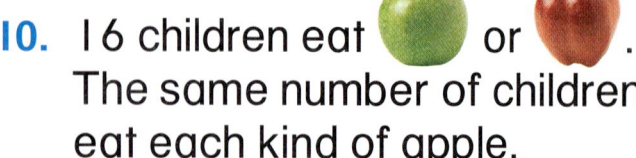 or . How many eat ? _____
    The same number of children
    eat each kind of apple.   How many eat ? _____

 Write About It • Explain your answer for Exercise 10.

🏠 **HOME ACTIVITY** • Say an addition doubles fact, such as 6 + 6 = 12. Have your child say the subtraction fact that is in the same fact family. (12 − 6 = 6)

Name _____

Algebra: Related Addition and Subtraction Facts

Learn

You can use related facts to help you find sums and differences.

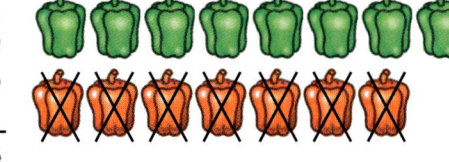

Check

Write the sum and difference for each pair.

1. 9   14
   +5   − 9

2. 5   11
   +6   − 6

3. 6   14
   +8   − 8

4. 6   15
   +9   − 6

5. 7   14
   +7   − 7

6. 6   13
   +7   − 7

7. 8   13
   +5   − 5

8. 9   12
   +3   − 9

9. 8   16
   +8   − 8

Explain It • Daily Reasoning

What addition fact can help you find the difference for 17 − 9? Explain how it can help.

Chapter 19 • Subtraction Facts and Strategies

Practice and Problem Solving

Write the sum and difference for each pair.

1. 8   11
  +3   − 3
  --- ---
  11   8

2. 9   16
  +7   − 9
  --- ---

3. 9   17
  +8   − 8
  --- ---

4. 8   12
  +4   − 8
  --- ---

5. 9   13
  +4   − 4
  --- ---

6. 6   10
  +4   − 4
  --- ---

7. 7   12
  +5   − 5
  --- ---

8. 2   11
  +9   − 2
  --- ---

9. 9   18
  +9   − 9
  --- ---

10. 8   15
   +7   − 8
   --- ---

11. 6   12
   +6   − 6
   --- ---

12. 7   11
   +4   − 7
   --- ---

Problem Solving
Application

Write a number sentence to solve.

13. 18 children are at a party.
    9 children go home.
    How many children
    are at the party now?

_____ children   _____ ◯ _____ ◯ _____

 Write About It • Look at Exercise 13.
Write about how you solved the problem.

🏠 **HOME ACTIVITY** • Have your child tell the addition fact that can help find the difference for 14 − 6. (6 + 8 = 14)

322 three hundred twenty-two

Name _____

Problem Solving Skill
Estimate Reasonable Answers

Tim has 10 carrots.
Bev has 9 carrots.
About how many carrots do they have in all?

about 5   about 10   (about 20)

> Each number is larger than 5. So **about 5** is too little.

> There are 9 more than 10. So **about 10** is too little.

> 10 + 9 is almost 10 + 10. So, **about 20** is the best estimate.

Circle the best estimate.

1. Betty has 10 plums. She gives away 4 plums. About how many plums does Betty have now?

   > Will 10 − 4 be more than 10 or less than 10?

   about 5   about 10   about 15

2. 6 children work in the garden. 10 more come. About how many children are in the garden?

   about 5   about 10   about 15

3. Mark picks 4 peppers. He needs 13 in all. About how many more peppers does Mark need?

   about 1   about 10   about 20

4. Elena waters her garden for 16 minutes. Don waters his garden for 9 minutes. About how many more minutes does Elena water than Don?

   about 5   about 10   about 20

Chapter 19 • Subtraction Facts and Strategies

Problem Solving Practice

Circle the best estimate.

THINK: Which estimate makes sense?

1. Tom plants 8 seeds. Then he plants 3 more. About how many seeds does he plant?

   about 5   about 10   about 15

2. Kris has 10 flowers. Mike brings 8 more. About how many flowers do they have in all?

   about 5   about 10   about 20

3. Becky picks 18 tomatoes. She gives 9 of them away. About how many tomatoes does Becky have left?

   about 2   about 10   about 20

4. Jason finds 4 ladybugs. Seena finds 10 more. About how many ladybugs do they find in all?

   about 5   about 10   about 15

5. Keesha picks 9 carrots. She eats 3 of them. About how many carrots does she have now?

   about 5   about 10   about 15

 HOME ACTIVITY • Ask your child how he or she chose the answer for each problem.

Name _____

Extra Practice

Write the difference.
Use the number line to help.

0 1 2 3 4 5 6 7 8 9 10 11 12 13 14 15 16 17 18 19 20

1. 12
   − 3
   ___

2. 14
   − 7
   ___

3. 16
   − 7
   ___

4. 15
   − 9
   ___

5. 13
   − 6
   ___

Write the sum and difference for each pair.

6.   6   12
    +6   − 6
    ___   ___

7.   7   14
    +7   − 7
    ___   ___

8.   5   11
    +6   − 6
    ___   ___

9.   7   15
    +8   − 8
    ___   ___

Problem Solving

Circle the best estimate.

10. Drew planted 10 seeds. Jess planted 9 seeds. About how many did they plant altogether?

about 5   about 10   about 20

Chapter 19 • Subtraction Facts and Strategies

Name _____

✓ Review/Test

Concepts and Skills

Write the difference.
Use the number line to help.

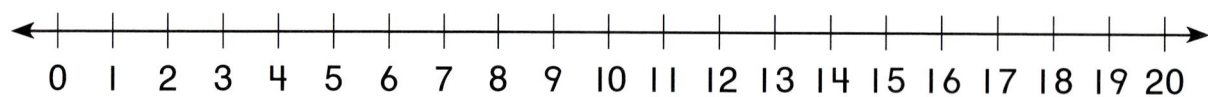

1. 15 − 9
2. 18 − 9
3. 14 − 6
4. 16 − 8
5. 17 − 8

Write the sum and difference for each pair.

6. 8 + 8   16 − 8
7. 9 + 9   18 − 9
8. 8 + 6   14 − 6
9. 8 + 9   17 − 9

Problem Solving

Circle the best estimate.

10. Juan has 8 flowers. Joe has 3 flowers. About how many flowers do they have in all?

about 5   about 10   about 20

Name _____

★Standardized Test Prep
Chapters 1–19

Choose the answer for questions 1–5.

1. Which does the number line show?

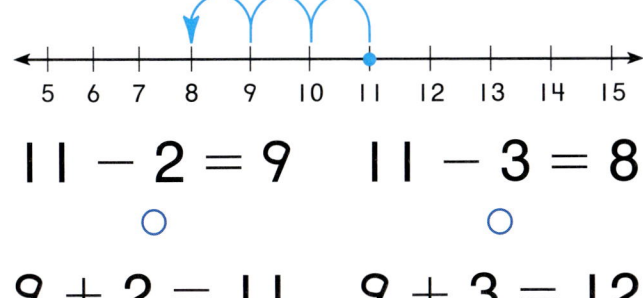

○ 11 − 2 = 9   ○ 11 − 3 = 8

○ 9 + 2 = 11   ○ 9 + 3 = 12

2. Which does the number line show?

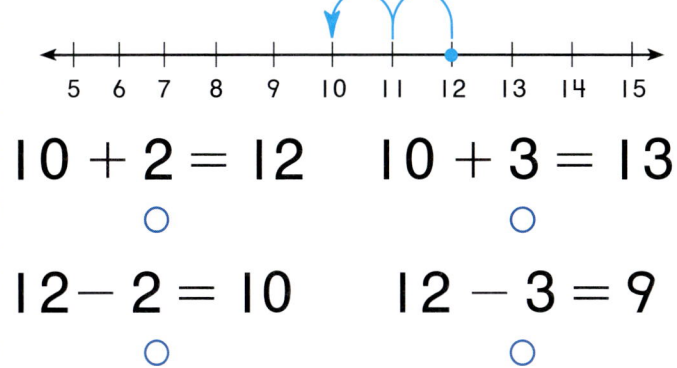

○ 10 + 2 = 12   ○ 10 + 3 = 13

○ 12 − 2 = 10   ○ 12 − 3 = 9

3. Which subtraction fact is in the same family as 9 + 9 = 18?

○ 18 − 9 = 9   ○ 17 − 9 = 8

○ 16 − 9 = 7   ○ 9 − 9 = 0

4. Which is the best estimate?

Jack has 20 crayons.
He gives 6 away.
About how many crayons does Jack have left?

about 5   about 15   about 50
○   ○   ○

5. Which is a different way to show 30 + 2?

         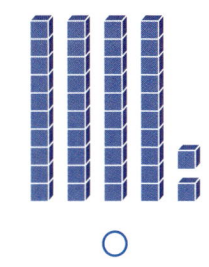

○   ○   ○   ○

Show What You Know

6. Find the sum and difference. Draw a picture to explain how the facts are related.

Chapter 19   three hundred twenty-seven **327**

MATH GAME

Fact Family Bingo

Play with a partner.

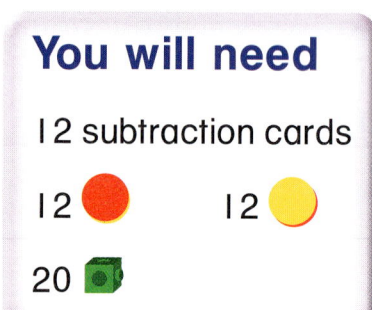

You will need

12 subtraction cards

12 🔴   12 🟡

20 🟩

1. Put 12 subtraction cards face down.
2. One player uses 🔴. The other player uses 🟡.
3. Take a card. Subtract. Use 🟩 to check.
4. If you are correct, cover 1 space with a counter.
5. Give an addition fact from that fact family.
6. If you are correct, cover 1 more space.
7. Play until all the spaces are covered.
8. The player with more counters wins.

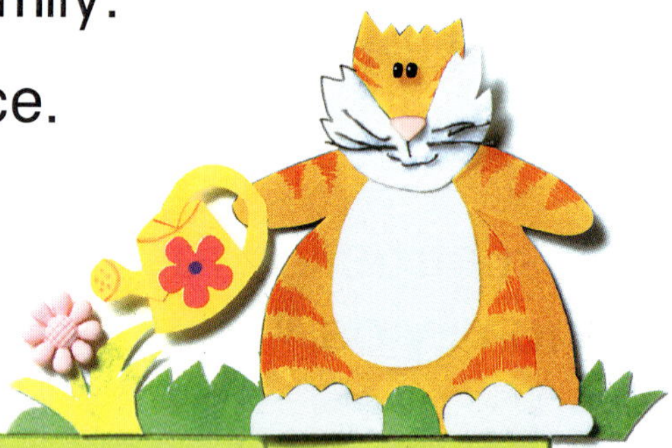

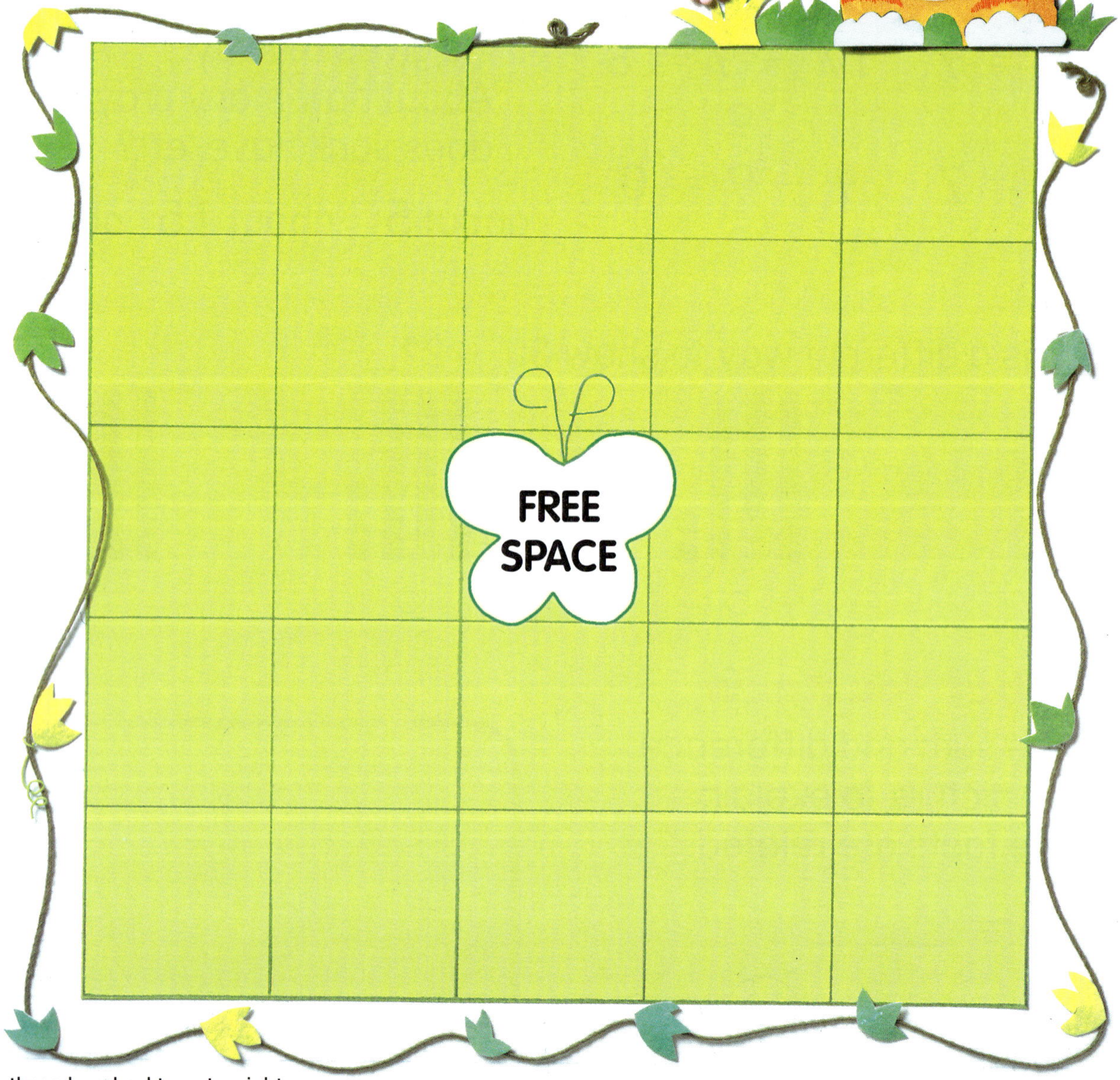

FREE SPACE

CHAPTER 20

Addition and Subtraction Practice

FUN FACTS

Emperor penguin dads keep the eggs on top of their feet for up to 63 days without food, waiting for chicks to hatch.

Theme: Arctic Life

Name _____

✓ Check What You Know

Fact Families to 12

Add or subtract.
Write the numbers in the fact family.

1. 3 + 8 = ____

   8 + 3 = ____

   11 − 3 = ____

   11 − 8 = ____

   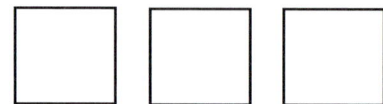

2. 3 + 9 = ____

   9 + 3 = ____

   12 − 3 = ____

   12 − 9 = ____

Sums and Differences to 12

Write the sum or difference.

3. 6 + 4 = ____

4. 9 − 3 = ____

5. 10 − 6 = ____

6. 7 + 2 = ____

7. 8 + 4 = ____

8. 3 + 9 = ____

9. 9
   +2
   ___

10. 12
    − 8
    ___

11. 11
    − 4
    ___

12. 12
    − 6
    ___

13. 5
    +4
    ___

14. 10
    −10
    ___

330 three hundred thirty   Use this page to review important skills needed for this chapter.

Name _____

Practice the Facts

Learn

There are many ways to find sums and differences!

I can count on, make a ten, or use doubles or doubles plus one to add.

I can count back or use a related fact to subtract.

Check

Add or subtract.

1. 9
   +5
   ——
   14

2. 12
   − 3
   ——

3. 7
   +9
   ——

4. 13
   − 8
   ——

5. 14
   − 5
   ——

6. 9
   +9
   ——

7. 5
   +8
   ——

8. 11
   − 4
   ——

9. 6
   +6
   ——

10. 10
    − 4
    ——

11. 13
    − 6
    ——

12. 4
    +7
    ——

13. 8
    +4
    ——

14. 14
    − 7
    ——

15. 5
    +7
    ——

16. 18
    − 9
    ——

17. 18
    − 8
    ——

18. 10
    + 9
    ——

Explain It • Daily Reasoning

What ways could you use to find the sum for 7 + 6? What ways could you use to find the difference for 12 − 3?

Chapter 20 • Addition and Subtraction Practice

three hundred thirty-one **331**

Practice and Problem Solving

1. Solve the number puzzle.
   Write each sum or difference.
   The problems go across and down.

16	−	8	=	8		15	−	7	=	
−		9		+		2			+	5
7					+	8	=			
							−	9		
	10	+	5	=		17				
+	8				−	8				
		−	9	=				+	7	=

Problem Solving

Logical Reasoning

2. The sum for two of these numbers is 14.
   The difference for the same two numbers is 2.
   What are the two numbers?

   5   8
   6   9

   _____ and _____

 Write About It • Look at Exercise 2.
The sum for two other numbers is also 14.
What are the two numbers?
What is the difference for those numbers?

HOME ACTIVITY • With your child, make flash cards for the addition facts with sums of 10 through 20. Ask your child to choose a card, say the sum, and then tell you a related subtraction fact. (For example: 8 + 7 = 15, 15 − 7 = 8)

332   three hundred thirty-two

Name _____

Fact Families to 20

Vocabulary
fact family

Learn

Fact Family
9 + 8 = 17

So, 8 + 9 = 17
17 − 8 = 9
17 − 9 = 8

You can use one fact in a fact family to help you write the other facts in the same family.

Check

Write the sum or difference.
Circle the two facts if they are in the same fact family.

1.
   6 + 7 = __13__
   13 − 6 = __7__

2.
   18 + 2 = ____
   20 − 10 = ____

3.
   9 + 3 = ____
   12 − 9 = ____

4.
   10 + 9 = ____
   10 − 3 = ____

5.
   15 − 7 = ____
   7 + 8 = ____

6.
   5 + 9 = ____
   14 − 5 = ____

7.
   18 − 9 = ____
   9 + 9 = ____

8.
   19 − 9 = ____
   9 + 2 = ____

Explain It • Daily Reasoning

Which facts are in the same family as 13 − 9 = 4? How do you know?

Chapter 20 • Addition and Subtraction Practice

Practice and Problem Solving

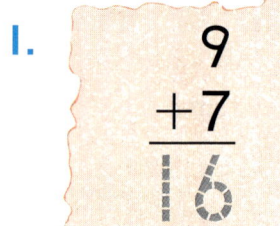

Write the sum or difference.
Color all the facts in the same fact family to match.

1. 9
   +7
   ―――
   16

2. 6
   +8
   ―――

3. 17
   − 9
   ―――

4. 6
   +9
   ―――

5. 15
   − 6
   ―――

6. 16
   − 9
   ―――

7. 8
   +6
   ―――

8. 17
   − 8
   ―――

9. 8
   +9
   ―――

10. 9
   +6
   ―――

11. 16
   − 7
   ―――

12. 14
   − 6
   ―――

13. 14
   − 8
   ―――

14. 9
   +8
   ―――

15. 15
   − 9
   ―――

16. 7
   +9
   ―――

Problem Solving
Application

17. Write the number sentence that is missing from this fact family.

    ____ ◯ ____ ◯ ____

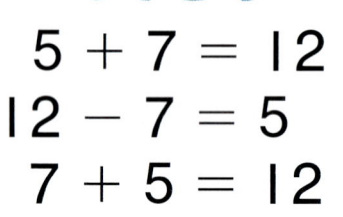

5 + 7 = 12
12 − 7 = 5
7 + 5 = 12

Write About It • Look at Exercise 17.
Explain how you figured out the missing number sentence.

HOME ACTIVITY • Say an addition or subtraction fact to your child. Ask him or her to tell another fact that is in the same fact family. (For example: 7 + 6 = 13, 13 − 6 = 7)

Name _____

Algebra: Ways to Make Numbers to 20

Explore

You can make the number 19 in different ways.

4 + 9 + 6

20 − 1

15 + 4

You can add or subtract to make 19.

Connect

Use .
Circle all the ways to make the number at the top.

1.
18
(9 + 9)
8 + 4 + 4
19 − 1
5 + 5 + 7
20 − 8
15 + 2
20 − 2

2.
20
13 + 6 + 1
5 + 4 + 10
20 − 0
14 + 6
5 + 7 + 8
12 + 7
2 + 8 + 7

Explain It • Daily Reasoning

Look at Exercise 2. What are three other ways to make 20?

Chapter 20 • Addition and Subtraction Practice

Practice and Problem Solving

Use 🟥🟦🟨.
Circle all the ways to make the number at the top.

1.
15
(6 + 4 + 5)
8 + 2 + 5
10 + 5
7 + 9
15 − 0

2.
17
6 + 10
17 − 0
5 + 5 + 7
18 − 0
7 + 10

3.
14
4 + 10
19 − 9
2 + 3 + 9
14 − 0
7 + 5 + 1

4.
16
6 + 4 + 6
10 + 6
17 + 1
8 + 8
7 + 3 + 5

Problem Solving
Application

5. Circle ways to show 12.

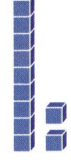   6 + 7   twelve   ❄❄❄❄❄❄❄❄

 Write About It • Use pictures, words, and numbers to show 13.

 HOME ACTIVITY • Ask your child to tell you three ways to make 20.

336 three hundred thirty-six

Name _____

Problem Solving Strategy
Make a Model

10 girls are sledding.
7 more come.
How many girls are sledding?

UNDERSTAND

What do you need to find out?

Circle the question.

PLAN

How will you solve this problem?

You can make a model.
Use 🟥 and 🟦 to show the groups of girls.

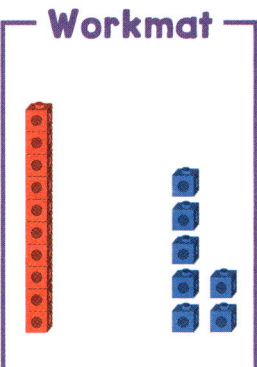

Workmat

SOLVE

I have 10. I can count 7 more.

There are __17__ girls.

CHECK

Does your answer make sense? Explain.

Use Workmat 1, 🟥, and 🟦.
Draw the 🟥 and 🟦 you use.
Write the answer.

THINK:
I have 17. How many more do I count to get to 20?

1. Tom's class has 20 children. 17 children are here today. How many children are absent?

   _____ children

Chapter 20 • Addition and Subtraction Practice

Problem Solving Practice

Use Workmat 1, 🟥, and 🟦.
Draw the 🟥 and 🟦 you use.
Write the answer.

Keep in Mind!
Understand
Plan
Solve
Check

1. 10 boys are skating.
   There are 18 boys in all.
   How many boys are not skating?

   _____ boys

2. Robin sees 9 children.
   9 more are hiding.
   How many children are there in all?

   _____ children

3. Kate makes 8 snowballs.
   Then she makes 7 more.
   How many snowballs does she have now?

   _____ snowballs

4. 15 mittens are missing.
   Jan finds 5 mittens.
   How many mittens are still missing?

   _____ mittens

HOME ACTIVITY • Ask your child how he or she decided to solve each problem.

Name _____

Extra Practice

Add or subtract.

1.	2.	3.	4.	5.	6.
7 +8	11 − 4	6 +6	16 − 7	13 − 8	5 +9

Write the sum or difference.
Circle the two facts if they are in the same fact family.

7. 10 + 0 = _____

    17 − 8 = _____

8. 7 + 9 = _____

    16 − 7 = _____

---

9. Use 🟥🟦🟨.
Circle all the ways to make the number at the top.

20
10 + 10
9 + 9
7 + 3 + 10
12 − 3
3 + 4 + 3

Problem Solving

Use Workmat 1, 🟥, and 🟦.
Draw the 🟥 and 🟦 you use.
Write the answer.

10. Ms. Lee sees 8 children. 7 more are hiding. How many children are there in all?

   _____ children

Chapter 20 • Addition and Subtraction Practice   three hundred thirty-nine **339**

Name _____

✓ Review/Test

Concepts and Skills

Add or subtract.

1. 6   2. 15   3.   9   4. 14   5. 17   6. 10
   +7   − 5   +9   − 6   − 9   + 8
   ___   ___   ___   ___   ___   ___

Write the sum or difference.
Circle the pair of facts if they are in the same fact family.

7. 8 + 7 = ____   8. 19 − 9 = ____

    15 − 8 = ____   9 + 9 = ____

9. Use 🟥🟦🟨.
   Circle all the ways
   to make the number
   at the top.

11
6 + 5
11 − 0
4 + 2 + 6
8 + 3
5 + 5 + 1

Problem Solving

Use Workmat 1, 🟥, and 🟦. Draw the
🟥 and 🟦 you use. Write the answer.

10. There are 15 children marching.
    Some children leave. 9 children
    are still marching. How many
    children left?

    _____ children

340 three hundred forty

Standardized Test Prep
Chapters 1–20

Choose the answer for questions 1–5.

1. Which object is shaped most like a sphere?

   ○   ○   ○   ○

2. What is the difference?

   $18 - 9 =$ _____

6	7	8	9
○	○	○	○

3. What is the sum?

   $10 + 6 =$ _____

13	15	16	20
○	○	○	○

4. Which fact is in the same family as $8 + 9 = 17$?

$17 - 8 = 9$	$17 - 7 = 10$	$9 - 8 = 1$	$1 + 8 = 9$
○	○	○	○

5. Which is a way to make 18?

$9 + 8$	$9 + 4 + 5$	$10 + 7$	$10 - 6$
○	○	○	○

Show What You Know

6. Solve. Draw ▢ to explain. Write a number sentence.

   14 children play in the snow.
   6 children are still playing.
   How many children went home?

   children

Chapter 20

IT'S IN THE BAG
The Hungry Prince's Crown

PROJECT You will make a crown with your hardest math facts.

You Will Need

- Paper plate
- Pattern tracer
- Crayons
- Scissors

Directions

1. Put the paper plate upside down in front of you. Write your hardest math facts around the outside. Fold the paper plate in half.

2. Place the pattern on top of your plate. Trace the cut lines on your plate.

3. Cut on the lines you traced.

4. Open the plate. Fold back the points to make the top of the crown. Decorate your crown.

The Hungry Prince

written by Lucy Floyd
illustrated by Alexi Natchev

🔹 This book will help me review doubles plus one.

This book belongs to _____.

Once there was a very hungry prince.
"I have only 5 muffins," said the prince.
"I need MORE!"

The cook gave him 5 more.

"Now I have 5 + 5 = _____ muffins,"
said the hungry prince. "I still need more."

The cook gave him 1 more muffin. "Goody!" said the hungry prince.

"Now I have 5 + 6 = _____ muffins!"

He ate every one of them.

"I am still hungry," said the prince.
The cook gave him 6 rolls.
"I need MORE!" said the prince.

The cook gave him 6 more rolls.

"Now I have 6 + 6 = ____ rolls!" said the hungry prince. "I still need more."

The cook gave him 1 more roll.
"Goody!" said the hungry prince.

"Now I have 6 + 7 = _____ rolls!"

He ate every one of them.

"I am still hungry," said the prince.
The cook gave him 7 bagels.
"I need MORE!" said the prince.

The cook gave him 7 more bagels.

"Now I have 7 + 7 = _____ bagels!"
said the hungry prince. "I still need more."

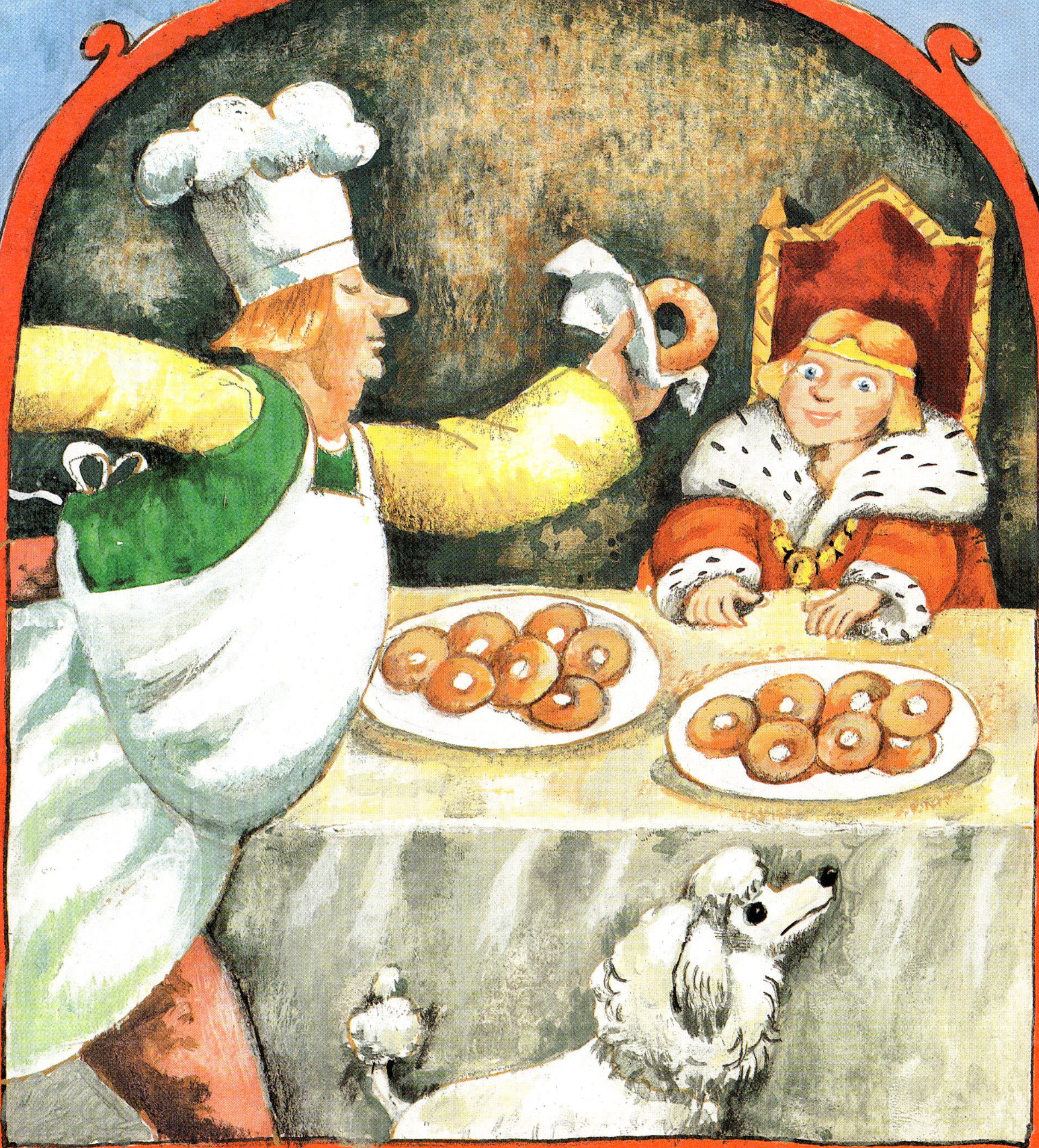

The cook gave him 1 more bagel. "Goody!" said the hungry prince.

"Now I have 7 + 8 = _____ bagels! Should I eat them all?"

WHAT DID THE PRINCE DO?

The prince did eat them all!

Then he was a sick prince, but he was NOT a hungry prince any more!

Name _____

PROBLEM SOLVING ON LOCATION

At the Park

Each year, more than 20 million people visit Central Park in New York City.

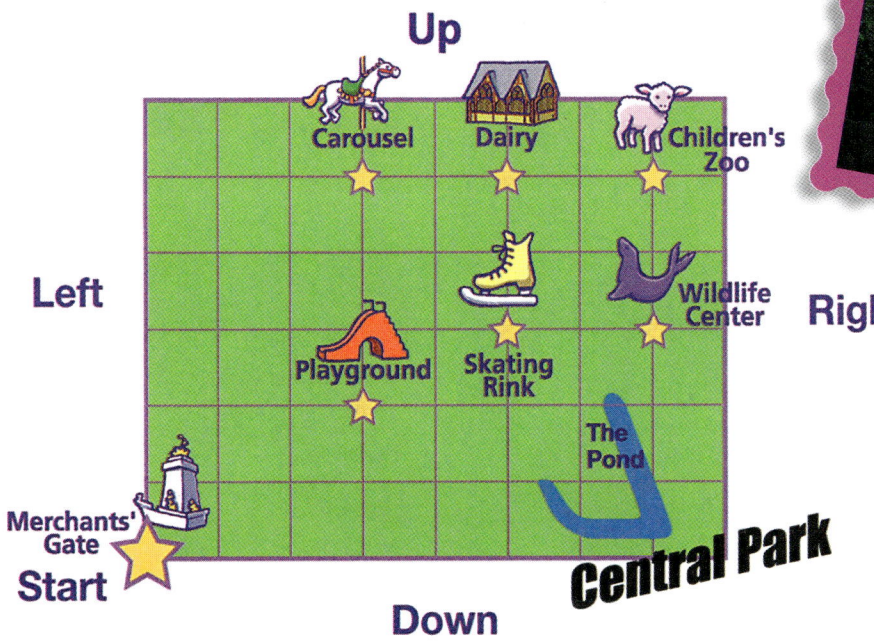

Visit some places in Central Park.
Fill in the blanks to show your path.

1. Go _____. Go _____.

   Where are you? _____

2. Go _____. Go _____.

   Where are you? _____

3. Go _____. Go _____.

   Where are you? _____

Unit 4 • Chapters 15–20   three hundred forty-three **343**

Name _____

CHALLENGE

Repeated Addition

Each bike has 2 wheels.
How many wheels are there in all?

__2__ + __2__ + __2__ + __2__ = __8__

You can add to find how many wheels there are.

Complete the number sentence.

1. Each boat has 2 sails.
   How many sails are there in all?

   ____ + ____ + ____ + ____ + ____ = ____

2. Each car has 4 wheels.
   How many wheels are there in all?

   ____ + ____ + ____ + ____ + ____ = ____

3. Each swing set has 3 swings.
   How many swings are there in all?

    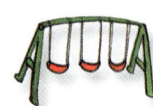  

   ____ + ____ + ____ + ____ = ____

Name _____

✓ Study Guide and Review

Vocabulary

Use 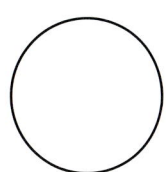 to color the **circles**.
Use 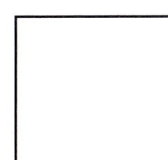 to color the **triangles**.
Use  to color the **rectangles** and **squares**.

1.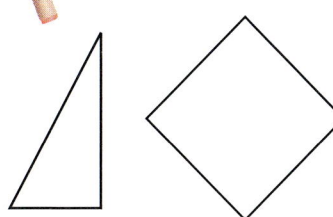

Skills and Concepts

Color each solid that will stack.

2.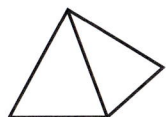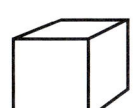

3. Write how many sides and vertices.

   _____ sides

   _____ vertices

4. Draw a line of symmetry to show two matching parts.

Write the sum.

5. 9
   +5
   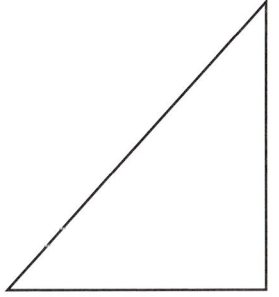

6. 8
   +4
   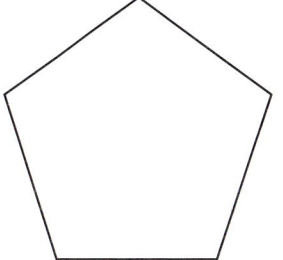

Add.

7. 9   10
   +6   +5

8. 7   10
   +4   +1

9. 8   10
   +5   +3

Unit 4 • Study Guide and Review   three hundred forty-five **345**

Subtract.

10. 15   11. 18   12. 20
    − 7   − 9   −10

13. 13   14. 17   15. 16
    − 5   − 8   − 8

Write the sum for the doubles addition fact.
Write the subtraction fact that is in the same family.

16. 9 + 9 = ____   ____ ◯ ____ ◯ ____

17. 7 + 7 = ____   ____ ◯ ____ ◯ ____

18. 8 + 8 = ____   ____ ◯ ____ ◯ ____

Problem Solving

Find the pattern. Circle the mistake.
Draw the correct shape.

19.  ▢

20. 🔺 🔺 🔺 🔺 🔺 🔺 🔺 🔺 ▢

Name _____

✓ Performance Assessment

How to Make a House

Sal had these blocks.

| 10 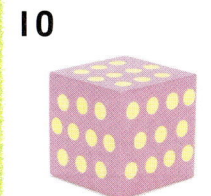 | 7  | 10  | 8 |

- He used 16 blocks to build a house.
- All the blocks he used had faces that were squares or triangles.

Draw 16 blocks Sal could have used. Write the number sentence to show the blocks he used.

Show your work.

Unit 4 • Performance Assessment

Name _____

TECHNOLOGY

The Learning Site • Addition Surprise

1. Go to **www.harcourtschool.com**.
2. Click on 🐻.
3. Drag the first number tile to start.

Practice and Problem Solving

Use 🟩 🟧 🟦.
Circle all the ways to make the number at the top.

1. **16**

   8 + 9
   4 + 14
   8 + 8
   14 + 2 + 2
   11 + 5

2. **20**

   11 + 9
   10 + 10
   12 + 7
   7 + 12 + 1
   8 + 5 + 6

Write the sums. Circle the pair of facts if they are in the same fact family.

3. 9 + 6 = _____

   10 + 5 = _____

4. 6 + 7 = _____

   7 + 6 = _____

Dear Family,

In Unit 4 we learned about geometry and about addition and subtraction to 20. Here is a game for us to play together. This game will give me a chance to share what I have learned.

Love,

_____

Directions
1. Put a game piece at START. Cover each button with a coin.
2. Your partner gives you directions such as, "Go down 2. Go left 1. Where are you?"
3. Move the game piece. Give your partner the coin where you land.
4. Take turns.
5. Play until all of the coins are taken.
6. The player with more coins wins.

Materials
- 10 pennies
- 10 nickels
- 10 dimes
- 2 game pieces or beans

Find the Pattern

START

Unit 5 • Unit Game

three hundred forty-nine A **349A**

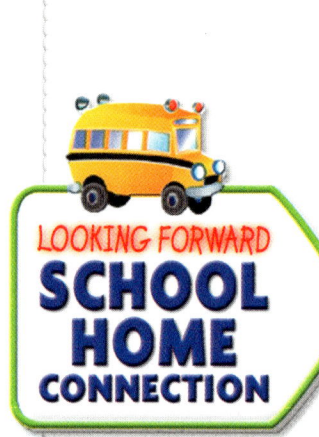

Dear Family,

During the next few weeks, we will learn about fractions, money, and time. Here is important math vocabulary and a list of books to share.

Love,

_____

Vocabulary

$\frac{1}{2}$ one half

$\frac{1}{3}$ one third

$\frac{1}{4}$ one fourth

minute hand

hour hand

Vocabulary Power

Two equal parts are halves.

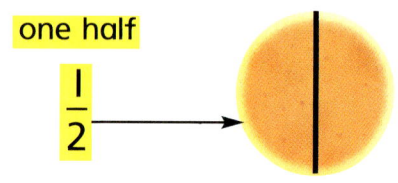
one half $\frac{1}{2}$

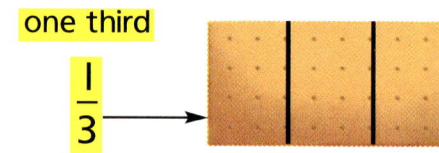
one third $\frac{1}{3}$

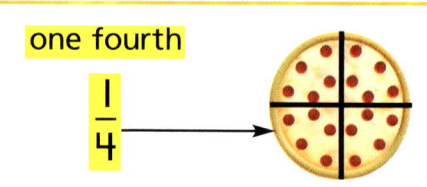
one fourth $\frac{1}{4}$

minute hand — hour hand

BOOKS TO SHARE

To read about fractions, money, and time with your child, look for these books in your library.

Eating Fractions,
by Bruce McMillan,
Scholastic, 1991.

Fraction Action,
by Loreen Leedy,
Holiday House, 1996.

26 Letters and 99 Cents,
by Tana Hoban, William Morrow, 1995.

Isn't It Time?
by Judy Hindley,
Candlewick, 1996.

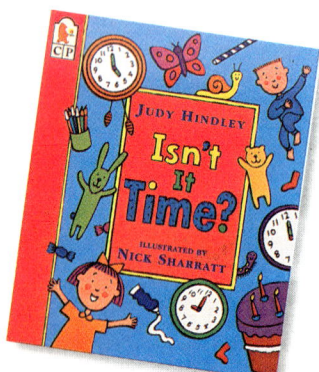

Visit *The Learning Site* for additional ideas and activities. www.harcourtschool.com

CHAPTER 23 Using Money

FUN FACTS

You get 25 pellets of goat food for a quarter.

Theme: What's for Sale?

Name _____

✓ Check What You Know

Pennies and Nickels

Count by ones or fives. Write the amount.

1.

   ____¢, ____¢, ____¢, ____¢, ____¢, ____¢   ☐ ¢

2.

   ____¢, ____¢, ____¢, ____¢, ____¢   ☐ ¢

Pennies and Dimes

Use . Draw and label them.
Count by tens. Write the amount.

3. 3 dimes

   ☐ ¢

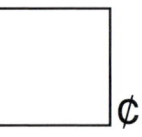

Count by tens. Write the amount.

4.

   ____¢, ____¢, ____¢, ____¢   ☐ ¢

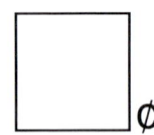

5.

   ____¢, ____¢, ____¢, ____¢, ____¢, ____¢   ☐ ¢

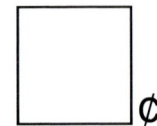

Name _____

Trade Pennies, Nickels, and Dimes

Vocabulary
trade

Explore

You can trade pennies for nickels and dimes.

5 pennies equal 1 nickel.   10 pennies equal 1 dime.   15 pennies equal 1 dime and 1 nickel.

Connect

Use coins. Trade pennies for nickels and dimes.
Draw and label the coins.

1.

   5¢

2.

3.

4.

5.

6.

Explain It • Daily Reasoning

For what coins would you trade 20 pennies if you wanted the fewest coins in your pocket? Explain.

Chapter 23 • Using Money   three hundred eighty-three **383**

Practice and Problem Solving

Each group shows 15¢, but this group has the **fewest** coins.

Use coins. Trade for nickels and dimes.
Use the fewest coins. Draw and label the coins.

1. 10¢ 10¢

2.

3.

4.

Problem Solving
Application

Draw the same amount with the fewest coins.

5.

 Write About It • Look at Exercise 5.
What are two other ways you could show 20¢?

HOME ACTIVITY • Have your child show you different groups of coins that equal the same amount of money as 20 pennies.

Name _____

Quarters

Vocabulary
quarter

Explore

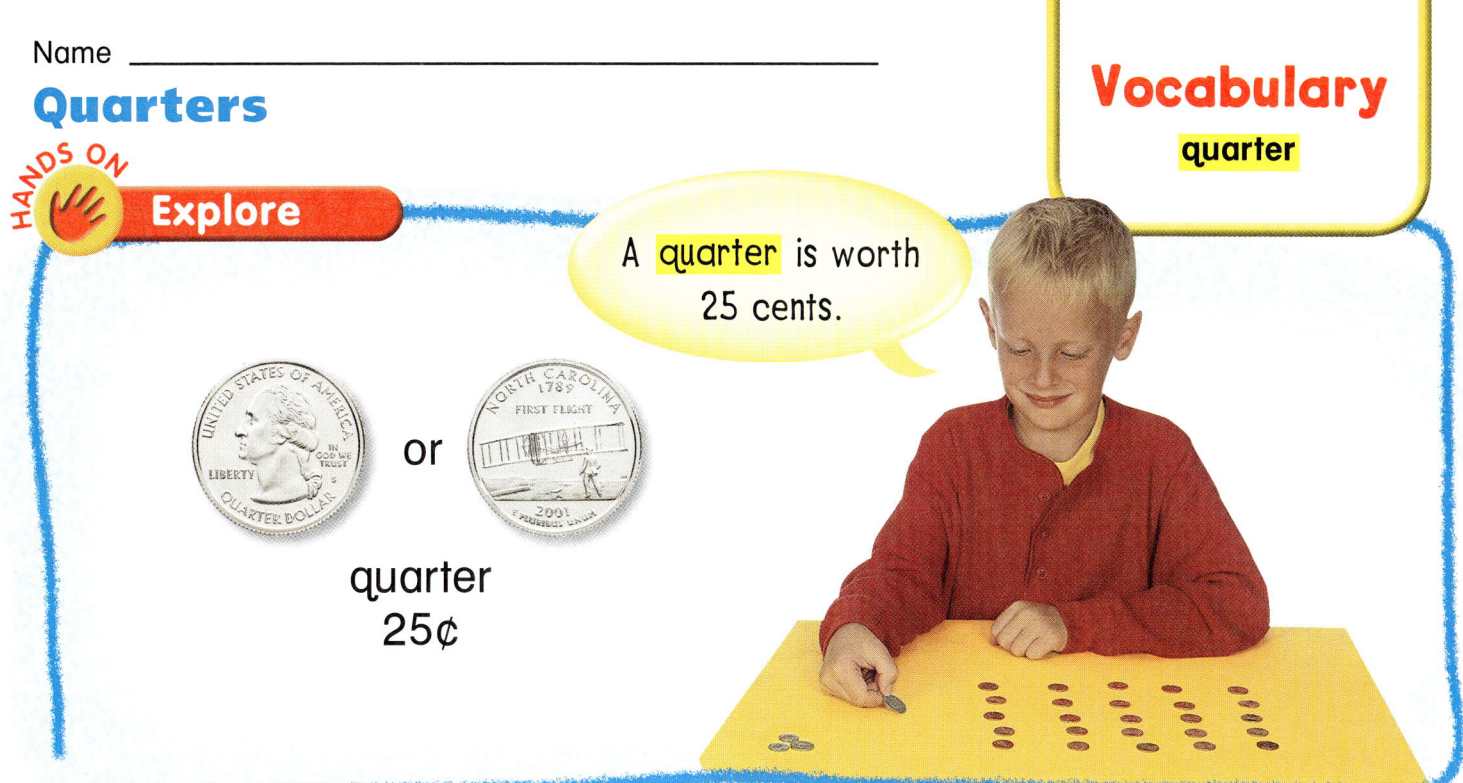

A quarter is worth 25 cents.

quarter
25¢

Connect

Show ways to make 25 cents.
Draw and label the coins.

Use only nickels.

1.

Use dimes and nickels.

Show two ways.

2.

3.

Explain It • Daily Reasoning

How many nickels would you need to equal 2 quarters? Explain how you know.

Practice and Problem Solving

Say 25. Count on by tens. Count on by fives.

25 ¢, 35 ¢, 45 ¢, 50 ¢, 55 ¢   55 ¢

Count on from the quarter. Write the total amount.

1.

_____ ¢, _____ ¢, _____ ¢, _____ ¢, _____ ¢   ☐ ¢

2.

_____ ¢, _____ ¢, _____ ¢, _____ ¢, _____ ¢   ☐ ¢

Problem Solving

Logical Reasoning

Use coins to solve.
Draw and label the coins.

3. Zoe has 4 coins that equal 50 cents in all. Which coins does she have?

 Write About It • Explain the best way to count the coins you drew.

HOME ACTIVITY • Show your child a quarter. Ask your child to show the same amount of money, using dimes, nickels, and pennies.

386 three hundred eighty-six

Name _____

Half Dollar and Dollar

Vocabulary
half dollar
dollar

Explore

or

1 half dollar = 50¢

1 dollar = 100¢

Connect

Draw and label the coins. Write how many.

1. Show how many quarters equal 1 dollar.

_____ quarters = 1 dollar

2. Show how many dimes equal 1 half dollar.

_____ dimes = 1 half dollar

Explain It • Daily Reasoning

Explain how you could find out how many nickels equal 1 dollar.

Practice and Problem Solving

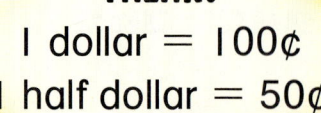

THINK:
1 dollar = 100¢
1 half dollar = 50¢

Draw and label the coins. Write how many.

1. Show how many dimes equal 1 dollar.

_____ dimes = 1 dollar

2. Show how many quarters equal 1 half dollar.

_____ quarters = 1 half dollar

3. Show how many nickels equal 1 half dollar.

_____ nickels = 1 half dollar

Problem Solving
Mental Math

Solve. Write the amount.

4. Kevin saved 4 dimes in one week. In the next week, he saved 1 half dollar. How much money did he have then?

_____ ¢

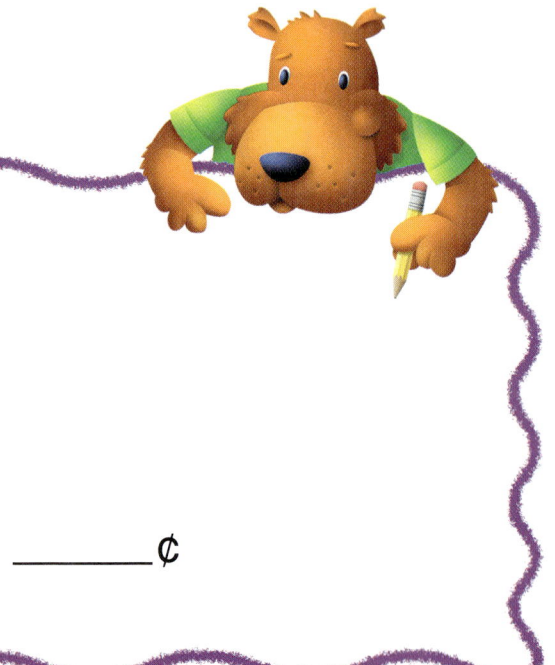

Write About It • Look at Exercise 4. Kevin saves one dime this week. Draw a picture to show how much money Kevin has now.

HOME ACTIVITY • Show your child a dollar bill. Ask him or her to show the same amount of money, using quarters, dimes, and nickels.

Name _____

Compare Values

Learn

Write the value for each group.
Which amount is greater? Circle it.

Check

Write the value for each group.
Circle the amount that is greater.

1.

   _____ ¢   _____ ¢

2.

   _____ ¢   _____ ¢

Explain It • Daily Reasoning

Compare the values of 1 dollar, 1 quarter, and 1 half dollar.
Put them in order from least value to greatest value.

Chapter 23 • Using Money

Practice and Problem Solving

Write the amount for each group.
Circle the amount that is greater.

1.    _____ ¢      _____ ¢

2.     _____ ¢        _____ ¢

3.  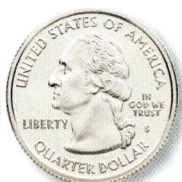     _____ ¢      _____ ¢

Problem Solving
Application

4. Cary wants quarters.
He has 6 dimes and 3 nickels.
Draw quarters to show the
same amount.

 Write About It • Cary gets one more coin.
Now he has 1 dollar. Draw and label the coin.
Tell how you know.

HOME ACTIVITY • Show your child two groups of coins, each worth one dollar or less. Have your child tell you the amount for each group. Then ask which amount is greater.

Name _____

Same Amounts

Explore — HANDS ON

I can show the amount in two ways. I can circle the way that uses fewer coins.

Connect

Use coins. Show the amount in two ways.
Draw and label the coins.
Circle the way that uses fewer coins.

1.

2.

Explain It • Daily Reasoning

How could you show this amount using fewer coins? Is there more than one way? Explain.

Chapter 23 • Using Money

Practice and Problem Solving

Use coins. Show the amount in two ways.
Draw the coins.
Circle the way that uses fewer coins.

1.  60¢

2.  80¢

3.  75¢

Problem Solving
Visual Thinking

4. Luis shows the same amount in two ways. One way has 1 quarter and 2 dimes. One way has 9 nickels.

Draw another way to show the same amount.

 Write About It • Look at Exercise 4. Use words to tell which group uses the fewest coins.

HOME ACTIVITY • Name an amount of money that is less than 50¢. Have your child use pennies, nickels, and dimes to show the amount in different ways. Then have your child point to the way that uses the fewest coins.

Name _____

Problem Solving Strategy
Act It Out

You want to buy these two things. What coins could you use?

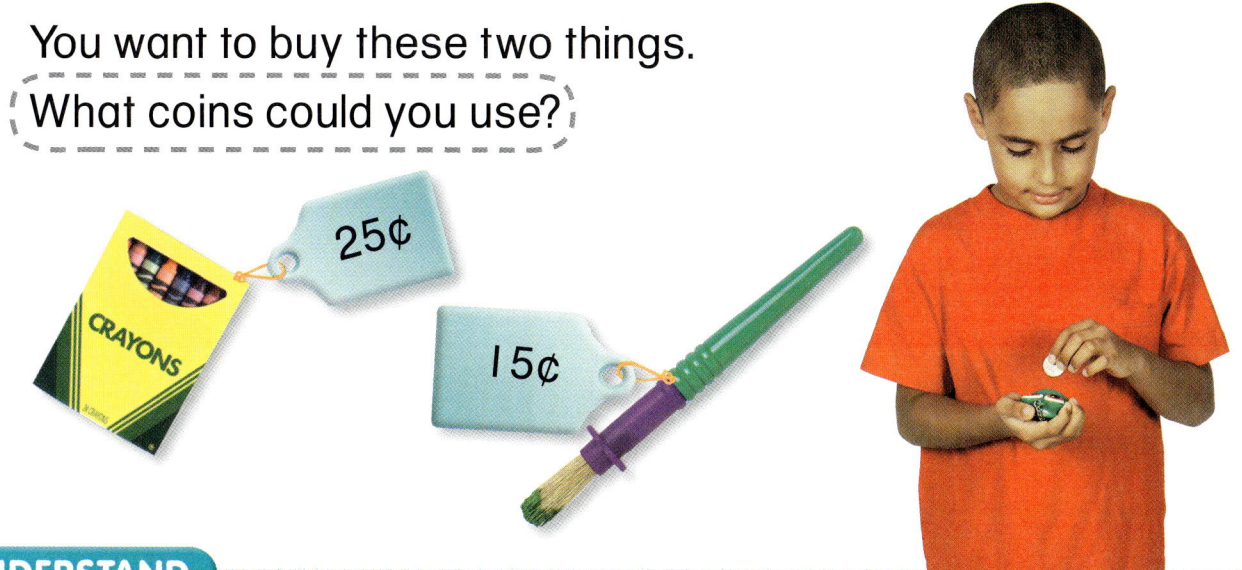

UNDERSTAND

What do you want to find out?
Circle it.

PLAN

How will you solve the problem?
Act it out. Use coins.

SOLVE

Show the coins you would use.
Draw and label the coins.

CHECK

Does your answer make sense?
Explain.

Show the coins you would use.
Draw and label the coins.

1.

Chapter 23 • Using Money   three hundred ninety-three **393**

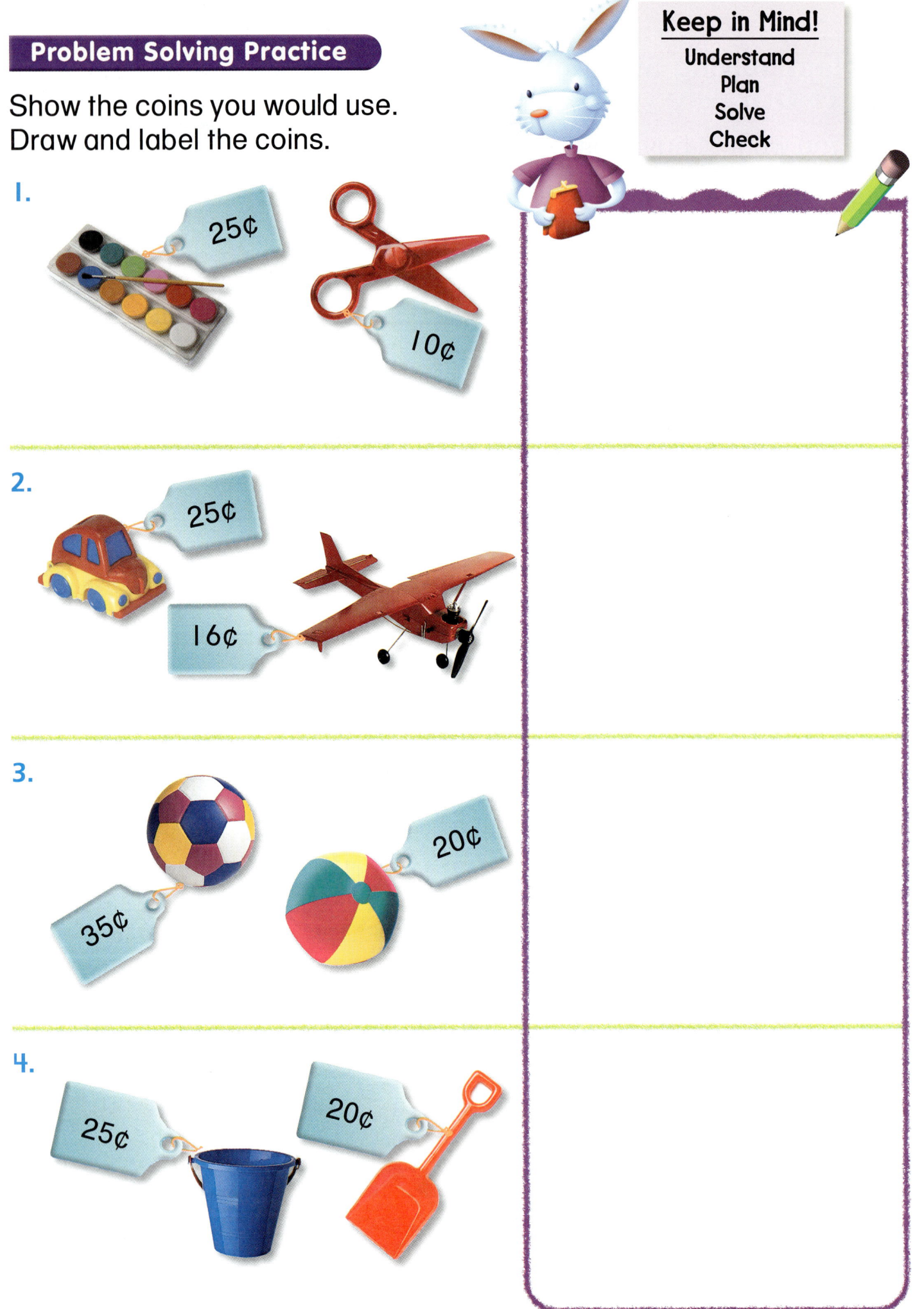

Problem Solving Practice

Show the coins you would use. Draw and label the coins.

Keep in Mind!
Understand
Plan
Solve
Check

1. paints 25¢, scissors 10¢

2. car 25¢, airplane 16¢

3. soccer ball 35¢, beach ball 20¢

4. bucket 25¢, shovel 20¢

HOME ACTIVITY • Set out two items, and write a price under 30¢ for each item. Then have your child use coins to act out buying the items.

Name _____

Extra Practice

Use coins. Show the amount in two ways. Draw and label the coins. Circle the way that uses fewer coins.

1.

Count on from the quarter. Write the total amount.

2.

_____ ¢, _____ ¢, _____ ¢   ☐ ¢

Draw and label the coins. Write how many.

3. Show how many quarters equal 1 half dollar.

_____ quarters = 1 half dollar

4. Show how many quarters equal 1 dollar.

_____ quarters = 1 dollar

Problem Solving

Show the coins you would use. Draw and label the coins.

5.

Chapter 23 • Using Money

three hundred ninety-five **395**

✓ Review/Test

Concepts and Skills

Use coins. Show the amount in two ways. Draw and label the coins. Circle the way that uses fewer coins.

1.

Count on from the quarter. Write the total amount.

2.

   _____ ¢, _____ ¢, _____ ¢, _____ ¢   ☐ ¢

Draw and label the coins. Write how many.

3. Show how many dimes equal 1 half dollar.

   _____ dimes = 1 half dollar

4. Show how many dimes equal 1 dollar.

   _____ dimes = 1 dollar

Problem Solving

Show the coins you would use. Draw and label the coins.

5.

396 three hundred ninety-six

Name _____

★Standardized Test Prep
Chapters 1–23

Choose the answer for questions 1–4.

1. 5 + 3 = _____

   2   4   8   9
   ○   ○   ○   ○

2. How many make  ?

   2   4   5   8
   ○   ○   ○   ○

3. Which is a way to make 25¢?

○ ○ ○ ○

4. Which amount can you trade to equal the amount shown?

○ ○ ○ ○

Show What You Know

5. Write a price on each toy that is less than 50¢. Draw coins to show each price. Explain which toy costs less. Circle it.

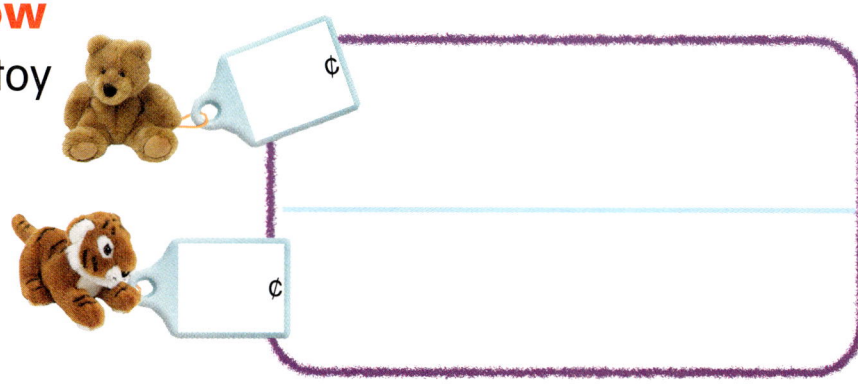

Chapter 23   three hundred ninety-seven **397**

Name _____

MATH GAME

Shopping Basket

Play with a partner.

1. Each player turns up 1 card.
2. Each player uses coins to show the total amount for the two cards.
3. The person who shows the correct amount with fewer coins keeps the two cards.
4. If both players use the same number of coins, each keeps one card.
5. Play until all the cards are used.
6. The player with more cards wins.

You will need

12 cards with prices

pile of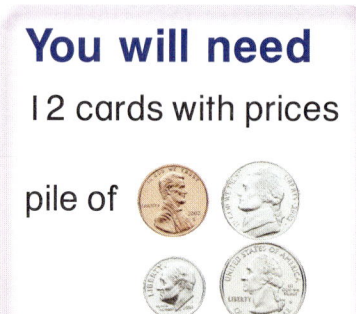

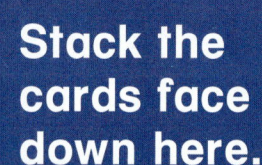
Stack the cards face down here.

Turn up 1 card here.

Turn up 1 card here.

CHAPTER 24
Telling Time

FUN FACTS

This clock has 2 hands like most clocks. It is special because it is made of foam material which does not break.

Theme: What Time Is It?

Name _____

✓ Check What You Know

More Time, Less Time

Circle the activity that takes more time.

1.

Circle the activity that takes less time.

2.

Use a Clock

Write the number that tells the hour.
Circle the two clocks that show the same time.

3.    4.    5.

_____ o'clock   _____ o'clock   _____ o'clock

400 four hundred   Use this page to review important skills needed for this chapter.

Name _____

Read a Clock

Vocabulary
minute hand
hour hand
o'clock

 **Explore**

Write the missing numbers on the clock.

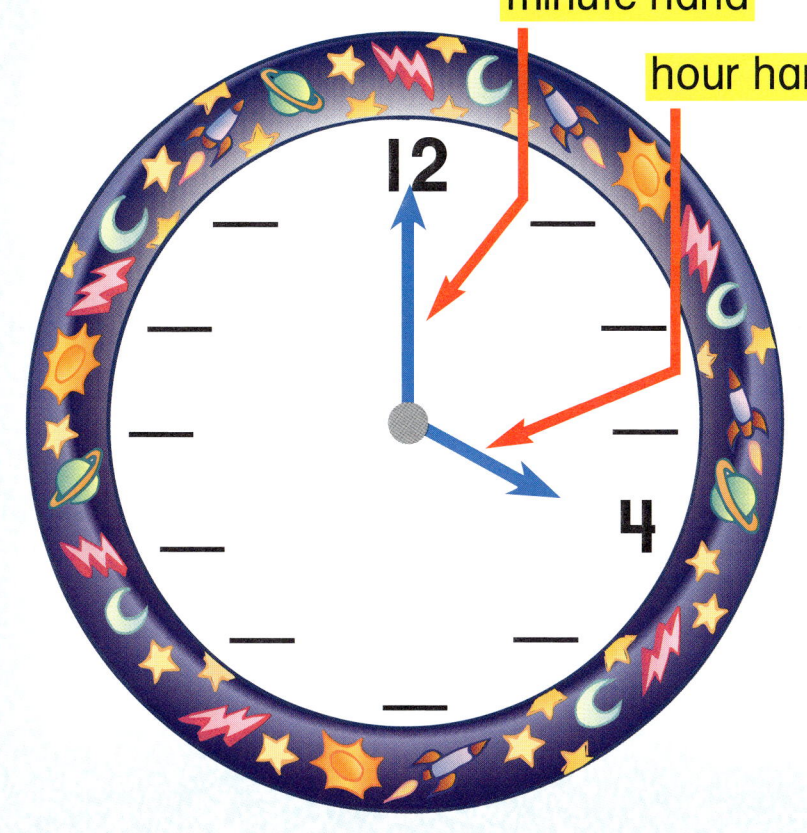

The time is 4 o'clock.

Connect

Use a 🕐. Show each time.
Trace the hour hand. Write the time.

1.

   __9__ o'clock

2.

   _____ o'clock

3.

   _____ o'clock

Explain It • Daily Reasoning

How are the minute hand and the hour hand different?

Chapter 24 • Telling Time

Practice and Problem Solving

Use a ⊙. Show each time.
Trace the hour hand. Write the time.

1.

   __4__ o'clock

2.

   _____ o'clock

3.

   _____ o'clock

4.

   _____ o'clock

5.

   _____ o'clock

6.

   _____ o'clock

Problem Solving
Visual Thinking

Write the time.

7.

   _____ o'clock

8.

   _____ o'clock

 Write About It • Write about what you do at 2 o'clock on a school day.

HOME ACTIVITY • At times on the hour, have your child show you the minute hand and the hour hand on a clock and tell what time it is.

Name _____

Problem Solving Skill
Use Estimation

Vocabulary
minute

How long is a minute?
You can estimate it.

Close your eyes.

Estimate when 1 minute has passed. Raise your hand.

Was your estimate too long or too short?
Try again. Was your estimate closer this time?

About how long would it take?
Circle your estimate.
Then act it out to check.

1. snap your fingers

more than a minute
less than a minute

2. wave goodbye

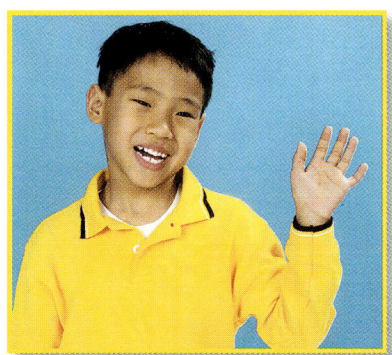

more than a minute
less than a minute

3. write a story

more than a minute
less than a minute

Chapter 24 • Telling Time

four hundred three **403**

Problem Solving Practice

About how long would it take?
Circle your estimate.
Then act it out to check.

1. write 1 to 50

(more than a minute)

less than a minute

2. clap your hands

more than a minute

less than a minute

3. draw a picture

more than a minute

less than a minute

4. say your name

more than a minute

less than a minute

5. read a book

more than a minute

less than a minute

6. write your name

more than a minute

less than a minute

HOME ACTIVITY • Have your child name an activity that he or she thinks will take about one minute. Time the activity to see if it takes about one minute, more than one minute, or less than one minute.

Name _____

Time to the Hour

Vocabulary
hour

Explore (Hands On)

These clocks show time to the **hour**.

"Both clocks show 9 o'clock."

9:00

Connect

Use a 🕐. Show each time. Write the time.

1.  12:00

2.  _:_

3.  _:_

4.  _:_

5.  _:_

6.  _:_

Explain It • Daily Reasoning

How far does each clock hand move in one hour?

Chapter 24 • Telling Time   four hundred five **405**

Practice and Problem Solving

Use a 🕐. Show each time. Write the time.

1.

11:00

2.
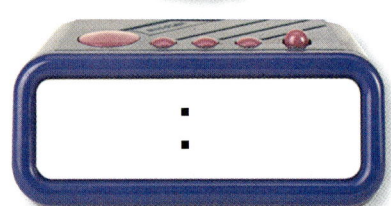

3.
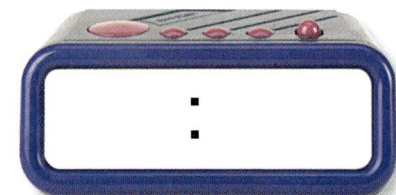

4.
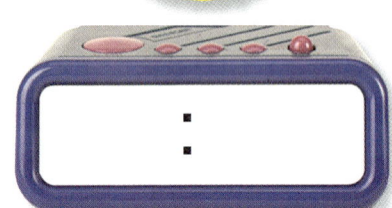

5.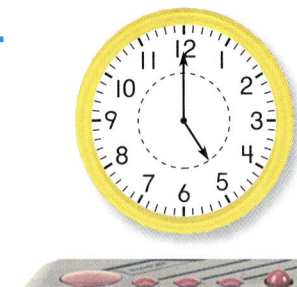
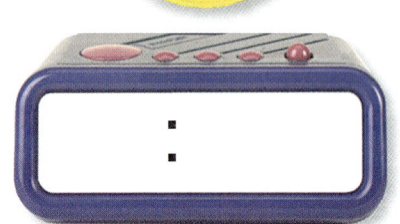

6.

Problem Solving
Mental Math

Solve. Write the time.

7. Matt wakes up at 6 o'clock. Linda wakes up 1 hour later. What time does Linda wake up?

_____ o'clock

 Write About It • Look at Exercise 7. You wake up 3 hours later than Matt. What time is it? Tell how you know.

🏠 **HOME ACTIVITY** • Ask your child to say the times on the hour in order, beginning with 1 o'clock (1 o'clock, 2 o'clock, 3 o'clock, and so on).

Name _____

Tell Time to the Half Hour

Vocabulary
half hour

Explore

There are 60 minutes in an hour.

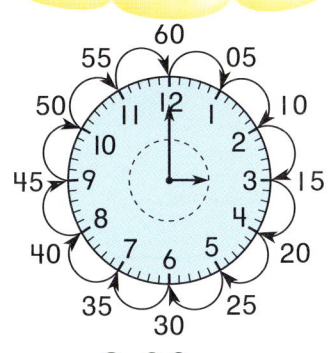

3:00 or
3 o'clock

There are 30 minutes in a half hour.

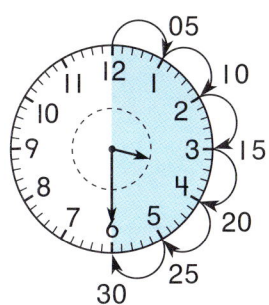

3:30 or
30 minutes after 3 o'clock

Connect

Use a 🕐 to show the time. Where are the hands?
Write the numbers. Write the time.

1. The hour hand is between __2__ and __3__.

   The minute hand is at __6__.

2:30

2.
   The hour hand is between _____ and _____.

   The minute hand is at _____.

___:___

3.
   The hour hand is between _____ and _____.

   The minute hand is at _____.

___:___

Explain It • Daily Reasoning

How far does each clock hand move in a half hour?

Practice and Problem Solving

Use a 🕐 to show the time.
Write the time.

1.

   12:30

2.

   ___:___

3.

   ___:___

4.

   ___:___

5.

   ___:___

6.

   ___:___

Problem Solving
Estimation

Estimate. Circle **half hour** or **hour**.
Then measure with a clock.

	Activity	Estimate.	Measure.
7.	 eat lunch	half hour / hour	_____
8.	 math class	half hour / hour	_____

Write About It • Write a list of things you can do in 30 minutes.

HOME ACTIVITY • At times on the half hour, have your child show you the minute hand and the hour hand on a clock and tell what time it is.

Name _____

Practice Time to the Hour and Half Hour

Learn

3:00

The hour hand points to a number. The minute hand points to 12.

3:30

The hour hand points half way between numbers. The minute hand points to 6.

Check

Draw the hour hand and the minute hand.

1.
4:30

2.
9:00

3.
10:30

4.
8:00

5.
2:30

6.
11:00

Explain It • Daily Reasoning

At 1:30, where is the hour hand? Explain.

Chapter 24 • Telling Time   four hundred nine **409**

Practice and Problem Solving

Draw the hour hand and the minute hand.

1.

2.

3.

4.

5.

6.

7.

8.

9.

Problem Solving
Algebra

10. Continue the pattern.
    Write the times that are missing.

    1:00, 1:30, 2:00, ___:___, ___:___, 3:30, ___:___, ___:___

Write About It • Look at Exercise 10.
What is the pattern?

HOME ACTIVITY • At times on the hour, have your child read the time on a clock and then tell what time it will be in half an hour.

Name _____

Extra Practice

Write the time.

1.

   _____ o'clock

2.

   _____ o'clock

3.

   _____ o'clock

4.

5.

6.
   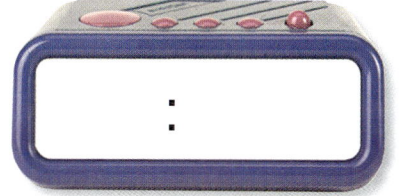

7.

   __:__

8.

   __:__

9.

   __:__

Problem Solving

10. About how long would it take to write the alphabet? Circle your estimate.

    more than a minute

    less than a minute

Chapter 24 • Telling Time

four hundred eleven 411

Name _____

✓ Review/Test

Concepts and Skills

Write the time.

1.

   _____ o'clock

2.

   _____ o'clock

3.

   _____ o'clock

4.
   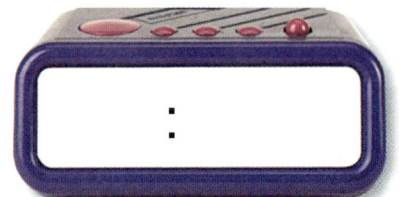

5.

6.
   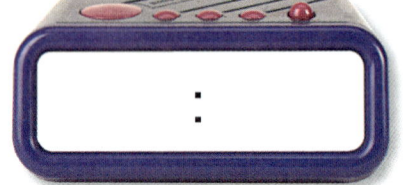

7.

   ___ : ___

8.

   ___ : ___

9.

   ___ : ___

Problem Solving

10. About how long would it take to write the numbers from 1 to 100? Circle your estimate.

    more than a minute

    less than a minute

412 four hundred twelve

Name _____

★Standardized Test Prep
Chapters 1–24

Choose the answer for questions 1–3.

1. Which object has 1 face?

○ ○ ○ ○

2. Which takes less than 1 minute?

write your name write a story eat lunch read a book

○ ○ ○ ○

3. Which clock shows the same time?

○ ○

○ ○

Show What You Know

4. Draw the hour hand and the minute hand on the clock.

Fill in the blanks to explain where the hands belong.

The hour hand is between

_____ and _____.

The minute hand is at _____.

Chapter 24   four hundred thirteen **413**

MATH GAME

Clock Switch

Play with a partner.

1. One player uses 🔴. The other player uses 🟡.
2. Your partner picks any space.
3. You show that time on the other kind of clock.
4. If you are correct, put a counter there.
5. Play until all the spaces are covered.
6. The player with more counters wins.

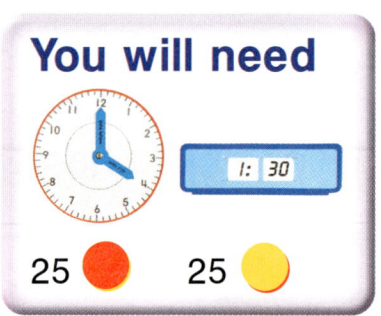
You will need

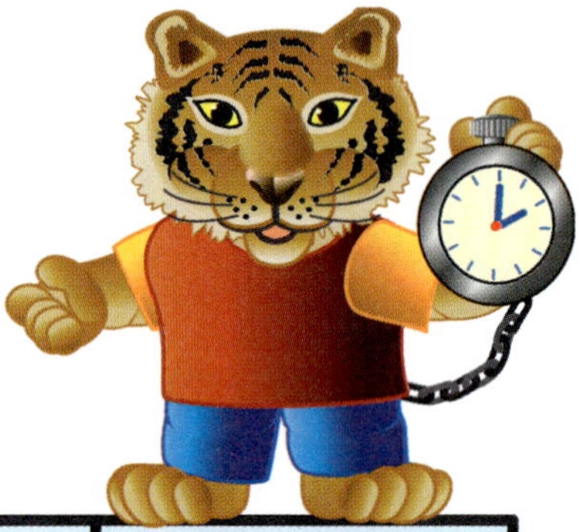

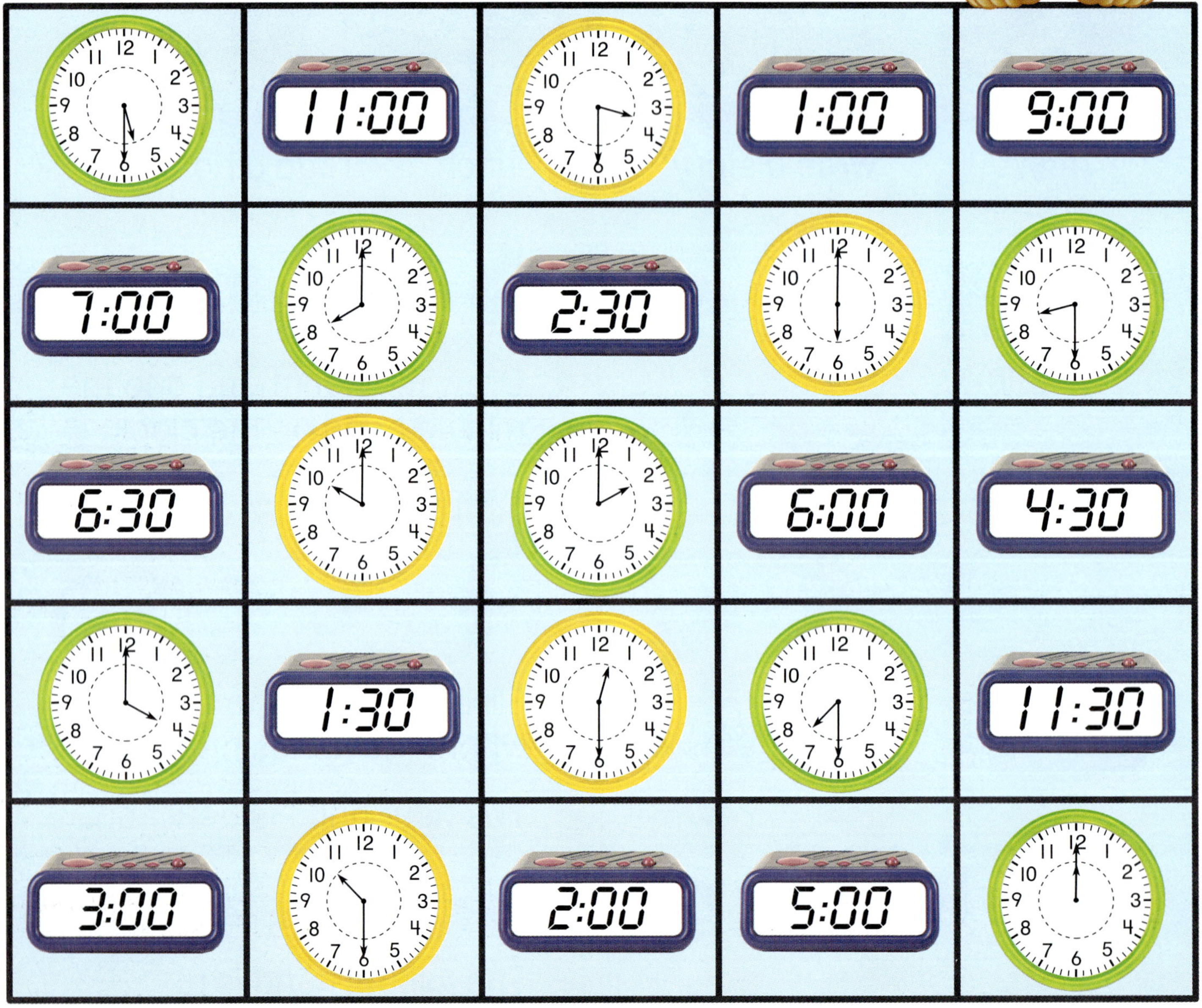

25 🔴   25 🟡

CHAPTER 25

Time and Calendar

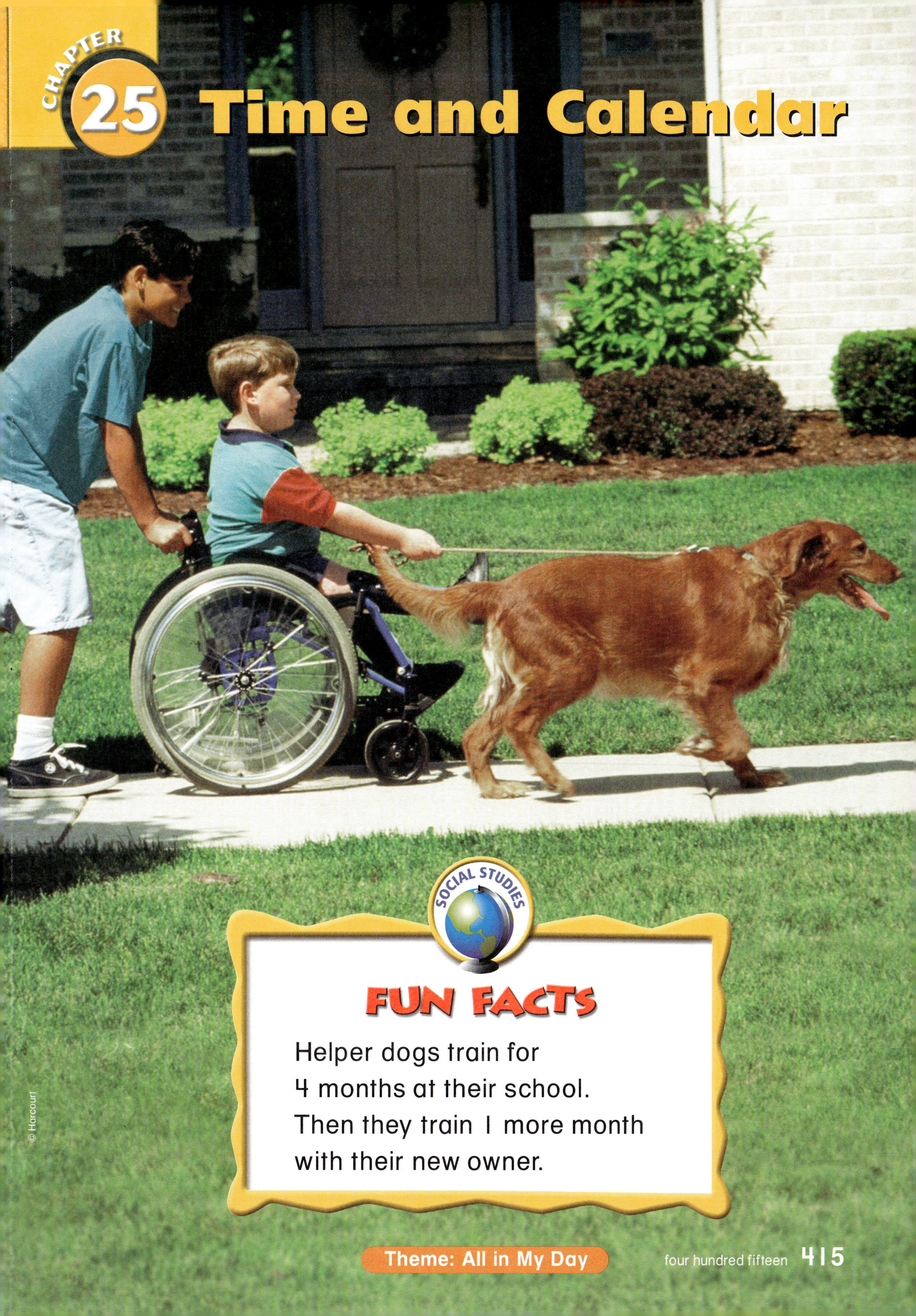

SOCIAL STUDIES

FUN FACTS

Helper dogs train for 4 months at their school. Then they train 1 more month with their new owner.

Theme: All in My Day

Name _____

✅ Check What You Know

Morning, Afternoon, and Evening

Identify the times of day.
Circle the time of day that is missing.

Use a Calendar: Identify Parts

			DECEMBER			
Sunday	Monday	Tuesday	Wednesday	Thursday	Friday	Saturday
			1	2		4
5	6		8	9	10	11
12	13	14	15	16	17	
19	20	21	22	23	24	25
	27	28	29	30	31	

Fill in the missing numbers.
Circle the name of the month.
Color the first day of the month red.

Count the Mondays. _____   Count the Thursdays. _____

416 four hundred sixteen   Use this page to review important skills needed for this chapter.

Name _____

Use a Calendar

Vocabulary
month

Learn

These are the months of the year in order.

This month is May.

Check

Use the calendar to answer the questions.

1. How many days are in a week? _____ days

2. What day of the week is May 14? _____

3. How many days are in May? _____ days

4. What month comes before May? _____

5. What is the first month of the year? _____

Explain It • Daily Reasoning

How many months are left in the year after the month of May? Tell how you know.

Chapter 25 • Time and Calendar

Practice and Problem Solving

Fill in the calendar for next month.
Use the calendar to answer the questions.

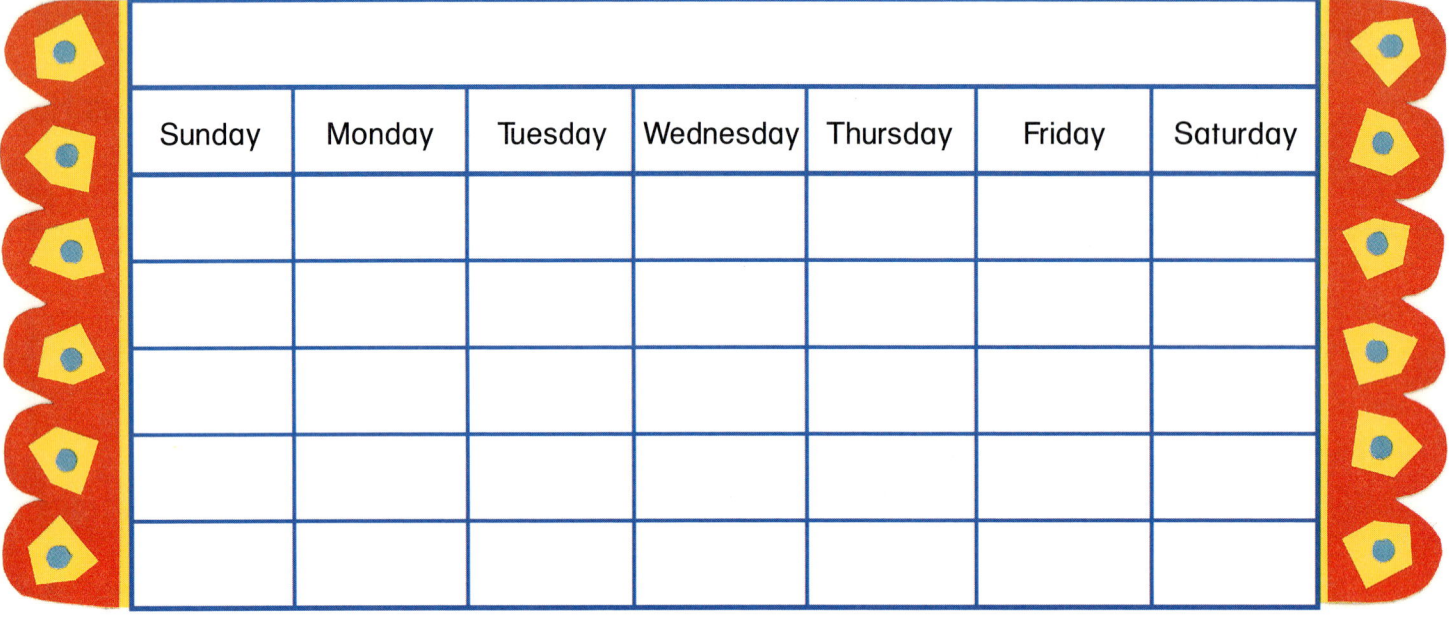

1. Color the Tuesdays 🖍.

2. Color the Saturdays 🖍.

3. What day of the week is the thirtieth? _____

4. On what day does the month end? _____

5. What is the date of the first Thursday? _____

6. How many days are in the month? _____ days

Problem Solving
Application

Look at the calendar above.
Suppose today is the twentieth.

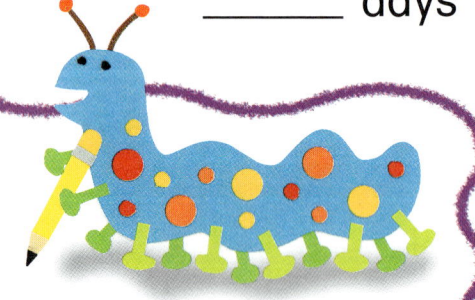

7. What day of the week was yesterday? Circle it in 🖍.

8. What day of the week is tomorrow? Circle it in 🖍.

 Write About It • Write about your favorite day of the week. Tell why it is your favorite.

🏠 **HOME ACTIVITY** • Have your child draw pictures of special events in his or her life and label each with the month of the year in which it happens.

418 four hundred eighteen

Name _____

Daily Events

Vocabulary
morning
afternoon
evening

Learn

I do this in the morning. I do this in the afternoon. I do this in the evening.

Check

Draw pictures of things you do in the morning, in the afternoon, and in the evening.

Morning

Afternoon

Evening

Explain It • Daily Reasoning

How are the things you do in the morning different from the things you do in the evening?

Chapter 25 • Time and Calendar

four hundred nineteen **419**

Practice and Problem Solving

1. Today is Saturday. Draw something you could do at these times.

In the morning yesterday	In the afternoon today	In the evening tomorrow

Problem Solving

Visual Thinking Write **day** or **night**.

2.

   _____

3.

   _____

 Write About It • Write about something you like to do in the afternoon.

HOME ACTIVITY • Have your child list activities from his or her school day in the order in which they happened.

Name _____

Problem Solving Strategy
Make a Graph

Which time of day is the favorite of the most classmates?

UNDERSTAND

What do you want to find out? Circle it.

PLAN

How will you solve the problem?

SOLVE

Ask 10 classmates to choose their favorite time of day. Make a tally mark for each choice. Then make a picture graph.

Our Favorite Times		Total
☀️ morning		
☀️ afternoon		
🌙 evening		

CHECK

Which time of day is the favorite of the most classmates?

_____

_____

Explain.

Our Favorite Times

Chapter 25 • Time and Calendar

four hundred twenty-one **421**

Problem Solving Practice

Ask 10 classmates to choose their favorite season. Make a tally mark for each choice. Then make a picture graph.

Our Favorite Seasons		Total
🌷	spring	
☀️	summer	
🍁	autumn	
⛄	winter	

1. Draw a picture to show each person's choice.

Our Favorite Seasons

	0	1	2	3	4	5	6	7	8	9	10
🌷 spring											
☀️ summer											
🍁 autumn											
⛄ winter											

2. Which season did the most classmates choose? _____

3. Which season did the fewest classmates choose? _____

4. How many classmates in all chose summer or winter?

_____ classmates

5. How many classmates in all chose spring or autumn?

_____ classmates

🏠 **HOME ACTIVITY** • Ask your child if there are any season totals that are greater than, less than, or equal to the total for spring.

Name _____

Read a Schedule

Vocabulary
chart

Learn

The chart shows when each subject begins and ends.

Subject	Start	End
math	 (clock)	 (clock)
language arts	 (clock)	 (clock)
music	 (clock)	 (clock)

Check

Use the chart to answer the questions.

1. Which subject is before language arts? _____

2. Which subject is after language arts? _____

3. Which subject lasts the shortest time? _____

Explain It • Daily Reasoning

How did you find out how long a subject lasts?

Chapter 25 • Time and Calendar

four hundred twenty-three **423**

Practice and Problem Solving

Activity	Start	End
games	9:00	11:00
crafts	11:00	12:00
lunch	12:00	12:30

Use the chart to answer the questions.

1. Which activity is before crafts? _____

2. Which activity is after crafts? _____

3. Which activity lasts the longest time? _____

Problem Solving

Logical Reasoning Solve. You can use a 🕐 to help.

4. How long do the games and crafts last altogether? _____ hours

Write About It • Look at Exercise 4. Explain how you got your answer.

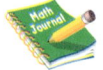 **HOME ACTIVITY** • Help your child make a chart to show what he or she does on Saturday mornings. Use times to the hour or half hour.

Name _____

Problem Solving Skill
Make Reasonable Estimates

Circle the best estimate for each activity.

1. tie a shoe

(about one minute)

about one hour

about one week

2. play a game of baseball

about one minute

about one hour

about one week

3. plant a seed

about one minute

about one hour

about one week

4. measure a plant

about one minute

about one hour

about one week

Chapter 25 • Time and Calendar

Problem Solving Practice

Circle the best estimate for each activity.

1. wash your hands

   - (about one minute)
   - about one hour
   - about one week

2. take a vacation

   - about one minute
   - about one hour
   - about one week

3. put a puzzle together

   - about one minute
   - about one hour
   - about one week

4. eat a cracker

   - about one minute
   - about one hour
   - about one week

5. clean up your room

   - about one minute
   - about one hour
   - about one week

HOME ACTIVITY • Name an activity, such as brushing teeth. Ask your child to choose the best estimate for the amount of time that activity takes: about one minute, about one hour, or about one week.

Name _____

Extra Practice

March						
Sunday	Monday	Tuesday	Wednesday	Thursday	Friday	Saturday
	1	2	3	4	5	6
7	8	9	10	11	12	13

Use the calendar to answer the questions.

1. What day of the week is March 4? _____

2. How many Tuesdays are shown? _____

Use the chart to answer the question.

3. Which activity lasts the shortest time?
   _____

Activity	Start	End
storytime	(clock)	(clock)
swimming	(clock)	(clock)

Problem Solving

Circle the best estimate for the activity.

4. go for a bike ride

about one minute

about one hour

about one week

Chapter 25 • Time and Calendar

Name _____

✓ Review/Test

Concepts and Skills

April						
Sunday	Monday	Tuesday	Wednesday	Thursday	Friday	Saturday
				1	2	3
4	5	6	7	8	9	10

Use the calendar to answer the questions.

1. On what day does the month begin?

2. What day of the week is April 5?

Use the chart to answer the question.

3. Which subject lasts the longest time?

Subject	Start	End
math	9:00	10:00
science	12:00	12:30

Problem Solving

Circle the best estimate for the activity.

4. paint a picture

about one minute

about one hour

about one week

428   four hundred twenty-eight

Name _____

Standardized Test Prep
Chapters 1–25

Choose the answer for questions 1–4.

1. 4 children share a muffin. Each gets an equal part. Which shows how the muffin is cut?

○ ○ ○ ○

2. Which day comes after Friday?

   Monday   Tuesday   Friday   Saturday
   ○   ○   ○   ○

3. Which is the best estimate?
   About how long does it take to play a soccer game?

   about 1 minute   about 1 hour   about 1 week
   ○   ○   ○

4. Which subject lasts the shortest amount of time?

   math   music
   ○   ○

Subject	Start	End
music		
math		

Show What You Know

5. Draw pictures to explain something you do in the morning, in the afternoon, and in the evening.

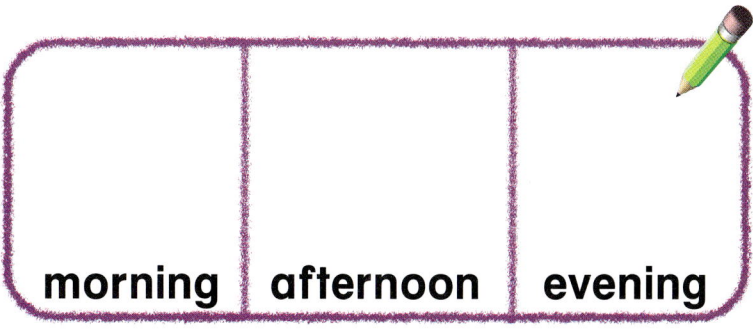

Chapter 25

four hundred twenty-nine **429**

IT'S IN THE BAG
Brown-Bag Grandfather Clock

PROJECT You will make a grandfather clock to practice telling time.

You Will Need

- Brown paper bag
- Crayons
- Glue
- Scissors
- Brass fastener
- Pattern tracer
- Blackline patterns

Directions

1. Trace around the clock outline. Then trace over your lines and add details.

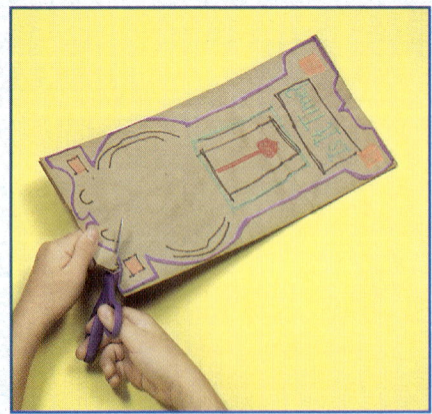

2. Cut out the top part of the clock, the clock face, and the hands.

3. Glue on the face.

4. Use a fastener to attach the hands.

5. Practice telling the time with your clock.

Is It Time?

written by Lucy Floyd
illustrated by Liz Conrad

🏠 This book will help me review telling time.

This book belongs to _____.

It can't be time so soon!
Tick-tock. Tick-tock. Tick-tock.
Do I need to get up now?

Yes! It's _____ o'clock!

_____ : _____

A half hour later . . .

I like to walk to school.
I walk just one short block.
Is it time for school to start?

Yes! It's _____ o'clock!

A half hour later . . .

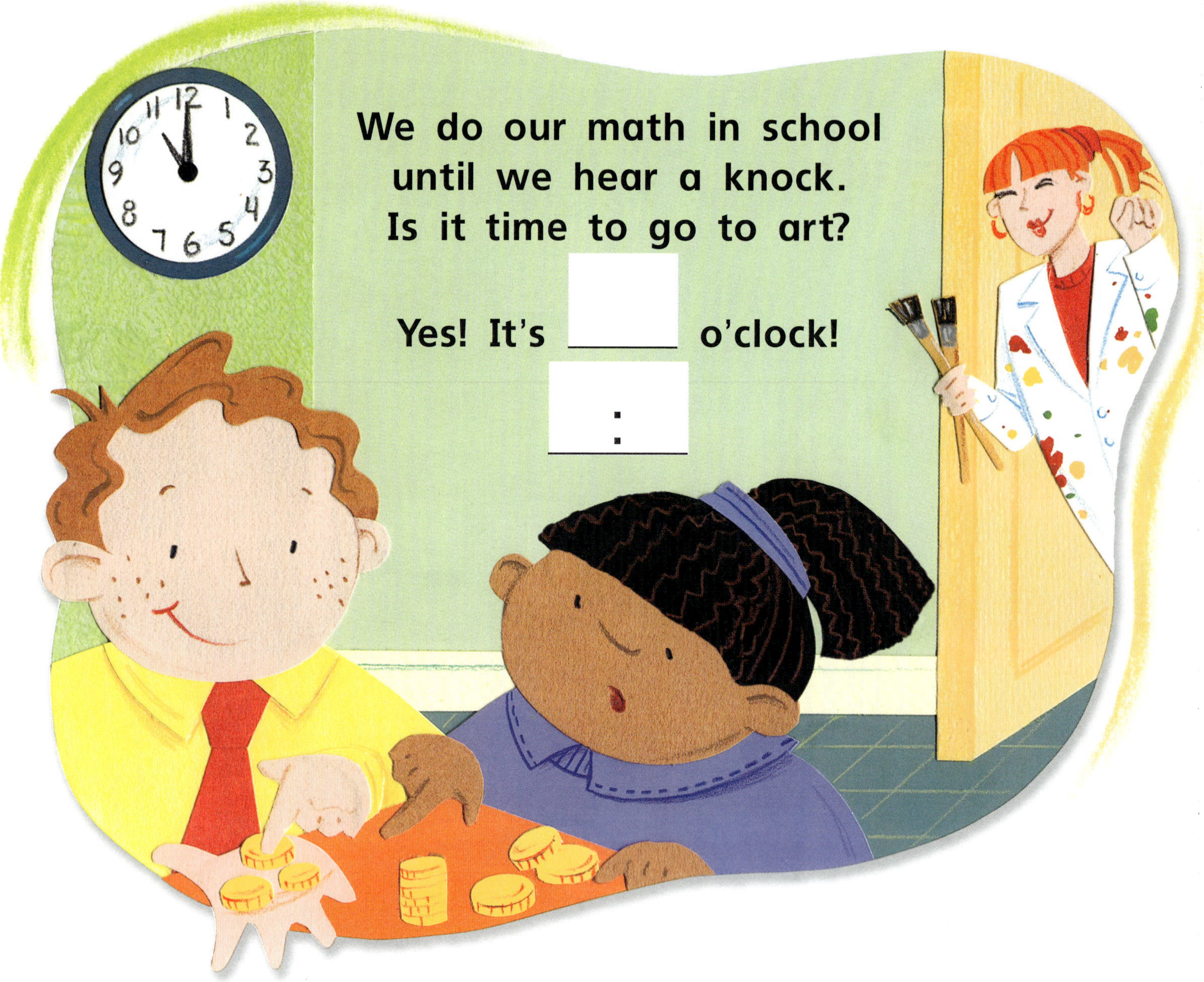

We do our math in school
until we hear a knock.
Is it time to go to art?

Yes! It's ☐ o'clock!

☐ : ☐

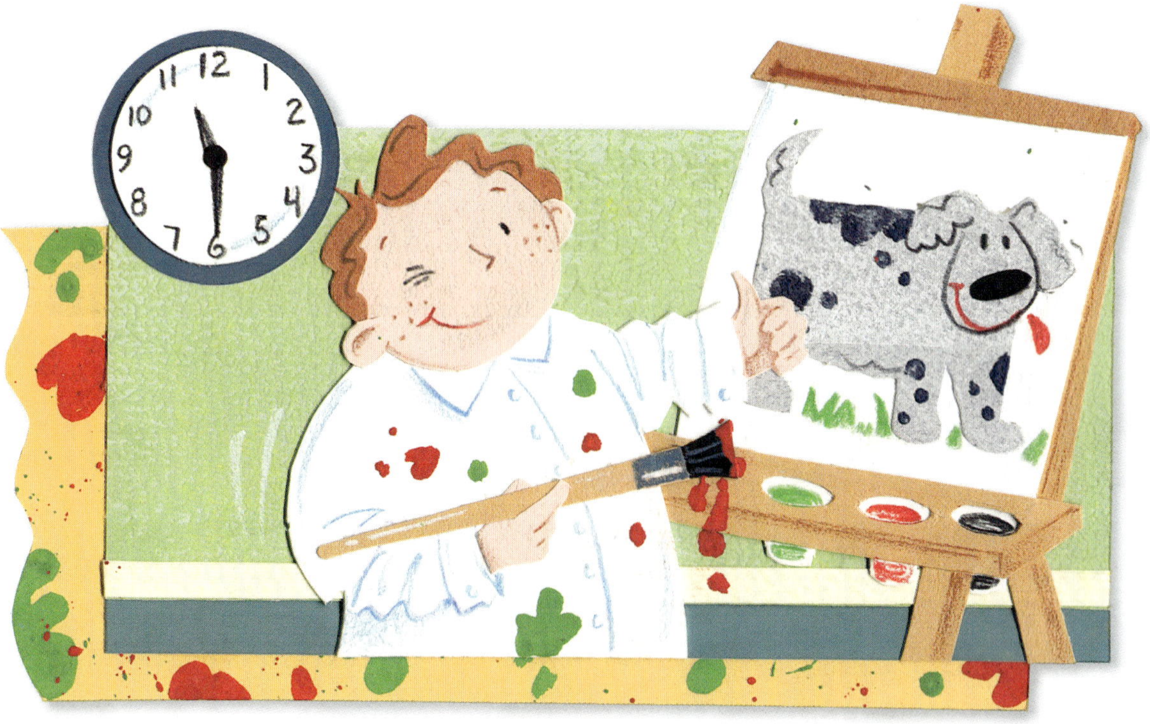

A half hour later . . .

When school is out, we play.
I show a friend my rock.
Is it time for me to go?

Yes! It's _____ o'clock!

_____ : _____

A half hour later . . .

Dad cooks some beans for us.
He stirs them in a wok.
Is it time for supper now?

Yes! It's ___ o'clock!

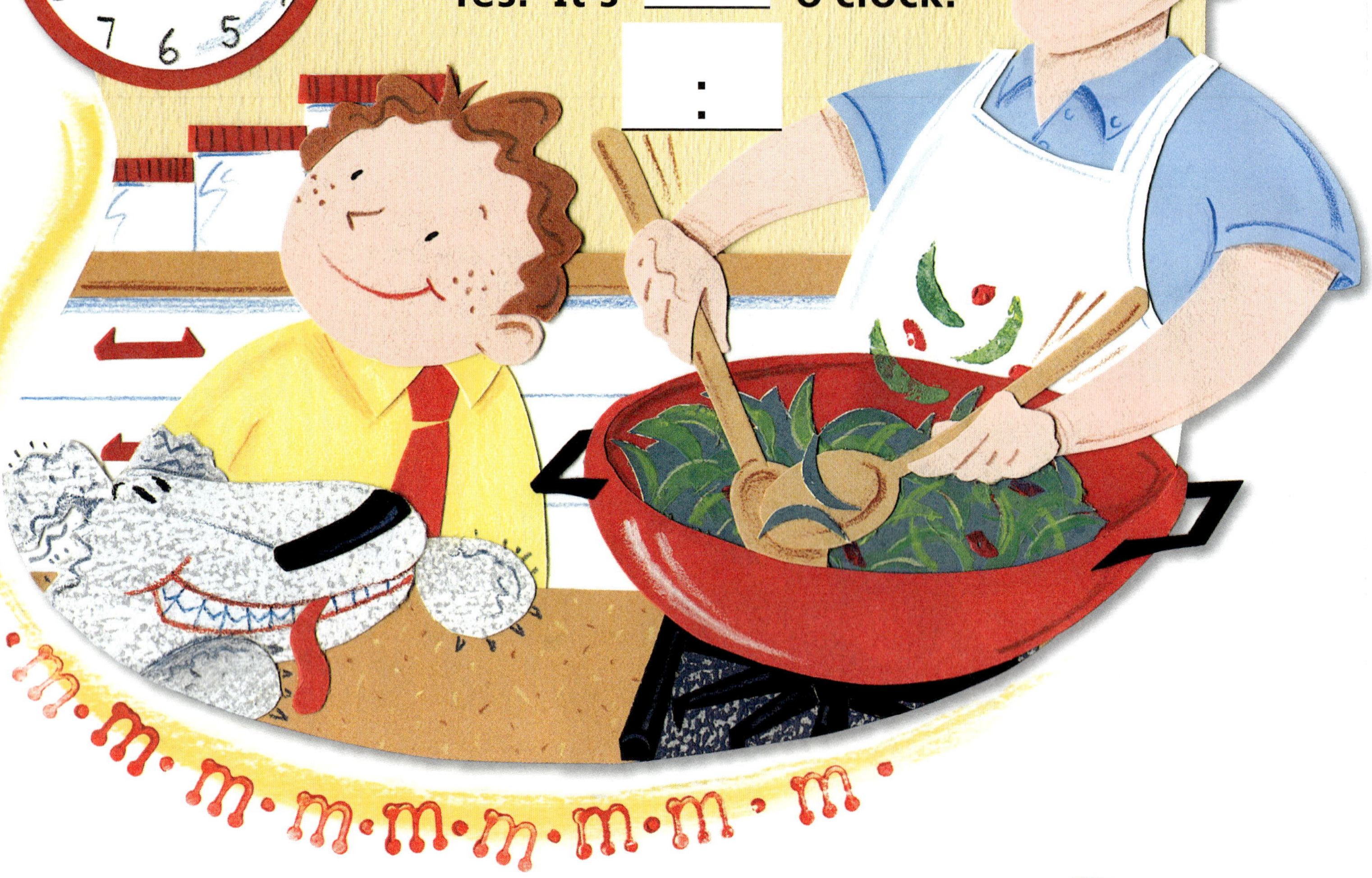

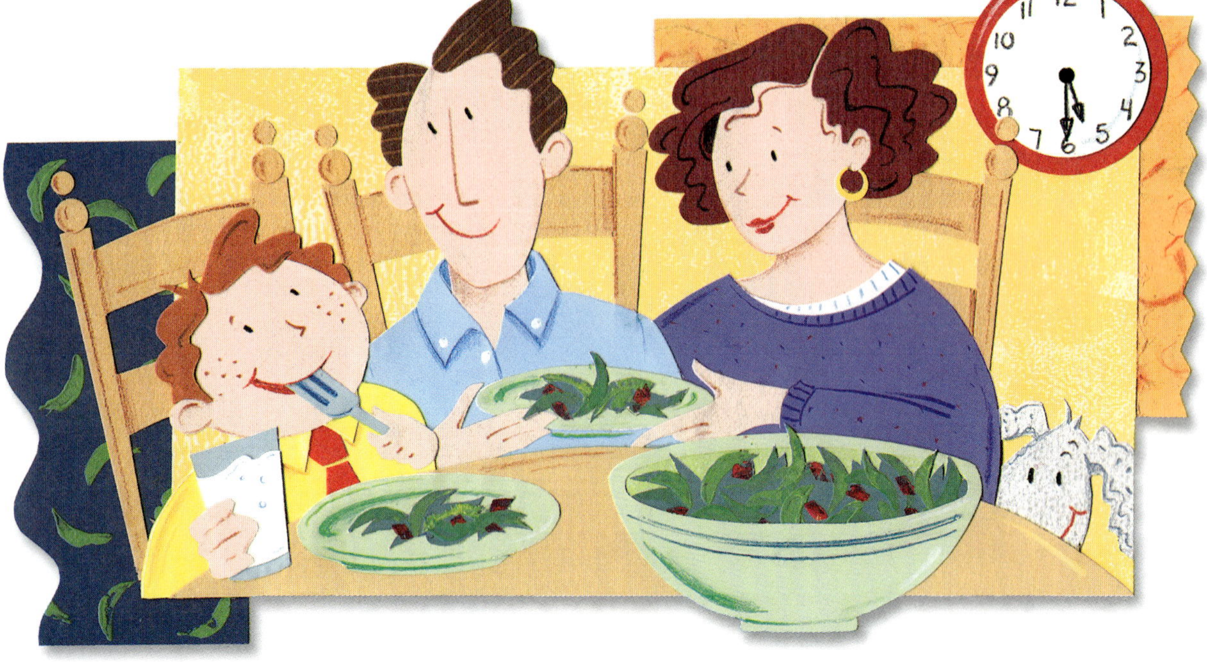

A half hour later . . .

I sit with Mom at night.
We like to sing and rock.
Is it time to read a book?

Yes! It's ___ o'clock!

A half hour later . . .

Now it's time to
go to sleep . . .

Tick-tock. Tick-tock.

Name _____

PROBLEM SOLVING ON LOCATION

At the Jazz Festival

New Orleans, Louisiana, has a jazz festival each year. People come to enjoy the music.

The musical groups ♥, ◆, and ■ are playing at the festival.

Use the calendar to answer the questions.

APRIL

Sunday	Monday	Tuesday	Wednesday	Thursday	Friday	Saturday
					1	2
3	4	5	6	7	8 ♥	9
10	11	12 ◆	13	14	15 ■	16
17	18	19	20	21	22	23
24	25	26	27	28	29	30

1. On what day of the week is ◆ playing? _____

2. Color the day of the week that has two groups playing.

3. Which group is playing on April 8?

Name _____

CHALLENGE

Writing Fractions

What fraction is shaded?

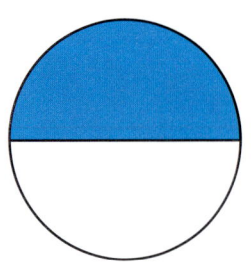

|1| 1 part is shaded out of
|2| 2 equal parts.

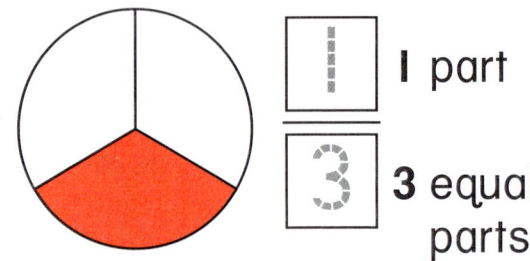 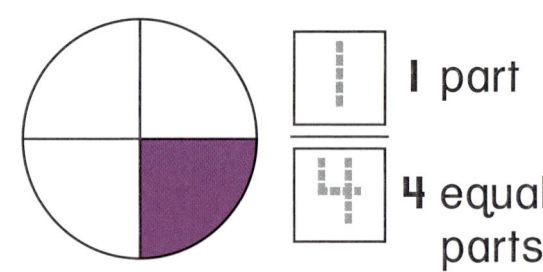

Is the shaded part $\frac{1}{2}$, $\frac{1}{4}$, or $\frac{1}{3}$?
Write the fraction.

1.

2.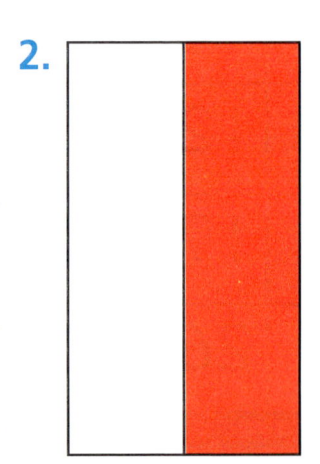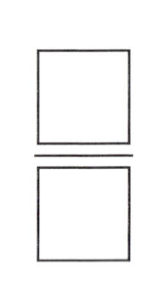

3.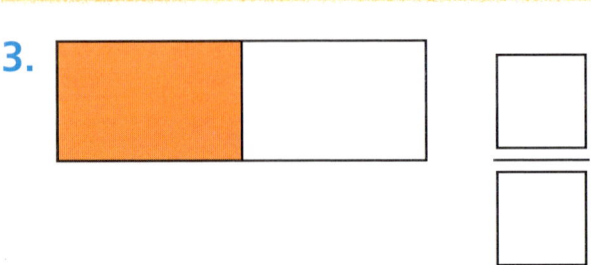

4.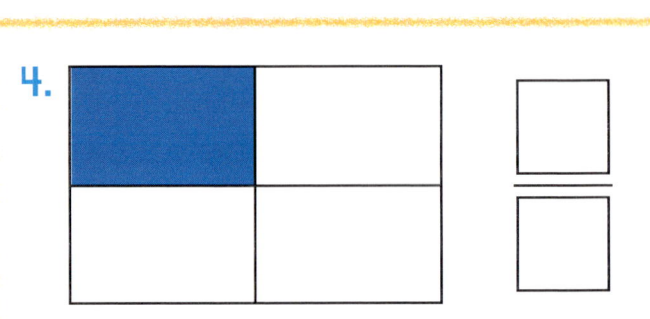

✓ Study Guide and Review

Vocabulary

Circle the **penny**. Circle the **dime**.
Circle the **quarter**. Circle the **nickel**.

1.

Skills and Concepts

Count the coins. Write the amount.

2.

   _____ ¢, _____ ¢, _____ ¢, _____ ¢, _____ ¢   ☐ ¢

3.

   _____ ¢, _____ ¢, _____ ¢, _____ ¢, _____ ¢   ☐ ¢

Use coins. Show the amount in two ways. Draw and label the coins. Circle the way that uses fewer coins.

4.

Draw and label the coins. Write how many.

5. Show how many dimes equal 1 dollar.

_____ dimes = 1 dollar

Unit 5 • Study Guide and Review   four hundred thirty-three **433**

Write the time.

6.
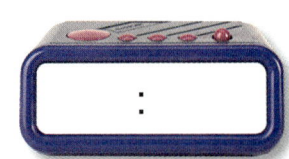

7.
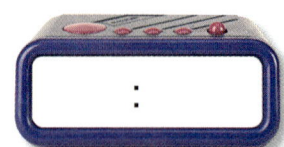

8.
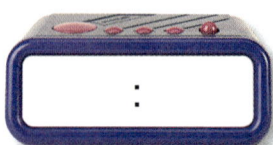

Color one part. Circle the fraction for the shaded part.

9.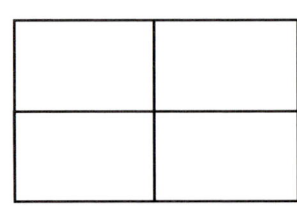

$\frac{1}{2}$ $\frac{1}{3}$ $\frac{1}{4}$

10.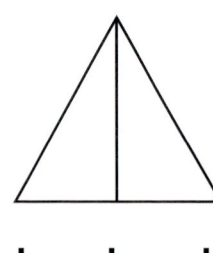

$\frac{1}{2}$ $\frac{1}{3}$ $\frac{1}{4}$

11.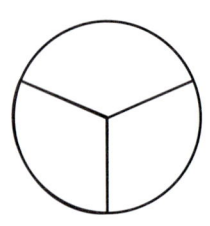

$\frac{1}{2}$ $\frac{1}{3}$ $\frac{1}{4}$

Problem Solving

Circle the best estimate for the activity.

12. Take a walk in the park.

about one minute

about one hour

about one week

Name _____

✓ Performance Assessment

Party Favors

Ed had these hats and blowers to give to friends at his party.

Choose one of the objects in the picture.

Use a fraction to tell what part of a group the object is.

Show your work.

Draw a picture to show the group.
Color the object you chose.

What part of the group does your fraction show?

Unit 5 • Performance Assessment

four hundred thirty-five **435**

Name _____

TECHNOLOGY

**The Learning Site •
Willy the Watchdog**

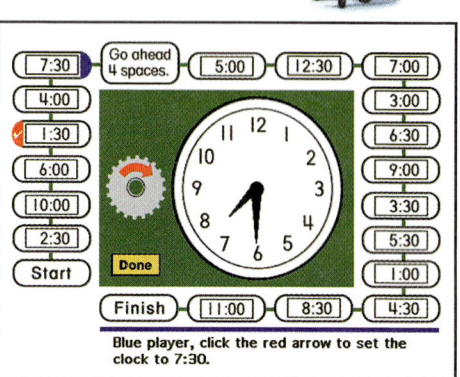

1. Go to **www.harcourtschool.com**.
2. Click on .
3. Play with a friend.
4. Set the clock to match each time.
5. Play again.

Practice and Problem Solving

Write the time.

1.

   3:00

2.

   ~~10~~:30

3.

   ~~12~~:30

Draw the hour hand and the minute hand.

4.

   11:00

5.

   2:30

6.

   6:30

7. Draw the hands on the clock to show 30 minutes later than 5:00.

   5:30

436 four hundred thirty-six

**LOOKING BACK
SCHOOL HOME CONNECTION**

Dear Family,

In Unit 5 we learned about money, time, and fractions. Here is a game for us to play together. This game will give me a chance to share what I have learned.

Love,

_____

Directions
1. Put your game piece at START.
2. Your partner hides 3 pennies in one hand and 2 pennies in the other.
3. Tap on one of your partner's hands. Your partner opens that hand.
4. Count the pennies. Move forward that many spaces.
5. Tell about the picture you land on.
   - Show the value with coins.
   - Tell what fraction is shown.
   - Tell what time the clock shows.
6. Take turns.
7. The first person to get to END wins.

Materials
- pile of pennies, nickels, dimes, and quarters
- 2 game pieces or 2 rocks

Tell About It

Unit 6 • Unit Game

four hundred thirty-seven A **437A**

Dear Family,

During the next few weeks, we will learn about measurement. We will also learn about adding and subtracting 2-digit numbers. Here is important math vocabulary and a list of books to share.

Love,

_____

Vocabulary
- inch
- foot
- pound
- cup

Vocabulary Power

An **inch** is a customary unit for measuring short lengths.

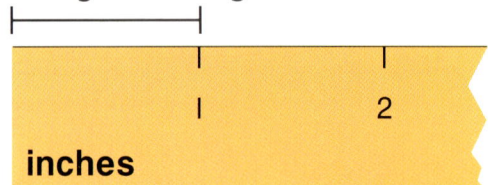

A **foot** is a customary unit for measuring longer lengths.

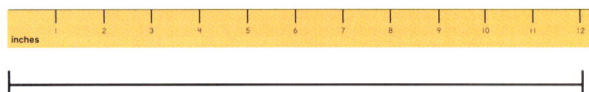

This bag of sugar weighs 1 **pound**.

A **cup** is a customary unit for measuring how much an object holds.

BOOKS TO SHARE

To read about measurement and about 2-digit numbers with your child, look for these books in your library.

Koala Lou, by Mem Fox, Harcourt, 1994.

Stone Soup, by Ann McGovern, Scholastic, 1986.

Lulu's Lemonade, by Barbara deRubertis, Kane Press, 2000.

One Hundred Hungry Ants, by Elinor J. Pinczes, Houghton Mifflin, 1999.

 Visit *The Learning Site* for additional ideas and activities. www.harcourtschool.com

Name _____

✓ Check What You Know

Compare Length

Circle the longer object.
Draw a line under the shorter object.

1.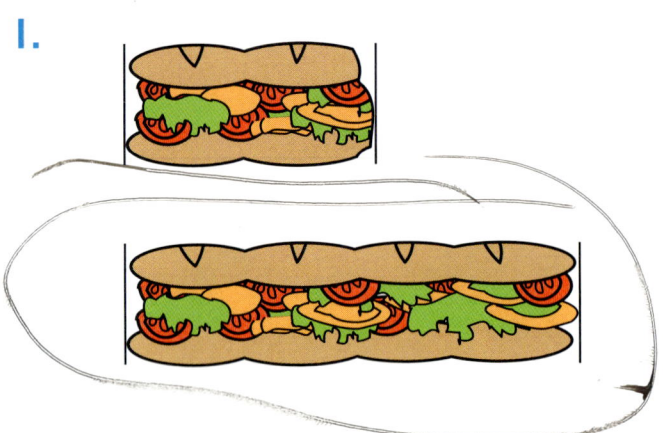

2.

3.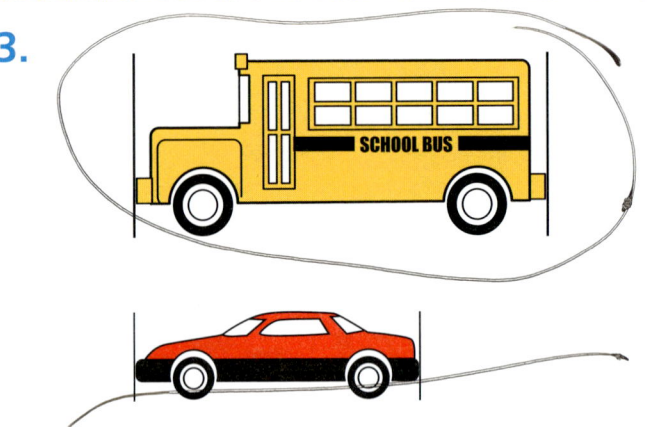

4.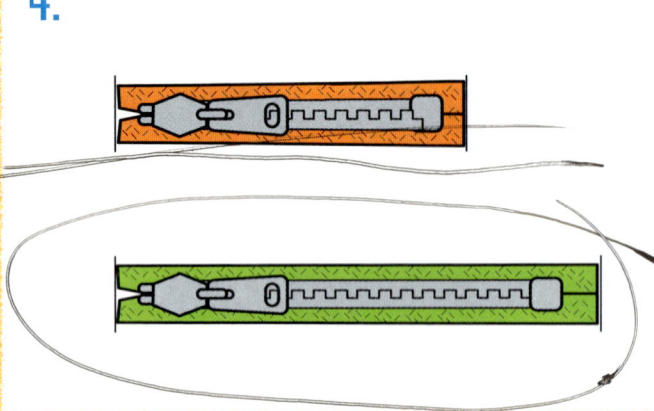

Order Length

Circle the objects that are in order from shortest to longest, starting at the top.

5.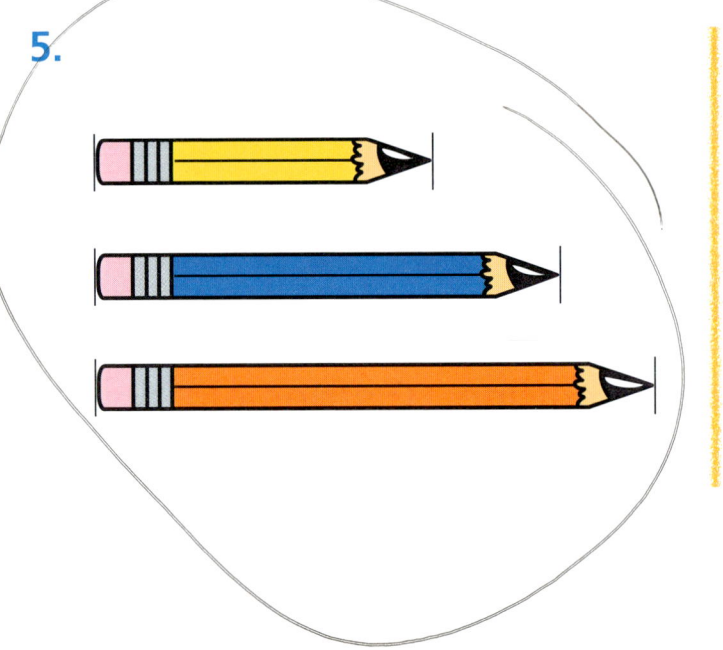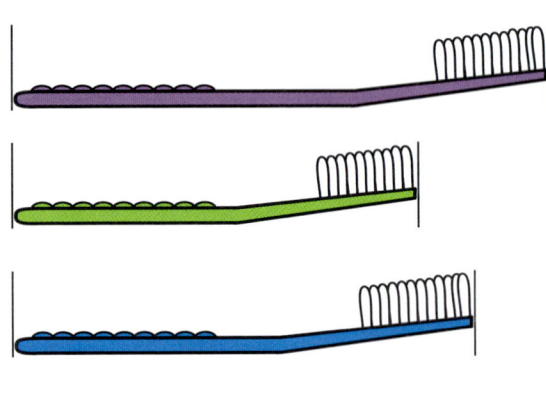

Name _____

Compare Lengths

Vocabulary
shortest
longest

HANDS ON Explore

These paper strips are in order from **shortest** to **longest**.

shortest

longest

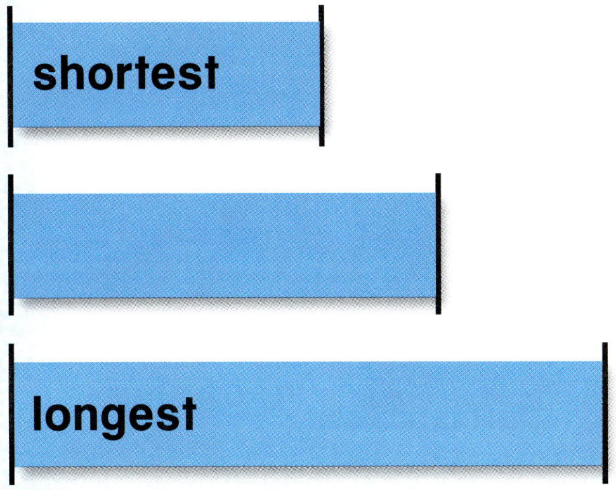

Connect

Put three paper strips in order from shortest to longest. Draw them.

1. shortest

2.

3. longest

Explain It • Daily Reasoning

In what other way could you put the paper strips in order?

Chapter 26 • Length

four hundred thirty-nine **439**

Practice and Problem Solving

Use real objects. Cut yarn to show each length. Use different colors. Then compare the pieces of yarn. Tell which object is the longest and which is the shortest.

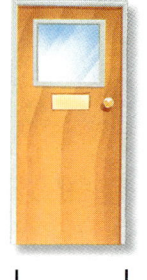  

Circle the object to answer the question.

1. Which is longer?

2. Which is shorter?

3. Which is longer?

4. Which is the longest?

Problem Solving
Visual Thinking

5. Circle the string that is longer. Use real string to check.

 **Write About It** • Look at Exercise 5. Explain your answer.

HOME ACTIVITY • Give your child three small objects of different lengths. Ask him or her to put them in order from shortest to longest.

Name _____

Use Nonstandard Units

Explore (HANDS ON)

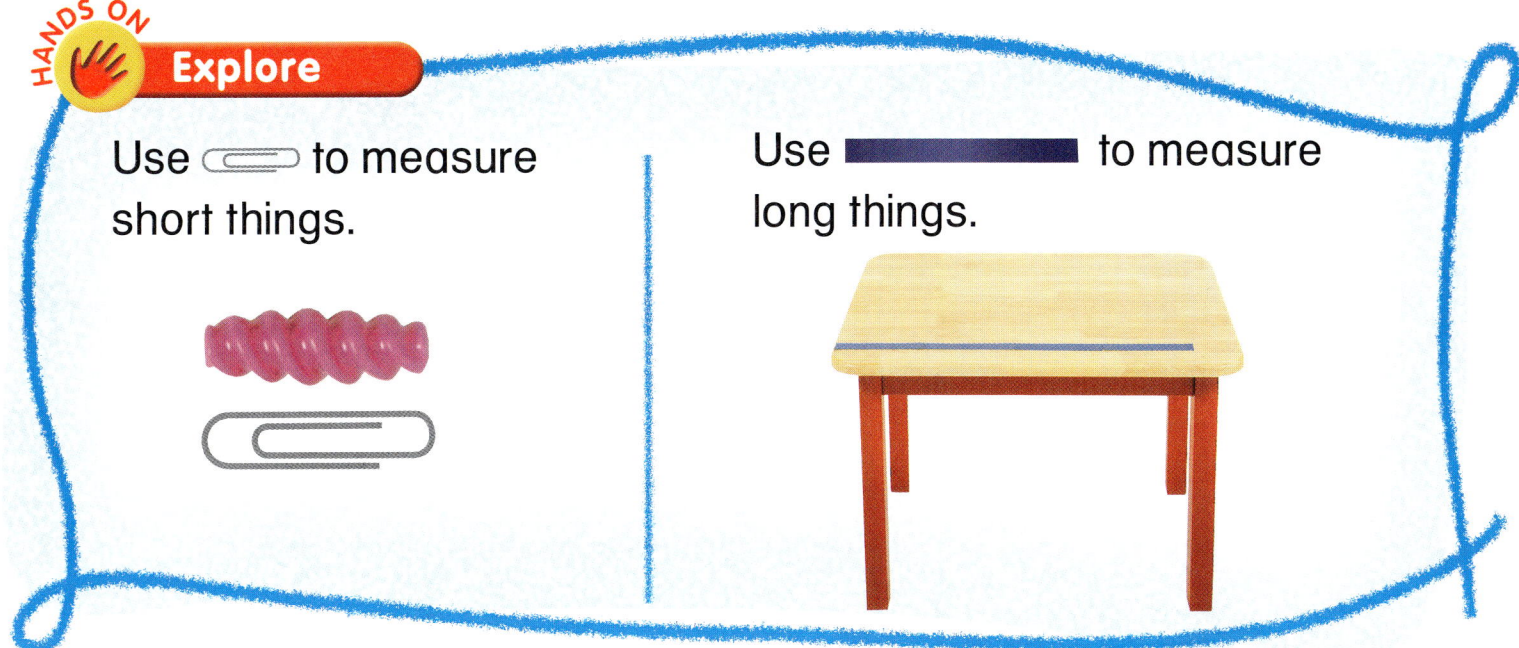

Use 🖇 to measure short things.

Use ▬ to measure long things.

Connect

Use real objects. Circle the unit you would use to measure. Then measure.

Object	Unit	Measurement
1. 🪑	🖇 / ▬	about _____
2. ✂️	🖇 / ▬	about _____
3. 📚	🖇 / ▬	about _____
4. ✏️	🖇 / ▬	about _____

Explain It • Daily Reasoning

How do you decide which unit to choose?

Practice and Problem Solving

Use real objects and .
Estimate. Then measure.
Circle the shortest object with 🖍️ (orange).
Circle the longest object with 🖍️ (blue).

	Object	Estimate	Measurement
1.	(crayon)	about _____	about _____
2.	(book)	about _____	about _____
3.	(footstool)	about _____	about _____
4.	(desk)	about _____	about _____

Problem Solving
Logical Reasoning

5. Circle your answer.

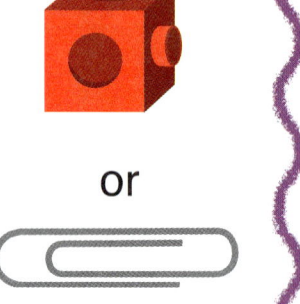

Carol measured with 📎.
Then she measured with 🟥.
Did she use more 📎 or 🟥?

Write About It • Look at Exercise 5. Draw an object that is longer. Draw an object that is shorter.

HOME ACTIVITY • Give your child some paper clips or other small objects that are all the same length. Have him or her use them to measure things around the house.

Name _____

Inches

Explore

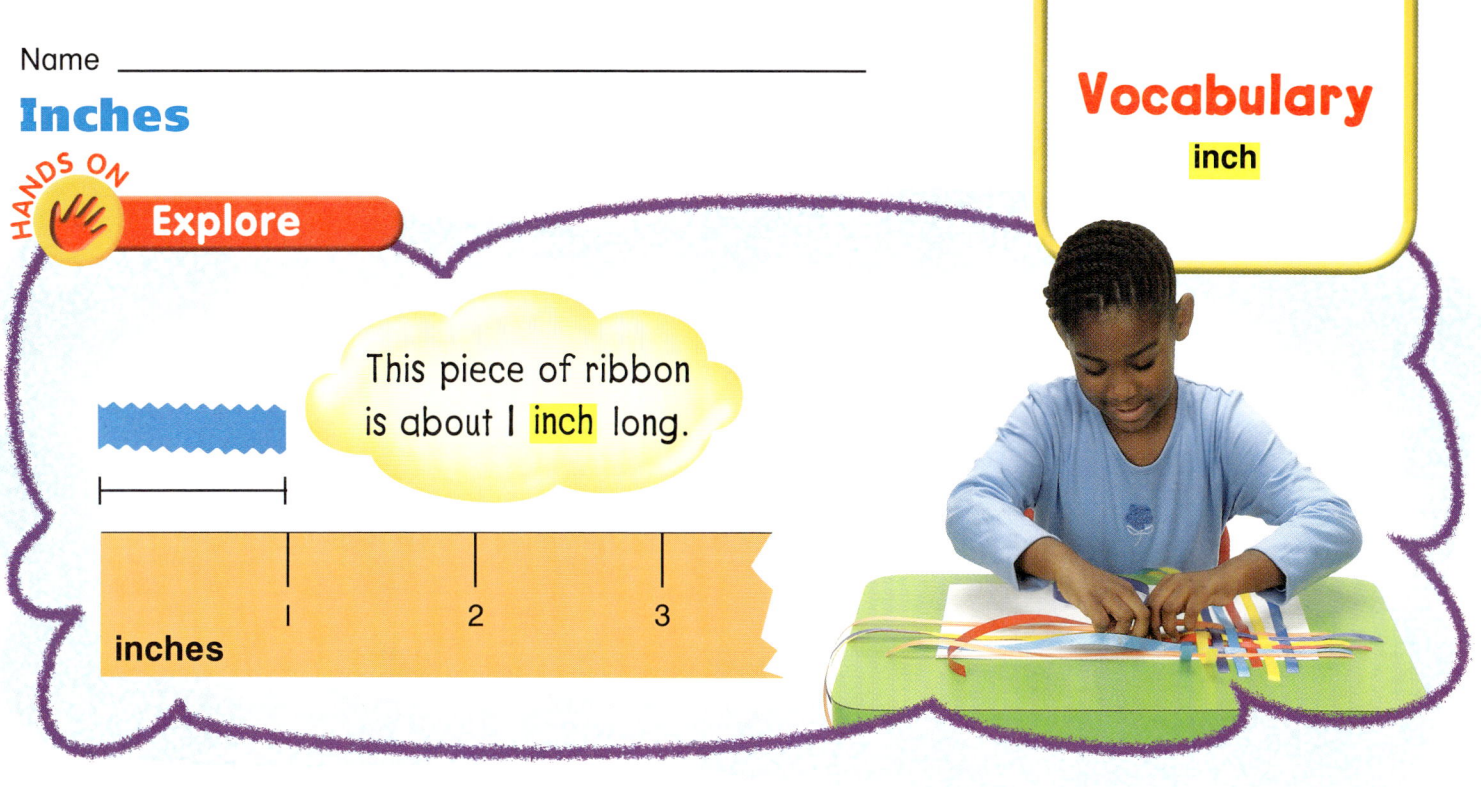

Vocabulary
inch

Connect

Use an inch ruler to measure.
Circle the longest ribbon.
Underline the shortest ribbon.

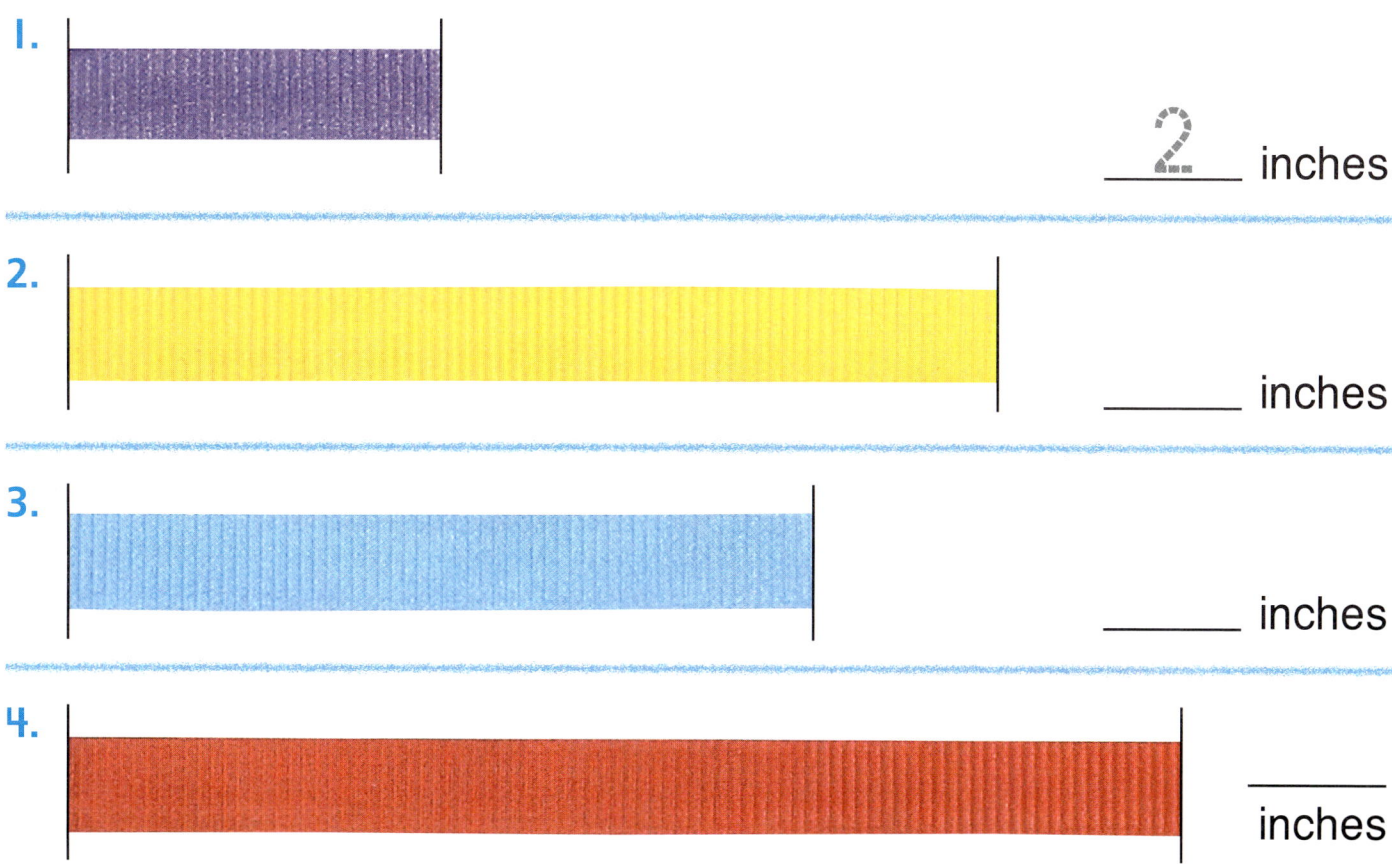

1. ___2___ inches
2. _____ inches
3. _____ inches
4. _____ inches

Explain It • Daily Reasoning

How did you know which ribbons were the longest and the shortest?

Practice and Problem Solving

Use real objects and an inch ruler.
Estimate. Then measure.

	Object	Estimate	Measurement
1.		about _____ inches	about _____ inches
2.		about _____ inches	about _____ inches
3.		about _____ inches	about _____ inches
4.		about _____ inches	about _____ inches

Problem Solving
Estimation

5. Rita's pencil is 6 inches long.
   About how long is Ben's pencil?

Rita's pencil

Ben's pencil   about _____ inches

 **Write About It** • Look at Exercise 5.
Explain your estimate.

🏠 **HOME ACTIVITY** • Have your child estimate the lengths in inches of some small objects. Together, use a ruler to check.

Name _____

Inches and Feet

Vocabulary
foot
feet

Explore (Hands On)

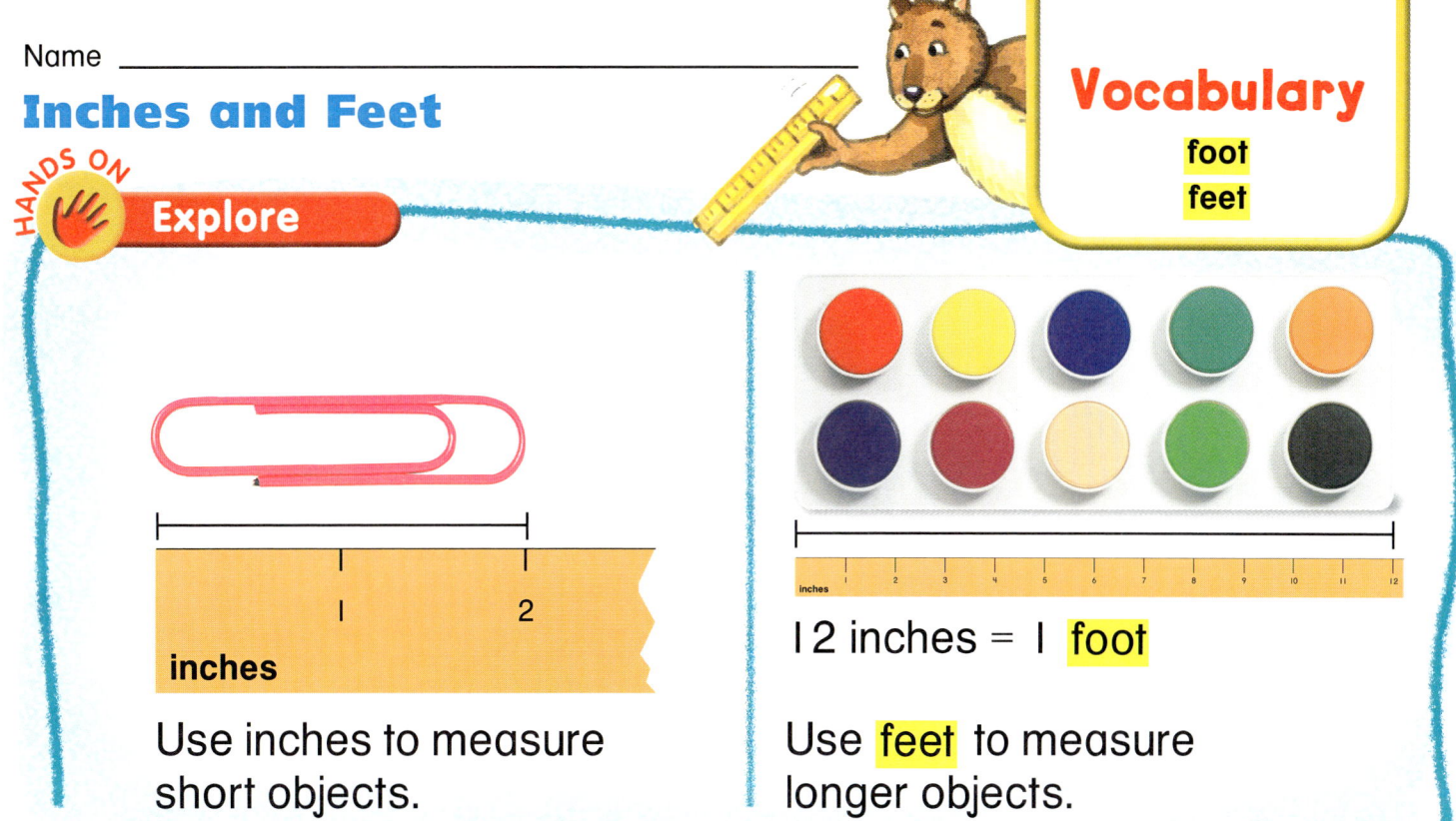

Use inches to measure short objects.

12 inches = 1 foot

Use feet to measure longer objects.

Connect

Use real objects. Circle the units you would use to measure.

1.  inches / (feet)

2. 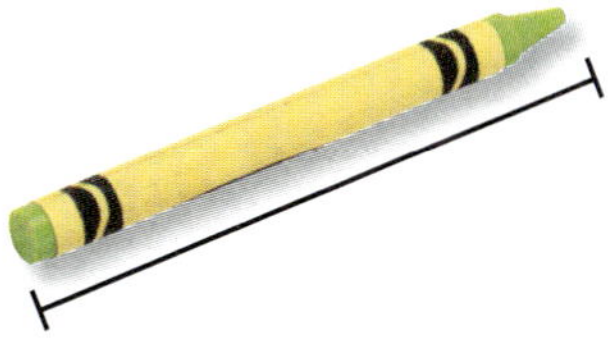 inches / feet

3. 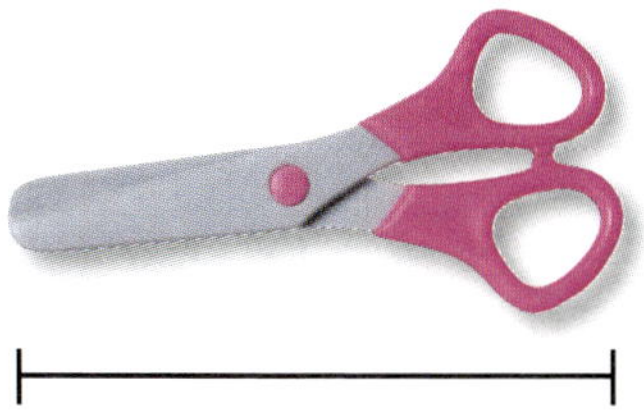 inches / feet

4.  inches / feet

5.  inches / feet

6. 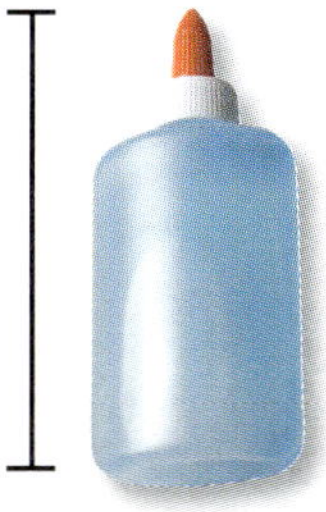 inches / feet

Explain It • Daily Reasoning

Estimate the measurements of the door. How could you check?

Chapter 26 • Length

four hundred forty-five **445**

Practice and Problem Solving

About how long is the real object? Circle the answer that makes sense.

THINK: A paper clip is about 1 inch. Your math book is about 1 foot.

1.  6 inches / 6 feet

2. 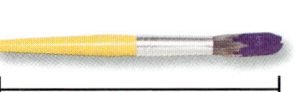 1 inch / 1 foot

3.  12 inches / 12 feet

4. 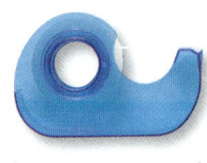 4 inches / 4 feet

5.  3 inches / 3 feet

6.  5 inches / 5 feet

Problem Solving
Application

7. Look around your classroom. Draw one object you can measure in feet. Draw one object you can measure in inches.

 Write About It • Look at Exercise 7. Write a sentence about each of the objects you drew. Use the words **feet** and **inches**.

HOME ACTIVITY • Gather some objects of different lengths. Have your child choose the objects that can be measured in feet.

Name _____

Centimeters

Vocabulary
centimeter

Explore

This bead is about 1 centimeter long.

Connect

Use a centimeter ruler to measure.
Circle the longest object. Underline the shortest object.

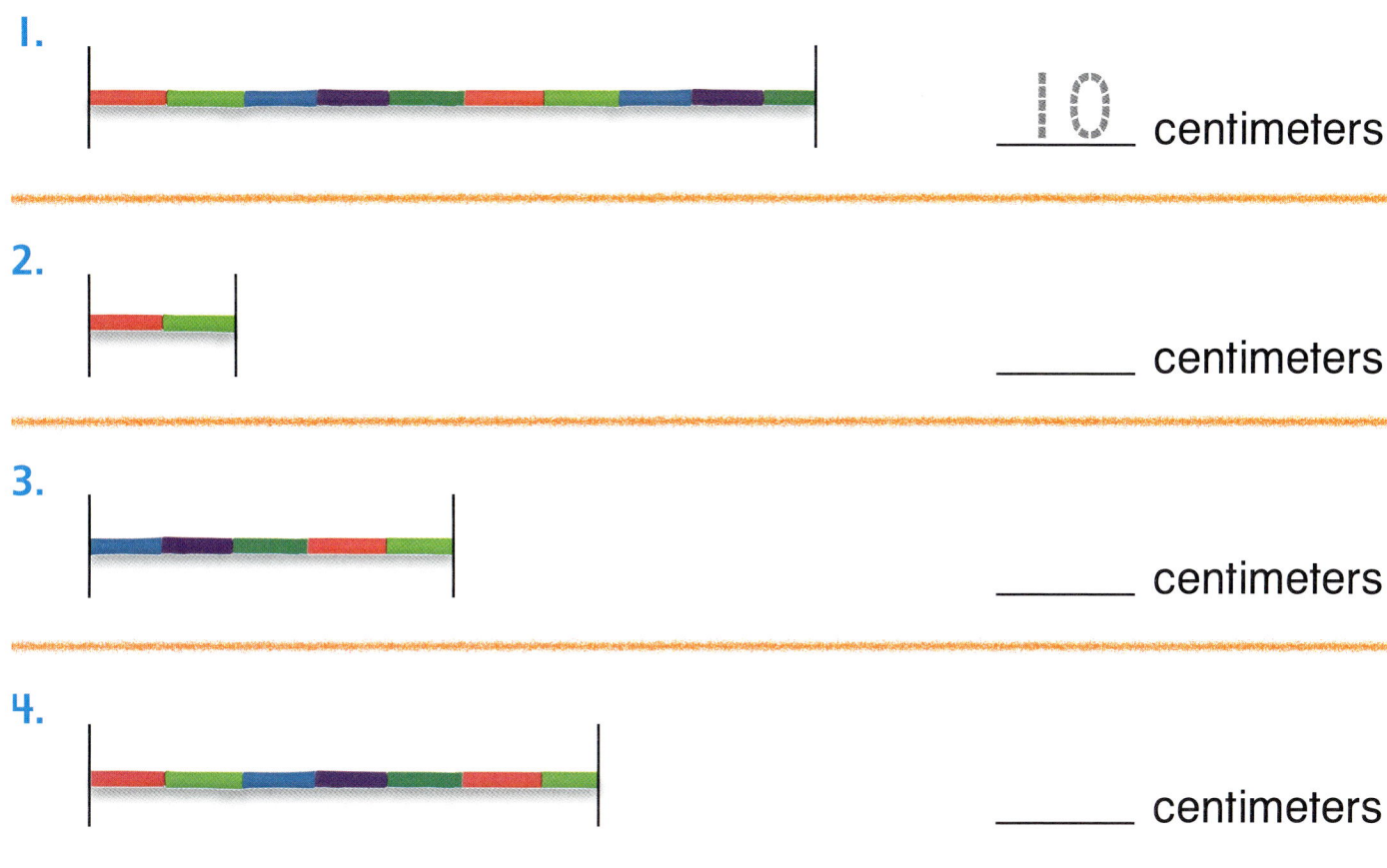

1. _10_ centimeters
2. _____ centimeters
3. _____ centimeters
4. _____ centimeters

Explain It • Daily Reasoning

How did you know which objects were the longest and the shortest?

Practice and Problem Solving

Use real objects and a centimeter ruler. Estimate. Then measure.

Object	Estimate	Measurement
1. (crayon)	about _____ centimeters	about _____ centimeters
2. (paper clip)	about _____ centimeters	about _____ centimeters
3. (eraser)	about _____ centimeters	about _____ centimeters
4. (pencil)	about _____ centimeters	about _____ centimeters

Problem Solving

Estimation

5. Anna's string of beads is 10 centimeters long. About how long is Tia's string of beads?

Anna's string

Tia's string

about _____ centimeters

 **Write About It** • Look at Exercise 5. How did you decide how long Tia's string of beads is?

HOME ACTIVITY • Give your child two objects of different lengths. Tell him or her how long in centimeters one of them is. Have your child tell you which object he or she thinks is that length.

Name _____

Problem Solving Skill
Make Reasonable Estimates

Lydia makes necklaces.
About how many beads long is the string?

about 2   about 4   about 6

2 beads long is   4 beads long   6 beads long
too short.   is about right.   is too long.

About how many beads long is the string?
Circle the answer that makes sense.

1.

   about 5   about 8   about 10

2.

   about 2   about 6   about 10

3.

   about 3   about 10   about 15

4.

   about 3   about 5   about 10

Chapter 26 • Length

Problem Solving Practice

About how many beads long is the string?
Circle the answer that makes sense.

THINK: Look at the choices to help you decide.

1.

about 2   about 3   (about 5)

2.

about 5   about 10   about 15

3.

about 2   about 3   about 7

4.

about 3   about 10   about 15

5.

about 2   about 4   about 6

HOME ACTIVITY • Ask your child to explain how he or she chose each answer.

Name _____

Extra Practice

Circle the string that is the shortest.

1.

Use the real object and . Estimate. Then measure.

2.

Estimate about _____

Measurement about _____

Use the real object and an inch ruler. Estimate. Then measure.

3.

Estimate about _____ inches

Measurement about _____ inches

Use the real object and a centimeter ruler. Estimate. Then measure.

4.

Estimate   about _____ centimeters

Measurement about _____ centimeters

Problem Solving

About how many beads long is the string?
Circle the answer that makes sense.

5.

about 2   about 6   about 10

Chapter 26 • Length

Name _____

✓ Review/Test

Concepts and Skills

Circle the string that is the longest.

1.

Use the real object and ⌐▭. Estimate. Then measure.

Use the real object and an inch ruler. Estimate. Then measure.

2.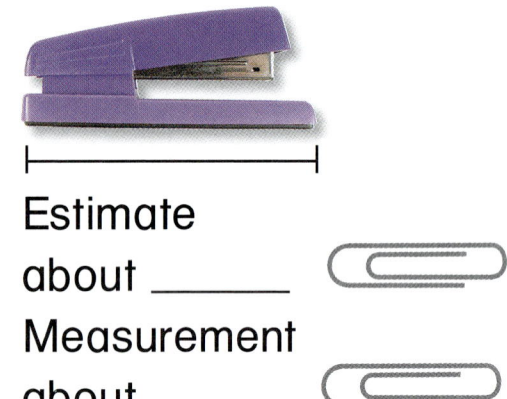

Estimate about _____ ⌐▭
Measurement about _____ ⌐▭

3.

Estimate about _____ inches
Measurement about _____ inches

Use the real object and a centimeter ruler. Estimate. Then measure.

4.

Estimate   about _____ centimeters

Measurement   about _____ centimeters

Problem Solving

About how many beads long is the string?
Circle the answer that makes sense.

5.

about 3   about 5   about 7

Name _____

Standardized Test Prep
Chapters 1–26

Choose the answer for questions 1–5.

1. Which crayon is the shortest?

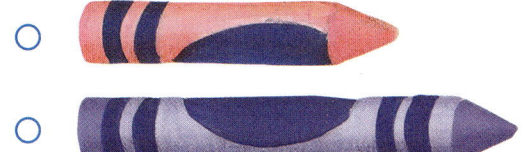

○   ○
○   ○

2. Use a  to measure.
   About how long is the paint brush?

   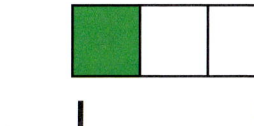

   2   3   4   8
   ○   ○   ○   ○

3. What fraction does the green part show?

   $\frac{1}{2}$ $\frac{1}{3}$ $\frac{1}{4}$ $\frac{1}{5}$
   ○   ○   ○   ○

4. Which unit would you use to measure a door?

   ○ inch
   ○ centimeter
   ○ foot

5. Which is the best estimate?
   About how many beads long is the string?

   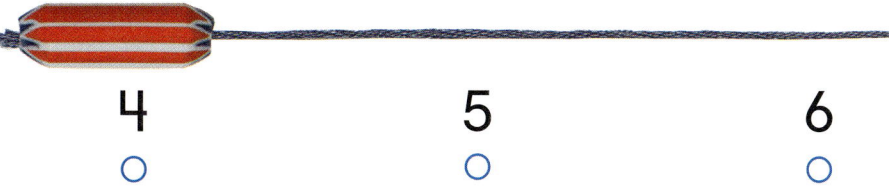

   4   5   6   7
   ○   ○   ○   ○

Show What You Know

6. Draw a ruler that is 3 inches long. Mark each inch. Use your ruler to measure your thumb. Draw a line to show how long it is.

   Is your thumb longer or shorter than your ruler? Circle to explain.

Chapter 26   four hundred fifty-three **453**

Name _____

MATH GAME

Ruler Race

Play with a partner.

1. Put your 🎯 at START.
2. Spin the 🎯. 
3. Use a ruler to find an object about that many inches long.
4. Move your 🎯 that many spaces.
5. The first player to get to END wins.

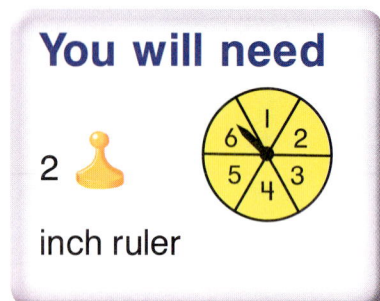

You will need

2 🎯

inch ruler

Name _____

✓ Check What You Know

Compare Weight

Circle the object that is heavier.
Mark an X on the object that is lighter.

1.

2.

3.

4.

5.

6.

Use this page to review important skills needed for this chapter.

Name _____

Use a Balance

Vocabulary
balance

Explore

It takes 6 bears to **balance** the crayons.

It takes a lot of paper clips to balance the crayons.

Connect

Use a  and real objects.
Circle the unit you would use to measure.
Then measure.

	Object	Unit	Measurement
1.	scissors	paper clip / bear	about _____
2.	dime	paper clip / bear	about _____
3.	sharpener	paper clip / bear	about _____
4.	glue	paper clip / bear	about _____

Explain It • Daily Reasoning

How did you decide which unit to use?

Chapter 27 • Weight

Practice and Problem Solving

About how many ⌒ does it take to balance?
Use real objects, a ⚖, and ⌒.
Estimate. Then measure.

Object	Estimate	Measurement
1. ✏️	about _____ ⌒	about _____ ⌒
2. 📏	about _____ ⌒	about _____ ⌒
3. (chalk)	about _____ ⌒	about _____ ⌒
4. (eraser)	about _____ ⌒	about _____ ⌒

5. Circle the heaviest object in blue.
6. Circle the lightest object in red.

Problem Solving

Logical Reasoning

7. 2 boxes of ⌒ balance a 🧀.

    6 boxes of ⌒ balance a 📘.

    How many 🧀 will balance the 📘? _____ 🧀

**Write About It** • Look at Exercise 5.
Draw a picture to show your work.

🏠 **HOME ACTIVITY** • Give your child some cans or boxes. Ask him or her to put them in order from heaviest to lightest.

Name _____

Pounds

Vocabulary
pound

 **Explore**

This bag of sugar weighs about one **pound**.

This bag of flour weighs about 5 pounds.

Connect

Look at each object.
Circle the better estimate.

1.

   (about 1 pound)

   about 10 pounds

2.

   about 1 pound

   about 10 pounds

3.

   about 1 pound

   about 10 pounds

4.

   about 1 pound

   about 10 pounds

Explain It • Daily Reasoning

Explain how you estimated what the objects would weigh.

Chapter 27 • Weight   four hundred fifty-nine **459**

Practice and Problem Solving

Find three items to weigh. Draw them. Estimate how much each object weighs. Then measure.

Object	Estimate	Measurement
1.	about _____ pounds	about _____ pounds
2.	about _____ pounds	about _____ pounds
3.	about _____ pounds	about _____ pounds

4. Circle the heaviest item in blue.
5. Circle the lightest item in red.

Problem Solving
Visual Thinking

Does each object weigh more than or less than 1 pound? Circle the better estimate.

6.

| more than 1 pound | more than 1 pound | more than 1 pound |
| less than 1 pound | less than 1 pound | less than 1 pound |

 Write About It • Draw three things that weigh less than a pound. Tell how you know.

 HOME ACTIVITY • Ask your child to read you the weights, in pounds, of some grocery items.

Name _____

Kilograms

Explore (Hands On)

This large book is about 1 kilogram.

This paper clip is about 1 gram.

Vocabulary
kilogram
gram

Connect

Circle the unit you would use to measure the real object.

1. (grams)   kilograms
2. grams   kilograms
3. grams   kilograms
4. grams   kilograms
5. grams   kilograms
6. grams   kilograms
7. grams   kilograms
8. grams   kilograms
9. grams   kilograms

Explain It • Daily Reasoning

What kind of objects did you choose to measure in grams? Why?

Chapter 27 • Weight

Practice and Problem Solving

Estimate how much the real object will measure. Use grams or kilograms. Then measure.

Object	Estimate	Measurement
1.	about _____ kilograms	about _____ kilograms
2.	about _____ grams	about _____ grams
3.	about _____ kilograms	about _____ kilograms
4.	about _____ grams	about _____ grams

Problem Solving
Visual Thinking

Think about the real objects. Which would you measure in grams? Circle in 🖍.

5.

 **Write About It** • Draw three things that weigh more than 1 kilogram. Tell how you know.

HOME ACTIVITY • Ask your child to read you the weights, in grams, of some grocery items.

462 four hundred sixty-two

Name _____

Problem Solving Strategy
Predict and Test

How many grams is this marker?

UNDERSTAND

What do you want to find out?
How many grams is the marker?

PLAN

How will you solve the problem?
I will predict how many grams it is.
To test, I will use the balance to measure.

SOLVE

Predict.
Then use large 🖇 as grams to balance.

THINK:
A large paper clip is about 1 gram.

Predict _____ grams   Test __9__ grams

CHECK

Was your prediction close?
Explain.

~~~~~~~~~~~~~~~~~~~~~~~~~~~~~~~~~~~~~~

How many grams is the object?
Use the real object and 🖇.

Predict. Then test.

1.

   Predict _____ grams   Test _____ grams

Chapter 27 • Weight

four hundred sixty-three **463**

Problem Solving Practice

How many grams is the object?
Use the real object and ⌒.
Predict. Then test.

Keep in Mind!
Understand
Plan
Solve
Check

1.  Predict _____ grams   Test _____ grams

2.   Predict _____ grams   Test _____ grams

3.  Predict _____ grams   Test _____ grams

4. Predict _____ grams   Test _____ grams

5. Predict _____ grams   Test _____ grams

HOME ACTIVITY • Ask your child to explain his or her answers for Exercises 1–4.

Name _____

Extra Practice

1. Choose the unit you would use to measure.
   Circle 🖇 or 🧸.
   Use a ⚖ to measure the real object.

Object	Unit	Measurement
(sharpener)	🖇  🧸	about _____

2. Find an object to weigh. Draw it.
   Estimate how much the object weighs.
   Then measure.

Object	Estimate	Measurement
	about _____ pounds	about _____ pounds

3. Estimate how much the real object will measure.
   Then measure.

Object	Estimate	Measurement
(bottle)	about _____ kilograms	about _____ kilograms

Problem Solving

4. How many grams is the object?
   Use the real object and 🖇.
   Predict. Then test.

   Predict _____ grams   Test _____ grams

Chapter 27 • Weight   four hundred sixty-five **465**

Name _____

✓ Review/Test

Concepts and Skills

1. Choose the unit you would use to measure.
   Circle 🖇 or 🐻.
   Use a ⚖ to measure the real object.

Object	Unit	Measurement
👟	🖇 🐻	about _____

2. Find an object to weigh. Draw it.
   Estimate how much the object weighs.
   Then measure.

Object	Estimate	Measurement
	about _____ pounds	about _____ pounds

3. Estimate how much the object measures.
   Then measure.

Object	Estimate	Measurement
📘	about _____ kilograms	about _____ kilograms

Problem Solving

4. How many grams is the object?
   Use the real object and 🖇.
   Predict. Then test.

   Predict _____ grams   Test _____ grams

Name _____

Standardized Test Prep
Chapters 1–27

Choose the answer for questions 1–4.

1.
```
   20
 − 10
```
   9   10   11   29
   ○   ○   ○   ○

2. Which object weighs about 1 kilogram?

   ○   ○   ○   ○

3. Which object weighs about 1 pound?

   ○   ○   ○   ○

4. Which is the heaviest?

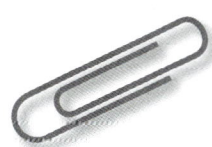   
   1 gram   5 grams   5 grams   10 grams
     ○   ○   ○   ○

Show What You Know

5. How many grams is the object? Predict. Then test.

Predict _____ grams

Test _____ grams

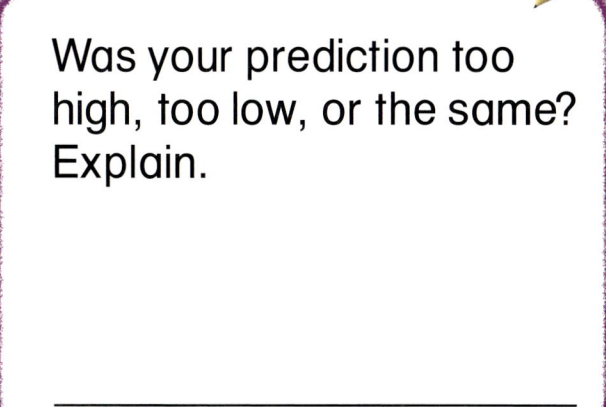

Was your prediction too high, too low, or the same? Explain.

_____

MATH GAME

Gram Grab

Play with a partner.

1. Put your 🔲 at START.
2. Toss the 🎲.
3. Move your 🔲 that many spaces.
4. Measure the object shown on that space in grams.
5. Take that many ⚪.
6. When both players get to END, count ⚪.
7. The player with more ⚪ wins.

You will need

2 🔲 ⚪
🎲 ⚖
large 📎

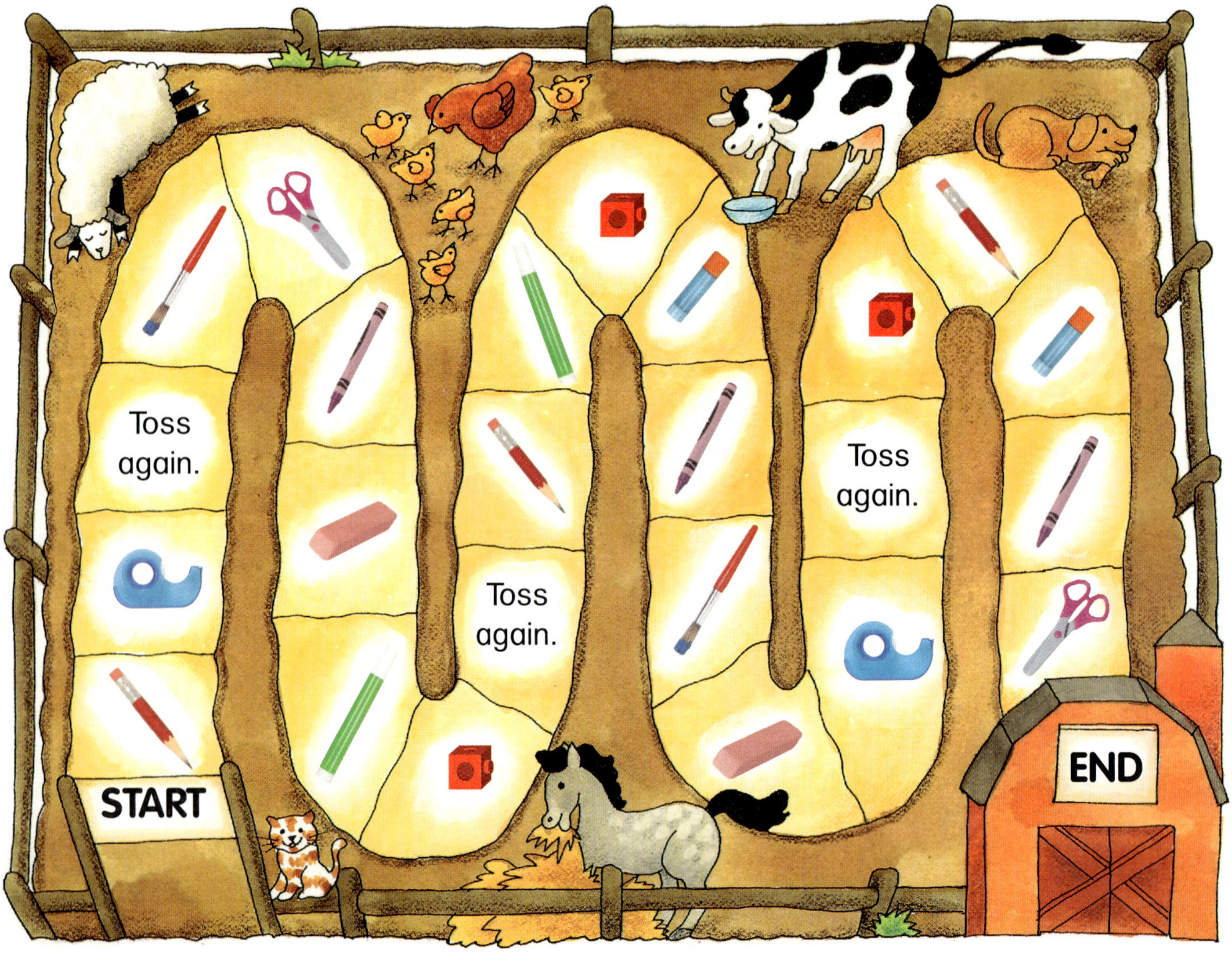

CHAPTER 28 Capacity

FUN FACTS

Each starfish needs 30 liters of saltwater to live in.

Theme: Fill It Up

Name _____

✓ Check What You Know

Compare Capacity

Circle the container that holds more.
Mark an X on the container that holds less.

1.

2.

3.

4.

5.

6.

Name _____

Nonstandard Units

Explore (Hands On)

"It took 3 of these scoops to fill the container."

"It took 6 of these cups to fill the container."

Connect

Choose the unit you would use to measure.
Circle 🥄 or ☕. Measure.

	Container	Unit	Measurement
1.	yogurt cup	scoop mug	about _____
2.	milk carton	scoop mug	about _____
3.	cottage cheese tub	scoop mug	about _____
4.	orange juice carton	scoop mug	about _____

Explain It • Daily Reasoning

How did you decide which units to use?

Chapter 28 • Capacity

Practice and Problem Solving

Use the real container and a 🥄.
Estimate. Then measure.

	Container	Estimate	Measurement
1.		about _____ 🥄	about _____ 🥄
2.		about _____ 🥄	about _____ 🥄
3.		about _____ 🥄	about _____ 🥄
4.		about _____ 🥄	about _____ 🥄

Problem Solving

Estimation

Circle your answer.

5. Which container do you think will hold the most 🥄 of rice?

Write About It • Look at Exercise 5. Explain how you chose your answer.

HOME ACTIVITY • Show your child three containers. Ask him or her to estimate which will hold the most water. Together, use a small cup or scoop to find out.

Name _____

Cups, Pints, and Quarts

Vocabulary
cup
pint
quart

Explore

You can use a cup to measure how much a container holds.

"This pint container will hold 2 cups."

"This quart container will hold 4 cups."

Connect

Use a 🥛 and containers.
Estimate. Then measure.

	Container	Estimate	Measurement
1.	(pan)	about _____ cups	about _____ cups
2.	(half & half carton)	about _____ cups	about _____ cups
3.	(measuring cup)	about _____ cups	about _____ cups
4.	(milk carton)	about _____ cups	about _____ cups

Explain It • Daily Reasoning

Which container holds about 2 cups?
Which containers hold about 4 cups?

Chapter 28 • Capacity

Practice and Problem Solving

Estimate. Then measure.
Trace to name the size of the container.

Container	Estimate	Measurement	Size
1. MILK	about ___ cups	about ___ cups	pint
2. WATER	about ___ cups	about ___ cups	pint
3. Milk carton	about ___ cups	about ___ cups	quart

Problem Solving
Logical Reasoning

4. Circle what you would use to measure a quart of milk.

5. Circle what you would use to measure a cup of juice.

Write About It  Look at Exercises 4 and 5. Explain how you decided which unit to use to measure.

 HOME ACTIVITY • Show your child three containers, and ask him or her to estimate which will hold more than a pint. Together, use a cup measure to find out.

474 four hundred seventy-four

Name _____

Liters

Vocabulary
liter

Explore

This **liter** bottle will hold a little more than 4 cups.

This liter bottle will hold a little more than 1 quart.

Connect

Estimate whether the container holds less than or more than a liter. Then use a liter bottle to measure.

	Container	Estimate	Measurement
1.		less than a liter / more than a liter	less than a liter / more than a liter
2.		less than a liter / more than a liter	less than a liter / more than a liter
3.		less than a liter / more than a liter	less than a liter / more than a liter
4.		less than a liter / more than a liter	less than a liter / more than a liter

Explain It • Daily Reasoning

Would you use a liter bottle to fill a fish tank with water? Why or why not?

Practice and Problem Solving

Does the container hold less than or more than 2 liters? Estimate. Then measure.

Container	Estimate	Measurement
1.	less than 2 liters more than 2 liters	less than 2 liters more than 2 liters
2.	less than 2 liters more than 2 liters	less than 2 liters more than 2 liters
3.	less than 2 liters more than 2 liters	less than 2 liters more than 2 liters

Problem Solving

Logical Reasoning

4. A liter bottle holds a little more than 4 cups. About how many cups will there be in 2 liter bottles?

   about _____ cups

 **Write About It** • Look at Exercise 4. Explain how you got your answer.

🏠 **HOME ACTIVITY** • Help your child find a 1-liter container and a 1-quart container. Ask him or her to tell you if a liter is less than or more than a quart. Then use water to check.

Name _____

Temperature

Vocabulary
temperature

Learn

A thermometer measures **temperature**.

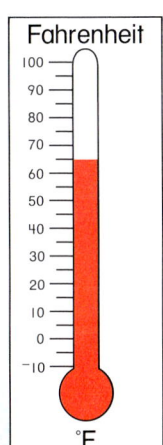

The temperature is 65 degrees.

It is __85__ °F.

It is __50__ °F.

Check

Read the thermometer.
Write the temperature.

1. 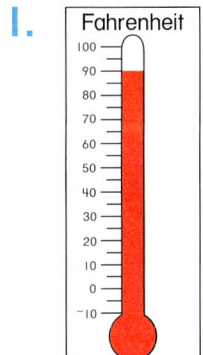   ____ °F

2. 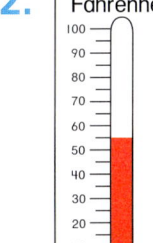   ____ °F

3. 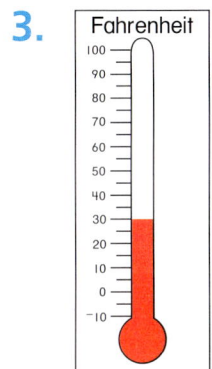   ____ °F

4.   ____ °F

Explain It • Daily Reasoning

What happens to a thermometer when the temperature gets warmer?

Chapter 28 • Capacity

Practice and Problem Solving

Read the temperature.
Color the thermometer to show the temperature.

1. 60°F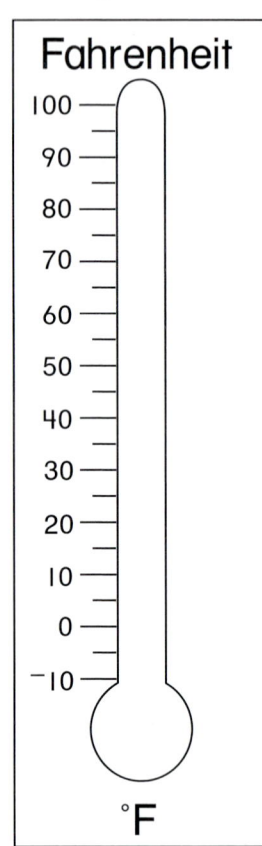
2. 20°F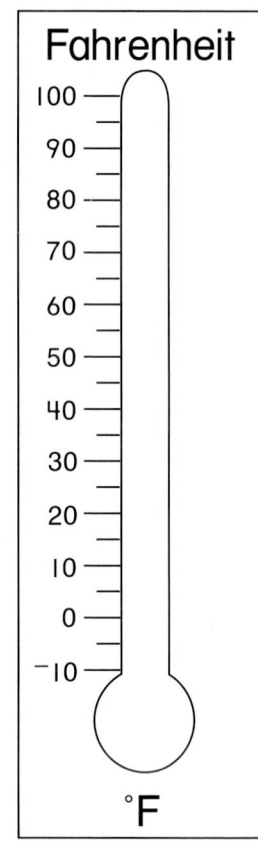
3. 75°F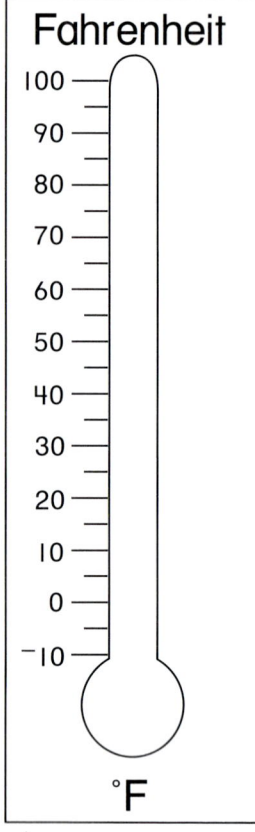
4. 95°F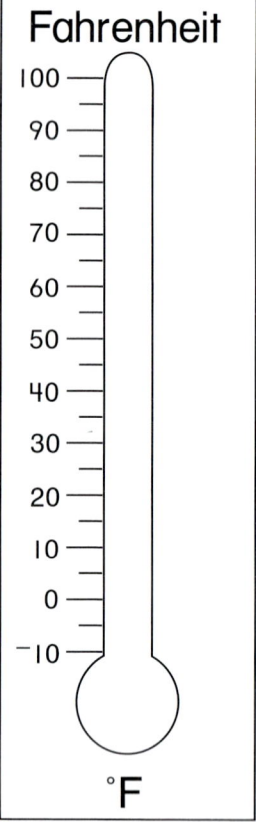

Problem Solving
Visual Thinking

5. The thermometer shows the temperature is 80 degrees. The sun goes down, and the temperature gets cooler. Circle the thermometer that shows what the temperature might be now.

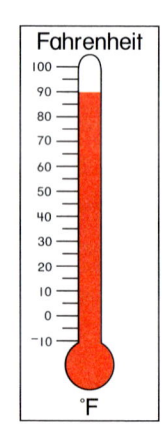 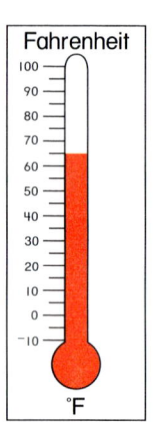

 Write About It • Tell what you would wear if the temperature was 85 degrees and what you would wear if it was 40 degrees.

HOME ACTIVITY • With your child, look at an outdoor thermometer or a weather report. Talk together about what the temperature is today.

Name _____

**Problem Solving Skill
Choose the
Measuring Tool**

"I use different tools to measure in different ways."

Find five objects to measure in different ways.
Choose the correct tool to measure in each way.
Draw and write to complete the chart.

	What to Find Out	Object	Tool	Measurement
1.	How tall is it?			
2.	How wide is it?			
3.	How much does it hold?			
4.	How much does it weigh?			
5.	How hot or cold is it?			

Chapter 28 • Capacity

Problem Solving Practice

Circle the correct tool to measure.

1. How tall is the plant?

2. Which book is heavier?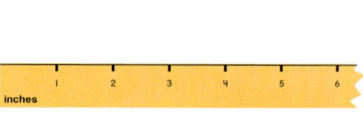

3. How much will the jar hold?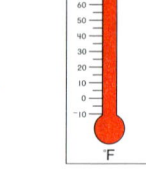

4. How wide is the chair?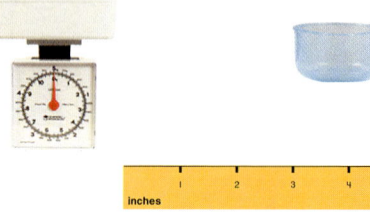

5. Which container holds more?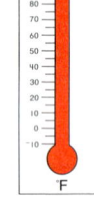

6. How cold is the water?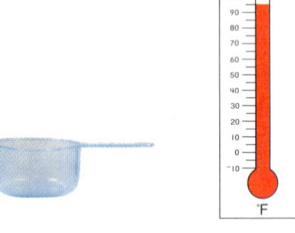

HOME ACTIVITY • Give your child an object, such as a book, and ask him or her to tell about all the different ways to measure it.

Name _____

Extra Practice

1. Use the real container and a 🥄.
   Estimate. Then measure.

Container	Estimate	Measurement
(cottage cheese)	about _____ 🥄	about _____ 🥄

2. Estimate how many cups it will take to fill the container. Then measure.

Container	Estimate	Measurement
(cup)	about _____ cups	about _____ cups

3. Estimate whether the container holds less than or more than a liter. Then use a liter bottle to measure.

Container	Estimate	Measurement
(thermos)	less than a liter more than a liter	less than a liter more than a liter

Read the temperature. Color the thermometer to show the temperature.

4. 80°F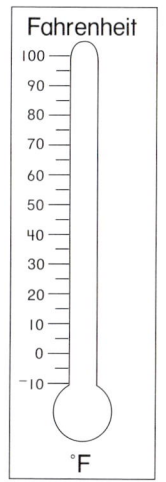

Problem Solving

5. Circle the correct tool to measure how hot the water is.

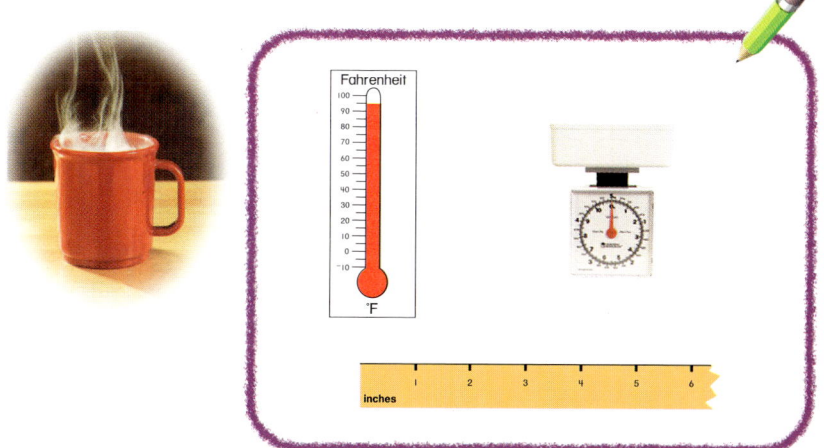

Chapter 28 • Capacity

four hundred eighty-one **481**

Name _____

✓ Review/Test

Concepts and Skills

1. Use the real container and a 🥄.
   Estimate. Then measure.

Container	Estimate	Measurement
(oats)	about _____ 🥄	about _____ 🥄

2. Estimate how many cups it will take to fill the container. Then measure.

Container	Estimate	Measurement
(half & half carton)	about _____ cups	about _____ cups

3. Estimate whether the container holds less than or more than a liter. Then use a liter bottle to measure.

Container	Estimate	Measurement
(water bottle)	less than a liter more than a liter	less than a liter more than a liter

Read the temperature.
Color the thermometer
to show the temperature.

4. 45°F

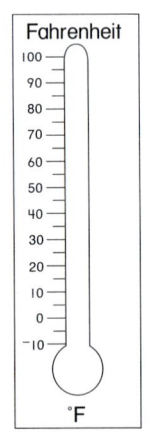

Problem Solving

5. Circle the correct tool to measure how tall the notebook is.

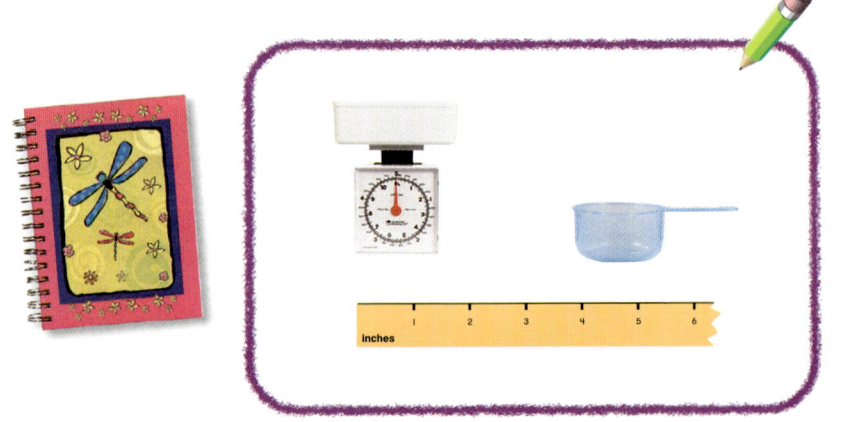

482 four hundred eighty-two

Name _____

Standardized Test Prep
Chapters 1–28

Choose the answer for questions 1–5.

1. 15 − 8 = _____

   6 ○   7 ○   8 ○   9 ○

2. Which one would you use a small 🥄 to measure?

    ○    ○    ○    ○

3. Which container holds about 1 cup?

    ○    ○    ○    ○

4. Which container holds more than 1 quart?

    ○    ○    ○    ○

5. What is the temperature?

   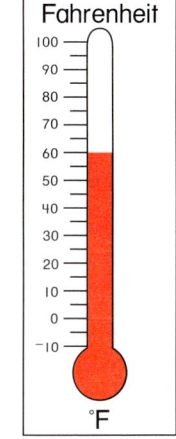

   20°F ○   32°F ○

   60°F ○   90°F ○

Show What You Know

6. How much will the glass hold? Circle the correct tool to explain how you would measure.

   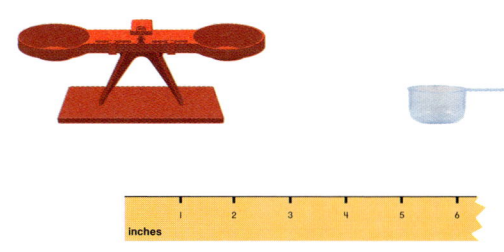

Chapter 28   four hundred eighty-three **483**

MATH GAME

How Many Cups?

Play with a partner.

1. Put your 🎳 at START.
2. Spin the 🎯.
3. Move your 🎳 to the next space that matches that color.
4. Measure to find how many cups that container holds.
5. Take 1 🔴 for each cup it holds.
6. Take turns until both players get to END.
7. The player with more counters wins.

You will need

2 🎳   70 🔴

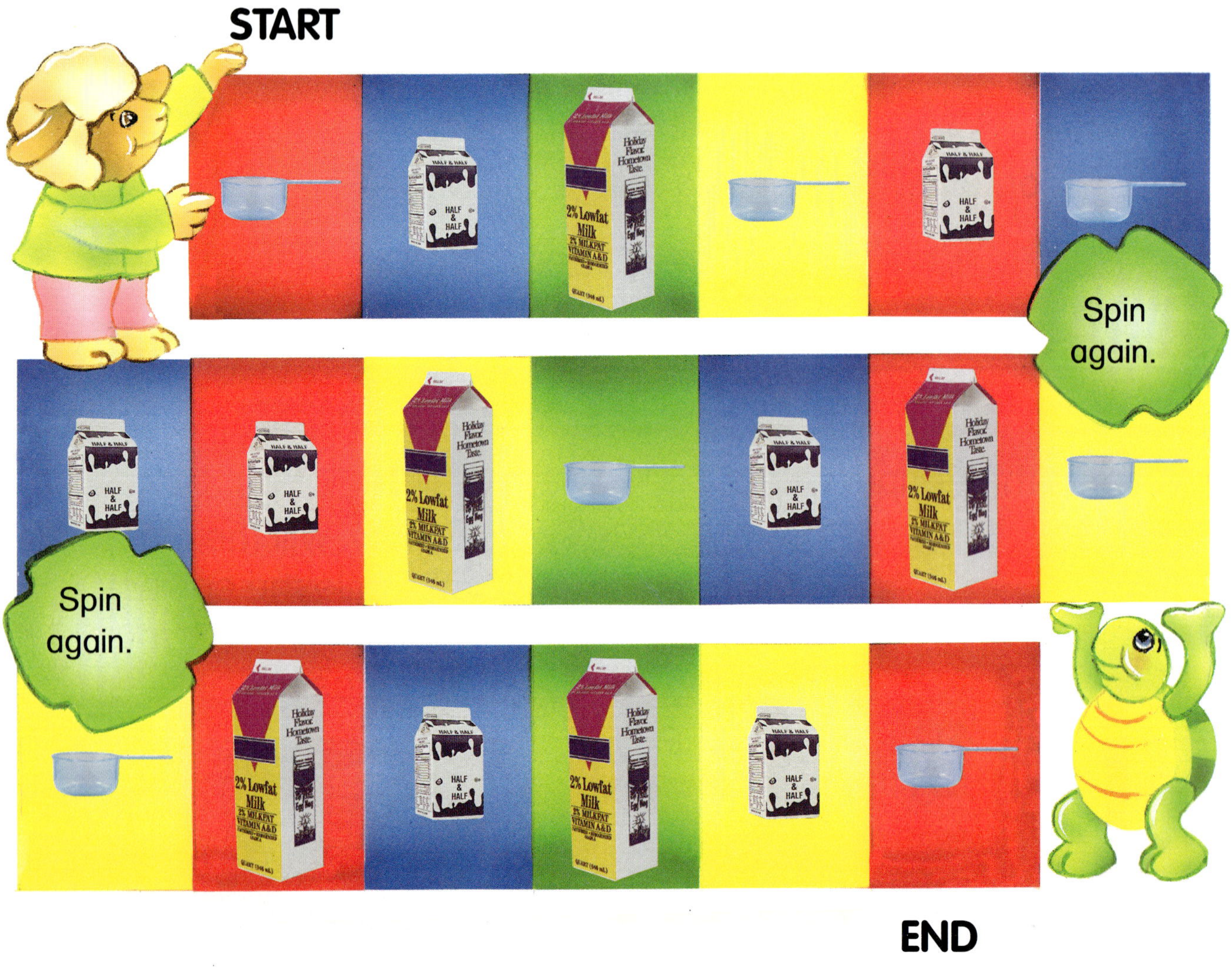

START

END

CHAPTER 29

Adding and Subtracting 2-Digit Numbers

FUN FACTS

A toucan's huge beak is almost the length of its body which is from 13 to 25 inches long.

Theme: In the Rain Forest

Name _____

✓ Check What You Know

Tens and Ones to 100

Write how many tens and ones.
Write the number.

1.

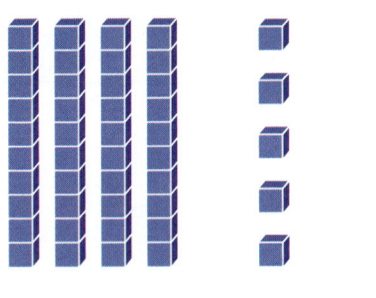

___ tens ___ ones = ___

2.

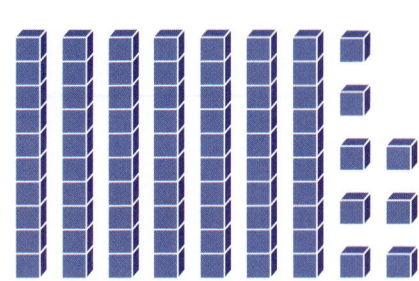

___ tens ___ ones = ___

Addition and Subtraction Facts to 20

Add or subtract.

3. 7
  +8

4. 9
  +7

5. 20
  −10

6. 18
  − 9

7. 10
  + 9

8. 17
  − 9

Fact Families to 20

Write the sum or difference. Circle the two facts if they are in the same fact family.

9. 6 + 9 = ___

16 − 9 = ___

10. 15 − 8 = ___

15 − 7 = ___

11. 9 + 8 = ___

17 − 9 = ___

12. 7 + 6 = ___

14 − 7 = ___

Name _____

Use Mental Math to Add Tens

Learn

A red panda eats 20 leaves.
Then it eats 10 more leaves.
How many leaves does it eat in all?

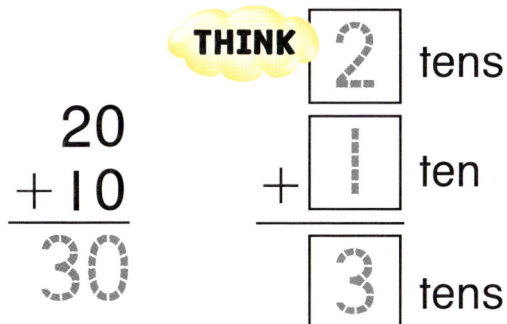

THINK: 2 tens + 1 ten = 3 tens

Start with two tens and add one more ten.

It eats __30__ leaves in all.

Check

Write how many tens. Then add.

1. 30
   +40

   THINK ☐ tens
   + ☐ tens
   ☐ tens

2. 50
   +10

   THINK ☐ tens
   + ☐ ten
   ☐ tens

3. 20
   +70

   THINK ☐ tens
   + ☐ tens
   ☐ tens

4. 40
   +40

   THINK ☐ tens
   + ☐ tens
   ☐ tens

Explain It • Daily Reasoning

How does knowing 7 + 2 = 9 help you find the sum for 70 + 20?

7 + 2 = 9

Chapter 29 • Adding and Subtracting Two-Digit Numbers

four hundred eighty-seven **487**

Practice and Problem Solving

40 + 30 means
4 tens + 3 tens.

THINK

```
  40      4 tens
 +30     +3 tens
 ───     ───────
  70      7 tens
```

Add.

1. 50   2. 30   3. 50   4. 10   5. 20
   +40   +30   +30   +30   +60

6. 10   7. 20   8. 80   9. 10   10. 70
   +70   +20   +10   +10   +20

11. 10   12. 20   13. 40   14. 30   15. 60
   +50   +30   +10   +50   +10

Problem Solving

Visual Thinking

Draw what was added.
Complete the number sentence.

16.  + =

___ + ___ = ___

 Write About It • Look at Exercise 16. Explain how you figured out how many tens to add.

 HOME ACTIVITY • Ask your child to explain how to find the sum for 30 + 20.

Name _____

Add Tens and Ones

Add.   32
     + 4

STEP 1 Show 32. Show 4.

STEP 2 Add the ones.

STEP 3 Add the tens.

	tens	ones
	3	2
+		4

	tens	ones
	3	2
+		4
		6

	tens	ones
	3	2
+		4
	3	6

Connect

Use Workmat 3 and 🟥 to add. Write the sum.

1.
	tens	ones
	2	5
+		3

2.
	tens	ones
	4	5
+		2

Explain It • Daily Reasoning

How could you find the sum for 64 + 3 without using blocks?

Practice and Problem Solving

Use Workmat 3 and 🟥 to add. Write the sum.

1.
tens	ones
4	1
+	4
4	5

tens	ones

2.
tens	ones
1	6
+	3

tens	ones

3.
tens	ones
3	5
+	2

tens	ones

4.
tens	ones
2	3
+	3

tens	ones

Problem Solving
Algebra

Write the missing numbers.

5.
tens	ones
3	1
+	☐
3	6

6.
tens	ones
5	3
+	☐
5	9

7.
tens	ones
2	2
+	☐
2	5

8.
tens	ones
6	4
+	☐
6	8

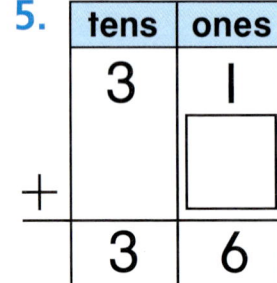

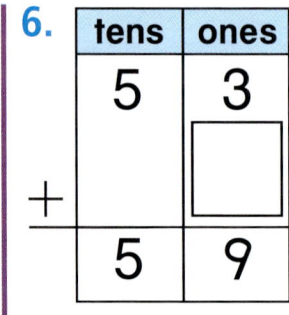

 Write About It • What are two ways you could show 19 + 1 with blocks?

 **HOME ACTIVITY** • Ask your child to draw pictures to show how to find the sum for 24 + 5.

Name _____

Add Money

Learn

> Add money amounts the same way you add other numbers.

Add the ones. Then add the tens.

Add numbers.

```
  23          23
+ 15        + 15
-----       -----
   8         38
```

Add money.

```
  23¢         23¢
+ 15¢       + 15¢
-----       -----
   8¢        38¢
```

Check

Add.

1. 32¢
   +27¢
   ____
      ¢

2. 17¢
   +10¢
   ____
      ¢

3. 75¢
   +22¢
   ____
      ¢

4. 43¢
   +16¢
   ____
      ¢

5. 55¢
   +31¢
   ____
      ¢

6. 61¢
   +18¢
   ____
      ¢

7. 24¢
   +33¢
   ____
      ¢

8. 82¢
   + 6¢
   ____
      ¢

9. 10¢
   +29¢
   ____
      ¢

10. 52¢
   + 7¢
   ____
      ¢

11. 53¢
   +15¢
   ____
      ¢

12. 36¢
   +41¢
   ____
      ¢

13. 65¢
   +23¢
   ____
      ¢

14. 24¢
   +50¢
   ____
      ¢

15. 32¢
   +47¢
   ____
      ¢

Explain It • Daily Reasoning

How are pennies like ones?
How are dimes like tens?

Practice and Problem Solving

Add.

1. 40¢ + 50¢ = 90¢
2. 72¢ + 23¢ = ___¢
3. 25¢ + 24¢ = ___¢
4. 35¢ + 4¢ = ___¢
5. 19¢ + 20¢ = ___¢

6. 53¢ + 46¢ = ___¢
7. 64¢ + 14¢ = ___¢
8. 75¢ + 3¢ = ___¢
9. 39¢ + 50¢ = ___¢
10. 81¢ + 17¢ = ___¢

11. 44¢ + 33¢ = ___¢
12. 24¢ + 42¢ = ___¢
13. 10¢ + 5¢ = ___¢
14. 61¢ + 8¢ = ___¢
15. 50¢ + 25¢ = ___¢

Problem Solving
Algebra

Write the missing numbers.

16. 42¢ + ☐☐¢ = 64¢

17. ☐☐¢ + 33¢ = 66¢

18. 35¢ + ☐¢ = 39¢

Write About It • Look at Exercise 18. Tell how you can subtract to find the missing number.

HOME ACTIVITY • Have your child add a group of 9 or fewer pennies and a group of 9 or fewer dimes.

492 four hundred ninety-two

Name _____

Use Mental Math to Subtract Tens

Learn

A bird finds 40 seeds.
It eats 30 of them.
How many seeds are left?

Start with 4 tens and subtract 3 tens.

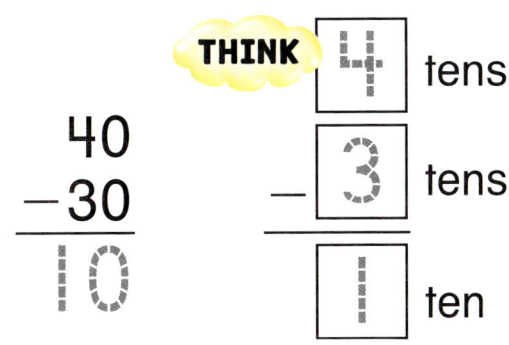

THINK: 4 tens − 3 tens = 1 ten

40
−30
―――
10

There are __10__ seeds left.

Check

Write how many tens. Then subtract.

1. 90
   −30

   THINK: ☐ tens − ☐ tens = ☐ tens

2. 30
   −10

   THINK: ☐ tens − ☐ ten = ☐ tens

3. 80
   −40

   THINK: ☐ tens − ☐ tens = ☐ tens

4. 70
   −20

   THINK: ☐ tens − ☐ tens = ☐ tens

Explain It • Daily Reasoning

How does knowing 6 − 4 = 2 help you find the difference for 60 − 40?

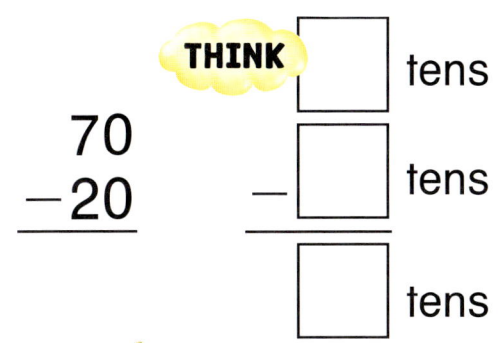

Chapter 29 • Adding and Subtracting Two-Digit Numbers

Practice and Problem Solving

50 − 20 means
5 tens − 2 tens.

THINK

```
  50      5 tens
 −20     −2 tens
  30      3 tens
```

Subtract.

1. 70 − 50
2. 40 − 40
3. 60 − 30
4. 80 − 70
5. 40 − 10

6. 90 − 20
7. 50 − 30
8. 20 − 10
9. 60 − 20
10. 70 − 40

11. 80 − 50
12. 30 − 20
13. 90 − 60
14. 50 − 10
15. 40 − 20

Problem Solving

Visual Thinking

Write the number sentence that tells about the picture.

16. ___ ◯ ___ ◯ ___

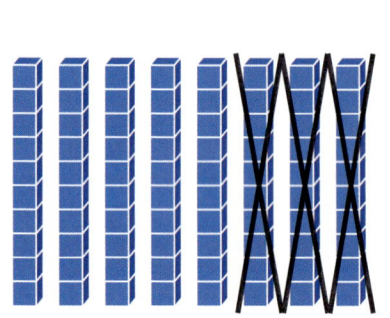

Write About It • Look at Exercise 16. Write a math story to go with your number sentence.

HOME ACTIVITY • Ask your child to explain how to find the difference for 70 − 40.

Name _____

Subtract Tens and Ones

Explore

Subtract.   28
          − 5

STEP 1 Show 28.

STEP 2 Subtract the ones.

STEP 3 Subtract the tens.

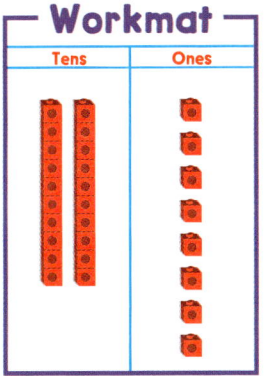
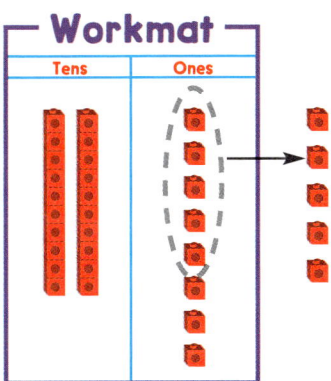
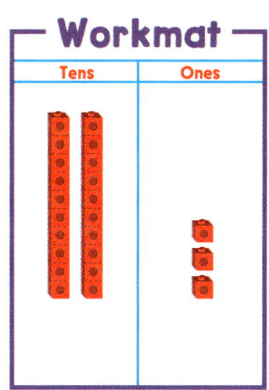

Connect

Use Workmat 3 and 🟥 to subtract. Write the difference.

1.
tens	ones
4	7
−	5

2.
tens	ones
1	9
−	4

Explain It • Daily Reasoning

How could you find the difference for 27 − 4 without using blocks?

Chapter 29 • Adding and Subtracting Two-Digit Numbers

Practice and Problem Solving

Use Workmat 3 and 🟥 to subtract.
Write the difference.

1.
tens	ones
3	9
−	2
3	7

2.
tens	ones
4	5
−	2

3.
tens	ones
2	6
−	5

4.
tens	ones
1	7
−	3

Problem Solving
Algebra

Write the missing numbers.

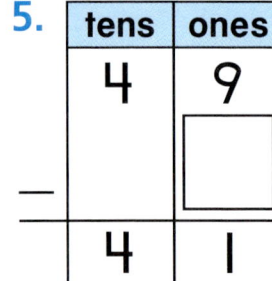

5.
tens	ones
4	9
−	
4	1

6.
tens	ones
8	6
−	
8	0

7.
tens	ones
1	8
−	
1	4

8.
tens	ones
7	5
−	
7	2

 Write About It • Look at Exercise 5. How could you draw 🟥 to prove your answer?

🏠 **HOME ACTIVITY** • Ask your child to explain how to find the difference for 48 − 3.

Name _____

Subtract Money

Learn

Subtract money amounts the same way you subtract other numbers.

Subtract the ones. Then subtract the tens.

Subtract numbers.   Subtract money.

```
  34       34        34¢       34¢
 −13      −13       −13¢      −13¢
 ———      ———       ————      ————
   1       21         1¢       21¢
```

Check

Subtract.

1. 26¢ − 13¢ = ___¢
2. 39¢ − 22¢ = ___¢
3. 68¢ − 32¢ = ___¢
4. 54¢ − 30¢ = ___¢
5. 93¢ − 62¢ = ___¢

6. 69¢ − 7¢ = ___¢
7. 77¢ − 33¢ = ___¢
8. 97¢ − 76¢ = ___¢
9. 29¢ − 19¢ = ___¢
10. 48¢ − 18¢ = ___¢

11. 86¢ − 23¢ = ___¢
12. 56¢ − 25¢ = ___¢
13. 45¢ − 12¢ = ___¢
14. 69¢ − 45¢ = ___¢
15. 39¢ − 22¢ = ___¢

Explain It • Daily Reasoning

What happens when both numbers have the same ones and tens? Why?

Chapter 29 • Adding and Subtracting Two-Digit Numbers

Practice and Problem Solving

Subtract.

1. 68¢ − 25¢ = 43¢
2. 75¢ − 50¢ = ___¢
3. 89¢ − 64¢ = ___¢
4. 45¢ − 44¢ = ___¢
5. 35¢ − 12¢ = ___¢

6. 56¢ − 36¢ = ___¢
7. 64¢ − 14¢ = ___¢
8. 90¢ − 40¢ = ___¢
9. 28¢ − 24¢ = ___¢
10. 65¢ − 20¢ = ___¢

11. 95¢ − 70¢ = ___¢
12. 83¢ − 22¢ = ___¢
13. 17¢ − 6¢ = ___¢
14. 75¢ − 25¢ = ___¢
15. 88¢ − 28¢ = ___¢

Problem Solving
Application

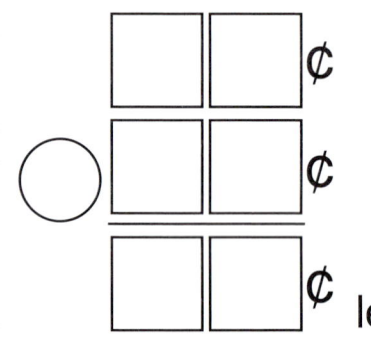

Write the problem. Solve it.

16. Greg has 49¢. He spends 24¢ for bird food. How much does he have left?

 Write About It • Suppose Greg has 68¢ and buys something different. Write your own story problem and solve it.

HOME ACTIVITY • Write a two-digit subtraction problem. Have your child show it with pennies and dimes and solve it.

Name _____

Problem Solving Skill
Make Reasonable Estimates

Without adding or subtracting, circle the best estimate.

THINK: Using tens can help me estimate.

1. Jon picks 14 flowers. Sam picks 5 flowers. About how many do they pick in all?

   Too few.   about 2 flowers

   (about 20 flowers)

   Too many.   about 200 flowers

2. The school has 30 books about animals. Kim takes out 13 books. About how many are left?

   about 2 books

   about 20 books

   about 200 books

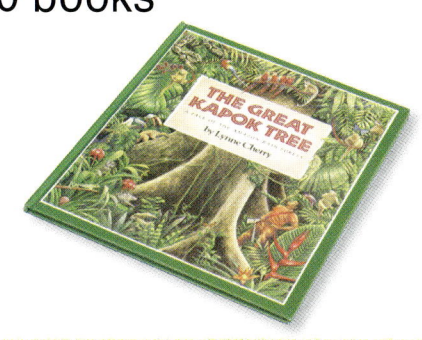

3. Aman saw 10 monkeys. Carla counted 10 more. Logan saw 6 other monkeys. About how many did they see in all?

   about 10 monkeys

   about 20 monkeys

   about 30 monkeys

4. 40 birds are in the forest. 12 fly away. About how many birds are left in the forest?

   about 5 birds

   about 30 birds

   about 100 birds

Chapter 29 • Adding and Subtracting Two-Digit Numbers

Problem Solving Practice

THINK: I do not need an exact answer.

Without adding or subtracting, circle the best estimate.

1. Lana's bird eats 5 seeds for breakfast.
   It eats 5 seeds for lunch.
   It eats 7 more seeds for dinner.
   About how many seeds does it eat in one day?

   about 5 seeds

   about 20 seeds

   about 100 seeds

2. Cam walks 22 steps in the forest.
   She walks 26 more.
   About how many steps does she walk in all?

   about 5 steps

   about 50 steps

   about 500 steps

3. Connor has 50¢.
   He buys a banana for 26¢.
   About how much money does he still have?

   about 5¢

   about 15¢

   about 25¢

4. 100 people are at the park.
   52 of them leave.
   About how many people are still at the park?

   about 50 people

   about 75 people

   about 100 people

HOME ACTIVITY • Ask your child how he or she chose the answer for each problem.

Name _____

Extra Practice

Add or subtract.

| 1. | 30
+50 | 2. | 70
+10 | 3. | 20
+50 | 4. | 90
−30 | 5. | 60
−10 |

Use Workmat 3 and 🟥 to add or subtract.

6.
tens	ones
1	5
+	4

7.
tens	ones
1	9
−	7

Add or subtract.

| 8. | 13¢
+35¢
___¢ | 9. | 20¢
+47¢
___¢ | 10. | 83¢
−21¢
___¢ | 11. | 65¢
− 3¢
___¢ | 12. | 52¢
−11¢
___¢ |

Problem Solving

Without adding or subtracting, circle the best estimate.

13. Juan sees 12 frogs. Elsa sees 11 more frogs. About how many frogs do they see in all?

about 5 frogs

about 20 frogs

about 100 frogs

Name _____

✓ Review/Test

Concepts and Skills

Add or subtract.

1. 70
  +20

2. 40
  +30

3. 50
  +40

4. 80
  −10

5. 60
  −20

Use Workmat 3 and 🎲 to add or subtract.

6.
tens	ones
2	4
+	5

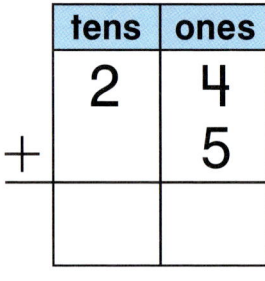

7.
tens	ones
2	8
−	4

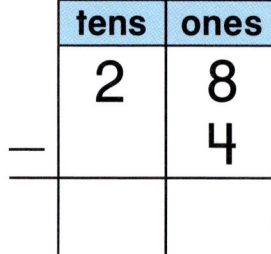

Add or subtract.

8. 31¢
  +26¢
  ___¢

9. 15¢
  +32¢
  ___¢

10. 65¢
  −43¢
  ___¢

11. 58¢
  −27¢
  ___¢

12. 26¢
  − 4¢
  ___¢

Problem Solving

Without adding or subtracting, circle the best estimate.

13. Sam sees 25 lizards. Then he sees 12 more. About how many lizards does Sam see?

about 10 lizards

about 40 lizards

about 100 lizards

502 five hundred two

Name _____

⭐Standardized Test Prep
Chapters 1–29

Choose the answer for questions 1–4.

1. 53   35   57
   + 4   ○   ○
   ____
             45   81
             ○   ○

2. 85¢   15¢   21¢
   −63¢   ○   ○
   ____
             22¢   34¢
             ○   ○

3. Which shows 50¢?

○   ○   ○   ○

4. Which is the best estimate?

Rachel jumps rope 23 times. She jumps rope 33 more times. About how many times does she jump rope in all?

about 5   about 55
○   ○

about 15   about 500
○   ○

Show What You Know

5. Use ▭▭▭▭. Explain two ways to make 90. Write the numbers.

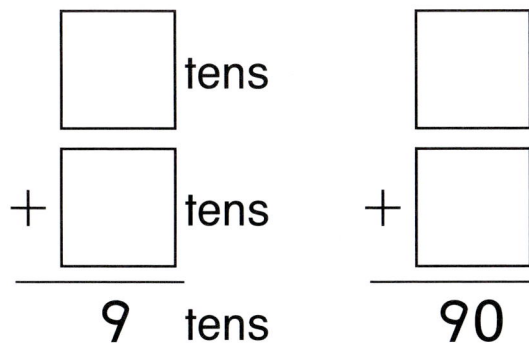   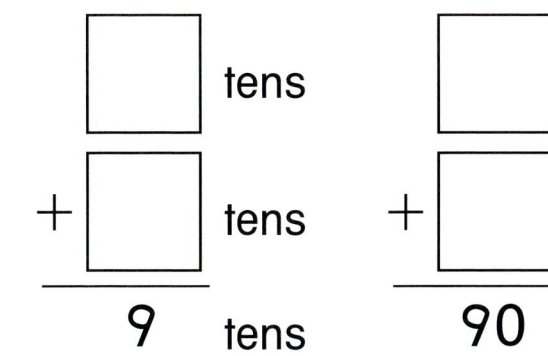

Chapter 29   five hunded three **503**

Name _____

MATH GAME

Math Path

Play with a partner.

You will need
2 pawns
1 number cube (0–6)
2 sets of 0–6 cards

1. Stack the number cards face down.
2. Put your pawn on START. Toss the number cube. Move your pawn that many spaces.
3. Take 2 cards. Use the numbers to make a two digit number to complete the problem.
4. Write the problem on paper.
5. Solve. Your partner will check your answer.
6. If you are not correct, lose a turn.
7. The first player to get to END wins.

504 five hundred four

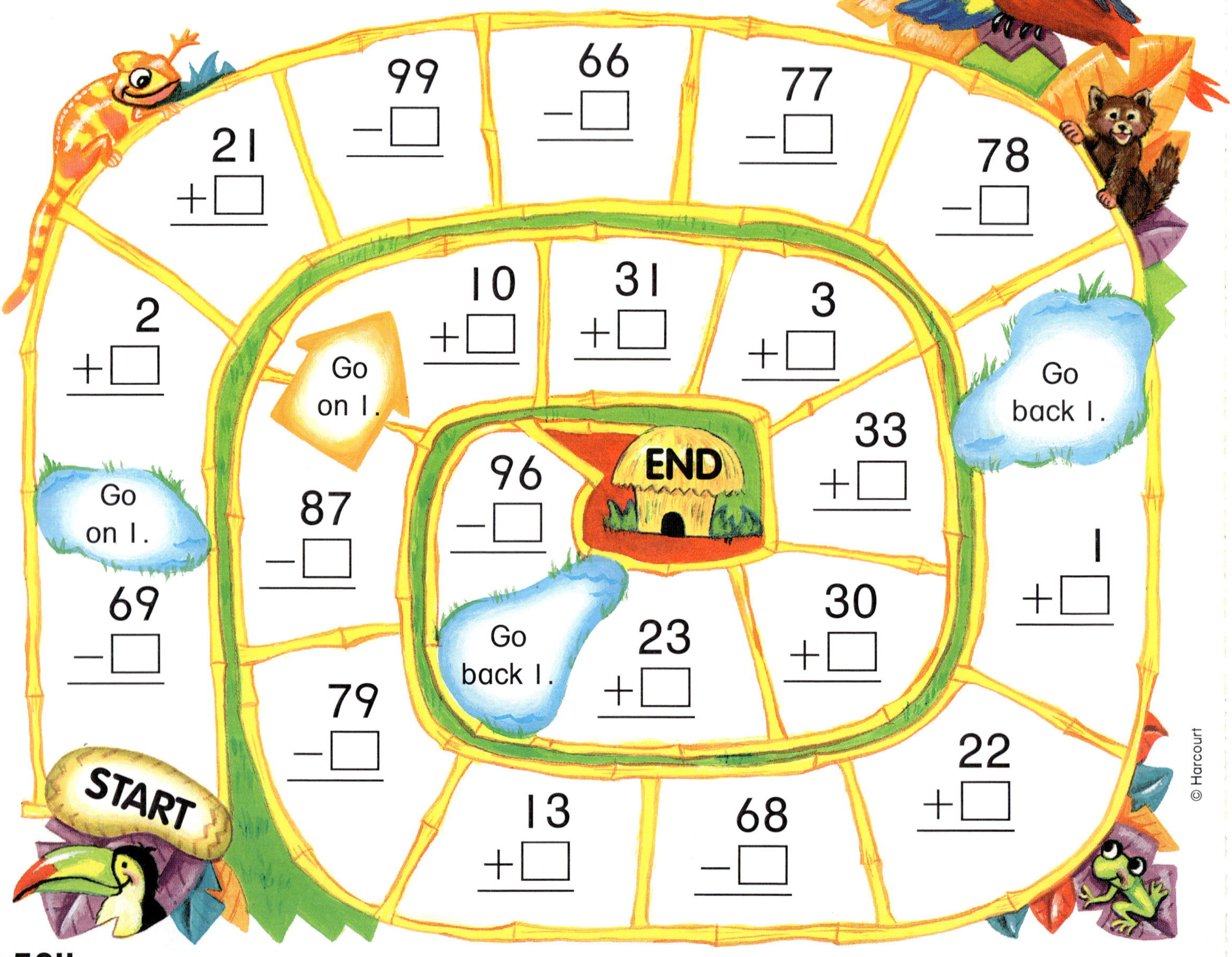

CHAPTER 30 Probability

FUN FACTS

These puppies are red, and black and tan. For every 3 puppies born, 2 are red, and 1 is black and tan.

Theme: Chances

Name _____

✓ Check What You Know

Could It Happen?

1. Circle the picture that shows which is more likely to happen.

2. Circle the picture that shows which is less likely to happen.

Chance

Use a paper clip and a pencil to make a spinner.
Spin 10 times.
Mark a tally mark in the table after each spin.
Circle the color the paper clip landed on more often.

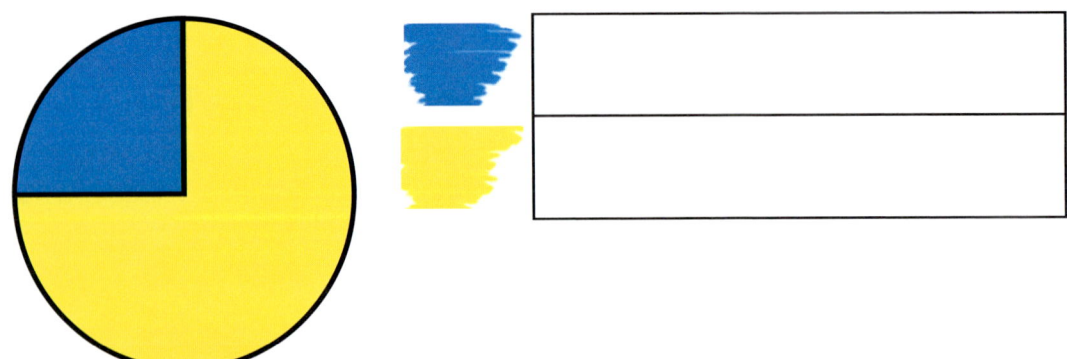

506 five hundred six   Use this page to review important skills needed for this chapter.

Name _____

Certain or Impossible

Vocabulary
certain
impossible

Learn

Pulling a green is certain.

Pulling a red is impossible.

Check

Mark an X to tell if pulling the cube from the bowl is certain or impossible.

			Certain	Impossible
1.	blue	(bowl of blue cubes)	X	
2.	red	(bowl of red cubes)		
3.	yellow	(bowl of green cubes)		
4.	green	(bowl of blue cubes)		

Explain It • Daily Reasoning

Suppose a bowl had only yellow cubes in it. What color would be certain to be pulled? Explain.

Chapter 30 • Probability

five hundred seven **507**

Practice and Problem Solving

Mark an X to tell if pulling the cube from the bowl is certain or impossible.

			Certain	Impossible
1.	yellow	(bowl of yellow cubes)		
2.	red	(bowl of green cubes)		
3.	green	(bowl of red cubes)		
4.	blue	(bowl of blue cubes)		

Problem Solving
Application

5. Circle the bowl from which pulling a 🟥 is certain.

   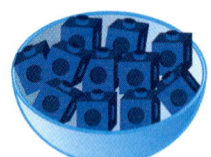

Write About It • Draw a bowl from which pulling a 🟨 is certain. Then draw a bowl from which pulling a 🟥 is impossible. Write **certain** or **impossible** under each bowl.

🏠 **HOME ACTIVITY** • Put some pennies in a bowl. Ask your child if pulling a dime from the bowl is certain or impossible. Have him or her explain.

Name _____

More Likely, Less Likely

Vocabulary
more likely
less likely

Learn

Pulling yellow is **more likely** than pulling green.

Pulling green is **less likely** than pulling yellow.

Check

Write **more** or **less** to tell how likely each color is to be pulled from the bowl.

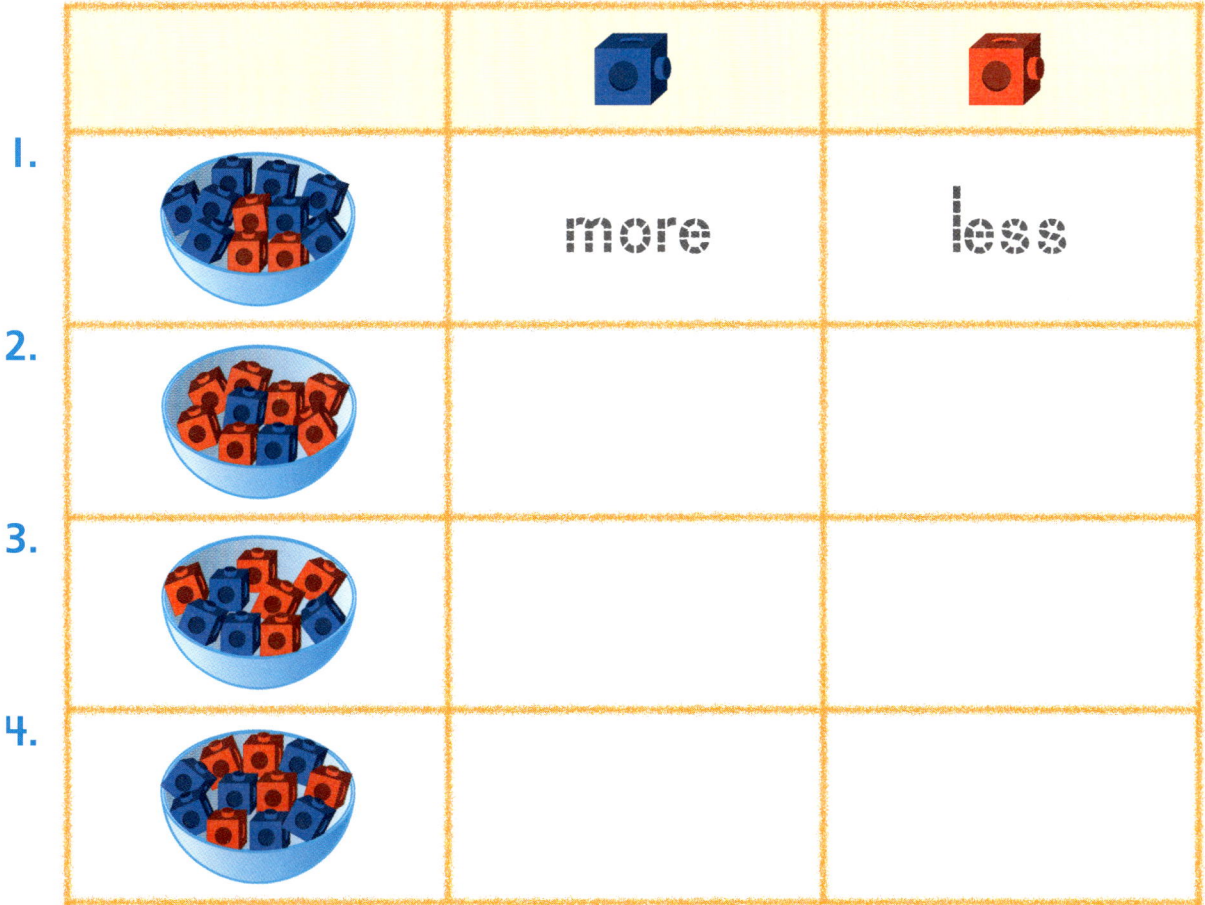

	🟦	🟥
1.	more	less
2.		
3.		
4.		

Explain It • Daily Reasoning

How can you tell which color is more likely to be pulled?

Chapter 30 • Probability

Practice and Problem Solving

Draw 🟦 and 🟥 to tell how likely each color is to be pulled from the bowl.

	More Likely	Less Likely
1.		
2.		
3.		
4.		

Problem Solving

Visual Thinking

5. How could you change the cubes so that pulling a 🟨 is more likely than pulling a 🟩? Draw and color a picture to show your answer.

Write About It • Draw and color a bowl from which pulling a 🟥 is more likely than pulling a 🟦. Then draw and color a bowl from which pulling a 🟦 is more likely than pulling a 🟥.

🏠 **HOME ACTIVITY** • Put 6 pennies and 3 dimes in a bowl. Ask your child if pulling a dime is more likely or less likely than pulling a penny. Have him or her explain.

Name _____

Equally Likely

Vocabulary
equally likely

Learn

Pulling yellow and pulling red are equally likely.

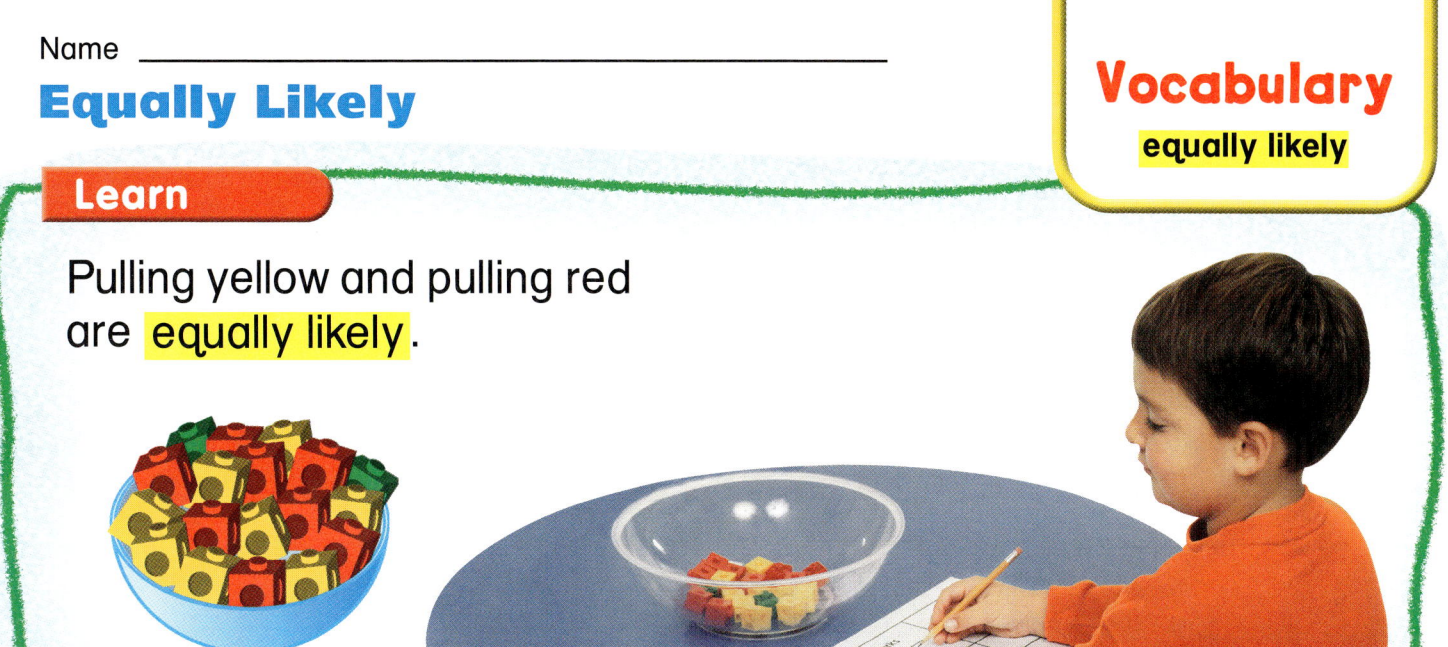

Check

Draw cubes to show which colors are equally likely to be pulled from the bowl.

1.
2.
3.

Explain It • Daily Reasoning

What 2 cubes could you add to the last bowl so that pulling 🟥 is less likely than pulling 🟨 or 🟦?

Chapter 30 • Probability

five hundred eleven **511**

Practice and Problem Solving

Draw cubes to show which colors are equally likely to be pulled from the bowl.

1.
2.
3.
4.

Problem Solving
Visual Thinking

5. How could you change the cubes so that pulling  and pulling  are equally likely? Draw and color a picture.

Write About It • Draw and color a bowl from which pulling a  and pulling a  are equally likely. Write **equally likely** under the bowl.

 HOME ACTIVITY • Put 6 pennies and 6 dimes in a bowl. Ask your child if a dime is more likely or less likely to be pulled or if both coins are equally likely to be pulled.

Name _____

Problem Solving Skill
Make a Prediction

Use a ✏️ and a 📎 to make a spinner.

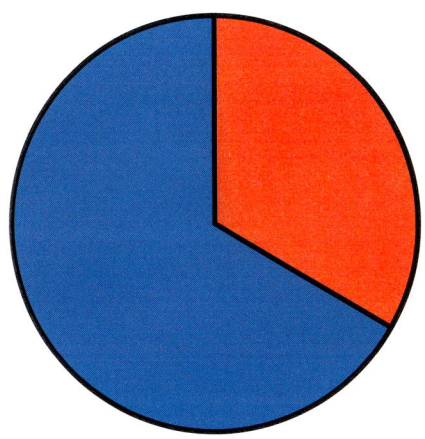

Predict. If you spin the pointer 10 times, on which color will it stop more often?

Circle that color.

red   blue

Check. Spin 10 times.
Make a tally mark after each spin.
Write the totals.

On which color did your pointer stop more often?

	Tally Marks	Total
red		
blue		

1. Predict. If you spin the pointer 10 more times, on which color will it stop more often?
Circle that color.

   red   blue

   Then spin to check.

Chapter 30 • Probability

PROBLEM SOLVING

Problem Solving Practice

1. Use a ✏️ and a 📎 to make a spinner.

Predict. If you spin the pointer 15 times, on which color will it stop most often?

Circle that color.

green   yellow   blue

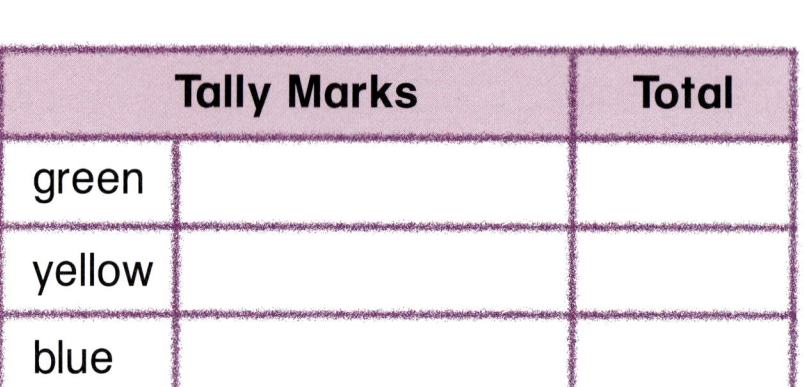

Check. Spin 15 times. Make a tally mark after each spin. Write the totals.

On which color did your pointer stop most often?

	Tally Marks	Total
green		
yellow		
blue		

2. Predict. If you spin the pointer 10 more times, on which color will it stop most often?
Circle that color.

green   yellow   blue

Then spin to check.

🏠 **HOME ACTIVITY** • Make a spinner divided into 4 equal parts. Color two parts the same color and each of the other parts a different color. Have your child predict on which color the pointer will land most often. Spin 10 times to check.

Name _____

Extra Practice

Mark an X to tell if pulling the cube from the bowl is certain or impossible.

		Certain	Impossible
1.	blue		

Draw 🟩 and 🟥 to tell how likely each color is to be pulled from the bowl.

		More Likely	Less Likely
2.			

Draw cubes to show which colors are equally likely to be pulled from the bowl.

3.		

Problem Solving

4. Use a ✏️ and a 📎 to make a spinner. Predict. If you spin the pointer 15 times, on which color will it stop most often? Circle that color.

blue   red   yellow

Check. Spin 15 times. Make a tally mark after each spin. Write the totals.

	Tally Marks	Total
blue		
red		
yellow		

Chapter 30 • Probability

Name _____

✓ Review/Test

Concepts and Skills

Mark an X to tell if pulling the cube from the bowl is certain or impossible.

		Certain	Impossible
1. yellow	[bowl of yellow cubes]		

Draw 🟨 and 🟦 to tell how likely each color is to be pulled from the bowl.

	More Likely	Less Likely
2. [bowl of mostly blue cubes with some yellow]		

Draw cubes to show which colors are equally likely to be pulled from the bowl.

| 3. [bowl of yellow and red cubes] | |

Problem Solving

4. Use a ✏️ and a 📎 to make a spinner. Predict. If you spin the pointer 10 times, on which color will it stop more often? Circle that color.

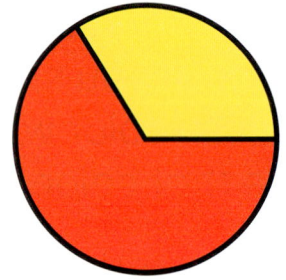

   yellow   red

   Check. Spin 10 times. Make a tally mark after each spin. Write the totals.

	Tally Marks	Total
yellow		
red		

Name _____

⭐Standardized Test Prep
Chapters 1–30

Choose the answer for questions 1–4.

1. Amanda's mom baked some cookies. Amanda ate 2. Her friend ate 3. How many cookies did they eat altogether?

   8 ○   7 ○   6 ○   5 ○

2. Which completes the sentence?

   It is impossible to pull a _____.

   ○   ○   ○   ○

3. Predict. If you spin the pointer 10 times on which color will it stop more often?

   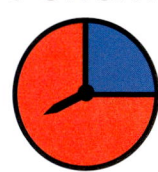

   red ○   green ○

   yellow ○   blue ○

4. Which completes the sentence?

   I am least likely to pull a _____.

   ○   ○   ○

Show What You Know

5.

   Color the cubes to explain which cubes are equally likely and less likely to be pulled from the bowl.

   I am equally likely to pull a 🎲 or a 🎲.

   I am less likely to pull a 🎲 than a 🎲.

Chapter 30   five hundred seventeen **517**

IT'S IN THE BAG
Cool Cat Hat

PROJECT You will make a hat and measure with paper clips how far it flies.

You Will Need

- Lunch-size bag
- Paper plate
- Crayons
- Scissors
- Tape
- Paper clips

Directions

1 Cut the circle out of the paper plate. Decorate the hat.

2 Decorate the bag on all sides.

3 Cut slits around the bag. Push them through the paper plate and tape them to it.

4 Throw your hat in the air. Measure with paper clips how far your hat flew.

"Good morning, Turtle," said Cat.
"How do you like my cool hat?"

"It's very nice," said Turtle.
"You do look cool!"

The wind blew Cat's hat into the pond.
"Help!" called Cat.
"I need a long stick to reach my hat."

Turtle said, "Cat, I can get your hat."

Squirrel got a stick.

About how long is this stick?

about ____ 📎 long

Squirrel's stick wasn't long enough.

Turtle said, "Cat, I can get your hat."

Rabbit got a stick.
It wasn't long enough.

About how long is this stick?

about _____ 🖇 long

Cat was not cool now.
"I'll never get my hat back!" he said.

Turtle said, "Cat, I can get your hat."

"Oh, Turtle, I don't think so," said Cat.
"There aren't any sticks long enough."

But Turtle didn't need a stick.
He swam out to the hat.
Then he swam back with
the hat on his back.

"Oh, thank you, Turtle!" said Cat.
"You are the coolest one of all!"

Name —

PROBLEM SOLVING ON LOCATION

At the Amusement Park

You can ride two big wooden roller coasters at Camden Park. It is near Huntington, West Virginia.

You can play games to win prizes at the park.

Use the spinners below to decide if your chances of winning are **more likely, less likely** or **equally likely** than your chances of losing. Circle your answer.

roller coaster

1

How likely are you to win if the spinner lands on green?

more likely   less likely   equally likely

2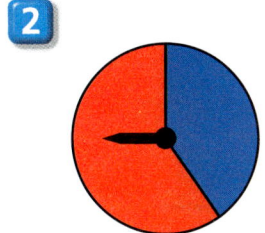

How likely are you to win if the spinner lands on blue?

more likely   less likely   equally likely

3

How likely are you to win if the spinner lands on green?

more likely   less likely   equally likely

Name _____

CHALLENGE

Area

How many units does it take to cover this shape?

____4____ units

How many units does it take to cover the shape? Use ▮. Then count.

1.

_____ units

2.

_____ units

3.

_____ units

4.

_____ units

Name _____

✓ Study Guide and Review

Vocabulary
Draw a line to the tool you use to measure with each unit.

1. **centimeter**

2. **inch**

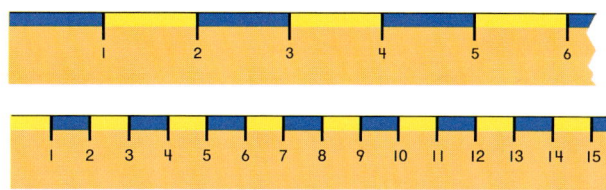

Skills and Concepts
About how long is this?

3. Use an inch ruler to measure.   _____ inches

4. Now use a centimeter ruler to measure.   _____ centimeters

Look at each object.
Circle the better estimate.

Object	Estimate
5. (butter)	about 1 pound / about 10 pounds
6. (oranges)	about 1 pound / about 10 pounds

Draw cubes to show which colors are equally likely to be pulled from the bowl.

7.

Read the temperature. Color the thermometer to show the temperature.

8. 20°F

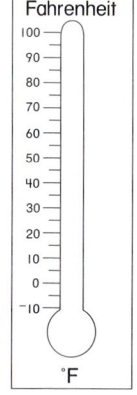

Unit 6 • Study Guide and Review

Add or subtract.

9. 20
  + 40

10. 60
   − 30

11. 50
  + 30

12. 71¢
  + 23¢
  ____¢

13. 87¢
   − 25¢
   ____¢

14. 98¢
   − 50¢
   ____¢

Use Workmat 3 and 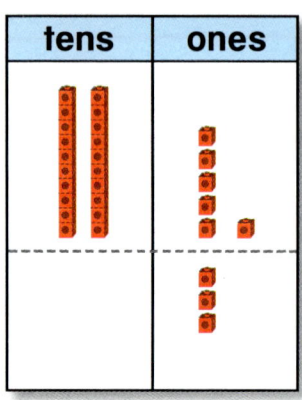 to add.

15.
tens	ones
2	6
+	3

16.
tens	ones
3	3
+	5

Use Workmat 3 and 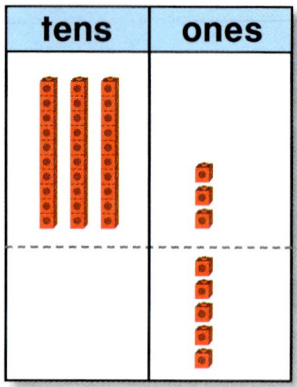 to subtract.

17.
tens	ones
2	9
−	4

18.
tens	ones
4	7
−	3

Problem Solving

Circle the best tool for finding each measurement.

19. Which shoe is heavier?

 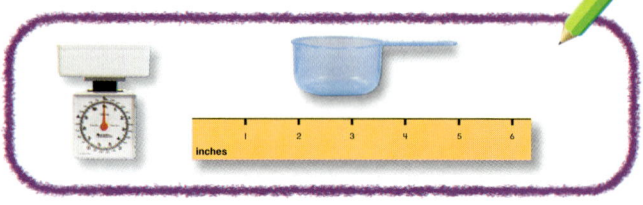

20. Which holds more?

  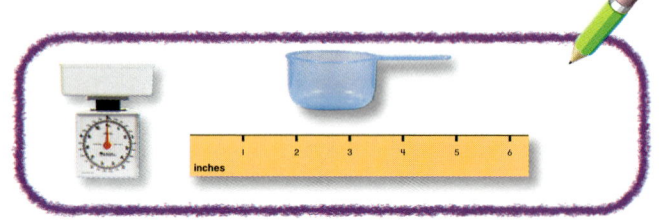

✔ Performance Assessment

Hannah's New Lunch Box

Hannah wants to measure her new lunch box.

Here are the tools she can use.

- Circle one of the tools.
- Draw a picture to show how Hannah can use the tool.
- Use this tool to measure a real lunch box.
- Estimate what you think your measurement will be.
- Then measure.

Show your work.

Estimate _____   Measurement _____

Name _____

TECHNOLOGY

Calculator • Find the Greatest Sum

$25 + 35 + 16 = 76$
$65 + 11 + 23 = 99$
$70 + 12 + 14 = 96$

Which has the **greatest** sum?

Use a 🖩. Add.

Press [ON/C] [2] [5] [+] [3] [5] [+] [1] [6] [=]

Write the answer. [76]

Press [ON/C] [6] [5] [+] [1] [1] [+] [2] [3] [=]

Write the answer. [ ]

Press [ON/C] [7] [0] [+] [1] [2] [+] [1] [4] [=]

Write the answer. [ ]

Compare. _____ is the greatest sum.

Practice and Problem Solving

Use a 🖩. Find each sum. Circle the greatest sum.

1. $15 + 23 + 31 =$ _____

   $44 + 11 + 13 =$ _____

   $10 + 24 + 65 =$ _____

   Which place value shows which sum is greatest? Underline it.

   tens   ones

2. $21 + 22 + 23 =$ _____

   $51 + 10 + 15 =$ _____

   $45 + 19 + 11 =$ _____

   Which place value shows which sum is greatest? Underline it.

   tens   ones

PICTURE GLOSSARY

above (page 269)

add (page 5)

$3 + 2 = 5$

addition sentence (page 9)

$4 + 1 = 5$

after (page 181)

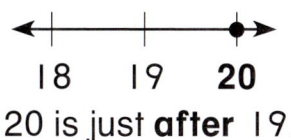

20 is just **after** 19.

afternoon (page 419)

are left (page 33)

3 **are left**.

balance (page 457)

bar graph (page 145)

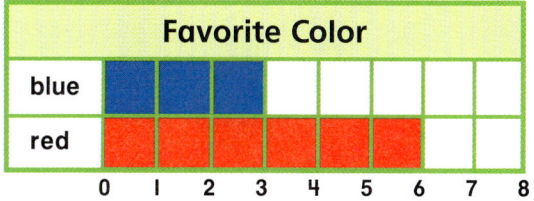

before (page 181)

18 is just **before** 19.

below (page 269)

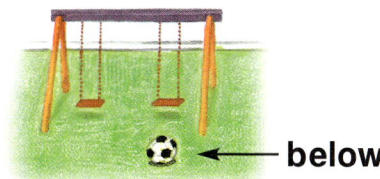

beside (page 270)

between (page 181)

19 is **between** 18 and 20.

centimeter (page 447)

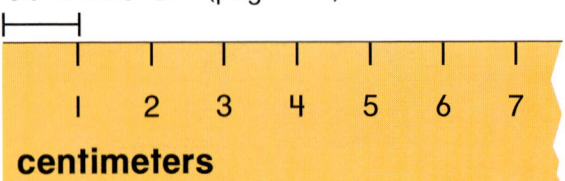

certain (page 507)

Pulling green is **certain**.

chart (page 423)

Subject	Start	End
math		
science		

circle (page 255)

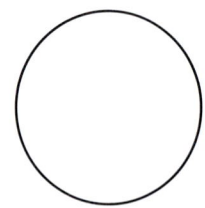

close by (page 269)

close by

closed figure (page 267)

concrete graph (page 139)

The Fruit Bowl				
🍎 apples	🍎	🍎	🍎	
🍊 oranges	🍊	🍊		
🍌 bananas	🍌	🍌	🍌	

cone (page 251)

526 five hundred twenty-six

count back (page 101)

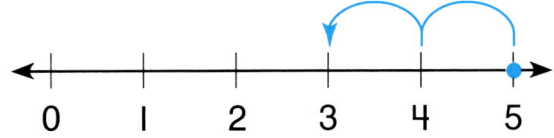

$5 - 2 = 3$

Start at 5. **Count back** two.
You are on 3.

count backward (page 183)

52, 51, 50

Count backward from 52.

count forward (page 183)

52, 53, 54

Count forward from 52.

count on (page 71)

$8 + 2 = 10$

Say 8. **Count on** two.
9, 10

cube (page 251)

cup (page 473)

cylinder (page 251)

day (page 417)

The **days** of the week are: **Sunday, Monday, Tuesday, Wednesday, Thursday, Friday,** and **Saturday.**

difference (page 35)

$9 - 3 = 6$

difference

dime (page 369)

 or  10¢
10 cents

dollar (page 387)

1 dollar = 100¢

doubles (page 75)

$4 + 4 = 8$

doubles plus one (page 213)

$4 + 4 = 8$, so $4 + 5 = 9$

five hundred twenty-seven **527**

down (page 271)

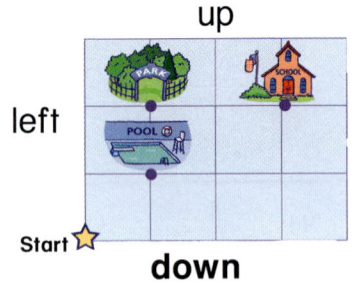

equal parts (page 351)

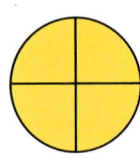

equally likely (page 511)

Pulling blue and red are **equally likely**.

equals = (page 5)
the same as

4 + 1 = 5

4 plus 1 **equals** 5.

estimate (page 167)

about 10 buttons

even numbers (page 199)

0, 2, 4, 6, 8, 10 . . .

evening (page 419)

face (page 253)

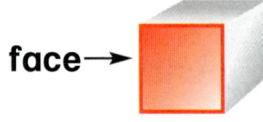

fact family (page 121)

5 + 3 = 8   3 + 5 = 8

8 − 3 = 5   8 − 5 = 3

far (page 269)

feet (page 445)

Use **feet** to measure longer objects.

fewest (page 384)

20   30   40

20 has the **fewest** tens.

foot (page 445)

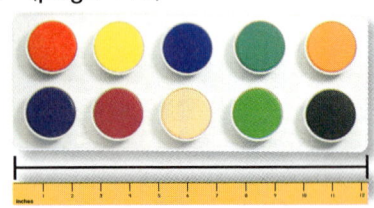

12 inches = 1 **foot**

gram (page 461)

This paper clip is about 1 **gram**.

half dollar (page 387)

 or  50¢ **half dollar**

half hour (page 407)

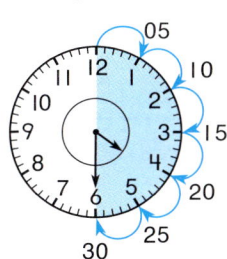

4:30

There are 30 minutes in a **half hour**.

hour (page 405)

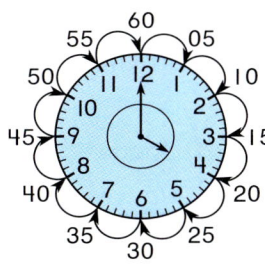

4:00

There are 60 minutes in an **hour**.

hour hand (page 401)

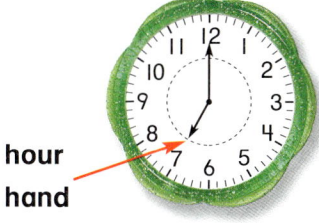

hundred (page 163)

impossible (page 507)

Pulling red is **impossible**.

in all (page 3)

There are 3 **in all**.

inch (page 443)

inches

is equal to (page 180)

25 **is equal to** 25.

25 = 25

is greater than (page 175)

5 **is greater than** 1.

5 > 1

is less than (page 177)

3 **is less than** 5.

3 < 5

kilogram (page 461)

This large book is about 1 **kilogram**.

left (page 271)

less likely (page 509)

Pulling red is **less likely** than pulling blue.

line of symmetry (page 273)

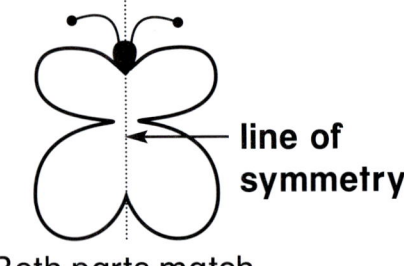

Both parts match.

liter (page 475)

longest (page 439)

make a ten (page 303)

Move 1 counter into the ten frame. **Make a ten.**

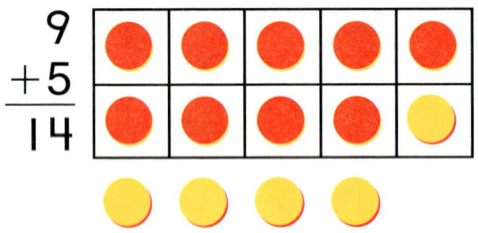

minus (page 35)

3 − 2 = 1

3 **minus** 2 equals 1.

minute (page 403)

You can estimate a **minute**.

minute hand (page 401)

month (page 417)

December						
Sunday	Monday	Tuesday	Wednesday	Thursday	Friday	Saturday
			1	2	3	4
5	6	7	8	9	10	11
12	13	14	15	16	17	18
19	20	21	22	23	24	25
26	27	28	29	30	31	

more (page 143)

40   30

40 has **more** tens than 30.

more likely (page 509)

Pulling red is **more likely** than blue.

morning (page 419)

near (page 270)

next to (page 270)

nickel (page 367)

 or 5¢
5 cents

number line (page 101)

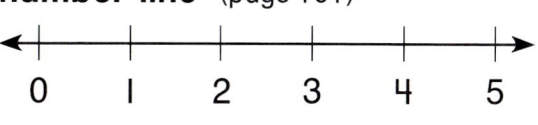

o'clock (page 401)

The clock shows 1 **o'clock**.

odd numbers (page 199)

1, 3, 5, 7, 9 . . .

$\frac{1}{4}$ **one fourth** (page 353)

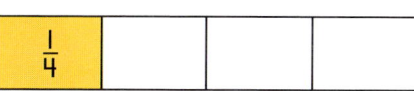

$\frac{1}{2}$ **one half** (page 351)

$\frac{1}{3}$ **one third** (page 355)

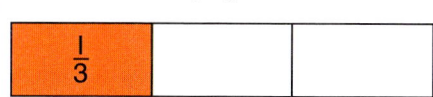

ones (page 157)

There are 3 **ones**.

open figure (page 267)

Order Property (page 17)

2 + 3 = 5 and 3 + 2 = 5

You can add in any **order** and still get the same sum.

ordinal numbers (page 203)

first   second   third

over (page 269)

pattern (page 283)

pattern unit (page 285)

penny (pennies) (page 367)

 or    1¢
1 cent

picture graph (page 141)

Our Pets			
dog	🐕	🐕	
cat	🐈	🐈	🐈
rabbit	🐇		

pint (page 473)

plus + (page 5)

4 + 3 = 7

4 **plus** 3 equals 7.

pound (page 459)

This weighs one **pound**.

pyramid (page 251)

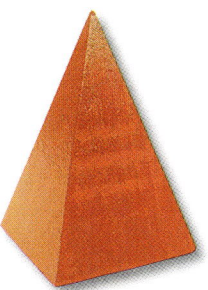

quart (page 473)

quarter (page 385)

 or    **25¢**
25 cents

rectangle (page 255)

rectangular prism (page 251)

related facts (page 105)

2 + 3 = 5 is **related** to

5 − 3 = 2 and 5 − 2 = 3.

right (page 271)

rule (page 91)

Add 2	
4	6
6	8
8	10

The **rule** is add 2.

shortest (page 439)

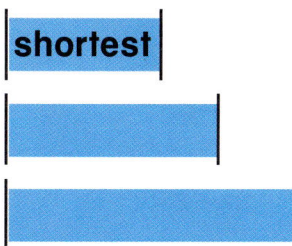

side (page 257)

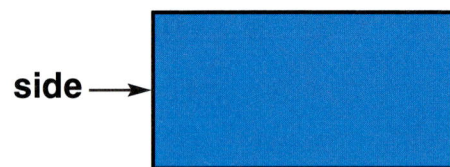

slide (page 275)

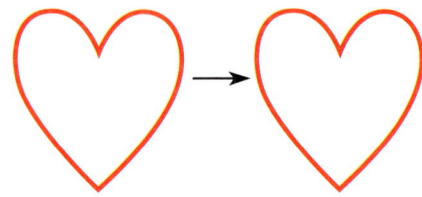

sort (page 137)

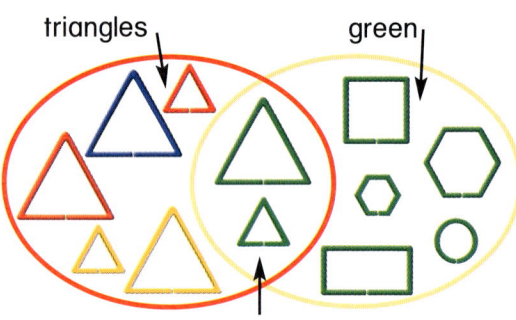

You can **sort** these shapes.

sphere (page 251)

square (page 255)

subtract (page 35)

$6 - 2 = 4$

subtraction sentence (page 37)

$8 - 2 = 6$

sum (page 5)

$5 + 1 = \mathbf{6}$ ← **sum**

tally mark (page 143)

卌 | ← tally mark

tally table (page 143)

Colors of Butterflies		Total
red	卌	5
blue	卌 ||	7

temperature (page 477)

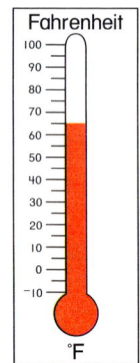

The **temperature** is 65 degrees.

ten less (page 185)

| 25 | 35 | 45 |

25 is **ten less** than 35.

ten more (page 185)

| 25 | 35 | 45 |

45 is **ten more** than 35.

tens (page 157)

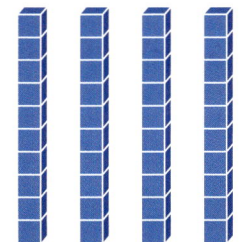

to the left of (page 270)

to the left of

to the right of (page 270)

to the right of

trade (page 383)

triangle (page 255)

turn (page 275)

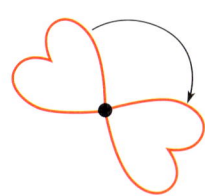

up (page 271)

up

left   right

Start   down

vertex (page 253 and 257)

← vertex →

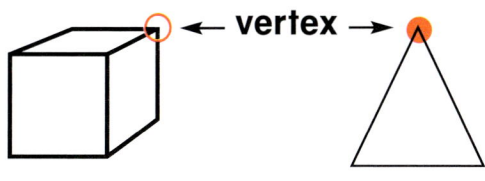

zero 0 (page 7)

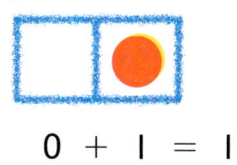

0 + 1 = 1

five hundred thirty-five **535**

Photography Credits

Page placement key: (t) top, (c) center, (b) bottom, (l) left, (r) right, (bg) background, (i) inset

Chapter Opener Photography Credits by Chapter:
Chapter: 1 Superstock; 2 Dana White/Photo Edit; 3 Gary Braasch/Stone/Getty Images; 4 Charles Gupton/Corbis; 5 David Fleetham/FPG/Getty Images; 6 Ariel Skelley/Corbis; 7 Tom Stewart/Corbis; 8 Corbis; 9 Harcourt; 10 Richard Cummins/Corbis; 11 Bill Bachman/Photo Edit; 12 Image State; 13 Raymond Gehman/Corbis; 14 Ariel Skelley/Corbis; 15 Scott Barrow, Inc../SuperStock; 16 William Dow/Corbis; 17 Photo Safari/Animals Animals/Earth Scenes; 18 Johnny Johnson/Stone/Getty Images; 19 David Cavagnaro/Peter Arnold, Inc.; 20 Art Wolfe/Stone/Getty Images; 21 J.Silver/SuperStock; 22 Harcourt; 23 Kim Karpeles; 24 Harcourt; 25 Don Smetzer/Stone/Getty Images; 26 Jose Luis Pelaez, Inc./Corbis; 27 Tom Stewart/Corbis; 28 Bill Tucker/International Stock/ImageState; 29 Frans Lanting/Minden Pictures; 30 Allison Barnes/Masterfile.

Stock photographs provided by:
37 (t) Gail Shumway/FPG International; 37 (c) E.R. Degginger/Animals Animals; 37 (b) Rod Williams/Bruce Coleman, Inc.; 38 (c) Doug Perrine/Innerspace Visions; 38 (b) Tom Brakefield/The Stock Market; 62a (t) R. Kord/H. Armstrong Roberts, Inc; 62a (c) Michael J. Pettypool/Dave G. Houser; 62a (b) Dr. D. E. Degginger/Color-Pic; 62b (both) Riverbanks Zoo Society; 73 (c) Arthur C. Smith/Grant Heilman Photography; 74 (t) Ron Kimball Photography; 74 (b) Chris Luneski/Natural Selection Stock Photography; 74 (tc) Rosemary Calvert/Tony Stone Images; 74 (bc) David W. Hamilton/The Image Bank; 75 (c) Mark Newman/Bruce Coleman, Inc.; 87 (t) Ron Kimball Photography; 87 (tc) J. C. Carton/Bruce Coleman, Inc.; 87 (b) Phil Savoie/Bruce Coleman, Inc.; 87 (bc) J & D Bartlett/Bruce Coleman, Inc.; 88 (t) Runk/Schoenberger/Grant Heilman Photography; 88 (c) Index Stock Photography; 88 (b) Chris Collins/The Stock Market; 89 (bc) J & D Bartlett/Bruce Coleman, Inc.; 124a (t) Ty Smedes Nature Photography; 124b (t) Bradley Simmons/Bruce Coleman, Inc.; 124b (b) Stan Shoneman/Omni-Photo Communications; 176 (b) G K & Vicki Hart/The Image Bank; 177 (t) Stock South/PictureQuest; 201 (c) Chris Collins/The Stock Market; 201 (b) Roy Morsch/The Stock Market; 202 (t) Mark Newman/Bruce Coleman, Inc.; 202 (c) Barbara Wright/Animals Animals; 202 (b) George Godfrey/Animals Animals; 210a Tom Stillo/Omni-Photo Communications; 210b (t) W. Bertsch/H. Armstrong Roberts; 284a (l) R. Harris/H. Armstrong Roberts, Inc.; 284a (c) J. Blank/H. Armstrong Roberts, Inc.; 284a (r) Dr. D. E. Degginger/Color-Pic; 284b (t) Indiana Historical Society; 370a (t) Bill Ross/Corbis; 370b (t) Howard Ande Photography; 446a Francis & Donna Caldwell/Affordable Photo Stock; 446b (t) Lowell Georgia/Corbis.

Problem Solving on Location Credits:
Page 63(t), Mike Booher / Transparencies; 63(c), Susan Ley / Animals Animals; 63(b), Fritz Prenzel / Animals Animals; 129, Richard Bryant / Tennessee Aquarium; 243(both), James P. Rowan Photography; 431, Alex Demyan Photography; 519(both), Joel Rogers / CoasterGallery.com.

All other photographs by Harcourt photographers listed below,

© Harcourt: Weronica Ankarorn, John Bateman, Victoria Bowen, Ken Kinzie, Ron Kunzman, Allan Maxwell, Sheri O'Neal, Quebecor Digital Imaging, Sonny Senser, Terry Sinclair.

ILLUSTRATION CREDITS:
Page: 8, Bernard Adnet; 49, 50, 52, 73, 74, 270, 277, 279, 317, 318, Ellen Appleby; 172, Pam Barcita; 50, 55, 56, 221, 222, 418, 427, Shirley V. Beckes; 101, 102, 112, 248, 474, 478, Rose Mary Berlin; 235, 236, 301, 305, 311, 355, 356, 361, 442, 445, 446, Linda Howard Bittner; 407, 408, 409, 410, 411, 371, 372, 376, 489, 490, 495, 496, 504, Carly Castillon; 89, 90, 269, 275, David Christensen; 46, 55, 56, 370, 377, Chi Chung; 158, 163, 164, 183, 184, Liz Conrad; 122, 166, 207, 232, 321, 356, 360, 432, 454, 458, 460, 520, Diana Craft; 213, 216, 223, K. Michael Crawford; 169, 187, Justine Dowling; 5, 6, 231, 232, 239, Kathi Ember; 335, 336, Dagmar Fehlan; 53, 68, 159, 319, 325, Rusty Fletcher; 137, 138, 141, 143, 149, 150, 233, 234, Elaine Garvin; 122, 125, Claudine Gévry; 134, 419, 420, 423, 424, Peter Grosshauser; 139, 140, 144, 146, 148, 151, 153, 171, 364, Franklin Hammond; 380, Eileen Hine; 33, 34, 491, 492, 497, 498, Mark Jarman; F, G, I, 35, 72, 181, 182, 193, 253, 254, 257, 264, 414, 507, 508, 509, 510, 511, 512, 515, 516, 517, Ken Laidlaw; 388, 390, 392, 395, Chris Lensch; 226, 289, 290, 296, 510, 515, Lyn Martin; 157, Claude Martinot; E, 18, 20, 27, 88, 367, 368, 373, 374, Bob Masheris; 292, 293, Christine Mau; 14, 43, 133, 507, 508, 512, Deborah Melmon; 87, 95, 175, 176, 179, 180, Cheryl Mendenhall; 260, Judith Moffatt; 115, 116, 197, 198, 205, Keiko Motoyama; 201, 202, 206, Yuri Motoyama; 79, 177, 178, 439, 440, 451, 468, Susan Nethery; F, H, I, 85, 86, 92, 321, 322, 460, 465, Ana Ochoa; 30, Laura Ovresat; 59, 60, 314, 487, 488, 493, 494, 501, Peter Pahl; 118, Mike Reed; 59, 98, 472, 476, 481, Scott A. Scheidly; 75, 76, 348, 351, 353, 359, Dan Sharp; 37, 82, 103, 106, 280, 303, 307, 457, 458, 461, 462, 484, Janet Skiles; 267, 268, 273, 274, 278, Jamie Smith; 190, 195, 196, 199, 203, Tammy Smith; 104, 106, Jackie Snider; 154, Susan Synarski; 107, 108, 256, 398, Peggy Tagel; 328, Pamela Thomson; 442, Gary M. Torrisi; 3, 4, 208, 215, 219, 220, Marshall Woksa.